The Early Years Professional's Complete Companion

We work with leading authors to develop the strongest
educational materials in education, bringing cutting-edge
thinking and best learning practice to a global market.

Under a range of well-known imprints, including Longman,
we craft high quality print and electronic publications
which help readers to understand and apply their content,
whether studying or at work.

To find out more about the complete range of our
publishing, please visit us on the World Wide Web at:
www.pearsoned.co.uk

The Early Years Professional's Complete Companion

Pam Jarvis, Jane George
and Wendy Holland

PEARSON
Longman

Harlow, England • London • New York • Boston • San Francisco • Toronto
Sydney • Tokyo • Singapore • Hong Kong • Seoul • Taipei • New Delhi
Cape Town • Madrid • Mexico City • Amsterdam • Munich • Paris • Milan

Pearson Education Limited

Edinburgh Gate
Harlow
Essex CM20 2JE
England

and Associated Companies throughout the world

Visit us on the World Wide Web at:
www.pearsoned.co.uk

_____

First published 2010

© Pearson Education Limited 2010

ISBN: 978-1-4082-0369-9

British Library Cataloguing-in-Publication Data
A catalogue record for this book is available from the British Library

Library of Congress Cataloging-in-Publication Data
Jarvis, Pam.
   The early years professional's complete companion / Pam Jarvis, Jane George, and Wendy Holland.
       p. cm.
   Includes index.
   ISBN 978-1-4082-0369-9 (pbk.)
   1. Early childhood education—Handbooks, manuals, etc.   2. Early childhood teachers—Professional
relationships—Handbooks, manuals, etc.   I. George, Jane.   II. Holland, Wendy,   III. Title.
   LB1139.23.J.37 2009
   372.21—dc22

                                                                    2009027403

10 9 8 7 6 5 4 3 2 1
14 13 12 11 10

Typeset in 9.5/13 pt Stone Serif by 73.
Printed and bound in Great Britain by Ashford Colour Press Ltd, Gosport, Hants

The publisher's policy is to use paper manufactured from sustainable forests.

This book is dedicated to:

My mother, Norma Watts Crouch, who was born two days after British women finally achieved the franchise on the same basis as men: what a long way both you and we have travelled in your lifetime!

Pam Jarvis

To my parents, Mary and Leslie Robinson, who knew that a good childhood relies upon parents who freely give unconditional love and limitless time to their children. They invested their hopes in me and offered me many of the opportunities that they had been denied, I hope I have made good use of them.

Jane George

This book is dedicated to all those young children it has been my delight to know and share with the 'awe and wonder' that is early childhood. During my time in Early Years Education, the insight, honesty and imagination of young children have never ceased to amaze and encourage me. I would like to make this dedication especially to my grandchildren, Joseph, George and Alice, whose young lives continue to reinforce for me the richness in every child.

Wendy Holland

Contents

About the authors

Dr Pam Jarvis is a graduate psychologist, social scientist and educational researcher, with many years of experience of creating and teaching developmental, social science and social policy modules for Education/Child Development programmes for community, further and higher education, most recently within the area of Early Years Professional training. She has qualified teacher status and has taught in school within her specialist subject areas of psychology, sociology and history. She is currently working on the Early Years and Children's Agenda team at Bradford College and as an Open University tutor, supporting education and child development students on a wide range of programmes at undergraduate and masters level. She is also an active researcher in child development and education, who has most recently focused on the areas of play-based learning and 'student voice'. Dr Jarvis was awarded a PhD by Leeds Metropolitan University in 2005 for her thesis 'The Role of Rough and Tumble Play in Children's Social and Gender Role Development in The Early Years of Primary School'. Her recent publications include:

Jarvis, P. (2009, in press) '"Born to Play": The biocultural roots of "rough and tumble" play, and its impact upon human development' in P. Broadhead, E. Wood and J. Howard (eds) *Play and learning in early years settings; from research to practice*. London: Sage.

Jarvis, P. (2009) 'Play, narrative and learning in education: a biocultural perspective'. *Educational and Child Psychology*, 26(2), pp. 66–76.

Brock, A., Dodds, S., Jarvis, P. and Olusoga, Y. (eds) (2008) *Perspectives on Play*. Harlow: Pearson Longman.

Jarvis, P. (2007) 'Monsters, Magic and Mr. Psycho: Rough and Tumble Play in the Early Years of Primary School, a Biocultural Approach' *Early Years, An International Journal of Research and Development*, 27(2) pp. 171–88.

Jarvis, P. (2007) 'Dangerous activities within an invisible playground: a study of emergent male football play and teachers' perspectives of outdoor free play in the early years of primary school'. *International Journal of Early Years Education*, 15(3), pp. 245–59.

Jane George (MEd) has extensive experience in the voluntary sector, in toddler groups and playgroups and managing and teaching for the Pre-School Learning Alliance. She has worked in Community Education developing and delivering Parent and Toddler at Play classes in areas of social deprivation and to various cultural groups. Working in colleges across West Yorkshire, she has developed and delivered a variety of Early Years programmes across the range of further and higher education. She was awarded an MEd in 2002. In her current role of Programme Manager for Early Years and Children's Agenda at Bradford College she

teaches and manages the curriculum across the [...]
Studies programmes, which includes CACHE levels [...]
and Education, the Foundation Degree in Early Years, the [...]
hood Studies, the Postgraduate Certificate in Early Years Practi[...]
Years Professional Pathway. She is also an Early Years Professional Sta[...]
Her recent publications include:

Jarvis, P. and George, J. (2008) 'Play, Learning for Life: the vital role of play in human development'. In A. Brock, S. Dodds, P. Jarvis and Y. Olusoga (eds) *Perspectives on Play: Learning for Life,* pp. 251–71. Harlow: Pearson Longman.

Wendy Holland (MA) has experience of teaching in mainstream nurseries, primary and special schools for over 30 years. From the 1970s onwards, her focus has been around inclusive provision and practice for childen 0 to 8 years. Through the establishment of mother and toddler groups and playgroups for children with particular needs, integrated mainstream provision for hearing and hearing-impaired nursery and primary aged children, she has pursued her particular interests around the inclusion of parents/carers in the caring and educative process. The importance of the role of reflective practitioner as an agent for change is another of her interests and she is at present involved in the training and assessing of Early Years Professionals at Bradford College. She is also currently working in the Teaching, Health and Care sector at Bradford College developing and producing modules for the BA(Hons) with Qualified Teacher Status degree and the BEd Studies degree, as well as supporting students engaged in a range of undergraduate and masters level programmes.

Jane Guilfoyle has taught in school, adult, further and higher education. She is a qualified, experienced Primary teacher and was a Registered *Ofsted* Nursery Inspector. She has substantial and varied experience of training and development for Early Years staff, both pre-service and in-service. For many years, she developed, led and managed a range of full- and part-time courses in further and higher education. More recently, she has been involved in the 'training of trainers' and the updating and development of tutors within the sector. She has substantial experience of a range of assessment processes and is currently an External Verifier and outside examiner for Early Years and Child Development for national awarding bodies. She has played a major role, on a consultancy basis, in the setting up and implementation of the EYPS project at Bradford College and is currently acting as the Project Co-ordinator and Senior Assessor. She is Vice-Chair of Governors of a Primary School, which has just gained designation as a Children's Centre.

Poonam Cant gained Early Years Professional Status in June 2007 and now works as a trainer, mentor and assessor for Bradford College with EYPS candidates. She has worked voluntarily with children since she was 15 years old and now owns and manages her own childcare business. Her experiences over the years have led her to work with children with English as a second language, children with special needs and children with unique family circumstances. This significant experience coupled with leadership and managerial skills obtained from her previous career as a chartered accountant and training manager have given her the appropriate skills to work with and understand EYP candidates.

Sarah Procter has worked in the Health and Social Care sector for over 20 years and has substantial experience of working with families and their children as well as with the multi-agency teams. Sarah has worked on a number of area-based initiatives, including New Deal for Communities where her passion for families and young children resulted in the creation of two Neighbourhood Nurseries as well as an award-winning project to encourage representatives from South Asian Communities into careers in Speech and Language therapy. In 2002, Sarah moved to be the Programme Manager of SureStart Bierely, Holmewood and Tyersal in Bradford where key successes involved the development of three new Children's Centres integrated into Primary School provision. Sarah has worked on two national programmes aimed at developing Early Years Settings leadership – the National Professional Qualification in Integrated Centre Leadership and EYPS. Currently, she is the course leader for the EYPS Programme based at Sheffield Hallam University. Sarah is also a Trustee of a local charity which provides full daycare in Bradford; this keeps her focused on the reality of providing high-quality education and care services for children and their families.

Dr Clive Opie was, until recently, the Deputy Director of the Institute of Education at Manchester Metropolitan University where he had overall responsibility for staffing and finances. It was here that he came to appreciate the importance and significance of the EYPS initiative in his position as Chair of the EYPS Executive Committee. He moved to Bradford College to take up the position of Assistant Director for the School of Teaching, Health and Care which includes an extensive EYPS programme. His research interests have centred on the use of ICT to support and enhance teaching and learning in a range of settings. These have included teachers and pupils within schools, initial teacher education students in Science and Educational Studies, and students on higher degree courses. He has had substantial experience of teaching students on MEd courses where, among other areas, he has taught research procedures and data analysis, both of which have included the exploration of using computers to assist in such work. His most recent publications include a text jointly authored with Judith Bell, *Learning from Research – Getting More from your Data*, Open University (2002), and acting as editor/author for *Doing Educational Research – A Guide to First Time Researchers*, Sage (2004).

Lynn Bradley is currently the Director of Services for three Children's Centres and Daycare Nurseries in Bradford, West Yorkshire. Lynn has a varied background in community regeneration, having worked within and across the voluntary and statutory sectors for the past 18 years. In the early 1990s Lynn was involved in a number of large regeneration programmes and her experiences and frustration fuelled her commitment to addressing inequalities in terms of the access to and the quality of services which negatively affected children and families despite improvements to their external surroundings.

Over the past 15 years she has convened and facilitated multi-agency working groups to develop ways of delivering service priorities at both district-wide and locality levels within Bradford. Lynn is committed to integrated working and service delivery but is pragmatic about the difficulties that need to be mediated to enable effective integrated working.

Lynn believes that workforce development underpins successful integrated service delivery that places the needs and aspirations of children and families first, together with the development of shared understanding and respect for different roles and contributions. She is committed to enabling all practitioners to contribute routinely to improved outcomes for families and children.

Lynn is an NPQICL graduate, and a member of the national Ministerial Reference Group for Children's Centre Leaders.

Foreword

I can't remember exactly when but some time around autumn 2006 I recall sitting in an extremely emotive meeting with 40 or so other University colleagues from around the country discussing the implementation of the newly announced Early Years Professional Status (EYPS). Not being an expert in Early Years I initially could not see why emotions were running so high. I very quickly came to learn that being a development dear to the heart of many in the room, long overdue and so eagerly awaited it was now, apparently, going to be jeopardised by the way it was to be implemented. Rarely had I seen colleagues so galvanised yet equally polarised in their feelings towards the future of EYPS.

Turn the clock forward almost three years and EYPS has not only survived (not that there was really any doubt that it would) but has grown and matured to the point where it has around 35 training providers covering the whole of the UK, delivering a range of routes to suit particular needs. I am still far from an expert in this age range but as a senior manager chairing EYPS meetings I quickly came to appreciate the structure and ethos underpinning EYPS. So, terms such as validation, short, long and full pathways and their suggested duration of study slipped off my tongue, and necessary prerequisites in the area of Early Years educare such as Children's Learning and Development; Social Policy for Early Years; Children's Rights and Diversity; Multi-professional Perspectives in Work with Children and Promoting Emotional Security all made more sense – in my management role.

What though if I wanted to attain EYPS? How did, or indeed, *did* these pathways link together? I might possess high levels of practitioner competence and dedication but with little received education and training at University level where might I find material to start to help me overcome my almost certain apprehension of academic study? Or material to help me engage with theoretical perspectives and so help me to better understand my existing practice and help me to make it more effective? Or even material couched within a context that also explored those areas important to me as a practitioner: communicating and working in partnership with families and carers; teamwork and collaboration; and providing an environment for play and learning? Material, perhaps even more crucially, which could provide words of support from those who have achieved EYPS, who through their stories could help me to achieve my goal? That material is all in this book.

The authors, all highly experienced in different roles in Early Years, have admirably addressed all of the points in the last paragraph but have done so in a format which guides the learner carefully and cogently through its contents. Starting with an overview of EYPS standards it moves in to an introduction to the EYPS framework, explaining the basis for its inception, its structure and critically what it implies for the range of learners who are seeking the qualification. It then moves on to consider various theoretical perspectives and at the beginning of each chapter helpfully identifies which of the EYPS standards will be covered within it. Throughout the book, these and other chapters are structured to invite the learner to explore and reflect upon their own practice through the use of appropriate contextual material and they conclude with the provision of a comprehensive set of references for further reading. While the latter chapters engage more specifically with the EYPS process considering such aspects as working with your Placement Supervisor and Leadership and Partnership in Early Years, it is perhaps the last chapter – Early Years Professionals Talking – that will convince even the most reticent learner that they can achieve EYPS.

This material recognises the base from which many seeking to achieve EYPS commence and skilfully guides them through what initially must seem like a labyrinth of EYPS terminology and academic theory. The material typifies the enthusiasm and encouragement of its authors and will no doubt help those wishing to attain EYPS achieve their goal and in so doing help them become the future leaders of Early Years practice.

Dr Clive Opie
Assistant Director
School of Teaching, Health and Care
Bradford College

Acknowledgements

Pam Jarvis:

As always, my first acknowledgements are for my family who put up with me while I write and edit! Many thanks are offered to all the people who have participated in my research over the years, various aspects of which are referred to throughout the chapters of this book. I am very grateful to my colleagues Wendy Holland, Jane Guilfoyle, Poonam Cant, Sarah Procter and Lynn Bradley for agreeing to be part of the unique collaboration that produced this book, and subsequently trusting me to edit their excellent chapters. Jane George deserves a very special mention all to herself as a long-standing colleague and very dear friend who has been unfailing in her professional and personal support since we began our journey together in the mid-1990s: 'a friend hears the song in my heart and sings it to me when my memory fails'. Thanks go to Maggie Smith who, alongside Jane Guilfoyle, initially set up the Early Years Professional Status programme at Bradford College that inspired us all to create this book. A very big 'thank you' goes to Dr Clive Opie Assistant Director (Teaching Health and Care) Bradford College University Centre for his ongoing encouragement and support, and (despite his modest comments in his forward!) his very deep understanding of contemporary early years issues. Thanks also go to all of Clive's team in Teaching Health and Care, many of whom have offered valuable professional support and encouragement over the period that this book was conceived and produced. We are housed in McMillan Building, named for Margaret McMillan, an early twentieth century pioneer of early years educare; her memory and her ethos continue to inspire us all. Especial thanks go to the four Early Years Professionals without whose participation there would have been no chapter 11; subsequent history should also recognise all of them as pioneers in the ongoing struggle to develop a cohesive professional educare ethos for infants and young children in twenty first century England. I should also thank Chris Jarvis, Dr Simon George and Sarah George for their patient proof reading, Michelle Megson who has given much valuable admin support to the team and last but definitely not least, every single one of the Early Years Professionals we have trained over the last two and a half years, who have taught me at least as much as I have taught them!

Jane George:

To my husband Simon and children Sarah and Graham, their lives have been affected by my work, my study and my writing — from preparing and 'test-driving' activities to IT expertise and proof reading — you are always supportive towards my ideas even when you don't really understand them. To all the children and families I have worked with who have influenced my thinking and practice and allowed me to develop my skills and knowledge through them. To my colleagues at Bradford College and my former colleagues in other organisations, you have challenged me to challenge myself

Wendy Holland:

The very nature of Early Years Practice is founded on good team work, and I would like to acknowledge all the help and support and inspiration I've received from the dedicated Early Years teams I have worked with both in mainstream and special school settings here in Yorkshire and in Lancashire. I would also like to acknowledge the immense gratitude I feel for those parents and carers of young children, who have welcomed me into their homes and worked with me, sometimes in very difficult circumstances, to enhance the lives of children. To Barry Miller and Maggie Smith, a huge thank you for having the initial vision to see what a difference the Early Years Professional Status programme could mean for future Early Years Practice, and Jane Guilfoyle along with the tutors, mentors and assessors for turning that vision into the reality of a very effective EYPS programme at Bradford College. To Dr. Clive Opie, my sincere thanks for his enthusiastic support and encouragement of a once fledgling programme that now commends wide recognition and respect, proof of which is the quality of our newly qualified EYPs, the 'pioneers', as my colleague and co-author, Dr. Pam Jarvis, so rightly calls them. Finally, my thanks go to all my collaborators in this book for giving of their time, and sharing their knowledge and expertise to create something so uniquely knowledgeable and diverse for the Early Years Professionals of the future.

Guided tour

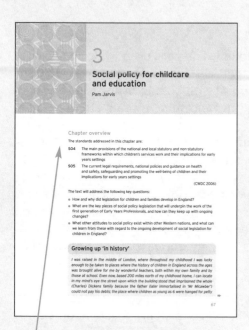

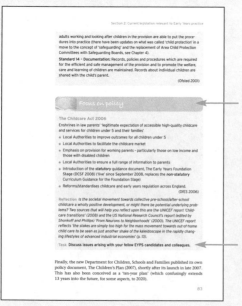

Chapter overviews begin by directing you to the standards that the chapter will address and highlighting some key questions that the chapter will cover.

Chapter introductions focus on the key themes and concepts that the chapter will build upon, often using mini-case studies.

The **subheadings** throughout the chapter highlight questions that you will need to consider as an early years leader.

The **Focus on practice** and **policy** features use real-life examples to help apply the theory of the chapter to a day-to-day context.

They typically close with a **Reflection** that will ask you to pause and engage in an activity and help you become a reflective practitioner.

Practical tasks throughout the book will help you to apply what you have learnt in each chapter.

Theory is applied to practice in short stories or **vignettes** highlighting practical situations in a variety of early years settings.

Figure 3.1 **Te Whariki: the woven mat**
Source: http://www.minedu.govt.nz/web/downloadable/dl3567_v1/WHARIKI.pdf p. 13.

Short **chapter conclusions** reflect on the topics the chapter has covered, and will help you to consolidate your learning. The conclusions summarise the key features of each chapter by looking back at the questions posed in the chapter overview.

At the end of each chapter, **further readings** and **relevant websites** are suggested to help you take your knowledge and understanding to the next level.

Publisher's acknowledgements

We are grateful to the following for permission to reproduce copyright material:

Figures
Figure 2.1 from *Psychology: the science of mind and behaviour*, Hodder & Stoughton (Gross, R. 1996) p. 888, Richard Gross, Psychology: The Science of Mind and Behaviour, 3/e (Hodder & Stoughton, 1996), (c) 1996 Richard Gross, reproduced by permission of Hodder & Stoughton Ltd"; Figure 2.2 from *Children's Language and Communication Difficulties: Understanding, Identification and Intervention* (Dockrell, J. and Messer, D. 1999), By kind permission of Continuum International Publishing Group.; Figure 3.1 from Te Whāriki is a metaphor for the curriculum, which weaves together the principles, strands, and goals defined in the document. The whāriki concept recognises the diversity of early childhood education in New Zealand. Different programmes, philosophies, structures, and environments will contribute to the distinctive patterns of the whāriki. Te Whariki: National Early Childhood Curriculum Guidelines, published by Learning Media Ltd for the Ministry of Education, Wellington 1996.

The publisher would like to thank the following for their kind permission to reproduce their photographs:

(Key: b-bottom; c-centre; l-left; r-right; t-top)

37 POD - Pearson Online Database: Pearson Education Ltd. Jules Selme (t); Pearson Education Ltd. Jules Selmes (c, b); **38 POD - Pearson Online Database:** Pearson Education Ltd. Jules Selmes (t, c); Pearson Education Ltd. Jules Selmes (b); **49 POD - Pearson Online Database:** Pearson Education Ltd. Jules Selmes; **52 Universal Press Syndicate:** ©1996 Watterson; **54 POD - Pearson Online Database:** Pearson Education Ltd. Jules Selmes. **59 POD - Pearson Online Database:** Creatas; **63 POD - Pearson Online Database:** Pearson Education Ltd. Jules Selmes. **69 Courtesy of the Thackray Museum, Leeds.:** (l, r); **72 Solo Syndication / Associated Newspapers Ltd:** By Permission of Llyfrgell Genedlaethol Cymru / The National Library of Wales and the British Cartoon archive, Kent; **96 Micheline Mason:** Alan Sprung; **105 Courtesy of Persona Doll Training.** www.persona-doll-training.org; **189 POD - Pearson Online Database:** Pearson Education Ltd. Malcolm Harris; **196 POD - Pearson Online Database:** Pearson Education Ltd. Jules Selmes; **197 POD - Pearson Online Database:** Pearson Education Ltd. Jules Selmes; **200 POD - Pearson Online Database:** Pearson Education Ltd. Jules Selmes; **206 POD - Pearson Online Database:** Pearson Education Ltd. Jules Selmes; **208 Milet Publishing:** From Chameleon Races / English-Somali by Laura Hambleton (Milet Publishing 2005) Copyright: Laura Hambleton & Milet Publishing; **216 Alamy Images:** ClassicStock (l); JUPITER IMAGES / BananaStock (r). **Corbis:** Gary Houlder (c); **231 Le Kinder Club:** Jane George

All other images © Pearson Education

Picture Research by Debra Weatherley

Every effort has been made to trace the copyright holders and we apologise in advance for any unintentional omissions. We would be pleased to insert the appropriate acknowledgement in any subsequent edition of this publication.

Introduction to
The Early Years Professional's Complete Companion

Pam Jarvis, Jane George and Wendy Holland

Welcome to *The Early Years Professional's Complete Companion*. This book provides a companion handbook for candidates currently engaged in Early Years Professional Status (EYPS) training, their mentors, work placement trainers and tutors. It will also help Early Years Professionals (EYPs) and Early Years teachers to reflect upon and develop their practice and leadership skills and to consider potential routes for continuing professional development. The book will initially outline what is required in terms of entry to EYPS training, and the four pathways that candidates may take. Its central focus will be upon the standards against which all Early Years Professional candidates are tested through the validation process. These standards are conceptually grouped in chapters (see below) in which experienced EYPS trainers take the reader on a holistic journey through the skills and knowledge that the candidate needs to develop to meet the standards required. Ideas for practical activities and further reading are suggested, and the text is interspersed with boxes outlining examples of practice, accompanied by reflection and advice.

The book is organised into four parts:

Part 1: Introducing Early Years Professional Status
Part 2: The Children's Agenda: principles in children's development, social policy and inclusion
Part 3: Leading practice in the Early Years setting
Part 4: Becoming an Early Years Professional: validation and beyond

The complex interface between EYPS training and the instigation of the Early Years Foundation Stage, the Common Core Skills, the Common Assessment Framework and the associated 'Lead Professional' role will be emphasised throughout the text. The text as a whole will also comprehensively reflect upon the role of the EYP in the new childcare/education settings currently being introduced in the UK, which include Extended Schools and Children's Centres. It depicts EYPS training as an integral part of the Every Child Matters initiative, and the EYP as a new professional role that is integral to the current transformation of practice in Early Years settings, underpinned by the new Early Years Foundation Stage, the Common Core Skills and

Common Assessment Framework. From the innovative basis of this approach, readers will be supported in their development of an organic, holistic perspective on childcare and education, where the EYPS standards are achieved in a synthesis of practical skills and knowledge development, not on a mechanical standard-by-standard basis. As such, readers will find that the standards are not always covered within the chapters in the exact order or within the same groupings in which they appear in the Children's Workforce Development Council (CWDC) documents (see http://www.cwdcouncil.org.uk/eyps).

The standards, in their initial presentation by CWDC, are as follows:

Knowledge and understanding

S01 The principles and content of the Early Years Foundation Stage and how to put them into practice

S02 The individual and diverse ways in which children develop and learn from birth to the end of the foundation stage and thereafter

S03 How children's well-being, development, learning and behaviour can be affected by a range of influences and transitions from inside and outside the setting

S04 The main provisions of the national and local statutory and non-statutory frameworks within which children's services work and their implications for early years settings

S05 The current legal requirements, national policies and guidance on health and safety, safeguarding and promoting the well-being of children and their implications for early years settings

S06 The contribution that other professionals within the setting and beyond can make to children's physical and emotional well-being, development and learning

Effective practice

S07 Have high expectations of all children and commitment to ensuring that they can achieve their full potential

S08 Establish and sustain a safe, welcoming, purposeful, stimulating and encouraging environment where children feel confident and secure and are able to develop and learn

S09 Provide balanced and flexible daily and weekly routines that meet children's needs and enable them to develop and learn

S10 Use close, informed observation and other strategies to monitor children's activity, development and progress systematically and carefully, and use this information to inform, plan and improve practice and provision

S11 Plan and provide safe and appropriate child-led and adult-initiated experiences, activities and play opportunities in indoor, outdoor and in out-of-setting contexts, which enable children to develop and learn

S12 Select, prepare and use a range of resources suitable for children's ages, interests and abilities, taking account of diversity and promoting equality and inclusion

S13 Make effective personalised provision for the children they work with

S14 Respond appropriately to children, informed by how children develop and learn and a clear understanding of possible next steps in their development and learning

S15 Support the development of children's language and communication skills

S16 Engage in sustained shared thinking with children

S17 Promote positive behaviour, self-control and independence through using effective behaviour management strategies and developing children's social, emotional and behavioural skills

S18 Promote children's rights, equality, inclusion and anti-discriminatory practice in all aspects of their practice

S19 Establish a safe environment and employ practices that promote children's health, safety and physical, mental and emotional well-being

S20 Recognise when a child is in danger or at risk of harm and know how to act to protect them

S21 Assess, record and report on progress in children's development and learning and use this as a basis for differentiating provision

S22 Give constructive and sensitive feedback to help children understand what they have achieved and think about what they need to do next and, when appropriate, encourage children to think about, evaluate and improve on their own performance

S23 Identify and support children whose progress, development or well-being is affected by changes or difficulties in their personal circumstances and know when to refer them to colleagues for specialist support

S24 Be accountable for the delivery of high-quality provision

Relationships with children

S25 Establish fair, respectful, trusting, supportive and constructive relationships with children

S26 Communicate sensitively and effectively with children from birth to the end of the foundation stage

S27 Listen to children, pay attention to what they say and value and respect their views

S28 Demonstrate the positive values, attitudes and behaviour they expect from children

Communicating and working in partnership with families and carers

S29 Recognise and respect the influential and enduring contribution that families and parents/carers can make to children's development, well-being and learning

S30 Establish fair, respectful, trusting and constructive relationships with families and parents/carers, and communicate sensitively and effectively with them

S31 Work in partnership with families and parents/carers, at home and in the setting, to nurture children, to help them develop and to improve outcomes for them

S32 Provide formal and informal opportunities through which information about children's well-being, development and learning can be shared between the setting and families and parents/carers

Teamwork and collaboration

S33 Establish and sustain a culture of collaborative and cooperative working between colleagues

S34 Ensure that colleagues working with them understand their role and are involved appropriately in helping children to meet planned objectives

S35 Influence and shape the policies and practices of the setting and share in collective responsibility for their implementation

S36 Contribute to the work of a multi-professional team and, where appropriate, coordinate and implement agreed programmes and interventions on a day-to-day basis

Professional development

S37 Develop and use skills in literacy, numeracy and information and communication technology to support their work with children and wider professional activities

S38 Reflect on and evaluate the impact of practice, modifying approaches where necessary, and take responsibility for identifying and meeting their professional development needs

S39 Take a creative and constructively critical approach towards innovation, and adapt practice if benefits and improvements are identified

(CWDC 2008)

They are covered within the chapters as follows:

Part 1: Introducing Early Years Professional Status

Chapter 1: Introducing Early Years Professional Status

In this chapter, Pam Jarvis introduces the role of 'Early Years Professional', how and why it was created, and how these initial concepts were developed into

39 standards, and thence a set of training programmes or 'pathways'. This chapter covers the following points:

- What is EYPS?
- Why was it developed?
- Who can enter training?
- What are the 'pathways'?
- What are the key similarities and differences between EYP training and teacher training?
- Is Early Years Professional training for *me*?

Part 2: The Children's Agenda: principles in children's development, social policy and inclusion

Chapter 2: Principles in childcare and education

In this chapter, developmental researcher Pam Jarvis and early years practitioner Jane George encompass the partnership in which they have designed and delivered child development modules for the past decade, synthesising the theoretical and the practical, and how these meet within the current early years guidance documents. This rather longer than average chapter is also used as a source of theoretical reference by the practice-based chapters throughout the book. The chapter incorporates:

S01 The principles and content of the Early Years Foundation Stage and how to put them into practice

S02 The individual and diverse ways in which children develop and learn from birth to the end of the foundation stage and thereafter

S03 How children's well-being, development, learning and behaviour can be affected by a range of influences and transitions from inside and outside the setting

Chapter 3: Social policy for childcare and education

In this chapter, Pam Jarvis not only outlines the current social policy for children and families, but, from her academic background as both historian and educational researcher, considers the concept of 'social policy' from both a historical and international perspective, to support students not only in building their knowledge in this area, but also their critical and analytical skills. This chapter incorporates:

S04 The main provisions of the national and local statutory and non-statutory frameworks within which children's services work and their implications for early years settings

S05 The current legal requirements, national policies and guidance on health and safety, safeguarding and promoting the well-being of children and their implications for early years settings

Chapter 4: Safe and equal, in the setting and beyond

In this chapter, Jane George reflects upon over 20 years of professional experience of supporting staff to ensure children's safety and equal opportunities in early years. This chapter incorporates:

S18 Promote children's rights, equality, inclusion and anti-discriminatory practice in all aspects of their practice

S19 Establish a safe environment and employ practices that promote children's health, safety and physical, mental and emotional well-being

S20 Recognise when a child is in danger or at risk of harm and know how to act to protect them

Part 3: Leading practice in the Early Years setting

Chapter 5: Leading in children's learning and development

In this chapter, Wendy Holland reflects upon over 30 years of experience as a nursery teacher and teacher/EYP trainer and assessor to outline the core daily work of an EYP in supporting children's learning in the Early Years. This chapter incorporates:

S10 Use close, informed observation and other strategies to monitor children's activity, development and progress systematically and carefully, and use this information to inform, plan and improve practice and provision

S13 Make effective personalised provision for the children they work with

S14 Respond appropriately to children, informed by how children develop and learn and a clear understanding of possible next steps in their development and learning

S15 Support the development of children's language and communication skills

S16 Engage in sustained shared thinking with children

S21 Assess, record and report on progress in children's development and learning and use this as a basis for differentiating provision

S22 Give constructive and sensitive feedback to help children understand what they have achieved and think about what they need to do next and, when appropriate, encourage children to think about, evaluate and improve on their own performance

Chapter 6: Promoting emotional security and positive behaviour

Moving directly on from Chapter 5, Wendy Holland now turns her attention to supporting children's emotional development, hence supporting positive behaviour within professional environments providing care and education for children from birth to 5. This chapter incorporates:

S07 Have high expectations of all children and commitment to ensuring that they can achieve their full potential

S17 Promote positive behaviour, self-control and independence through using effective behaviour management strategies and developing children's social, emotional and behavioural skills

S23 Identify and support children whose progress, development or well-being is affected by changes or difficulties in their personal circumstances and know when to refer them to colleagues for specialist support

S25 Establish fair, respectful, trusting, supportive and constructive relationships with children

S26 Communicate sensitively and effectively with children from birth to the end of the foundation stage

S27 Listen to children, pay attention to what they say and value and respect their views

S28 Demonstrate the positive values, attitudes and behaviour they expect from children

Chapter 7: Transforming the environment for play and learning

Wendy Holland considers a range of positive environments in which to support children's learning, reflecting upon resources, routines and activities and the responsibility of Lead Professionals to provide high-quality experiences for the children in their care. This chapter incorporates:

S08 Establish and sustain a safe, welcoming, purposeful, stimulating and encouraging environment where children feel confident and secure and are able to develop and learn

S09 Provide balanced and flexible daily and weekly routines that meet children's needs and enable them to develop and learn

S11 Plan and provide safe and appropriate child-led and adult-initiated experiences, activities and play opportunities in indoor, outdoor and in out-of-setting contexts, which enable children to develop and learn

S12 Select, prepare and use a range of resources suitable for children's ages, interests and abilities, taking account of diversity and promoting equality and inclusion

S24 Be accountable for the delivery of high-quality provision

Chapter 8: Leadership and partnership in Early Years

Experienced SureStart innovators and Children's Centre managers Sarah Procter and Lynn Bradley join Wendy Holland to produce this chapter. It reflects upon the broad range of partnerships required within the complex contemporary arena of early years education and care in the UK, encompassing nursery schools, children's centres and non-state sector settings. This chapter incorporates:

S06 The contribution that other professionals within the setting and beyond can make to children's physical and emotional well-being, development and learning

S29 Recognise and respect the influential and enduring contribution that families and parents/carers can make to children's development, well-being and learning

S30 Establish fair, respectful, trusting and constructive relationships with families and parents/carers, and communicate sensitively and effectively with them

S31 Work in partnership with families and parents/carers, at home and in the setting, to nurture children, to help them develop and to improve outcomes for them

S32 Provide formal and informal opportunities through which information about children's well-being, development and learning can be shared between the setting and families and parents/carers

S33 Establish and sustain a culture of collaborative and cooperative working between colleagues

S34 Ensure that colleagues working with them understand their role and are involved appropriately in helping children to meet planned objectives

S35 Influence and shape the policies and practices of the setting and share in collective responsibility for their implementation

S36 Contribute to the work of a multi-professional team and, where appropriate, coordinate and implement agreed programmes and interventions on a day-to-day basis

Part 4: Becoming an Early Years Professional: validation and beyond

Chapter 9: Managing your placement supervisor, mentor and your own continuing professional development

In this chapter, Early Years Professional and EYPS candidate mentor Poonam Cant focuses upon the workplace/work placement, considering how EYPS candidates can negotiate their way through the processes required to move successfully into validation, considering typical experiences of candidates on all four pathways. This chapter incorporates:

S37 Develop and use skills in literacy, numeracy and information and communication technology to support their work with children and wider professional activities

S38 Reflect on and evaluate the impact of practice, modifying approaches where necessary, and take responsibility for identifying and meeting their professional development needs

S39 Take a creative and constructively critical approach towards innovation, and adapt practice if benefits and improvements are identified

Chapter 10: Surviving validation

In this chapter, EYP project manager and lead assessor Jane Guilfoyle guides candidates clearly and succinctly through the validation process, outlining:

- What to expect from the validation process
- Preparing for 'Gateway'
- A holistic approach to the standards
- Guide to the written tasks
- Preparing for the assessment visit

Chapter 11: Concluding perspectives: Early Years Professionals talking – voices of the future

In this chapter, Pam Jarvis turns her research focus upon the experiences of Early Years Professionals in the first year of their careers. She interviews four EYPs who approached their validation on each of the four pathways, and who inhabit a range of professional roles in Early Years settings. They reflect upon their experience of validation, their current professional roles, how their training and achievement of EYP status have impacted upon their professional lives, and how they see their future careers in terms of challenges and opportunities.

Throughout the book, the reader is invited to engage in the carefully coordinated EYP training programme developed by this highly effective team, as the innovative programme that they deliver is communicated through the text. 'The Early Years Professional's Complete Companion' is a text that is unquestionably produced specifically for Early Years Professionals, by a team who has a sole focus on teaching and assessing Early Years Professionals, and informed by the opinions of those who have already entered this new professional arena as Early Years Professionals as products of this training programme. It is designed to become a key text for the growing number of potential and actual EYPS candidates, and for tutors, trainers, assessors and mentors currently contributing to EYPS training programmes across the UK.

References

CWDC (2008) Guidance to the standards for the award of Early Years Professional Status. Available at: http://www.cwdcouncil.org.uk/assets/0000/2398/EYP_Guidance_to_standards_web.pdf. Accessed on 2 January 2009.

Part 1

Introducing Early Years Professional Status

1

Introducing Early Years Professional Status

Pam Jarvis

Chapter overview

This chapter will address the following key questions that you are likely to ask as you consider your entry to Early Years Professional Status training:

- What is Early Years Professional Status?
- Why was EYPS developed?
- Who can enter training?
- What are the pathways?
- What is involved in the EYPS validation process?
- What are the key differences between EYPS training and teacher training?
- Is EYP training for *me*?

Introduction: what is Early Years Professional Status?

Early Years Professional Status (EYPS) is a graduate leadership role for Early Years settings in England, developed by the Children's Workforce Development Council (CWDC). The training programme was successfully piloted in 2006, and its first full year of operation commenced in January 2007. The introduction of this role into all professional settings providing care and education for children aged from birth to 5 was instigated by the Government with the intention that a graduate-led workforce would raise standards, skills, experience, commitment and effective leadership of practice across the range of Early Years provision. Early Years Professional Status is equivalent to Qualified Teacher Status (QTS); however, while the professional standards required for each status are related, they are not identical (see below).

Training providers deliver EYPS training programmes in accordance with CWDC guidelines. The current Government target is that there will be at least one Early Years Professional (EYP) leading practice in all children's centres offering childcare by 2010 (two in areas of disadvantage), and at least one EYP in every full daycare setting by 2015. It is intended that EYPs will 'lead and transform practice by modelling skills and behaviours that promote good outcomes for children' (CWDC 2006, online).

Within an EYPS 'validation' process (see below), candidates must demonstrate their competence in areas covered by the 39 EYPS Standards (see the Introduction to this book), which are both knowledge and practice based, and cover leading practice with babies and children from birth to the end of the Early Years Foundation Stage (EYFS). The EYFS concludes at the point that children enter Year 1 primary, which, in England, is the education stage for children who will have their sixth birthday between the September and August of the relevant education year.

EYPS Standards and requirements are *more* than the sum of their parts and the standards are designed to be assessed holistically. It cannot be emphasised strongly enough that EYPS training *cannot* be undertaken in a shallow outcome by outcome fashion; candidates should perceive the standards as 39 interlocking pieces of an integrated jigsaw of academic knowledge and practitioner skills. The status is awarded to highly competent senior practitioners who can demonstrate, through a rigorous set of written and oral assessments, that they are capable of reflexively leading practice within the complex arena of the contemporary Early Years setting, which aims to provide a 'one stop shop' for education, health and care services for young children and their families.

The standards (and the chapters that follow in this book) cover the following areas of Early Years practice:

- Principles in childcare and education
- Social policy for Early Years
- Safe and equal in the setting and beyond
- Leading in children's learning and development
- Promoting emotional security and positive behaviour.
- Transforming the environment for play and learning
- Leadership and partnership in Early Years
- Continuing professional development

Why was EYPS developed?

In October 2005, the Early Education Advisory Group in England agreed that the organisation and management of Early Years care and education services needed to be reviewed and reshaped. Their focus was to produce a role which, while it retained many of the very positive features of the existing nursery teacher role, also encompassed the multi-agency practitioner leadership of a childcare and education team in the new children's centres and extended schools, which would also provide services for children under 3 and their families. The other aspect that the Advisory Group wished to address was that services for children under 3 were, at that time, most frequently led by staff who, while typically possessing high levels of practitioner competence and dedication, had not received education and training at the university level (or Higher Education/HE). Many recent high-profile early years research projects, in particular, the British-based Effective Provision of Pre-School Education (EPPE) project (1997 ongoing, 2008 online), made a clear finding that outcomes for children, especially those from a background of disadvantage, were improved when the practice in the setting was led by a graduate. The role of the Early Years Professional was developed from this basis, representing an attempt to retain the best concepts and structures of Early Years practice in England, and developing it from this basis into a more flexible model for the twenty-first century, with some features drawn from the role of the 'pedagogue', which has a long record of success in Scandinavian countries.

The Early Years Professional is therefore a new professional role with the brief to lead practice within a re-designed Early Years Care and Education system. There are many challenges associated with entering such a new profession, but also many opportunities for the first generation of EYPs to proactively mould their professional role and the new Early Years settings in which they will be the leaders of practice.

Who can enter training?

Those applying to enter the validation only and short pathways must be graduates within disciplines relating directly to early years education and care. Applicants with the minimum of a Foundation Degree/HND in Early Childhood Studies or closely related subjects (e.g. Foundation Degree in Supporting and Managing Learning), or with a BA/BSc degree in a subject unrelated to early years and current professional experience in an early years care/education role are eligible to apply for EYPS training on the long pathway; centres providing the training will tailor the length and content of the programme to the qualifications and experience of successful applicants. Graduates who have no previous training or professional background in early years practice may also access training through the full-time professional development pathway.

EYPS candidates must have achieved both English and Maths GCSEs at grade 'C' or above. They may enter training and study towards these GCSEs simultaneously, but they must have achieved them before entering the validation process. Candidates have to provide a suitable Criminal Records Bureau enhanced clearance that indicates their fitness to work with young children, and a medical history that indicates that they are in sufficiently good physical and mental health to be suitable for the demanding pace and content of work within care and education settings dealing with young children. They also have to provide good references from previous employers/tutors, and those who have previous childcare and/or education experience will need to provide positive references from these specific employers. Finally, EYPS candidates must have the right to live and work in the UK; those who do not cannot be accepted on to the programme.

At the time of writing (early 2009), CWDC regulations do not allow training providers to accept applicants for EYPS training if they are employed in any capacity within a local authority maintained school or nursery; the long, short and validation only pathways are reserved for candidates working in private, voluntary or independent settings or within children's centres that provide care and education for children aged 0–6.

What are the 'pathways'?

The pathways are:

- The four-month part-time validation pathway
- The six-month part-time professional development (short) pathway
- The 15-month part-time professional development (long) pathway, which may be truncated to 12 months for some very experienced practitioner candidates
- The 12-month full-time professional development (full) pathway.

All pathways have financial support packages provided by the CWDC; the balance of funding is allocated between employer and candidate depending on the specific pathway taken. There are no course fees to pay for EYPS training. In 2008, up to £4000 supply cover costs were available to settings that released an employee for EYPS training, and candidates on the full pathway were entitled to a personal bursary of £5000. There is also funding available to pay for mentoring for EYPS students on all four pathways.

The validation only pathway (four months part-time) is probably for you if:

- You are currently employed in a senior role in a children's centre, or in a private, voluntary or independent childcare/education setting that deals with the full Early Years Foundation Stage age range (0–6), *and*
- You have a degree in a childcare/Early Years education related discipline in which you have achieved at least 60 credits at level 6 (HE level 3).

Validation only pathway students will usually need to attend college for training sessions that take place over a maximum of six full days; this programme will be spread over four months. Settings releasing a candidate for the validation only pathway received £500 in supply cover costs in 2008.

 Focus on practice

Validation only candidate Belinda trained as a nursery nurse 20 years ago. She has worked as a practitioner in Early Years since receiving her initial qualification, starting off in a nursery school and moving into private daycare eight years ago. She completed an HNC in Early Childhood Studies 10 years ago, and then undertook a 'top-up' programme five years later after which she was awarded a BA (Hons) in Child and Youth Studies. Last year, she opened a private daycare setting which she owns and manages in partnership with a long-standing colleague. The centre has a growing reputation for excellent practice, which has recently been recognised by their first full Ofsted report. Belinda has extensive experience of working with the whole EYFS age range and their families, and she leads and trains her own staff on an ongoing basis. Her most recent training initiative has involved participating in a collaborative project undertaken in partnership with other full daycare providers within the local area, to enhance practice in working with the parents and families who use their daycare provision.

Reflection *The most important aspect for validation only candidates is that they can clearly show complete coverage across the full EYFS age range and full range of standards, as both a current practitioner and as leader of practice. Belinda has such long experience of enacting, developing and leading practice across the full EYFS age range; she is clearly a strong candidate for this pathway.*

The short pathway (six months part-time) is probably for you if:

- You are currently employed in a senior role in a children's centre, or in a private, voluntary or independent childcare/education setting that deals with at least part of the age range within the Early Years Foundation Stage age range (0–6), *and*
- You have a degree in a childcare/Early Years education related discipline in which you have achieved at least 60 credits at level 6 (HE level 3).

Short pathway students will be provided with a range of training experiences tailored to their individual needs and availability. This may involve both college attendance and short placement experience; the programme will be spread over six months including the validation process. Settings releasing a candidate for the short pathway received £1000 in supply cover costs in 2008.

Focus on practice

Short pathway candidate Sanjay initially trained as a nursery teacher. He spent five years teaching in a nursery school, then, three months ago, he was appointed to lead practice in a newly opened children's centre. Sanjay was very familiar with the Curriculum Guidance for the Foundation Stage, but as he worked only with children over 3 in the nursery school he does not have any substantial knowledge of the Birth to Three Matters material that formed the guidance for working with younger children.

He has never worked professionally with children under 3 in any capacity, although he does have his own young family, and has assured the training provider that he has plenty of practical experience in nappy changing and bottle feeding! He is bilingual and worked as the home-school coordinator for families with English as an Additional Language when he was in post at the nursery school. It is agreed that Sanjay will join the short pathway, attending a programme of early evening sessions at college with other short pathway students, covering developmental theory from birth to 3, and the requirements of the Early Years Foundation Stage. Such sessions will also provide some opportunities for the candidates to 'network'. Sanjay will also undertake a one day a week placement over eight weeks in the baby room of a local private daycare centre, as his children's centre does not yet provide care for babies. His training provider has asked him to carry out a set of observations on the babies that he will be working with, and with the support of his mentor he will use these to develop some activities for them. Sanjay's employer will receive funding to provide cover for him while he attends placement.

Reflection *Sanjay is clearly very experienced at enacting and leading practice in one area of the relevant age range, but has recognised that he needs to develop his experience of provision for children under 3. He already has some basis for developing these skills in his experience as a parent, and his placement and study are arranged around a timetable that he can work with, thanks to the funding that CWDC have provided for his employer to cover his absence. He has a wealth of experience of working with parents and families. All of these are important indications that Sanjay is a strong candidate for the short pathway.*

The long pathway (15 months part-time, may be 12 months in some individual cases) is probably for you if:

- You are currently employed in a children's centre, or in a private, voluntary or independent childcare/education setting that deals with at least part of the age range of the Early Years Foundation Stage (0–6), *and*
- You have an HND or Foundation Degree in a childcare/Early Years education related discipline or an ordinary or honours degree in a non-childcare/early years education-related subject.

Long pathway students will study a range of HE childcare and development modules at level 6 (Stage 3 HE). To go forward to EYPS validation, non-graduate candidates must pass modules totalling a minimum of 60 Credits, leading to the award of a BA in Early Childhood Studies. Some candidates will opt to undertake the full 120 credit award of BA (Hons) in Early Childhood Studies. CWDC will provide the funding for non-graduate long pathway candidates to undertake 60 credits of childcare and development study at level 6 (HE level 3). Settings releasing a candidate for the long pathway also received £4000 in supply cover costs in 2008.

Long pathway candidate Sean finished his Foundation Degree in Playwork five years ago. He initially worked in an adventure playground with children over 7, but when that lost its funding and shut down three years ago, he opened a childminding business with his partner Jamelia; this is currently doing very well. They received a particular commendation on their last Ofsted report for their excellent liaison with families; this was due to a recording and information sharing system that Sean designed.

Jamelia did not initially have any qualifications in childcare, but she is currently just completing an NVQ 3 in Children's Care, Learning and Development (CCLD). Last year the business made enough money for the couple to employ an assistant, who Sean and Jamelia have encouraged to take an NVQ 2 in CCLD. As they now have an extra member of staff, and, given the funding attached to EYPS training, Sean can now spare the time to take the top-up year to convert his Foundation Degree into a BA (Hons) in Early Childhood Studies, followed by EYPS validation. He can cover the leading practice standards as he leads the practice of Jamelia and the childcare assistant in his setting. At the moment the setting does not care for any children under 2, but they have had some recent enquiries. Sean will keep his tutor informed about the progress of this situation, and, if a firm booking does not result, the college will arrange a short placement for him in the baby room of a local children's centre towards the end of his top-up programme, where he will carry out the same programme of observations and planning as Sanjay.

Reflection *Sean has organised his time to ensure that he can cope with the demands of the long pathway. He has recognised a possible pitfall in terms of covering the full age range and has made a contingency plan in case things do not work out as he might hope. Sean has a solid background in practice with children, and while 'lone' childminders sometimes struggle to demonstrate the leadership skills required for EYPS validation, Sean should not have a problem with this as he is clearly the leading practitioner in a setting with two other workers. He has shown particular aptitude for working with families, and this has been recognised and praised by an Ofsted inspector. All of these factors indicate that he is a strong candidate for the long pathway.*

The full pathway (12 months full-time) is probably for you if:

- You have limited, or no experience of working with children aged 0–6

- You have a strong ambition to develop or change your career in order to work in a leadership role in an early years setting, and you are in a position to undertake a year's unpaid intensive professional development in order to accomplish this. (In 2008, full pathway candidates were eligible for a CWDC bursary of £5000.)

- You have a degree in which you have achieved at least 60 credits at level 6 (HE level 3) in any subject or discipline.

Full pathway students attend college across one calendar year (which may run September–August or January–December), to undertake the academic study of child development, Early Years education and care. A substantial percentage of the year's programme will additionally be spent gaining work experience – the minimum time allocated for this is stipulated as 18 full weeks by CWDC, but many centres will judge that this needs to be substantially more for students to gain the necessary knowledge and skills, which must include leadership. Many centres will give students the opportunity to gain some credit for academic study undertaken during full pathway training, either at BA honours or masters level, depending upon the specific programme offered.

Focus on practice

Full pathway candidate Amelia always had an ambition to work with young children when she was at school, but her parents and teachers persuaded her that she could 'do better' particularly when she got very good GCSE and 'A' level grades, showing a particular aptitude in maths. Amelia eventually completed a BA (Hons) in Business Studies and went to work in a building society when she was 21, reaching the rank of deputy manager by the time she had her own two children, who are now 14 and 16. She returned to work in the building society part time as a section leader after her first maternity leave. Three months ago, she applied for voluntary redundancy as she calculated that this would give her enough money to take a year out from paid work. She plans to undertake the EYPS full pathway and then purchase a private daycare setting. Her husband Rob will be her business partner, and he is very supportive of her plans to re-train. Amelia has undertaken some recent voluntary work in her friend's private daycare setting, which she enjoyed very much. She also feels that she will bring many transferable skills to her studies. For example, she is an experienced parent; she was one of the founder members and coordinators of a parent and toddler club in her local area when her children were young, and she has a wealth of experience of team leadership and management from her role at the building society. She also has an excellent grasp of accounts and financial planning, and is looking forward to using these skills to benefit her own business. Last but not least, she is very used to the self-organisation and time-management that is an essential feature of coping as a working parent. She is looking forward to the course as a whole, but most particularly to returning to college to study child development – the subject that she wanted to take when she was 18. Her training provider has constructed an academic programme for full pathway students so that they can complete the first third of a masters qualification alongside their EYPS training, so Amelia should finish the year with a postgraduate certificate in Early Years in addition to her EYPS. The children are intrigued that mum is 'going back to school' and both they and Amelia are looking forward to all sitting down to do their 'homework' together.

Reflection *Amelia has clearly thought very hard about why she wants to undertake the full pathway; this is based on a long-term ambition and a realistic business plan* *for the future. Her redundancy pay means that the modest size of the bursary should not create financial problems for her over the year's training if she is unable to earn money during this period. She has undertaken voluntary work within the Early Years sector to make sure that she has realistic expectations of the childcare environment. She has clear plans relating to how she wishes to use her new qualifications, and she possesses a large set of transferable skills and experience to take forward into her new role, including some voluntary experience of organising and coordinating a serv-ice for children and their parents. Her family are very supportive, and her children are old enough to cope independently if she has to undertake placement during school holidays. Amelia also brings her strong time-management, self-organisation and aca-demic aptitude forward into a very intensive programme where she will need to progress very quickly. All of these factors indicate that Amelia is a strong candidate for the full pathway.*

Candidates for all pathways should carefully consider their individual needs and learning styles when choosing a training provider. There is a multitude of ways to provide EYPS training, and the candidate should choose wisely, considering which combination of face-to-face, open and blended learning offered by different train-ing providers they feel would best develop their skills, and how flexible different training providers are able to be with regard to offering individual programmes. There is also great variation in the amount of individual tuition offered by differ-ent training providers; full and long pathway candidates in particular should be wary of training programmes that rely almost exclusively on placement/workplace experience, with little time or tuition offered to develop early years related theo-retical skills, or for group reflection with fellow candidates, or for individual and small group interaction with tutors and mentors. Some training providers may also offer the chance to study for additional accreditation on conventional HE pro-grammes, for example to study relevant postgraduate modules as part of the train-ing programme, which obviously adds value to the training process. Candidates who need to achieve an English and/or Maths GCSE, or build writing skills before entering validation should also carefully research whether and how different train-ing providers may offer to support them in such endeavours, before committing themselves to sign on to a specific provider's programme.

What is involved in the EYPS validation process?

The validation process is described in detail in Chapter 10. Students on the early part of their EYPS training journey are advised to consider their training as a holistic process, engaging them in the development of both academic knowledge and practical skills, knitted together by engagement in reflection on practice, from which the EYP competencies will emerge. A highly summarised guide to validation is, however, provided below to give students a basic outline of what to expect.

Formal validation training will typically be provided over five days of college attendance which will be carefully staged over four months. Each centre will make its own arrangements for this; as such there is some element of flexibility for days/times to be agreed with individual candidate groups. The input is structured as follows:

- **Day 1**: Introduction to the standards
- **Day 2**: Introduction to the written tasks
- **Day 3**: Introduction to the Gateway review of skills
- **Day 4**: Gateway review of skills (½ day) – at this point candidates will receive formal feedback from the lead assessor at the centre relating to whether they have shown suitability to proceed to validation; those who have not will be advised where shortfalls have occurred, and be given targets to meet before re-entering the validation process at a later date
- **Day 5**: Introduction to the setting visit for those candidates who are proceeding to validation.

Candidates produce a *set of CWDC-stipulated written tasks*, which are a set of structured descriptions, reflections and evaluations on leading practice across the full EYFS age range, totalling approximately 6000 words. The written tasks are examined by an EYPS *assessor*, who will then subsequently undertake a *visit to the candidate's setting* over one working day where s/he will carry out a range of assessment activities for which the candidate must produce a *range of supporting evidence* (e.g. planning documents, centre policies developed by the candidate etc); this takes approximately 5½ hours. This includes the candidate hosting a 'tour' of the setting where, based on the evidence they have presented in the set tasks and supporting evidence, they illustrate to the assessor how they lead practice, and time for the assessor to interview some witnesses nominated by the candidate who can provide evidence that demonstrates the candidate's leadership skills.

The assessor makes a judgement on the written evidence presented and the evidence collected during the setting visit, and subsequently makes a recommendation as to whether the candidate has satisfactorily met all the standards, whether there is a minor shortfall on one or two, or whether the candidate has, in this instance, failed to meet a substantial proportion of the standards. This decision is internally verified by the team of assessors at the centre, and a sample of candidates' written evidence and matching assessor records are then sent to an external assessor for external verification. When this somewhat lengthy process is complete, candidates are advised of their result. Those receiving a result of 'minor shortfall' can usually address this by providing additional evidence to the centre, after which their result is revised to 'all standards met'; those with a 'major shortfall' will need to repeat validation at a later date. *It should be emphasised here that it is very rare for a candidate who has passed through Gateway to receive a result of 'major shortfall'*, so please do not worry unduly about this process at the outset of your training – place your trust in your centre's highly experienced lead assessor.

What are the key differences between EYPS training and teacher training?

There are actually a lot of *similarities* between EYPS and teacher training. Both require physical and psychological resilience, both confer a status which recognises the holder's competence to provide care and education for children and both require a candidate to demonstrate a mixture of academic knowledge and practical skills. It is in the balance between the content and uses of the academic knowledge concerned that we can locate our first difference: where teachers, particularly those who teach in the later years of secondary schools, are expected to possess a body of subject-based academic knowledge that crucially underpins the *content* of their teaching, EYPs are expected to possess a body of academic knowledge relating to the study of child development, and to bring this knowledge to bear in their *interactions* with young children. This is an excellent illustration of the EYP/QTS 'equal but different' situation. While the level of subject-specific knowledge required to support the development of young children's early reading, writing and numeracy skills is clearly not at the level required by a secondary school teacher delivering 'A' level English or mathematics to 17 year olds, EYPs work with children who are at a much earlier stage of their development; therefore they need a wealth of developmental knowledge to allow them to engage with such very young minds, and to structure play-based learning tasks that sustain young children's interest and enjoyment. EYPs also require a solid knowledge of child development to engage effectively in the physical and emotional care of very young children, which will additionally underpin their ability to develop closer (while still highly professional) relationships with the children and families that use their setting than will be the case for teachers working with higher ratios of older children to adults within formal classroom settings.

In terms of training, both trainee teachers and EYPS candidates will be expected to undertake a mixture of academic study at college and practical training in the classroom/setting. In this sense, there are some clear structural similarities between the Registered Teacher Programme and the long EYPS pathway, and the Graduate Teacher Programme and the full EYPS pathway. Training structures will of course continue to evolve, particularly with regard to EYPS as a new qualification, but currently the principal differences are as follows:

- Students in initial teacher training undergo continual formal assessment by a placement mentor and college tutors, both of whom work closely with the student during their training process, while EYPS assessment is carried out solely by an impartial stranger assessor, and this assessment is wholly located at the end of the programme of training.
- Teachers have to pass three Teacher Development Agency (TDA) skills tests in literacy, numeracy and information technology before they can become fully-fledged practitioners; EYPs do not. However, teachers do not have to undertake any nationally prescribed and moderated extended written tasks such as those that EYPs are required to present for the validation process.

- Teachers do not finish their training when they graduate with their Qualified Teacher Status; they have to satisfactorily complete a Newly Qualified Teacher year in employment before they are recognised as a fully-fledged teacher. Those who fail the NQT year are not permitted to retain their Qualified Teacher Status. At the time of writing (early 2009), EYP status is fully awarded at successful completion of the validation process.

- The practical training that teachers and EYPs undertake is necessarily different with regard to the different workplaces that each profession will inhabit when qualified. Teachers learn to break down curriculum content into discrete learning outcomes that are organised into schemes of work and individual lesson plans, while EYPs learn how to use the cycle of observation, assessment and planning in the pursuit of addressing young children's individual learning and development needs through play. Again, these skills are highly interrelated and transferable; for example, while teachers also need to recognise and plan for individual needs, EYPs need to plan for continuous provision in their setting that can be flexibly accessed by children at different levels of attainment and development.

It is possible to gain both QTS and EYPS. In February 2008 the Department for Children, Schools and Families (DCSF) proposed that children's centres should employ both a qualified Early Years teacher and an EYP; however, 'in most cases the qualified teacher should be able to work towards EYPS' (DCSF 2008, p. 4), indicating their belief that it is possible for one person to 'straddle' the necessary roles. The initial Government view of the difference between the role of the QTS and EYP was outlined to training providers as follows:

- EYPs will principally operate in the private, voluntary and independent sectors providing care and education for children under 6, and alongside Early Years teachers in children's centres/extended schools, leading provision for children under 6. Their work will be underpinned by the Early Years Foundation Stage (DCSF 2008), which began operation in September 2008.

- Primary and Secondary school teachers will operate within local authority maintained schools leading provision for children over 5 (and private schools providing education for children over 5). Their work will be underpinned by the Primary and Secondary National Curriculum, which have also been reviewed for 2008. The Primary Curriculum is currently being further scrutinised by The Primary Review (2008) and, as such, is likely to undergo further changes, at least up to 2010. If a decision is taken to create a more careful bridge between the child-led learning of the EYFS and the early stages of Key Stage 1 of the National Curriculum, EYPs may in future have some role to play in the care and education of children aged between 5 and 7.

Is EYP training for *me*?

The first issues to explore are whether you have the relevant qualifications to access EYPS training (see above). For those who have pre-HE qualifications and significant experience of working in childcare/Early Years education, but do not yet have credits at the HE level, do not give up at this point. Make enquiries with your local Foundation Degree in Early Years provider, as you may qualify for some Accreditation of Prior Experience and Learning (APEL), based on previous experience/qualifications, hence be eligible to undertake a truncated programme towards the award of a Foundation Degree. Many training providers may also allow such experienced, mature students who are employed within the Early Years sector as senior practitioners to undertake some or all of their study via open, distance and/or blended learning, which helps students to balance their work commitments with study.

For those who are just starting out on their careers, you will need to start at the relevant level of the qualifications ladder – for those who are sure they want to work with children from birth to 5, the most relevant qualifications at the 'A' level standard are currently (early 2009) an Edexcel BTEC or CACHE level 3 Diploma in Childcare and Education. You can then move on to a degree programme in Early Childhood Studies, taking every chance to build practical experience via either placement or paid work as you go. CWDC is currently engaged in aligning the standards across the full range of Early Years qualifications, so pre-HE qualifications in childcare and education are also currently undergoing change and development. Consequently, it is advisable to keep an eye on the CWDC website to keep pace with ongoing changes – **www.cwdcouncil.org.uk**.

For those with the relevant HE qualifications and experience, you need to make sure that you meet the health and CRB requirements (see above) and that you have the relevant GCSEs or are willing/able to undertake extra study to complete these before or during your EYPS training programme. Those who have a degree in a different discipline from Childcare/Early Years/Early Years Education, and no previous work experience in Early Years childcare/education settings should seriously contemplate the following advice before undertaking EYPS training, based on my experience over two years of leading the EYPS full pathway:

- The EYPS full pathway is a 'fast track' training programme for graduates. It assumes that full pathway candidates will possess solid graduate-level skills in terms of academic aptitude, self-motivation, self-organisation, personal and academic maturity and the potential for leadership. It puts considerable demands upon students in terms of an expectation that they will take in information very quickly and develop both academic knowledge and practical skills at a very fast pace. For this reason it is very much a full-time course, and those who take it on should expect placement and study to be their full-time occupation throughout the full year of their training.

- Bearing in mind the level of commitment outlined above, it is extremely advisable that entry on to the full pathway is undertaken only after consultation with people sharing the candidate's everyday life (e.g. partners, parents and children), particularly those who may be expected to provide financial support during the training year.

- The potential full pathway candidate should also consider very carefully whether they are fully aware of the substantial physical and psychological demands of a leadership role in Early Years childcare and education, and if they do not have previous experience of the collective care of children aged 0–6 they are strongly advised to obtain at least two weeks' full-time experience as a volunteer in a children's centre or private daycare setting before confirming their registration to the EYPS training programme.

With regard to candidates for the other pathways, they need to consider the following points:

- Do I work with children across the full EYFS age range (0–6)?
- Do I guide the work of other practitioners?
- Do I have a solid understanding of the requirements of the EYFS?
- Am I involved in leading/managing the delivery of the EYFS?
- Am I involved in monitoring/influencing the work of other practitioners, including giving them feedback/guidance?
- Do I interact with professionals inhabiting different roles from myself during the course of my regular duties?
- Do I confidently use literacy, numeracy and IT skills in my everyday work in the setting?
- Am I involved in team working within my setting?
- Do I have a good understanding of how to assess children's progress, and do I/could I support others in this endeavour?
- Do I work in partnership with parents/carers to support children's learning and development and do I/could I support other practitioners to do so?

Success at validation depends upon a 'yes' answer to all these points. Those joining the long pathway are unlikely to enter with all these attributes fully developed, but they must be able to extend to this point over the time during which they undertake EYPS training. Again, as a tutor who has been involved in supporting the long pathway over the past two years, I would advise aspiring long pathway candidates who do not have substantial work-based practitioner experience in Early Years setting(s) to make sure they can build this up to a sufficient level, and secure the opportunity to gain some leadership experience over the period of the training programme. If this seems unlikely, consideration should be given to completing the academic programme of study and gaining additional work experience before enrolling on the EYPS programme, as at the time of writing (early 2009) there is an ongoing opportunity to access the short or validation only pathway when the practitioner feels they have attained the commensurate level and mixture of professional experience. It is emphasised that EYPS is not awarded purely for practitioner competence; it requires the candidate to show evidence that they have led others in practice. This does not, however, mean that all EYPS candidates have to be line managers – it means that they need to be able to show that they are trusted by their setting's stakeholders to *model* good practice and therefore lead the work of others whose practice is not yet developed to such a high level.

Suitably experienced practitioners will need to consider whether they need to undertake the short or validation only pathway. Again, from my experience of supporting short pathway students, the most common reason for taking the short pathway is that, although the candidate can demonstrate that they can competently lead practice for part of the EYFS age range, they lack experience of working with children in the other part. Training providers construct individual programmes of placement and possibly academic input for such candidates, extending their training to six months part-time, which can usually be flexibly arranged. Employers receive CWDC funding for any cover costs incurred (see above). In the end, each potential candidate will need to decide in partnership with their training provider whether EYPS training is for them and, if so, which pathway. Whichever pathway is accessed, you should certainly expect to engage in a lot of hard work over the course of your training, which will also underpin some very rewarding professional and personal development.

Candidates undertaking training between approximately 2006 and 2012 will form the first generation of EYPs, those who undertook their training before all the planned children's centres and integrated services were fully in action, and, for those who trained during the first two years of the programme, even before the EYFS began operation. As such, they will form the cohort who will pilot and further develop a new profession; it is to these very special people that this book is addressed. The book is designed specifically to be a first port of call for those seeking advice on the basic knowledge and skills required by EYPs, and where to access further information with regard to both printed materials and online. We look forward to taking this 'maiden voyage' with all of you, and to producing a revised edition of this book in the not-too-distant future when you have collectively shaped the profession into its first working model. In the more distant future, we hope some of you will write your own books for the second generation of EYPs, creating a growing body of literature to more substantially underpin rich reflective practice within what will then be an increasingly established profession.

Focus on practice

Starting a reflective journal and Continuing Professional Development portfolio

Many of you will have kept reflective journals for previous qualifications. The EYP reflective journal is special, in that it is hoped that, once you start it, it will always be ongoing, acting as a cornerstone of your continuing professional development, long beyond your EYPS validation.

Initially, what you need to do is to produce a basic introduction to your setting and your role within it. This will need to be revised when inevitable changes occur (you move to a different role, move settings etc.). You should try to write an entry at least every three or four days, focusing on aspects of your work-based experience that caused you to reflect upon and develop your practice. Incidents that form the basis for your reflections may be positive, negative or neutral, and mundane, dramatic, funny or sad. You should not have to share your whole journal at any time (as this may inhibit the scope of your reflection), but it is useful from time to time to share edited extracts with fellow students, tutors and colleagues. *Do* make sure that your journal text is safely anonymised, particularly if you are storing it electronically – it is surprisingly easy to unwittingly stray outside the data protection legislation if you use full, real names for colleagues, children and locations!

Alongside your reflective journal, you should also maintain a Continuing Professional Development (CPD) portfolio where you keep records of training courses attended, job reviews/appraisals, possibly some samples of children's work (with their permission) and associated planning from activities you designed that went particularly well, letters/cards expressing thanks from parents and carers (you could even keep communications of complaint with associated notes relating to how you rectified the relevant issues!) and any other materials that you feel serve to document your continuing development as a practitioner.

Further reading

CWDC (2006) Early Years home page, available at:
  http://www.cwdcouncil.org.uk/projects/earlyyears.htm

DCSF (2008) The Early Years Foundation Stage, available at:
  http://www.standards.dfes.gov.uk/eyfs

References

CWDC (2006) Early Years home page, available at:
  http://www.cwdcouncil.org.uk/projects/earlyyears.htm Accessed on 2/4/08.

DCSF (2008) *Graduate Leader Fund – Information on purpose and implementation*, HMSO.

DCSF (2008) The Early Years Foundation Stage, available at:
  http://www.standards.dfes.gov.uk/eyfs/ Accessed on 24/3/08.

Early Education Advisory Group (EEAG) (2005) Annex 3, Paper 05/5/9, Item M available at:
  http://www.tda.gov.uk/upload/resources/doc/b/boardoct05_early_years_teachers_c.doc
  Accessed on 2/4/08.

The Effective Provision of Pre-School Education (EPPE) project (2008) 1997 ongoing, available at:
  http://k1.ioe.ac.uk/schools/ecpe/eppe Accessed on 29/3/08.

The Primary Review (2008), available at:
  http://www.primaryreview.org.uk/index.html Accessed on 2/4/08.

Part 2

The Children's Agenda: principles in children's development, social policy and inclusion

2

Principles in childcare and education

Pam Jarvis and Jane George

Chapter overview

The standards addressed in this chapter are:

S01   How to put the principles and content of the EYFS into practice

S02   The individual and diverse ways in which children develop and learn from birth to the end of the Foundation Stage and thereafter

S03   How children's well-being, development, learning and behaviour can be affected by a range of influences and transitions from inside and outside the setting

(CWDC 2006)

The text will address the following key questions:

- What are the EYFS principles, and how are they reflected in the content?
- What are the main theoretical perspectives that describe how children develop and learn, particularly between birth and their sixth birthday?
- What influences and experiences in the setting and beyond can impact on children's well-being, development, learning and behaviour and how can we connect these to the theoretical perspectives introduced in the previous section?

The culture of childcare – 'then' and 'now'

Caroline, an Early Years Professional, was very surprised at the level of distress that her mother, Jean, exhibited on being told that her three-year old granddaughter, Maisie, would have to undergo a series of treatments as a hospital in-patient. Jean had known that Maisie would need treatment since she was born; the situation was not life-threatening, and had a very positive prognosis: Maisie had a slight deformation of her feet, which would respond to a series of routine operations between the ages of 3 and 5. Caroline reassured her mother: 'she will be fine, Mum.'

'That's what my mum thought when I had my tonsils out in 1958', replied Jean, with tears in her eyes. 'I was only 3, too – she didn't see how much I cried when she wasn't there. I still remember a nurse who got very cross with me and told me to "pull myself together" – I didn't even know what that meant, so I asked my mum at visiting time. There was also the sister in charge of the ward – she wouldn't let your Auntie Sue come in because, your grandma told me later, she said "ten year olds are crawling with germs". Even your grandma got upset the first time she visited me – I don't re-member this, but she told me that I said "I don't live with you any more, mummy, do I?" She tried to explain, but she could only visit for an hour a day . . . apparently, I was only in for a week, too, but it seemed like a year to me . . . .'

'Oh, mum,' said Caroline, now feeling tears welling in her own eyes, 'don't be silly. This isn't the dark ages now. One of us will be with Maisie nearly all of the time when she is in hospital. She's also going to get a visit from one of the staff before she goes in, and she is going to visit the ward, so it won't seem so strange to her. There's a nursery nurse, an EYP and a teacher attached to the ward, so Maisie will be able to do nearly all the activities that she would be doing at nursery, and later at school if she ever needs to be in for longer periods of time. But they will only keep her in for the short-est time that they need to, hopefully not even a week after each operation, and her nursery have already discussed with the hospital how they are going to look after her while her feet are still in plaster.'

'She's going to nursery with her feet in plaster?' said Jean. 'They wouldn't have let you in my day . . . .'

'But an awful lot of things have changed since your day, like treating children as indi-vidual human beings with their own set of needs, for a start,' replied Caroline. 'Now . . . we need to discuss when you will be available to stay with Maisie when she is in hos-pital this time. I'm working out a rota, so all the people she is attached to can take a turn. Don't you remember, attachment theory? I did a project on it at college.'

'No', said Jean more cheerfully, 'I don't. But it sounds like an awful lot of things have changed for the better since I was three years old . . . . .'.

Introduction

Jean is certainly right about one thing – an awful lot of things *have* changed in the field of Early Years practice since she was three years old, including our under-standing of children's emotional development, and the capacity for practitioners to engage in multi-agency working, including ongoing liaison with parents, who are now seen as the most important 'experts' in the pursuit of defining their child's individual needs.

The underpinning principles of childcare and education require that leading practitioners have a solid, up-to-date working knowledge of the current national guidelines for early years practice, and of the theoretical principles that describe how children develop emotionally, socially and intellectually. This rather longer than average chapter will outline a summary of the principles of the current Early Years Foundation Stage (EYFS) guidance (DCSF 2008), followed by a summary of the core theoretical perspectives that have underpinned the huge changes in Early Years practice that have occurred over the last 50 years. The recommended reading list will give you a range of texts to study further on these topics. It is hoped that you will use this chapter as a reference base for the key underpinning theories of child development and the key content and principles of the EYFS, returning when necessary from the later chapters in the book to check (for example) developmental stage information or references to theoretical concepts.

What are the EYFS principles, and how are they reflected in the content?

The EYFS principles focus around four main themes which are:

- A unique child
- Positive relationships
- Enabling environments
- Learning and development.

They are reflected in the content as follows:

A unique child

The EYFS makes it very clear that children should not be expected to progress within a narrow, normative model of the human being. It emphasises that each child has his/her own specific likes, dislikes and **temperament** (see below), and that development does not always proceed in a staged, linear fashion. Carers should expect children to develop along a trajectory where there are sometimes irregular peaks and troughs in progress, and where particular aptitude is shown in some areas and difficulties experienced in others. The key focus for carers is to constantly support the child in their developmental processes, nurturing their self-confidence (hence resilience) at all times. This involves being sensitive to the child's family and cultural background, individual preferences and dislikes, their physical and psychological safety and physical and emotional health.

Positive relationships

The EYFS makes it very clear that the practitioner's responsibility is not only to the child, but also to the family, particularly the parents, in respect of working in partnership with them to support the child's development and learning. A core aspect of this is the provision of a key person within the professional setting, who works with both the child and the family. This is particularly important in the earliest days of the child's life when they are still forming their **internal working model** through their **bonded relationships** (see below).

Enabling environments

Early Years Professionals (EYPs) must be confident to lead practitioner teams in the operation of the ongoing cycle of observation, assessment and planning that should underpin practice within all Early Years settings (see Chapter 5). This cycle should underpin individually tailored provision for each child. This should include negotiation and interaction with the child's parents and, ideally, participation from them in full partnership with the centre and key worker. The EYP should be able to use his/her knowledge of child development to lead a team to plan suitable environments and activities for children, including continuous provision which contains the inherent flexibility for differentiation between individuals, and the inclusion of some activities that present surmountable challenges for children, including the potential to take carefully calculated risks. EYPs should also be prepared to support children sensitively through transitions as and when these arise in their lives.

Learning and development

EYPs should understand how to provide children with a wide variety of play experiences that support their physical, intellectual, social and emotional development. The adult role within such activities is to develop the child's understanding via 'sustained shared thinking' (EYFS 2008 online), an interaction which occurs when the adult meets the child 'where s/he is' at that point in their developmental process, sensitively providing the input that will help the child to move on to the next level of thinking about the issue at hand. This can often involve helping children to make connections between concepts, which will require adult sensitivity towards each individual child's personal 'style', and towards their family and cultural background. Children learn best when they actively engage with situations that make sense *to them*, and a successful setting will provide a range of such opportunities, under the leadership of an EYP. Activities should be carefully designed so that the provision within the setting addresses the six areas of learning and development:

- Personal, social and emotional development
- Communication, language and literacy
- Problem solving, reasoning and numeracy
- Knowledge and understanding of the world
- Physical development
- Creative development.

The EYFS principles 'in action' will be closely addressed in Chapters 5, 6 and 7.

Aspiring EYPs should also be centrally aware of The Key Elements of Effective Practice (KEEP) that senior practitioners need to 'develop, demonstrate and continuously improve' (DFES 2005). These are as follows:

- Relationships with both children and adults
- Understanding of the individual and diverse ways that children learn and develop

- Knowledge and understanding of how to actively support and extend children's learning in and across all areas and aspects of learning and development
- Practice in meeting all children's needs, learning styles and interests
- Work with parents, carers and the wider community
- Work with other professionals within and beyond the setting.

This will involve ongoing engagement in continuing professional development activities once qualified; see Chapter 9 for further information on this point. Senior practitioners also need to lead and liaise with other professionals in cross-agency practice, based on the guidelines contained in the Common Core of Skills and Knowledge for the Children's Workforce (DFES 2005). These are as follows:

- Effective communication and engagement with a wide range of colleagues, including those from other professional sectors that provide services for young children and their families
- Understand how children and young people develop and be clear about one's own professional role to support them in this process
- Safeguarding and promoting the welfare of the child based on a core knowledge of current legal procedures and frameworks
- Supporting transitions, being able to skilfully judge when and how to intervene in this process
- Multi-agency working from the basis of an understanding of one's own role and the complementary roles of other professionals
- Sharing information from the basis of an understanding of the complexities involved in this, balancing families' rights for confidential services with an understanding of when and how to share information and concerns with colleagues and professionals from other agencies, based on an underpinning knowledge of current policy guidance and legislation.

 Focus on practice

Henry: a 'naughty boy' or a difficult situation? A multi-agency response

Henry, aged 2½, caused some amount of concern to the staff at the playgroup he began attending for four mornings a week. He did not seem to have any problems in separating from his mother, but his attitude towards the other children in the group was very aggressive, pushing and biting. Josie, a nursery nurse and Henry's key-worker, found that if she responded to this by sitting Henry on her lap and talking quietly and calmly to him he would calm down very quickly and go back to play – until the next time. After Henry had a tantrum where he 'swiped' a set of quite heavy wooden toys off a table where several children were playing (luckily not resulting in any injuries), Josie spoke to Sam, the centre EYP, about how they should proceed.

Identifying good practice

Sam suggested that the centre staff should carry out a series of **focal child observations** (see Chapter 4) on Henry, so they might be able to discern some kind of pattern that indicated what might be the cause of Henry's temper tantrums, then they could discuss how they might respond. He asked Josie to talk to Henry's mother, Jan, about this, and to let her know that both Josie and Sam were always available to discuss ongoing issues. After this was done, Josie reported back to Sam that Henry's mother was relieved – she had put Henry's problems down to the 'terrible twos' stage on the advice of her own mother, but was now beginning to think that there was more to it than that, although she had been unsure. It had been agreed in this meeting that Jan would have full access to the observations and a regular weekly discussion with Josie.

Leading practice

Sam suggested that Josie share the task of carrying out the observations with Angie, the other nursery nurse in the setting, so that the collected data was not based only on the opinions of one person. After a fortnight, Josie, Sam and Angie met to discuss what had been observed. It emerged that Henry had no problems with other children if they approached him from the front, but both observers had recorded that if they came from the side, particularly the left, he would lash out. It was agreed that Sam and Josie would meet with Jan to discuss this. Sam's suggestion was that maybe Henry had some problem with his sight that meant he was being taken by surprise when children approached from the side, but he was unsure why this had not been picked up in Henry's two-year sight check. All was revealed when Jan informed him that Henry had not yet had his two-year sight check because the family had moved around this time, and been allocated to a different health visitor. She subsequently contacted her new health visitor, who carried out the test the following week. Henry was found to have some problems with the test, and was referred to an optician. The optician's diagnosis was a 'lazy' left eye.

Reflection *Sam's decision to investigate this situation properly created the positive result that, instead of becoming the setting's 'naughty boy', as might have happened in earlier times, Henry's underlying problems were diagnosed and treated. However, diagnosis does not always mean instant improvement. In Henry's case, the treatment the optician advised involved patching the 'good' eye for a time, so Henry's experience was that, for a short time, his sight got worse instead of better, and consequently his behaviour deteriorated to some extent. But the centre staff now knew about the underlying problem and Sam suggested various ways that they could cope with this, which included consideration for the safety of the other children in the setting. Due to other children leaving the setting to move on to nursery during this time, Sam managed to reduce Josie's keyworker caseload temporarily so that she was consistently available to give Henry the emotional support he needed while his eye was patched. When his eye was unpatched, Henry was prescribed a pair of glasses which gave him relatively normal vision, and his behaviour improved dramatically.*

The EYFS describes six overlapping phases of child development:

Birth to eleven months

The initial stage where babies are focused principally upon physical and social development. They learn to control the basic movements of their bodies, understand in basic terms the information that is being filtered through their senses, and begin to communicate with the other people who inhabit their world.

Eight months to twenty months

From eight months infants begin to learn about locomotion, rolling, crawling and eventually walking. From the middle of the first year they begin to show attachment to familiar people in their world, and as they move towards the final third of their first year, the first words are uttered; these are often the names of people who represent the infants' closest bonded attachments, e.g. 'mama', 'dada', 'gan'.

Sixteen months to twenty-six months

Children moving from babyhood to toddlerhood are frequently full of energy, using their new skills of mobility to investigate every inch of their surroundings. Safety considerations within everyday environments now become paramount; children of this age will have little understanding of everyday dangers, so, for example, fireguards, electric socket shields and stair gates will be necessary in order to protect them from potentially harmful results of such investigations. Children will also usually enter the two-word utterance stage of language development during this stage (see below), and, while they will become quite skilled at communicating meaning to familiar adults, there may be misunderstandings with people with whom they do not regularly interact. The will to do or communicate something may not always be matched by the necessary capacity at this stage, meaning that there may be frustration and temper tantrums that need skilful handling by carers.

Twenty-two to thirty-six months

Language continues to develop to the point that the child becomes more able to interact successfully with a wide range of others, including peers. If children have the opportunity to mix with a range of adults and peers during this stage they will become more socially competent, developing rudimentary skills of peer negotiation, although where difficult situations arise they will turn to bonded adults for help. Children in the later part of this stage will typically begin to deal with simple intellectual challenges such as shape-matching, simple counting, naming colours and learning simple songs and rhymes. Fine motor skills develop rapidly, meaning that children in this stage will typically enjoy mark making and simple construction activities.

Thirty to fifty months

Children's abilities to engage in peer interactions increase; in particular they are able to engage in, and enjoy increasingly intricate collaborative make believe scenarios with their peers. Gender preferences in play styles and play companions begin to emerge, as does recognition of cultural differences and curiosity relating to this. There is a growing independence in 'self-care' activities such as toileting and dressing. Children will be happy to leave bonded adults for increasing periods of time, while still needing readily available help from familiar adults when confused, or comfort when distressed. The first literacy skills emerge, usually starting with the child's ability to recognise and then write their own name, moving on to recognise and copy other familiar words and phrases.

Forty to sixty months

The child is now beginning to build an increasingly independent role in the peer group, typically engaging in literacy and numeracy activities with enjoyment and increasing understanding. Independent problem-solving and reasoning skills are now developing quickly and children of this age are very capable of having a simple (albeit usually quite brief!) reasoned debate. They are also increasingly capable of controlling their own behaviour towards a projected end; this includes a developing ability to delay gratification for short periods of time.

These stages have been drawn from many years of developmental research. We have provided a brief overview of such research below; however, you (especially those who do not have significant child development education and training prior to undertaking their EYPS pathway) are advised to read more widely on this point, using the recommended reading list at the end of the chapter as your starting point.

Additionally, those who work with disabled children can access a wealth of support from the Early Support Service, who have been commissioned by the government to achieve better coordinated services for young disabled children and their families across England as a whole. This service aims to integrate the work of the range of agencies who provide services for disabled children and their families. The programme was initially developed for children under 3, but has now been extended to children under 5. It is funded by the Department for Children, Schools and Families (DCSF) through SureStart, and is being further developed in partnership with the Department of Health and the voluntary sector. The Early Support Service's work and ongoing developments are explained on its website: http://www.earlysupport.org.uk/modResourcesLibrary/HtmlRenderer/welcomeview .html.

What are the main theoretical perspectives that describe how children develop and learn, particularly between birth and their sixth birthday?

The first questions to be asked about human psychology were posed by the ancient Greek philosophers. They proposed that human beings expressed individually different temperaments, which they named as sanguine (easy-going), phlegmatic (sluggish), choleric (irritable) and melancholic (depressive) (Galen, second century BC in Thomas 1990). Modern theorists reject such early conclusions, but the study of personality – in its infant guise, temperament – is still ongoing today (see below), increasingly underpinned by the biological knowledge that is continually being developed by studies in the field of human genetics and brain biology.

Modern studies of human development have their roots in the 'Enlightenment', the beginnings of scientific study that began in the late seventeenth century in Europe, following the Renaissance. Some of this research was carried out in the field of pedagogy, and you will read about this in Chapters 5, 6 and 7 which deal with early years education practice. This chapter will introduce you to the principal theorists and theories in the field of developmental psychology.

1 Introduction to emotional development: attachment theory

Attachment theory was originated by the British psychologist John Bowlby (1969) over the period directly following World War II (1939–45). It was based on a mixture of Freudian ideas and extrapolation of concepts from studies that biologists had carried out on non-human animals and their offspring. Bowlby's central proposal was that human mothers and babies have a natural, evolved instinct to form a strong emotional bond. While this fixed focus on mothers was later found to be highly problematic, Bowlby's concept of the 'Internal Working Model' is still a central facet of modern attachment theory. He proposed that, based on the earliest relationship (nowadays relationships), infants construct an Internal Working Model (IWM) of what to expect from other people, and of their own level of 'lovability'. Bowlby proposed that a positive mother–child relationship creates an 'other people are nice and I am lovable' IWM, whereas a troubled mother–child relationship creates an 'other people are unkind and I am *not* lovable' IWM. This basic belief, he proposed, was the basis of all subsequent interactions and relationships for the child.

Bowlby also carried out studies with James Robertson, a social worker (Robertson and Bowlby 1952), on the problems that children experienced in the hospitals of the time, where visits by parents were extremely limited (see Jean's memories of being in hospital during the late 1950s above). This research indicated that children went through a process of initial distress, followed by despair, and, if contact with attachment figures was lost altogether, they finally detached from the adult concerned. If the detachment stage was reached, the relationship became very difficult to rebuild. The younger the child at the time the relationship was put under strain, the more quickly they went through the stages and the greater the negative effect the process had upon their psychological health and subsequent emotional development.

Schaffer and Emerson (1964) found, in a longitudinal study of babies aged 0–2 that *several* bonds with adults were formed in the first months. The babies tended to have one primary attachment and several secondary attachments, being perfectly content to be cared for by any of these 'bonded' adults. Only approximately 50 per cent of these babies had the primary attachment to the mother; the other 50 per cent had formed a primary attachment to another member of the family (most commonly the father or grandmother). The primary attachment tended to be the person in the family who showed the most sensitive responsiveness to the baby. The studies of Mary Ainsworth (1970) also indicated that the quality of attachment that a child had to the main carer had a lasting effect on the IWM. However, later studies found her 'strange situation' methodology to be flawed, particularly in its tendency to diagnose problematic attachments in children from non-Western cultures, where, on examination of the child's life outside the laboratory situation that Ainsworth created for her tests, no such problems appeared to exist.

Modern studies of the attachments children build in daycare have produced complex and controversial findings, but the picture that emerges is that children in high-quality daycare do not suffer attachment problems, while those in low-quality daycare suffer a range of problems relating to both emotional and intellectual development (see Chapter 3). Such findings led directly to the Government's decision to fund dramatic improvements in daycare provision over the first decade of the twenty-first century; this includes developing the role of the EYP. A summary of findings is presented in Table 2.1.

Table 2.1 Recommendations for daycare drawn from attachment theory

Developmental psychology	Recommendations for daycare
Children under 3 (and preferably under 5) need **regular care** from adults to whom they are **attached**, and can **rely upon**.	Daycare settings need to do everything in their power to **avoid high staff turnover** e.g. good wages and working conditions; employment of well-qualified, dedicated staff.
Children need a lot of **individual attention** from adults, including one who sees the child as their 'especial' focus.	Daycare settings must have a **high number of adult staff** so that children can receive a lot of individual attention, much of which should be given by a **keyworker** whose role is to provide care for a small group of children.
. . . . who show **sensitive responsiveness** to the child, showing a genuine interest in their communications, and an understanding of what they want/need at different times and in different situations (sustained shared thinking).	Staff in daycare settings need to be **specifically trained to work with children under 5**, and to have enough **professionalism, personal maturity and experience** to be able to 'decentre' from their own thoughts and needs to understand and show interest in the sometimes mundane communications of small children.
Children need **developmentally appropriate play resources** and **help/encouragement from adults** to progress in their learning.	Daycare settings should be **well-resourced** with toys and large indoor and outdoor play equipment and **adults should be specifically trained to understand how young children learn,** particularly what levels of understanding to expect in children throughout the 0–5 developmental period.

Note: Basic hygiene/health and safety practices etc. are not noted here, but are still obviously important!

Focus on practice

Antony, his brothers and 'sensitive responsiveness'

(Author's observation. Note: this observation was undertaken in a time when Reception was still part of Key Stage 1, before the instigation of the Foundation Stage.)

Antony, just 4, who is three weeks into his reception year, is on the far side of the Key Stage 1 playground when I arrive, nearly into the older children's playground. He is in fits of giggles, being given a piggy-back by his oldest brother, while the next oldest one looks on. Antony has two older brothers, very close in age, one in Year 2 and another, the piggy-backer, who is in Year 4 and really should be in the older children's playground . . .

Later during the play session, the lunchtime supervisor rings the bell, which is the signal for 'stop play'. She gives the children a general reminder that they are not to push, or pull each others' coats, and tells them they are all to stand still for two minutes as a punishment for doing this. . . . Antony remains standing quite still for a moment after play resumes. Kirsty, his friend from Reception, was individually told off by the lunchtime supervisor for jigging around when the children were standing still, and she cried. She is now holding the lunchtime supervisor's hand and several of the children in her class are around her, Antony being one of these. This is interesting because Antony is usually very active at playtimes . . . . Some of the other reception children also seem quite subdued, probably because they are not used to being punished in this way.

Antony's oldest brother comes over; he is well into the Key Stage 1 playground now. He twists Antony's shoulders, making him 'dance', then rubs his nose against Antony's and they stand forehead to forehead. Antony then goes around behind his brother, puts his arms around him, the brother walks forward and Antony follows, arms around him, and then the older boy turns around and rubs Antony's hair. This is not the only time I have observed that, when some of the reception children become upset, concerned or worried, an older sibling will appear and offer some comfort and reassurance. The staff generally seem to turn a 'blind eye' to this . . . . The lunchtime supervisor has spotted Antony's brother, but she hasn't told him to go back to his own playground as yet . . .

Identifying good practice

I was a visitor in this school, carrying out observations of the children for a piece of extended research, so it took me a while to learn 'the rules', and even longer to learn that sometimes the staff allowed some rules to be stretched where they thought it would be of benefit to the children. While the formal rule in the school at that time was that the Key Stage 1 playground was for the children in Reception, Year 1 and Year 2, and the Key Stage 2 playground was for the children in Years 3, 4, 5 and 6, the unwritten rule seemed to be that staff did not reprimand or send an older child back to the Key Stage 2 playground if they were there to comfort a younger sibling, and the older children seemed to be fully aware of this. While all attempts were made by this school to ease the reception children into mainstream school as was the practice at that time, the staff fully recognised that children who are only just 4, while they are moving into a stage of development where they can manage to function for a large part of their day without immediate access to people to whom they have bonded attachments, may still crave such support in times of unhappiness and uncertainty. In this way, the older siblings were neatly providing a 'sensitively responsive' interaction by filling such an 'attachment gap' and the school's flexible approach to this situation also indicated 'sensitive responsiveness' to practice with their youngest pupils.

Leading practice

As I got to know the setting better, I found out that there had been some instances where support staff (typically those who were new and untrained) had tried to enforce the playground allocation rules, regardless of the older child's purpose in the younger children's playground – usually to great protest from the older child in the situation. The Key Stage 1 and lunchtime coordinators dealt with such situations with great tact, finding somewhere else for the siblings to go together, and explaining to the adult concerned at a later time that this rule was 'made to be broken' in *some*, very specific instances. This is actually quite a difficult and dichotomous message to communicate to a member of staff – how do you think you might go about this?

Reflection *What do you think about the existence of 'rules that are made to be broken' (in some circumstances) in Early Years settings?*

Task **Discuss this with your fellow EYPS candidates and colleagues. Where might you find a flexible rule like this in a non-school based setting? Do you think it would be easier to deal with, more difficult, or about the same?**

2 Introduction to individual differences: temperament theory

The underpinning idea for a concept of 'temperament' came from a very famous psychologist called Hans Eysenck. He was concerned with adult psychology and is the originator of the modern concepts of an extravert/introvert, neurotic/stable personality. Eysenck (1981) proposed that there were very subtle differences in the brain biology of individuals, rather like the setting of a thermostatic mechanism. This, he proposed, would underlie our outwardly expressed personality. Developmental researchers soon proposed that the origins of adult personality could be discerned within infant styles of interacting with the external environment; this area of individual difference was termed 'temperament'.

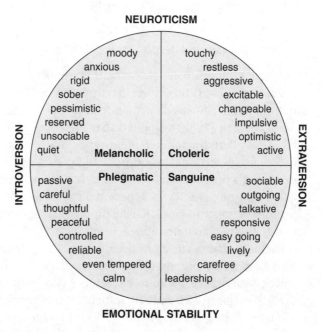

Figure 2.1 **Dimensions of personality**
Source: Gross 1996, p. 888.

Based on the New York Longitudinal Study of temperament, which began in the 1950s, Thomas and Chess (1977) proposed that they had discovered nine dimensions of infant temperament:

- Activity level
- Quality of mood
- Approach/Withdrawal
- Rhythmicity
- Adaptability
- Threshold of responsiveness
- Intensity of reaction
- Distractibility
- Attention span.

Not surprisingly, these proved difficult to define reliably in more short-term studies. It was subsequently proposed that these dimensions were not all fully independent of each other, and could be collapsed into three basic 'types': the 'Easy', 'Difficult' and 'Slow to Warm Up' child. Other researchers and practitioners did not necessarily find potentially judgmental labels such as 'easy' and 'difficult' particularly helpful, however!

Buss and Plomin (1984) proposed that they could simplify Thomas and Chess's temperament dimensions to three, and that these could be related to Eysenck's theory of adult personality:

- Emotionality (relates to Neuroticism)
- Activity (relates to Extraversion/Introversion)
- Sociability (also relates to Extraversion/Introversion).

Buss and Plomin further proposed that impulsivity and shyness might also be independent dimensions from the three named, although they maintained that their 'EAS' system was an adequate model of temperamental differences between infants. Kagan (1988) suggested that there was a firm physiological basis for differences underlying temperament types, due to regulation of neuronal activity in the limbic system – again, similarly to Eysenck's theory. Kagan's theory was based on strength of emotional reaction, a continuum which he proposed was principally responsible for levels of personality traits such as sociability, shyness, adventurousness, talkativeness. Kagan proposed that people could consciously try to modify their behaviour and reactions, but that they could not change the biological activity that occurred in their bodies, e.g. increased heart rate and pupil dilation; hence, he proposed, the basic temperament 'type' was determined by genetic inheritance. More recent studies (see below) have suggested that cortisol levels may not be 'set' only by individual inheritance, but also by external events occurring during gestation and early childhood.

Dunn and Kendrick (1982) suggested that events that the child was exposed to in infancy and early childhood (particularly the birth of a sibling) could have a large effect on their behavioural style, and that, as time went on, transactions in the relationships between the carers and the siblings would have an important impact on all the children's temperaments and eventual adult personalities. Chess and Thomas (1984) suggested that 'goodness of fit' between a child's temperament and that of their regular carers has a huge effect on the child's self-confidence and resilience. This leads back to the concept of 'sensitive responsiveness' evoked in attachment theory, and from there to the concept of 'sustained shared thinking' that is so centrally emphasised in the Early Years Foundation Stage documents.

Focus on practice

Kayleigh and Sarah: 'sustained shared thinking' with children *and* their parents

Kayleigh was a premature baby who spent three weeks in an incubator before coming home for the first time. Her mother Sarah had always been rather anxious about her, and as she has grown older Kayleigh has shown many of the signs of being what Thomas and Chess might call a 'difficult' child. She shows high emotion and great sensitivity to environment; she does not like to mix with strangers, either adults or children. Sarah has identified that Kayleigh seems very sensitive to her emotional responses, and realises that this can create a 'vicious circle', in the sense that Sarah will worry that Kayleigh will respond poorly to a situation, and her concerns will seem to communicate themselves to Kayleigh, so Kayleigh's emotional responses are heightened. Kayleigh is now just 3, and in good health, and Sarah is five months pregnant. She wants to settle Kayleigh into a private nursery class for four mornings a week before the baby arrives. She has taken Kayleigh for an introductory session, during which Kayleigh cried and clung to her mother most of the time, apart from a short period of interest at the painting table. Kayleigh is to return next week, and Sarah is already dreading the experience. Jenny, the EYP in the setting, who manages the transitions, is aware of the situation.

Identifying good practice

Jenny talks to Barbara, the nursery teacher, and Jill, the nursery practitioner who is to be Kayleigh's keyworker, about how to proceed. They decide the following:

- Jill will undertake another home visit, and talk to Sarah about Kayleigh's normal activities and routines, and how these might be a little more closely aligned with the activities and routines of the nursery class, so that Kayleigh feels some familiarity within the nursery environment.

- Jill will also try to ensure that Sarah feels as much at ease with her, and with the situation, as possible, so that Kayleigh is not picking up so many negative emotions from her mother about the situation.

- Amber, who lives next door to Sarah and Kayleigh, is attending the nursery for one more term before moving on to the reception class in the school in September. Kayleigh knows Amber a little, and they have sometimes 'visited' to play. Jill is going to suggest that, if possible, the parents take turns in bringing Kayleigh and Amber to nursery together (Sarah for the first couple of weeks if she prefers), so that Kayleigh does not come in alone.

- Jill will also find out if Kayleigh has a favourite toy that she would like to bring to nursery, one that can act as what attachment theorist Winicott (1951) called a 'transitional object', providing some comfort when people to whom she has bonded attachments are not physically present.

- Sarah and Jill will agree a schedule via which Sarah will leave Kayleigh for longer and longer periods over the first few weeks of her attendance until she is attending the whole session without Sarah. Jenny explains to Jill that this will not only involve providing reassurance for Kayleigh, but also for Sarah.

Leading practice

When Kayleigh has been at nursery for three weeks, Jill and Barbara inform Jenny that, while Kayleigh seems to be making good progress, despite Jill's efforts at reassurance that Kayleigh is happy and settled, Sarah seems unable to leave her in the setting for more than an hour without popping back to 'see if she is OK'. Barbara and Jenny decide that it would be a good idea for Jenny to talk to Sarah about this. If you were Jenny, how do you think you would approach this situation?

Reflection Such conversations with parents cannot be wholly planned, as the practitioner undertaking them needs to be able to respond to the situation as it unfolds, sometimes involving other staff on a 'need to know' basis. By this time Sarah will be nearly six months pregnant, and perhaps helping her to focus on how she will maintain Kayleigh's routine when the new baby arrives (which should include the three-hour session at nursery) might help Sarah to move on in the previously agreed schedule, leaving Kayleigh for progressively longer periods in the nursery. Jenny will try to help Sarah to consider that, if Kayleigh is used to spending the full session at nursery without her mother present by the time the baby arrives, the resulting changes will not unbalance Kayleigh's routine so dramatically, and thus minimise the unsettling events arising for her from the new arrival. If Jill (who is currently completing her Foundation Degree in Early Years, with a view to eventual EYPS validation) is informed and involved in this process, Jenny will also be able to model good practice in working with parents for her.

3 Introduction to social development

Uri Bronfenbrenner (1979) did not deny that genetics was very important in determining what children become in later life. However, he proposed that crucial interactions with the child's 'nature' were created by the 'nurturing' environment. Many highly influential childhood intervention and enrichment projects eventually grew from the basis of Bronfenbrenner's ideas. He proposed that children inhabited a series of systems that were nested one within the other like a set of Russian dolls.

- The innermost system is the *Microsystem* which describes the child's everyday environments (e.g. home, school).

- The *Mesosystem* provides the contacts between the structures of the microsystem e.g. a parent-teacher association or a local parent and toddler group.
- The middle system is the *Exosystem* which describes aspects that have a direct influence on the microsystem environment (e.g. parents' jobs, relationships with extended family and friends).
- The outer system is the *Macrosystem* which describes the cultural surroundings of these environments (e.g. language, culture, wealth and poverty, ethnicity and religion).

See Figure 2.2.

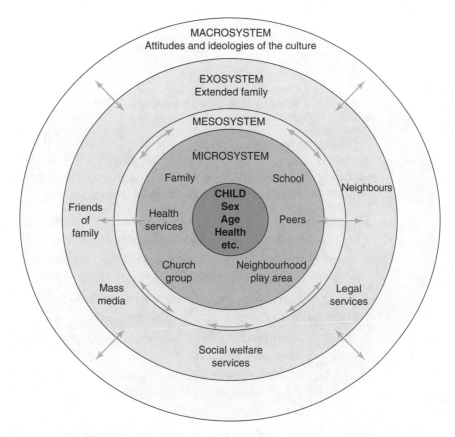

Figure 2.2 Bronfenbrenner's concept of 'systems'
Source: Dockrell and Messer (1999, p. 139).

At a time when many scientific discoveries were beginning to indicate that what we 'are' is determined to a great extent by genetics, Bronfenbrenner emphasised the still crucial influence of the environment. He made it clear that, while nature determined how 'long' individual human potential was, nurture determined how far it was going to be 'pulled' (see Figure 2.3). His theories have subsequently been the launching pad for two very high-profile childhood enrichment programmes on both sides of the Atlantic, HeadStart (US 1962–present, 2008 online) and SureStart (UK 1998–present, 2008 online).

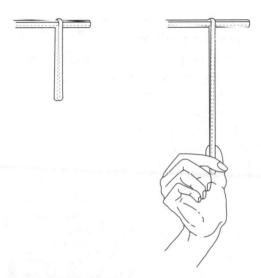

Figure 2.3 **Extending children's development**

Dunn and Kendrick (1982) considered children's development in family environments during the period when they were aged between 3 and 7 years. The following important environmental influences upon children's early social development were indicated by the findings of this study:

- Children's interactions with friends and family strongly impacted on their ability to understand emotions and 'other minds' ('theory of mind').
- Frequent discussion about why people do/feel what they do especially seemed to develop 'theory of mind' skills in young children.
- Young children very quickly learned to use different types of discussion and argument with different family members.
- Children who develop early skills of emotional understanding build on this and are more advanced at later stages.
- Child–child relationships were very important in their development of these skills, both with siblings and with friends.

 Focus on practice

Five-year old football play and resulting peer relationship learning

(Author's observations)

Over 2002–03, I carried out an ongoing series of observations in primary school, of which one of the aims was to study the relationships developed by the children through their outdoor free play. Some of the observations undertaken were of the 5 and 6 year old boys in the group when they engaged in football play. Here is an extract

Source: POD/Pearson Education Ltd. Jules Selmes

from one of the transcripts. At this time, Antony had just had the plaster removed from a recently broken arm, and was not really supposed to engage in football play at all:

'Antony gets the ball. The other boys are very careful not to tackle Antony and they let him have his turn with the ball. . . . . . He kicks it, and all the other boys run after it. I hear Leo's voice: "Tom, it's my turn". Tom kicks at goal, and Antony saves it in front of Benji. We seem to have three goalkeepers now, Aiden also standing by the goal post. Benji takes the ball from Antony and kicks it out. It hits Ashley on the hand and a cry goes up: "hand ball". Antony picks up the ball and takes it out of play. He says "I'm taking it, hand ball". (Chanting "score, score, score") He puts it down, takes a kick at goal and scores. He says "like Beckham".

'The ball rolls out of play down to the tarmac. Tom brings it back up. He is standing on the hill looking like he is going to throw in, but he kicks it instead. It goes behind the goal. Antony takes the next throw in. They seem very sure about the boundaries of their football pitch, but it is not clear to an adult observer . . . . He puts the ball down and kicks it through the goal sideways and then jumps up and down (children cheer). Benji says "no goal" as he was not in the goal at the time . . . But they are not counting the goals anyway. Benji is saying "no, no" and holding on to the ball. They all chant at him: "time waster". So he kicks the ball back out into play again'.

Identifying good practice

There are many aspects of social learning through peer relationships that can be identified in this short set of observation extracts. Though only 5, these children realised that Antony could not play unless they gave him some special consideration, and it is clear that they effectively managed to do this. This indicates some amount of ability to decentre from their own situations to understand the situation of another, currently recovering from injury. The children show some rudimentary knowledge of the rules underlying football in their invocation of 'hand ball', 'time wasting' and 'goal scoring', and their understanding that there is a designated area outside which the ball is no longer in play, but it is clear that this is still at a very basic level, indicated (for example) by the presence of three goalkeepers and a complete lack of team-based play. Benji indicates that, while he can evoke the rules as he understands them, he is also willing to acquiesce to majority opinion and send the ball back into play – a highly flexible response to social pressure, which also indicates some underlying 'Theory of Mind'. As these children play, they co-create rules and practices. My analysis, after several observations of this nature, was that their learning about the rules of the game was very much secondary to their learning about the social interactions that they had with each other, all underpinned by the impetus to achieve the continuation of a play situation that they were all enjoying. There is little that is required from adults in such a situation, apart from a discreet vigilance to ensure that physically dangerous or 'bullying' situations do not develop.

Leading practice

During my time on this piece of research, I occasionally saw adults intervening in the children's play in attempts to completely change the meanings that the children had created between themselves, with the inevitable result that such play broke down. For example, when a group of boys were playing a chasing game which involved Benji dragging a skipping rope while the other boys chased him, the female teacher on playground duty stopped their game, and gathered the group together to talk to them. She showed them how to turn the rope, with one child at each end. All the boys tried to skip, but none seemed to have any idea of when to jump as the rope swung around. The teacher then called to Miranda to demonstrate . . . she was very good at skipping, but the boys lost interest and wandered off. The chasing game soon began again, with Benji at the front, this time with a 'push wheel'. When the bell went, I asked him what they were playing. 'Fire engines', he replied. I wondered if that was also the game ongoing with the skipping rope. If so, the play narratives used by the boys and the adult were not at all compatible. It could also be theorised that some of these differences were underpinned by a cross-gender misunderstanding, something that all female Early Years Practitioners (who massively outnumber men within the profession) need to consciously consider (see Chapter 4).

As a leading practitioner, how would you explain to your staff how to judge when and how to intervene in children's play, to protect and enhance, without imposing a potentially destructive adult agenda?

Reflection

The only real 'rule' here is that each situation must be approached on its own merits, underpinned by an adult's aim to build on and extend the children's ideas, rather than attempting to impose his or her own agenda on top of them. There are many instances where building shared understandings with other children is the most important aspect of a play event, whether or not those understandings are judged as 'correct' by an adult. The key point here is to focus on the activity's processes rather than its outcomes. You need to consider this point deeply during the observations that you undertake in the early part of your training (see Chapter 4). Such a focus will develop your knowledge and sensitivity in this area, which will in turn help you to support other staff towards a greater understanding of the benefits of child-led play, as part of your evidence for the leadership standards as you move towards validation.

4 Introduction to cognitive developmental theory

Jean Piaget was the first theorist to produce a comprehensive theory of human intellectual development. In 'The Psychology of the Child' (1969) he outlined his theory that children learn in interaction with the *concrete* world (i.e. world of objects), with experiential learning underpinning the child's construction of a cognitive network of schemas, assimilating and accommodating new knowledge. A schema is, in Piaget's context, a set of mental connections. At the time of Piaget's research there was little evidence of how the living brain worked, but now we know that infants and children do indeed rapidly build up connections between brain cells called neurons over the developmental period. Piaget proposed that the child either assimilates a new experience (taking it into thought without creating a new concept, e.g. you lick an ice cream and you also lick an ice lolly) or accommodates it (creating a new concept in thought, e.g. you can't pick up spaghetti with just a spoon, or a knife and fork; you have to learn a new action with a spoon and a fork). The child moves towards accommodation by a process of 'equilibration', which means needing to balance all related schemas against one's current picture of reality.

Piaget proposed that building thought processes to adult competence continued until the child was 12. Nowadays, we know it takes much longer than this, and that there is a wealth of individual and cultural difference in such construction. However, Piaget's concept of stages is still useful as a rough guide to children's intellectual competence in the early years of life. He carried out an extensive series of experiments that indicated babies under about six months do not even realise that objects that they cannot immediately see still exist within the world; hence he proposed that such young infants have no concept of 'object permanence'. This, he proposed, relates to lack of mental connections within such an immature mind. Babies do not yet have the available symbols within their mind to 'hang' such concepts and memories upon. Achieving the concept of object permanence is one of the major goals of the sensori-motor stage (birth to 18 months), alongside organising information coming from the senses, and the achievement of basic motor skills (walking, holding objects etc.). Children aged approximately 18 months move on to the 'pre-operational' stage, where they will spend approximately 4½ years building schemas relating to developing linguistic and social competence and reducing egocentricity (a focus solely on the self and one's own point of view). Children in the earlier periods of this stage are unable to hypothesise logically with respect to social or intellectual situations, frequently showing 'centration' (a focus on only one simple, surface-based aspect of a situation). Margaret Donaldson (1978) outlined a series of experiments undertaken by her research team that indicated that, once a child understood the social situation in which a problem was embedded, they were much more likely to be able to work towards a successful solution. It is therefore common, but not inevitable, that children will show more sophistication in dealing with social situations than intellectual situations as they move through this stage. A Piagetian concept that can be used to describe this inconsistency is 'décalage' (literally 'gap' or 'interval'). Once children reach the next stage, that of 'Concrete Operations' 7–12 years), their ability to think logically about both social and intellectual situations becomes more flexible and mature.

Figure 2.4 An example of 'centration'

Source: CALVIN AND HOBBES © 1986 Watterson Dist. by UNIVERSAL PRESS SYNDICATE. Reprinted with permission. All rights reserved.

The Russian developmental psychologist, Lev Vygotsky, was also a theorist in the constructivist tradition, like Piaget, proposing that children built their understanding of the world on the basis of their interactions within it. However, Vygotsky (1978) placed more emphasis upon the role of interaction with other people, proposing that language was crucially important in learning, in that it was the principal medium through which a child would begin to 'internalise the external'. While Piaget proposed that cognition precedes language, Vygotsky proposed that language precedes cognition. While Piaget proposed that a child had to be 'ready' to grasp a particular skill or idea, Vygotsky proposed that interaction, particularly with an adult or a more able peer, could take a child one step further in their learning than they were able to move alone. He referred to the area into which a child could be 'coached' as a 'Zone of Proximal Development' (ZPD). Jerome Bruner, who brought Vygotsky's work to the attention of the West, proposed that the adult's ongoing role in a teaching and learning process is to progressively *scaffold* the child's learning at an appropriate level, i.e. within the ever-progressing ZPD (Wood, Bruner and Ross 1976). Building on this point, Wood and Middleton (1975) proposed that the best way adults can help children learn is by creating a contingency, by consciously and carefully tailoring adult input on a minute-to-minute basis so it is always contingent to the child's learning (i.e. supporting the child into the constantly moving zone of proximal development). This leads us back to the concept of 'sustained shared thinking' that is advocated in the EYFS.

Focus on practice

On a Bear Hunt with Pinky: developing contingency

Three year old Anastasia is constructing a picture based on a story that her teacher has read the group called 'Bear Hunt'. There is a box of pre-cut card bear shapes on the table, and a basket of brown furry material. Anastasia has spread glue on her bear shape, but she is looking around for some pink furry material, because she wants the bear to look like Pinky, her favourite teddy who sits on her bed at home. She goes to the trainee nursery practitioner, Vanessa, who has designed the activity and is work-ing with the children at the table. Anastasia holds out a piece of brown material to Vanessa and says 'where's the pink?' 'Can't you stick it on, Anastasia?' says Vanessa, 'here you are'. She sticks the material on to the middle of Anastasia's bear shape and says, 'there. Can you do the next one?' Anastasia shakes her head, and wanders off to the painting table, where she finds some pink paint. She is soon in conversation with Brenda, the centre EYP, about the picture she is painting of Pinky, her teddy bear. Vanessa finds the abandoned bear shape on the table at the end of the session when the children have gone home. She shrugs, and then puts it into the waste paper bin.

Identifying good practice

In order to access Anastasia's zone of proximal development, Vanessa needed to *listen* to what Anastasia was saying to her and respond appropriately. Anastasia was presenting her with a problem that she needed help to solve, but Vanessa provided her with a solution that Anastasia had already considered and rejected. In doing so, Vanessa has missed the opportunity to help the child to solve the problem in a way that she would comprehend as useful and effective. If Vanessa remembered that the abandoned bear shape belonged to Anastasia after the session, she might wrongly conclude that the task was 'too difficult' for the child; this is what frequently happens when adults do not try to consider the situation from the child's point of view. If Vanessa had responded to the situation with more insight, she might have moved on to consider that the activity itself was very limited, given the materials available to the children, and then towards some ideas on how to improve the activity next time by providing a wider range of materials for the children to use.

Leading practice

Brenda sees Vanessa put the unfinished bear picture into the bin. She has picked up from her conversation with Anastasia that the child had abandoned the activity; she also knows that Anastasia was not the only child in the setting to do so during that session. She has allowed Vanessa to design and run the activity in this way so that she can learn from the experience, but Vanessa's response to this indicates that she has not intuited that there is anything wrong with the activity; in fact, Brenda heard her telling another member of staff during the session that the children 'are not very good at sticking activities'. What would you say to Vanessa, if you were in Brenda's position?

Reflection *It can sometimes help with very young trainees to give them a very limited set of paints and ask them to paint a picture of themselves – they will very quickly comment that they haven't got the right colour for their hair/eyes etc. and from that personal, practical experience they can more easily move on to consider how every craft activity should offer children a choice and a chance to personalise their work. From there they can then move on to understand why the perennial Early Years prompt to 'tell me about your picture' is such a crucial interaction between young children and their carers, and why forcing children of this age into the 'Blue Peter' situation (where they are required to make a copy of something an adult has made earlier!) is not particularly helpful at this stage of their development.*

5 Introduction to language development

Words are *symbols*. Each word that we utter 'stands for' something, in our own minds, and (hopefully!) in the minds of the person we are talking to. Usually these meanings match – if they do not, there can be misunderstandings, which may be quite amusing. For example, in a very old joke:

'I say, I say, I say – my dog has no nose'.
'Your dog has no nose? How does he smell?'
'Terrible!'

Some words will stand for simple concrete objects, e.g. 'dog', 'cat', 'table'. Other words stand for complex abstract ideas, e.g. 'love', 'peace', 'justice'. However, the average 10 year old child will have a working (if not exact) idea of what all these words mean.

When we converse with someone we match the symbols in our heads with the symbols in theirs. This is usually possible when we use the same sounds (and squiggles, if we include written language) to stand for the same ideas and objects, although we may not always communicate exactly what we intend. If people use different sounds and squiggles from us to stand for the same ideas and objects (i.e. they speak a different language), translation is often possible, but this inserts an extra 'step' which makes communication even more imperfect.

The basic stages of language development proceed as follows:

Protoconversation

The 'protoconversation' was first described by Mary Bateson in the 1970s. She described 7-to-15 week old infants responding to their mothers' talk with appropriately timed smiles and coos in a give-and-take, dialogue-like pattern, hence 'proto' (stands for) conversation (Bateson 1975). The adult will often act as though the baby's 'responses' are intentional. In this way, Bateson proposed, the baby learns the turn-taking conventions of adult conversation.

Source: POD/Pearson Education Ltd. Jules Selmes

Stage 1

This is the one-word stage; the child develops a small repertoire of single words, usually the names of familiar people and objects, e.g. 'mum', 'dad', 'cup' [around 1 year to 18 months].

Stage 2

Two-word sentences which tend to be simple descriptions of actions and possessions now emerge, e.g. 'my ball', 'throw ball'. This stage was referred to as **'telegraphic speech'** (Oates and Grayson 2004); nowadays we might be more likely to call it 'text speech'; the point is that the child usually manages to convey a surprising amount of information in very few words (alongside gestures and facial expressions) [around 18 months to 2½ years].

Stage 3

Simple grammatical sentences are now beginning to be uttered, and towards the middle of this phase their content begins to encompass past tenses, reflecting a growing understanding of past and future. Children start to use grammatical constructions, e.g. 'I walked', but in doing this they sometimes inadvertently 'regularise' irregular verbs, e.g. 'that tree growed' instead of the grammatically correct 'that tree grew'. This indicates that they are not just simply repeating adult speech but learning (and sometimes stumbling on) grammatical rules to underpin their own original utterances. They also begin to learn to play with language in songs and rhymes [around 2½–3½ years].

Stage 4

The 'where, what, why' stage. The child becomes a competent language user, and begins to use this new skill to ask adults everything the child wants to know about the world. As any parent knows, some of these questions will be impossible to answer; for example, at this age my son once asked his father 'why elephants?' On further investigation this did not refer to *what* elephants were, or what they *did*, but simply *why* they 'were'. Children of this age sometimes appear to use their new linguistic competence to engage in a developmental stage of what could be termed basic philosophical enquiry! [around 3½ –4½ years].

Stage 5

Children may now use more complex sentences involving more than one clause. For example, they will begin to use the more grammatical 'who is playing with that ball?' structure, rather than the more babyish 'who play ball?' [around 4–5 years].

Stage 6

Children now join sentences smoothly together with conjunctions like 'and' and 'but', e.g. 'John and Asif came with me' and 'I used to like Samantha, but I don't like her now.' They can also turn the meanings of sentences around, e.g. 'is that your coat?' and 'that is your coat', and enjoy playing with language in this way; for example, see the joke at the beginning of this section! [around 4½–5½ years].

Children who have had other developmental problems also tend to have delayed development of linguistic competence. This may be particularly in evidence if hearing loss has been a problem. Children who have been diagnosed with, or are in the process of being investigated for, conditions within the autism spectrum disorder category also typically have a range of difficulties with language development.

The day-to-day adult role in assisting children with their language development is very important. As outlined above, carers and small babies show turn-taking behaviour in interactions that psychologists have labelled 'proto-conversation' (Dougherty 1999). Later on, when children begin to speak, adults and older children automatically simplify their speech when talking to small children, emphasising key words and often repeating key phrases. This has been referred to as 'parentese' or the 'baby talk register', but adults who are not parents, and even older children will usually instinctively do this when conversing with children under 2. Another instinctive adult technique is to introduce a 'frame', e.g. 'What is this? It's a frog. What is this? It's a fish'. A lot of toddler books are constructed in this fashion; a favourite with my children was 'Where's Spot?' (Hill 1980), which repeats 'Where's Spot? He's not in the . . .' over a few pages until Spot is found.

Traditional songs and rhymes that small children are taught to sing are also frequently constructed in this fashion as well, e.g. 'The Wheels on the Bus' and 'Ten Green Bottles'. This format presents a nugget of information in a familiar 'frame', so the child pays attention to and learns the new information without the pressure and confusion of a continually changing 'frame'. Such games can be very useful in extending children's language competency.

6 Introduction to biological perspectives of child development

The human central nervous system begins developing at two weeks gestation. The human brain weighs around 350 grams at birth; by the end of the first year it weighs 1000 grams. An adult brain weighs between 1200 and 1400 grams. This illustrates the huge importance of the first year of life for brain development. When we are born we have many more neurons (brain cells) than we actually need. Over the first few years of life, the human brain undergoes a huge neuronal connection programme. Those neurons that are not connected to others shrivel and eventually die. Most children have a 'good enough' environment, but if they experience extreme neglect their brains do not develop as they should; in particular, there is a fixed 'window' for some skills to be triggered (e.g. language). If this window is missed, the child may not be able to make up the lost ground at a later point in their life. A well-documented case of this type is that of 'Genie', a 13 year old American girl who was found locked in her bedroom in the early 1970s (Rymer 1994). The evidence that could be put together suggested that she had been locked away from other people since she was a very small child. Although she was unable to speak when she was discovered, she initially made good progress in learning individual words; however, she never progressed to putting these words together to form grammatical sentences. The researchers concluded that the developmental window for learning grammar and syntax had passed for 'Genie', that the neurons that should have been dedicated to this task had died away, and were not able to be reactivated. Modern research increasingly indicates that much early brain development, while underpinned by genetic programmes, is shaped by a child's early environments. A good example of this is how easily small children learn to be bi- or even multi-lingual, developing native competence in all languages learned in infanthood, while adults struggle to learn subsequent languages and seldom become accomplished enough to speak them without a foreign accent.

Recent biological research also suggests that the amount of stress that children are placed under in infancy has a crucial 'thermostat setting' effect on the biological mechanisms relating to the stress response, commonly known as 'fight or flight'. Children who have a lot of stress in infancy, in particular that created by experiences of being passed from carer to carer with little or no attention paid to the time to form bonded relationships, are vulnerable to developing abnormalities in the levels of the hormone cortisol, which mobilises the 'fight or flight' mechanisms in all animals. Children experiencing ongoing stress typically have abnormally high resting levels of cortisol and these take longer to return to baseline after individual stressful experiences.

Initial studies of children in Western daycare suggested that, across the board, they appeared to show cortisol levels that rose steadily throughout the day, a very worrying finding. However, Antipodean researchers Sims, Guilfoyle and Parry (2006) compared the cortisol levels of children in daycare settings judged as 'high quality' against the cortisol levels of children in daycare settings judged as 'satisfactory'. They found that, while the children's cortisol levels rose throughout the day in the satisfactory settings, they fell throughout the day in the high-quality settings. These researchers went on to outline what features defined a 'high-quality setting':

- **Staff relationships:** happy engaging atmosphere, with staff guiding children's behaviour positively.
- **Respect:** staff initiate and maintain communication with children, accommodating their individual needs, including the recognition of social and cultural differences.
- **Partnership:** staff and families exchange effectively both verbal and written information about the children, and about the centre's routines and expectations.
- **Staff interaction:** staff communicate effectively and function as a team.
- **Planning and evaluation:** the centre programmes reflect a clear centre philosophy and shared goals, which cater for the needs, interests and abilities of all the children, and all the children are helped towards successful learning.
- **Learning and evaluation:** the centre programmes encourage children to make confident choices and take on new challenges.
- **Protective care:** staff supervise children at all times, and individual needs for safety, rest and comfort are met. Children are appropriately dressed for indoor and outdoor play. Toileting and nappy procedures are positive experiences.
- **Managing to support quality:** staffing policies and practices facilitate continuity of care for each child.

(Sims *et al.* 2006)

These features lead us back to the beginning of the chapter, where similar aspirations can be found in the content of the EYFS and the Key Elements of Effective Practice.

Focus on practice

Providing a calm environment in a stressful world

It is a Monday morning, 9.20 a.m. Four year olds Jenna, Shaun and Olivia are hanging up their coats at the children's centre that they regularly attend. Jenna's father has just been made redundant, and her mother has just finished her nursing degree. Jenna's mother is currently working on a series of part-time temporary contracts, still looking for a permanent job. This morning, Jenna heard her parents arguing because her mother wanted her father to take Jenna to the setting, but he was still in bed. Both of Shaun's parents work long hours, and his father, who brought him to the centre, was running late today. He made a business call on his mobile phone as soon as he got out of the car outside the centre, and forgot to kiss Shaun, or to say goodbye. Shaun looks out of the window, watching his father pull quickly out of the car park. Olivia lives with her single mother and her 11 year old sister Amy. Amy has some important tests at school today and, when Olivia started to sing at the breakfast table this morning, Amy (who can be quite nice sometimes) screamed at her to 'shut up'.

The children all have their own pegs in the cloakroom, and they recognise the pictures that have been there since they started at the centre over a year ago. Although all their families were running a little late this morning, there is no pressure for the children to be exactly 'on time'; the morning starts with the children's self-registration, which is accomplished by their removing a name tag that hangs on their coat pegs so they can hang their coats up, and then putting the tag in a basket by the playroom door. The children are not called together as a group until 11.30 a.m., although it is standard practice for their keyworkers to greet them on arrival, and speak briefly to their parents.

As they hang up their coats and put their tags in the basket, the children can see their keyworkers interacting with other children playing with the activities on the tables in the playroom. The children know that they can ask any of the adults in the setting for help at any point, and that their request will meet with a calm and helpful response. A snack will be available shortly, and the children will be able to have this any time between 9.30 and 11.00 a.m. Lunch, afternoon snack and tea will also be served at regular intervals in the day, and there will be regular activities that punctuate the day, for example a story before lunch and a song with actions just before the afternoon snack is available.

The setting is light and roomy, and the staff try to ensure that no one pushes or shouts, although the children are allowed to be a little noisy when they are running around and laughing outside. The equipment is well maintained and the centre policy is to maintain a slightly higher adult–child ratio than the minimum required by law.

The adults work well as a team; all of them are fully aware of the centre practices and policies, and the children's parents are encouraged to engage with the children's activities in the centre; this is more often successful at the end of the day rather than at the beginning, when the parents' schedules may be very tight.

Shaun runs in and joins in a game with the 'matchbox' toy cars that has already begun between his friends Jon and Andrew. Olivia makes her way to the painting table, dips a brush into the red paint and begins spreading the paint across the paper. 'That's very bright, Olivia', says Rob, her keyworker. 'It's Amy, she's cross about her SATs', says Olivia. 'Oh dear', says Rob, 'I was cross when I had SATs, too. What other colours are sort of "cross" do you think?' Olivia thinks for a moment, and then dips her brush into the yellow paint. She applies it to the paper so that it drips into the red, creating a bright orange. 'That's great, Olivia', says Rob, 'all really sort of "cross" colours, look at that orange you've made with the red and the yellow.' Jenna goes into the Home Corner and picks up a doll. When Dominic follows her in she says, 'why can't you take her to school, Daddy? I'm busy'. 'OK', says Dominic. They begin to put the doll into the little buggy, which Jenna then takes outside.

Source: POD/Creatas

Identifying good practice

What stresses have the children been exposed to in their home lives, and how has the practice in the setting helped them to settle down more calmly to their day after a rather fraught start at home? Go through the description above, producing your own bullet-points relating to the relevant practices.

Leading practice

Task A new placement student in the setting runs after Jenna, intending to tell her not to take the doll and the pushchair outside. How would you respond to this situation? How would you explain to the student that it is important for the child to move through her narrative with the doll and the pushchair, even if it does end with the toys abandoned in the corner of the playground, when Jenna decides she would prefer riding around on a tricycle? Discuss this with your fellow EYPS candidates and colleagues.

Reflection In common with many other examples outlined in the activity boxes above, the key issues here focus around the adult decentring to the child's position, and sometimes offering the type of 'sustained shared thinking' response that Rob demonstrates, 'tapping in' to the art activity in which Olivia has engaged. In doing so, he manages to extend Olivia's understanding of colour mixing, while validating her feelings and those of her sister, and not interfering in a self-defined activity which appears to be offering Olivia some amount of emotional catharsis.

What influences and experiences in the setting and beyond can impact on children's well-being, development, learning and behaviour, and how can we connect these to the theoretical perspectives introduced in the previous section?

We have seen from the information above that the underpinning theory and the current early years guidelines indicate that young children need to gradually develop their knowledge and understanding of the world principally through self-selected play-based experiences. These should involve active learning, in calm, well-resourced environments where they are supported cognitively and emotionally by adults who have a sound underpinning knowledge of child development, and an understanding of each child's unique individual needs. While no setting is perfect, this chapter has led us to the consideration of what 'good practice' may actually entail, and how to define this against practice which is not so enlightened.

 Focus on practice

Developing the independent learners of the future

We are going to provide you with an example of two different (fictional and highly stereotyped) settings to consider:

Brilliant Babies	Jolly Jumpers
Has a fixed start time	Has a flexible start time
Has very fixed routines which serve the convenience of the adults	Has flexible routines which serve the needs of the children
Has set tasks that the children must complete	Has a range of activities from which the children can choose freely
Has a set routine that the adult staff must follow, whether or not this fits in with the needs of the children in their care	Expects adults to self-regulate their duties in partnership with others (including parents) and encourages them to be as flexible as possible

Brilliant Babies	Jolly Jumpers
Has a set regime for recording that the adults must follow, even where the procedures do not 'fit' with the information they wish to record	Allows the adults to record how and what they judge to be useful, as long as enough information on every child is collected via the processes undertaken
Adults tell the children what to do	Adults are emotionally and cognitively available to the children
Adults feel that their role is to direct and instruct	Adults feel that their role is to support the children's development and learning
The practice is driven by targets and 'box-ticking'	The practice views the current Early Years Framework as a set of useful guidelines
The leaders in the setting 'direct practice' and 'manage learning'	The leaders in the setting 'lead practice' and 'support learning'
The child is dependent upon the adults and learns to blindly obey	The child becomes an independent learner, building their knowledge and understanding of the world principally through a range of self-selected, play-based activities with sensitive adult support
The child enters later years of schooling unable to evaluate a situation in order to make judgements and choices	The child enters later years of schooling able to evaluate and make choices on the basis of their own judgements

Identifying good practice

Of course, you are unlikely to find a 'pure' example of 'Brilliant Babies' or 'Jolly Jumpers' in your own practice environment – most settings have features of both, although they may have more features of one than the other! By this point in the chapter, you should be very clear about which setting is exhibiting the best practice; however, the challenge remains as to how to achieve this in a 'real world' environment, where highly directive regimes in the later stages of education may have a 'top down' pressure that Early Years settings may sometimes find hard to completely resist.

Leading practice

At some stages of your career, you will be expected to defend your setting's practice in the face of some criticism, not least with regard to inspection.

Task How would you defend child-centred, play-based learning, even if it does not generate the 'correct' mechanical responses to fixed assessment measures that more structured practice may produce in very young children? Discuss this with your fellow EYPS candidates and colleagues.

Reflection *Even experienced professionals are likely to experience some qualms when considering the question above. Early Years practitioners must remain firm in their core understanding that an emotionally secure, reflective, independent learner is not quickly produced within the process of development and learning. We can look for inspiration to the Scandinavian countries and their measured 'educare' approach to Early Years education for support in this respect, particularly with regard to the excellent outcomes their children achieve in the later years of development (see Chapter 3).*

Conclusion

What are the EYFS principles, and how are they reflected in the content?

Summaries of the EYFS principles and content are detailed above, and we hope you will view this first, rather long chapter as a key source of reference as you move through the following chapters, returning to its pages where authors raise related points. You are also directed to the DCSF website, where you will find regular updates on the EYFS.

What are the main theoretical perspectives that describe how children develop and learn, particularly between birth and their sixth birthday?

While it was impossible to cover all theoretical perspectives that might be useful in this respect, this chapter has been designed to get you off to a good start, by introducing central theories and theorists in the areas of emotional, cognitive, social, language and biological development, and theories of individual difference underpinned by temperament. We hope that you will use the directions to further reading below to increase your knowledge in these areas, and engage in discussions with your fellow EYPS candidates and colleagues relating to the more controversial aspects of each area of theory. The more widely you read, the more confident you will become in such debates. You should also become a regular reader of at least one of the journals listed below, so you can keep up with theoretical, policy and practice developments in your chosen professional field.

What influences and experiences in the setting and beyond can impact on children's well-being, development, learning and behaviour, and how can we connect these to the theoretical perspectives introduced in the previous section?

You should now be beginning to make such connections, for example:

- Attachment theory with the keyworker system
- Scaffolding and contingency with sustained shared thinking
- Biological theory relating to the initial calibration of the arousal mechanisms within the infant brain with calm, flexible routines within childcare and education settings.

The wide range of concepts introduced within this chapter should serve as a platform from which to access the following chapters within this book; so please feel free to return to this base as many times as you wish to reflect upon the later ideas with which you are presented. You have now launched your journey towards becoming an expert and leader in child development, hence the hub around which the practice of a childcare and education setting will revolve: that is, an Early Years Professional.

Source: POD/Pearson Education Ltd. Jules Selmes

Further reading

Bee, H. (1997) *The Developing Child*. Harlow: Longman.

Brock, A., Dodds, S., Jarvis, P. and Olusoga, Y. (2008) *Perspectives on Play*. Harlow: Pearson.

Cohen, D. (2002) *How the child's mind develops*. London: Routledge.

David, T., Gooch, K., Powell, S. and Abbott, L. (2003) Birth to three matters, a review of the literature, available at:
http://www.standards.dfes.gov.uk/eyfs/resources/ downloads/rr444.pdf

Donaldson, M. (1978) *Children's Minds*. London: Fontana.

Flanagan, C. (1996) *Applying Psychology to Early Child Development*. London: Hodder & Stoughton.

Gerhardt, S. (2004) *Why love matters: how affection shapes a baby's brain*. London: Routledge.

Gopnik, A., Kuhl, P. and Meltzoff, A. (2001) *How Babies Think: The Science of Childhood*. London: Phoenix.

Johnson, J. and Nahmad-Williams, L. (2009) *Early Childhood Studies*. Harlow: Pearson.

Kehily, M.J. (ed.). (2004) *An Introduction to Childhood Studies*. Maidenhead: Open University Press.

Lindon, J. (2008) *Understanding Child Development: Linking Theory and Practice (2nd Edition)*. London: Hodder Arnold.

MacLeod-Brudenell, I. (ed.). (2008) *Advanced Early Years Care and Education (2nd Edition)*. Oxford: Heinemann.

Nutbrown, C. (2006) *Threads of Thinking: Young Children Learning and the Role of Early Education*. London: Sage.

O' Hagan, M. and Smith, M. (2002) *Early Years Child Care and Education: Key Issues*. London: Bailliere Tindall.

Smith, P.K., Cowie, H. and Blades, M. (2003) *Understanding Children's Development*. Oxford: Blackwell.

Some useful websites

DCSF (2007) The Children's Plan, available at:
http://www.dcsf.gov.uk/publications/childrensplan/

DCSF (2008) The Early Years Support Programme, available at:
http://www.earlysupport.org.uk/modResourcesLibrary/HtmlRenderer/welcomeview.html

DFES (2005) Common Core of Skills and Knowledge for the Children's Workforce, available at:
http://www.everychildmatters.gov.uk/publications/?asset=document&id=15510

The Effective Provision of Pre-School Education (EPPE) project (1998–ongoing), available at:
http://k1.ioe.ac.uk/schools/ecpe/eppe/

The Early Years Foundation Stage:
http://www.standards.dfes.gov.uk/eyfs/

Children's Workforce Development Council, EYPS information:
http://www.cwdcouncil.org.uk/projects/earlyyears.htm

Journals

Child Development

Children Now

Early Years – an International Journal of Research and Development

Educational Researcher

Early Years Educator

Nursery World

Psychological Review

References

Ainsworth, M.D.S. and Bell, S.M. (1970) 'Attachment, exploration, and separation: Illustrated by the behavior of one-year-olds in a strange situation'. *Child Development*, 41, pp. 49–67.

Bateson, M.C. (1975) 'Mother-infant exchanges: The epigenesis of conversational interaction'. In: D. Aaronson and R.W. Rieber (eds) *Developmental Psycholinguistics and Communication Disorders; Annals of the New York Academy of Sciences*, Vol. 263. New York: New York Academy of Sciences.

Bowlby, J. (1969) *Attachment and loss: Volume, Attachment*. New York: Basic Books.

Bronfenbrenner, U. (1979) *The Ecology of Human Development: Experiments by Nature and Design*. Cambridge, MA: Harvard University Press.

Buss, A. and Plomin, R. (1984) *Temperament and early developing personality traits.* Hillside, NJ: Lawrence Erlbaum.

Chess, S. and Thomas, A. (1984) *Origins and evolution of behaviour disorders*. New York: Brunner Mazel.

Dockrell, J. and Messer, D. (1999) *Children's Language and Communication Difficulties: Understanding, Identification and Intervention*. London: Continuum.

DCSF (2008) The Early Years Foundation Stage, available at: http://www.standards.dfes.gov.uk/eyfs/ Accessed on 24/3/08.

DCSF (2007) The Children's Plan, available at: http://www.dcsf.gov.uk/publications/childrensplan/ Accessed on 24/3/08.

DCSF (2008) The Early Years Support Programme, available at: http://www.earlysupport.org.uk/modResourcesLibrary/HtmlRenderer/welcomeview.html Accessed on 24/3/08.

DFES (2005) Common Core of Skills and Knowledge for the Children's Workforce, available at: http://www.everychildmatters.gov.uk/publications/?asset=document&id=15510 Accessed on 24/3/08.

DFES (2005) Key Elements of Effective Practice, available at: www.standards.dcsf.gov.uk/eyfs/resources/downloads/pns_fs120105keep.pdf Accessed on 24/3/08.

Donaldson, M. (1978) *Children's Minds*. London: Fontana.

Dougherty, D. (1999) *How to talk to your baby*. New York: Perigree.

Dunn, J. and Kendrick, C. (1982) *Siblings: love, envy and understanding.* London: Grant McIntyre Ltd.

Eysenck, H. (1981) *A Model for Personality*. Berlin: Springer Verlag.

Gross, R. (1996) *Psychology: the science of mind and behaviour.* London: Hodder Arnold.

Hill, E. (1980) *Where's Spot?* London: Heinemann Young Books.

Kagan, J. (1988) Temperamental contributions to social behaviour. *American Psychologist*, 44, pp. 668-74.

National Head Start Association (US) (2008) About the National Head Start Association, available at: http://www.nhsa.org/about/index.htm Accessed on 24/3/08.

Oates, J. and Grayson, A. (2004) *Cognitive and Language Development in Children*. Oxford: Blackwell.

Piaget, J. and Inhelder, B. (1969) *The psychology of the child*. New York: Basic Books.

Robertson, J. and Bowlby, J. (1952) 'Responses of young children to separation from their mothers'. *Courrier of the International Children's Centre,* Paris, II, pp. 131-40.

Rymer, R. (1994) *Genie, a scientific tragedy*. London: HarperPerennial.

Schaffer, H.R. and Emerson, P.F. (1964) 'The development of social attachments in infancy'. *Monographs of the Society for Research in Child Development,* 29 (Serial No. 94).

Sims, M., Guilfoyle, A. and Parry, T. (2006) 'Child care for infants and toddlers: where in the world are we going? The First Years - Nga Tau Tuatahi'. *New Zealand Journal of Infant and Toddler Education*, 8(1), pp. 12-19.

SureStart (UK) (2008) SureStart: About us, available at: http://www.surestart.gov.uk/ aboutsurestart/ Accessed on 24/3/08.

Thomas, A. and Chess, S. (1977) *Temperament and Development*. New York: Brunner/Mazel.

Thomas, K. (1990) 'Dimensions of Personality' in I. Roth (ed.) *Introduction to Psychology*, pp. 373–416. Hove: Lawrence Erlbaum.

Vygotsky, L. (1978) *Mind in Society*. Cambridge, MA: Harvard.

Watterson, B. (1995) Calvin and Hobbes, available at: http://www.calvinandhobbes.co.uk/ Accessed on 24/3/08.

Winnicott, D.W. (1951) 'Transitional objects and transitional phenomena. A study of the first not-me possession'. *International Journal of Psycho-Analysis,* 34, pp. 89–97.

Wood, D., Bruner, J. and Ross, G. (1976) The role of tutoring in problem solving. *Journal of Child Psychology and Psychiatry,* 17, pp. 89–100.

Wood, D.J. and Middleton, D.J. (1975) 'A Study of assisted problem solving'. *British Journal of Psychology,* 66, pp. 181–91.

3

Social policy for childcare and education

Pam Jarvis

Chapter overview

The standards addressed in this chapter are:

S04   The main provisions of the national and local statutory and non-statutory frameworks within which children's services work and their implications for early years settings

S05   The current legal requirements, national policies and guidance on health and safety, safeguarding and promoting the well-being of children and their implications for early years settings

(CWDC 2006)

The text will address the following key questions:

● How and why did legislation for children and families develop in England?

● What are the key pieces of social policy legislation that will underpin the work of the first generation of Early Years Professionals, and how can they keep up with ongoing changes?

● What other attitudes to social policy exist within other Western nations, and what can we learn from these with regard to the ongoing development of social legislation for children in England?

Growing up 'in history'

I was raised in the middle of London, where throughout my childhood I was lucky enough to be taken to places where the history of children in England across the ages was brought alive for me by wonderful teachers, both within my own family and by those at school. Even now, based 200 miles north of my childhood home, I can locate in my mind's eye the street upon which the building stood that imprisoned the whole (Charles) Dickens family because the father (later immortalised in 'Mr Micawber') could not pay his debts; the place where children as young as 6 were hanged for petty theft, and the streets around the area where my great-grandfather undertook trade union work that would eventually contribute in a small way to the birth of the Labour party and the Welfare State. Such a background has given me a life-long passion for social history and social policy relating to children and their families, which I will attempt to share with you in the pages of this chapter.

Introduction

The underpinning principles of childcare and education require that senior practitioners not only have a grasp of contemporary social policy and legislation relating to children's issues, but also the sociological grounding and flexibility to understand the reasoning behind the policy making. It is also a requirement that individuals invested with the responsibility for leading practice continually keep up to date with new legislation, and become able to engage in debate relating to ongoing changes, developing the potential to become one of those leading practice development both locally and nationally, as their career unfolds. This chapter will outline a brief history of social policy, focusing upon children's legislation, moving on to compare current Early Years policy structures in England with those of two different contemporary Western nations. It is constructed in three discrete sections:

- **Section 1:** outlines a brief summary of the history of social legislation in England relating to children and families
- **Section 2:** outlines current legislation relevant to Early Years practice
- **Section 3:** outlines a brief international comparison of social legislation and its relative impact on Early Years practice within the relevant nations.

The further reading list will introduce you to a range of texts and online resources in which to read more widely on these topics.

Section 1: A brief history of social legislation in England relating to children and families

How and why did social legislation and children's legislation develop in England?

The first formal poor law in England was established in 1598 by Queen Elizabeth I, who decreed that 'parish relief' would be distributed to the 'destitute'. A medieval parish covered an area served by a specific church, and it was proposed that 'parish relief' should be collected, managed and distributed by the church in every district. Sunday schools subsequently arose (particularly under the Cromwells' Puritan rule, between 1653 and 1660) and took a role in the education of the poor, teaching children 'moral' behaviour and, sometimes, basic reading and counting skills. Elizabeth initially created the parish relief legislation to deal with aggressive roving beggars who were causing concern, as illustrated by the following rhyme:

Hark, hark the dogs do bark
The Beggars are coming to town
Some in rags and some in jags
And one in a velvet gown

(Traditional)

(The Tudor meaning of 'jag' was a fashionable slit in a garment exposing a material of a different colour underneath.) The underlying reason for the law was to encourage each parish to 'look after its own' and avoid the violence that ensued when people in a particular town or village (with no formal law enforcement mechanisms beyond the village squire and priest) decided to run potentially undeserving strangers out of their territory! This mixture of compassion and practical governance can still be discerned in today's social legislation, as we will see later in this chapter.

The parish system operated for over three centuries, until industrialisation changed the ways that people were employed, creating a huge expansion in city-based living as people moved into the rapidly expanding towns to work in the new factories and mills. Parish relief was no longer practical in such large and impersonal communities, and in 1834 it was replaced by the unpopular workhouse system. 'Pauper' families were split up and sent to segregated male, female and

Focus on policy

There are a lot of old Victorian workhouse buildings still in existence in Britain, many of which have been converted to a wide variety of purposes. One of the pictures below shows one of the old workhouses in Leeds, which is today used as a medical museum.

In the workhouse: some inmates of the workhouse to the east of Leeds city centre, and the building today, which now serves as the Thackray Medical Museum.
Source: Courtesy of the Thackray Museum, Leeds

Task Why not see if you can find an old workhouse building in the city nearest to where you live, and learn something about its history?

children's sections in large institutions where they lived like prisoners, carrying out menial work for a place to stay and basic sustenance. Most families did everything they could to remain out of the workhouse system, even if it meant living in extreme poverty.

Trade Unions, created by working men, subsequently started 'friendly societies' where members donated a small percentage of their income to a collective insurance fund so that their families would be able to continue to receive an income (hence avoid the workhouse) for some length of time if they became unemployed, ill or died prematurely. The impersonal nature of life in the new cities underpinned many fundamental societal changes, including the creation of a statutory Policing system, which began in 1829 with the London 'Bow Street Runners', who were the original Metropolitan Police force.

Over the mid-19th century, successive Victorian governments became increasingly concerned about the poverty and squalor in the new cities. In 1870 a Public Health Act made it compulsory for Local Authorities to provide clean water and sewerage systems paid for by a new local tax on householders called 'the rates'. Fired by the example of charitable education institutions such as Thomas Barnardo's 'ragged school' for pauper boys in Stepney, East London, which opened its doors in 1867 (BBC 2001, online), the government passed the first Education Act in 1870, which set up publicly funded school boards to ensure that all children aged 5 to 12 were allocated a free school place and maintained their attendance to ensure that they received a basic primary education, principally inculcating basic literacy, numeracy, practical skills and moral understanding. Mid-Victorian Britain was fast developing a cultural understanding of children as 'special' vulnerable human beings who needed care, education and protection under the law. By 1870, Barnardo had extended his charitable efforts to a home for orphaned and 'pauper' children (Barnardo's 2008, online) and in 1884 The London Society for the Prevention of Cruelty to Children was created (BBC 2001, online). In 1889, the government passed the first Children Act to instigate legal procedures to protect children from physically abusive adults, and the London Society for the Prevention of Cruelty to Children became a national charitable institution, the NSPCC, which, alongside Barnardos, still continues to provide help for disadvantaged children and their families today.

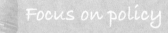

Focus on policy

The Children Act 1889

This act was the first to impose criminal penalties on those who mistreated children. It enabled the state to intervene, for the first time, in relations between parents and children. Police could arrest anyone found ill-treating a child, and enter a home if a child was thought to be in danger. The act included guidelines on the employment of children and outlawed begging, which frequently involved children.

(DoH 1889)

Throughout the nineteenth century, the British government extended the right to vote to working men (women had to wait until 1928 to get the vote on the same terms), which changed the political landscape, as politicians scrambled for working-class votes. This eventually resulted in the birth of the Labour party (emerging from the Trade Unions Congress as the political party for working men) in 1900, although it had to wait until 1924 for its first very short (nine-month) term of government. For most of the twentieth century, the Labour movement would bring a *collectivist* approach to government, raising taxation to fund services that acted to equalise the population, while the Conservative movement would bring an opposing *individualistic* orientation, cutting taxation on the basis that individuals and families had the right to decide upon the services that they required, and pay for them on a private basis.

Focus on policy

The Children's Charter 1908

- Established juvenile courts
- Introduced the registration of foster parents, which had the effect of regulating 'baby-farming' and wet-nursing, which in turn had the emergent effect of reducing infanticide (people secretly 'doing away' with unwanted children!)
- Prevented children working in dangerous trades and prevented them from purchasing cigarettes and alcohol
- Local authorities were granted powers to keep poor children out of the workhouse and protect them from abuse; this led to many councils setting up social services departments and county orphanages
- Raised the minimum age for execution to 16, later raised to 18 in the Children and Young Persons Act 1933 (see below)

(DoH 1908)

Over the early years of the twentieth century, the Liberal party's popularity began to fall behind that of the new Labour party. This revelation in the political landscape gathered pace in Britain once the Armistice ended World War I (1918), as all men over 21 and all women over 30 were given the right to vote. However, one of the last Liberal administrations set up the very first national insurance system in 1906, based upon the model created over the previous century by the Trade Unions. At this time, national insurance was only for men, who paid a compulsory small amount that was taken at source from their wages. The resulting fund was used to pay old age pensions, and to insure those who paid into the fund against sickness, unemployment and disability. Some money was also put aside to fund school health checks, free school meals for poor children and the setting up of 'labour exchanges' (early job centres). Unfortunately, an international economic slump during the early 1930s exposed the inadequacy of this initiative. Men were laid off work for long periods of time and, as their unemployment pay ran out, several child deaths due to starvation occurred in families who refused to endure the misery, separation and degradation of the workhouse. Full employment was only finally achieved in the late 1930s due to the armament production and military service opportunities that directly preceded and endured throughout World War II.

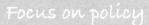

Focus on policy

The Children and Young Person's Act 1932/33

- The Children and Young Persons Act 1932 broadened the powers of juvenile courts and introduced supervision orders for children at risk.

- In 1933, a further Children and Young Persons Act collated all existing child protection legislation into one act.

(DoH 1932/1933)

As the Blitz raged over London in the mid-1940s, the war government, a coalition of all political parties, asked William Beveridge (1879–1963), who was an economist and social reformer, to create a plan for rebuilding British society after the war. Beveridge (1942) proposed that there were 'five giants' of deprivation to slay: want, ignorance, disease, squalor and idleness.

Beveridge's five giants
Source: Solo Syndication/Associated Newspapers Ltd: By Permission of Llyfrgell Genedlaethol Cymru/The National Library of Wales and the British Cartoon archive, Kent

Focus on policy

Task If you and/or your fellow EYPS candidates have elderly relatives who were children in pre-World War II Britain, ask them what they remember about education, health and family finance in the pre-welfare state society. Compare the situations and services that they tell you about with those that exist today.

As the war ended in 1945, the Labour party was voted in by a landslide. The franchise had now been extended to all Britons, male and female, aged over 21. Over their first three years in office, this government (with Clement Attlee as its Prime Minister) set up the **British Welfare State**, based on the recommendations of the Beveridge Report (1942). This comprised:

- The **National Health Service** to tackle **disease**
- A comprehensive, nationally funded **benefits and pensions** system to tackle **want**
- Free high-quality and compulsory **education** from 5–15 (16 from 1972) to tackle **ignorance**
- A national **housing** initiative to tackle **squalor**
- A national **employment** initiative to tackle **idleness**

Many major industries were also permanently *nationalised* (for example, the mines, the post office and the railways) so that the national administration procedures that had been created in the war years could continue to operate. At the time, it was the most ambitious set of collectivist national projects in the Western world, which shocked some political commentators in the USA into comparing the new British regime to those that operated in the Communist nations of Eastern Europe (Glennerster 2006).

Focus on policy

1940s social legislation

The Education Act 1944 was passed by the coalition World War II government, a year before the Attlee Labour government was voted into power. This Act set up a system of state schooling from age 5-11 (primary) and 11-18 (secondary). The minimum school leaving age rose to 15 (DfES 1944). This basic structure remains, although the leaving age became 16 in 1972 and will become 18 in 2010, although it is proposed that some 14-18 year olds will be in apprenticeships rather than in formal schooling.

Major legislative measures of the post-war Labour government:

- 1945 Family Allowances Act
- 1946 National Insurance Act

- 1946 National Insurance (Industrial Injuries) Act
- 1946 National Health Service Act (implemented July 1948)
- 1947 Town and Country Planning Act
- 1947 New Towns Act
- 1948 National Assistance Act
- 1948 Children Act
- 1949 Housing Act

(BBC 2008, online)

The Children Act 1948 established a children's committee and a children's officer in each local authority. It followed the creation of the Parliamentary Care of Children Committee in 1945 following the death of 13 year old Dennis O'Neill at the hands of his abusive foster parents (DoH 1948).

These health, benefits and education systems, although much 'worked upon' by subsequent administrations, still form the bedrock of all the UK nations' social policy today. They remained pretty much unsullied throughout the 1950s and 1960s, but by the early 1970s rising international oil prices sent the whole Western world into economic recession. Throughout the 1970s in Britain, a succession of both Conservative and Labour administrations battled with the Trade Unions, as inflation rapidly raised the cost of living and the unions called strike after strike in an attempt to force employers to raise wages to keep pace with prices. In 1978, Britain entered what was to thereafter be known as 'the winter of discontent' where nearly all workers in the public and nationalised industries went on strike. Dead bodies remained unburied and piles of rubbish lay uncollected in the streets, attracting swarms of rats (Marr 2007).

In 1979, Britons voted in the Conservative administration led by Margaret Thatcher, who subsequently became Britain's first woman Prime Minister. She undertook a comprehensive programme of de-nationalisation, and, while the welfare state remained materially intact, the value of benefits was slashed, and there were cuts and economies applied to nationally funded services including education and health. In The Housing Act of 1980, the Thatcher government gave tenants the 'right to buy' public housing stock that had largely been built in the period directly after World War II; in areas where this venture did not succeed, the management of public housing was subsequently largely removed from local authorities and sold on to private housing trusts. This government also denied government subsidies to unprofitable manufacturing industries, allowing them to close down altogether. By the early 1980s Britain experienced a 10 per cent unemployment level, which disproportionately hit manufacturing industries, raising the unemployment levels in areas that housed factories, mines and mills proportionally well beyond those that had been experienced in the 1930s, particularly among male workers (Marr 2007). Subsequent urban regeneration projects undertaken over the late 1980s and early 1990s eventually achieved some amount of re-employment by encouraging 'service' and financial industries to set up their offices within the old industrial areas. The resulting new jobs were frequently temporary, part-time and low-paid, and disproportionately filled by women.

Meanwhile, despite the Government's efforts to cut public spending in education and health, the advance of medical science hugely increased the costs of the NHS, as the range of treatments available increased, and in addition technological advances began to create a requirement for a more technically competent workforce; hence a longer mass education for young people became necessary. The Government increasingly began to contemplate how they could create a public education and social welfare support system that inculcated the 'correct' skills and attitudes in children to create a steady supply of 'useful citizens'. This eventually resulted in the Education Act 1988, which was swiftly followed by the Children Act 1989 as the Government's response to a string of high-profile and controversial debates about child protection, including the recognition of more insidious areas of child maltreatment including neglect, emotional and sexual abuse.

While the age for voting was dropped to 18 in 1970, the school leaving age was raised to 16 in 1972, and, as the 1970s drew to a close, increasing numbers of young people remained in education until they were 18. Numbers attending university also increased over the 1970s and 1980s; such individuals remained in education until they were 21. However, at the other end of education provision, pre-school opportunities remained largely within the private sector. The Conservatives remained in governance until 1997, with John Major replacing Margaret Thatcher as Prime Minister in 1990.

Focus on policy

Reflection *Were you a child and/or young person in Britain during the 1980s? What do you remember of the culture and society that formed the background to your childhood? For example, what do you remember about adult employment roles and experiences of unemployment, and its effects upon the family? Do you remember taking SATs at school? Did you attend pre-school education? I remember that my young twins were only able to attend pre-school for two days a week before they entered primary school in 1991, because the private fees were so high, and pre-school children had no guaranteed right to a nursery place, whether or not they were 'multiples'!*

Task Share your reflections of 'Thatcher's Britain' with your fellow students and tutors. How do you think life was different from (and/or similar to) life today for young children and their families?

Thatcher government legislation for children and families

The Education Reform Act 1988

Main provisions include:

- Devolution of responsibilities for managing each school to governing bodies-Local Management of Schools (LMS)
- Greater central control through instigation of the National Curriculum
- A system of national testing via 'Standard Assessment Tasks' (SATs)
- Parental choice (informed by notified SATs results)
- The basis for later regulation (e.g. this was followed by the **Education (Schools) Act (1992)** which set up Ofsted to inspect schools in England and Wales)

(DfES 1988)

The Children Act 1989

Part one outlines the Paramountcy Principle (the child's welfare is paramount) and the concept of Significant Harm.

Part two sets out measures which may be used by Social Services departments who are in dispute with parents of children within their designated area.

Part three sets out the principal responsibilities of local authorities regarding children in their area.

Part four sets out the grounds under which courts may make an order, which, in simplified form, relates to evidence that a child has been suffering significant harm, or that a court feels that there is a strong possibility that s/he may be likely to do so in the future in his/her current situation.

Part five outlines the introduction of a new Emergency Protection Order to replace the old Place of Safety Order, and stipulates how the new Order may be used, and by whom.

Parts six to twelve cover:

- guidelines regarding residential care
- guidelines regarding fostering
- standards concerning nursery and childcare arrangements for under 5s
- court arrangements for dealing with children's issues.

(DoH 1989)

By 1997, the British electorate had had enough of Thatcherist Conservatism, and they elected a Labour government. However, Labour politics had moved on considerably during their nearly two decades in opposition, and, while the new 'New Labour' government (with Tony Blair at its head between 1997 and 2007) had promised to protect the Welfare State, it did very little to reverse the cut-backs instigated by the previous Conservative administration. This heralded a less collectivist approach underlying its 'New' Labour label. Much of this government's work relating to welfare has subsequently consisted of the creation of 'deals' between the government and private sources of funding to manage health and education. Public funding has, however, been steadily pumped into education initiatives, still driven by the (originally Thatcherite) focus upon producing an educated workforce that will make Britain more internationally competitive. However, New Labour has an additional impetus to try to equalise the chances of children in the early years, embodied in an ambitious attempt to dramatically reduce the numbers of children living in poverty. To this end, they created the SureStart initiative in 1998 (2008 online), based upon the HeadStart initiative (2008 online) in the United States. SureStart Centres were set up across urban disadvantaged areas in England. Many of these have recently (early 2009) become Children's Centres, which aim to provide a 'one stop shop' for health, education and care services for young children and their families. The focus is upon supporting low income families (including single parents) to find their own way out of poverty through paid work. This 'workfare' concept was drawn from the political philosophy of the Clinton administration which governed the USA between 1992 and 2000, and has become internationally known as the 'third way' (i.e. between individualism and collectivism). Such a philosophy was clearly embodied in the Ten Year Plan for Childcare (2004, see below). In 2007, Gordon Brown took over the premiership and created a new Department for Children, Schools and Families (DCSF) headed by Ed Balls. In November 2007, it published the Children's Plan (see below). At the time of writing (early 2009) the Brown New Labour administration appears to maintain a similar commitment to the 'third way' philosophy which was unfurled under the premiership of Blair; however, it is beginning to struggle to keep its reform programme on target due to an international financial crisis and growing recession, which is threatening to become a full-blown depression.

Having covered 500 years of social policy at some speed above, you may now be asking what relevance this has to your work within the contemporary Early Years sector. The answer initially relates to the general place of history in everyday life – it allows us to find our own point on an unfolding timeline where continually changing social and political perspectives can otherwise seem very confusing. It also allows us to reflect upon the fact that governments and populations frequently have to respond in the best way they can to situations that have not been thoroughly planned and may not be entirely of their own making.

Those who work in the Early Years sector should be very aware that children are particularly vulnerable to the problems and uncertainties created by the constantly shifting social and economic forces that underpin their parents' lives within modern societies. Physical deprivation and familial stress can have more devastating results upon developing bodies and minds than upon those of adults, and the individualistic mantra to 'fend for oneself' cannot be sensibly applied to those who are not yet old enough to do so. Governments are often particularly interested in the fate of their nation's children, and not always for the most charitable reasons, being inclined to view them as 'projects' for a collective national future rather than as individuals. For the British government, the late nineteenth century discovery that city-raised men from poor families had frequently been so poorly nourished and cared for in childhood that they were unfit to be soldiers created a national imperative to provide aid for poor children at the beginning of the twentieth century; at the beginning of the twenty-first century Alderson (2008, p. 53) similarly proposed that the Every Child Matters charter (2003, see below) 'appears to be more concerned with the national economy than with the welfare and protection of young children'. This echoes the mixture of compassion and practical governance that was initially raised at the beginning of the chapter as an underlying factor of the Elizabethan Poor Law.

The role of senior childcare and education practitioners in any society in time or geography is to work within the systems that they inhabit at the time, with a view to doing the best they can for the children under their care. This crucially involves a large amount of independent, analytical thought, reconciling what the practitioner knows from experience and theoretical knowledge to be good practice with the opportunities and pitfalls present in the policies and guidelines with which they are currently presented. In this way the Early Years Foundation Stage (2008) and associated underpinning policies and guidance can be optimistically but cautiously viewed principally as opportunities, based as they are in the developmental knowledge gathered by the ongoing The Effective Provision of Pre-School Education (EPPE) project (1997–2008 online) and underpinned by the Birth to Three Matters review of the literature undertaken by David *et al.* (2003). However, the informed, reflective practitioner also needs to heed the ongoing warnings of dissenting voices such as Alderson's (2008 above), which perform the essential task of alerting us to what may happen when policy documents are slavishly instigated by practitioners who think 'two-dimensionally', taking little account of individual children's emotional, social and intellectual needs. With this word of caution in mind, the main areas of legislation and policy that will guide the work of the first generation of Early Years Professionals will be presented in summary below.

Section 2: Current legislation relevant to Early Years practice

What are the key pieces of social policy legislation that will underpin the work of the first generation of Early Years Professionals, and how can they keep up with ongoing changes?

In January 2003, Lord Laming published his report into the death of child abuse victim Victoria Climbié, which found that health, police and social services missed 12 opportunities to save Victoria. It recommended that the Children Act 1989 was to continue to function as the principal piece of child protection legislation but made the following additional recommendations: a minister for children; a national agency for children and families; local committees and management boards to oversee children's services; a national child database and a 24-hour helpline for the public to report concerns about children. A government green paper, Every Child Matters, followed in September. The Paper was presented to Parliament by the Chief Secretary to the Treasury and signalled a cross-sector approach to policy for children and young people. It proposed an electronic recording system to track the developmental and educational progress of England's 11 million children; 150 children's trusts; a children's director to oversee local children's services; statutory local safeguarding children boards and an independent children's commissioner for England, to protect young people's welfare and rights. An amalgamation of social services, education and child health was to be accomplished by 2006 (although there has since been some back-tracking on this), and a set of guidelines for those caring for the youngest children also emerged: The Birth to Three Matters guidelines (2003), which were later to feed into the Early Years Foundation Stage (2008).

Focus on policy

Every Child Matters: The key outcomes

The Every Child Matters (ECM) Green Paper of 2003 identified five key outcomes for children and young people that are to be met both through changes in individual public and independent agencies working with children and through Improved Inter-Agency Working:

- *Being healthy:* enjoying good physical and mental health and enjoying a healthy lifestyle
- *Staying safe:* being protected from harm and neglect
- *Enjoying and achieving:* getting the most out of life and developing the skills for adulthood
- *Making a positive contribution:* being involved with the community and society and not engaging in anti-social or offending behaviour
- *Economic well-being:* not being prevented by economic disadvantage from achieving their full potential in life.

(DfES 2003)

Every Child Matters currently remains a 'Green Paper' and has not resulted in a 'White Paper' (which takes it into a proposal for new legislation); in other words, it is not law. It has, however, become the basis for a huge number of policy developments relating to education, health and social care and workforce development, one major result of which was the setting up of the Children's Workforce Development Council in 2006.

In 2004, the Government passed a new Children Act to implement the main proposals of the Green Paper: electronic children's files, children's directors and the children's commissioner. It allowed local authorities some flexibility in organising their children's services, with the amalgamation of education and social services no longer mandatory. Councils were also given another two years to set up children's trusts.

Focus on policy

The Children Act 2004

Parts One and Two of The Act provide new structures and duties for England.

- To create a Children's Commissioner for England (already exists in Wales and Northern Ireland)
- To establish more effective information sharing through electronic means between public authorities for children at risk of abuse or who have been abused
- To establish a new structure for inter-agency cooperation in child protection – Local Safeguarding Children Boards (LSCBs)
- To establish Local Authority Directors of Children's Services and a lead member for children within Councils
- To establish a new inspection framework for children's services
- To establish Joint Area Reviews of services for children.

Parts Three and Four deal with the Welsh aspects of this legislation.

Part Five contains Miscellaneous provisions that include some updating of elements of the Children Act 1989, the main points of which remain very much 'live', and work in partnership with all new legislation.

Part Six deals with some necessary administrative details.

(DfES 2004)

Task Consider the principles of Every Child Matters and the contents of the Children Acts 1989 and 2004. Is there anything you think should be added, removed or more carefully defined? Make notes on this to discuss with your fellow EYPS candidates and colleagues.

The Ten Year Plan for Childcare, which was unveiled in 2004, arguably instigated a new era in social legislation. No government had previously legislated on care for pre-school children, or after-school care for older children; as such the Childcare Act 2006 which followed the Ten Year Plan can be viewed as the first major legislative extension of the Welfare State, nearly 60 years after its instigation. However, there was much less naivety relating to potential funding mechanisms among those creating these twenty-first century legislation plans than there had been among the enthusiastic but somewhat innocent social reformers of the 1940s.

Focus on policy

The Ten Year Plan for Childcare 2004

Choice and flexibility: parents to have greater choice about balancing work and family life

- A goal of 12 months' paid maternity leave
- A goal of legislation to give mothers the right to transfer a proportion of this paid leave to the child's father
- Every family to have easy access to integrated services through Children's Centres. 2500 Children's Centres to be in place by 2008 and 3500 by 2010.
- For all families with children aged up to 14 who need it, an affordable, flexible, high-quality childcare place that meets their circumstances.

Supply and demand: legislation for a new duty on local authorities in place by 2008 so that over time they will secure sufficient supply to meet the needs of families

- A goal of 20 hours a week of free high-quality care for 38 weeks for all 3 and 4 year olds
- An out-of-school childcare place for all children aged 3–14 between the hours of 8.00 a.m. and 6.00 p.m. each weekday by 2010.

Raising quality: high-quality provision with a highly skilled childcare and early years workforce

- All full daycare settings to be professionally led
- Transformation Fund of £125 million each year from April 2006 to invest in high-quality, sustainable, affordable provision
- Radical reform of the workforce, with the Children's Workforce Development Council consulting on a new qualification and career structure
- Reform of the regulation and inspection regime to improve standards and to give parents better information
- Affordability: families to be able to afford flexible, high-quality childcare that is appropriate for their needs
- The Government's long-term ambition is to reduce further the proportion of childcare costs paid by such families, making childcare increasingly affordable.

(DfES 2004)

Focus on policy

Ofsted Guidance to the National Standards for Daycare 2001

Ofsted created a set of national standards for daycare when the Government gave them the responsibility to inspect daycare settings. These standards are still 'live', and concepts within them have fed forward into the Early Years Foundation Stage

(2008) and the professional standards for Early Years Professionals created by the Children's Workforce Development Council. The National Standards for Daycare are as follows:

Standard 1 – Suitable Person: Adults providing daycare, looking after children or having unsupervised access to them should be suitable to do so.

Standard 2 – Organisation: The setting meets required adult:child ratios, ensures that training and qualifications requirements are met and organises space and resources to meet the children's needs effectively.

Standard 3 – Care, Learning and Play: The setting meets children's individual needs and promotes their welfare. Activities and play opportunities are planned and provided to develop children's emotional, physical, social and intellectual capabilities.

Standard 4 – Physical Environment: The premises are safe, secure and suitable for their purpose. They provide adequate space in an appropriate location, are welcoming to children and offer access to the necessary facilities for a range of activities which promote their development.

Standard 5 – Equipment: Furniture, equipment and toys are provided which are appropriate for their purpose and help to create an accessible and stimulating environment. They are of suitable design and condition, well maintained and conform to safety standards.

Standard 6 – Safety: The setting takes positive steps to promote safety within their premises and on outings, and ensures proper precautions are taken to prevent accidents.

Standard 7 – Health: The setting promotes the good health of children and takes positive steps to prevent the spread of infection and appropriate measures when they are ill.

Standard 8 – Food and Drink: Children are provided with regular drinks and food in adequate quantities for their needs. Food and drink is properly prepared, nutritious and complies with dietary and religious requirements.

Standard 9 – Equal Opportunities: The setting and its staff actively promote equality of opportunity and anti-discriminatory practice for all children.

Standard 10 – Special Needs (including special education needs and disabilities): The setting staff are aware that some children may have special needs and are proactive in ensuring that appropriate action can be taken when such a child is identified or admitted to the provision. Steps are taken to promote the welfare and development of the child within the setting in partnership with the parents and other relevant parties.

Standard 11 – Behaviour: Adults caring for children in the provision are able to manage a wide range of children's behaviour in a way that promotes their welfare and development.

Standard 12 – Working in Partnership with Parents and Carers: The setting and its staff work in partnership with parents to meet the needs of the children, both individually and as a group. Information is shared.

Standard 13 – Child Protection: The setting complies with local child protection procedures approved by the Area Child Protection Committee and ensures that all adults working and looking after children in the provision are able to put the proce-dures into practice (there have been updates on what was called 'child protection' in a move to the concept of 'safeguarding' and the replacement of Area Child Protection Committees with Safeguarding Boards, see Chapter 4).

Standard 14 – Documentation: Records, policies and procedures which are required for the efficient and safe management of the provision and to promote the welfare, care and learning of children are maintained. Records about individual children are shared with the child's parent.

(Ofsted 2001)

 Focus on policy

The Childcare Act 2006

Enshrines in law parents' 'legitimate expectation of accessible high-quality childcare and services for children under 5 and their families'

- Local Authorities to improve *outcomes* for all children under 5
- Local Authorities to *facilitate* the childcare market
- Emphasis on provision for working parents – particularly those on low income and those with disabled children
- Local Authorities to ensure a full range of information to parents
- Introduction of the **statutory** guidance document, The Early Years Foundation Stage (DCSF 2008) ('live' since September 2008, replaces the **non-statutory** Curriculum Guidance for the Foundation Stage)
- Reforms/standardises childcare and early years regulation across England.

(DfES 2006)

Reflection *Is the societal movement towards collective pre-school/after-school childcare a wholly positive development, or might there be potential underlying prob-lems? Two sources that will help you reflect upon this are the UNICEF report 'Child-care transitions' (2008) and the US National Research Council's report (edited by Shonkoff and Phillips) 'From Neurons to Neighborhoods' (2000). The UNICEF report reflects 'the stakes are simply too high for the mass movement towards out-of-home child care to be seen as just another shake of the kaleidoscope in the rapidly chang-ing lifestyles of advanced industrial economies' (p. 13).*

Task **Discuss issues arising with your fellow EYPS candidates and colleagues.**

Finally, the new Department for Children, Schools and Families published its own policy document, The Children's Plan (2007), shortly after its launch in late 2007. This has also been conceived as a 'ten-year plan' (which confusingly extends 13 years into the future, for some aspects, to 2020).

Focus on policy

The Children's Plan 2007

- Enhance children's and young people's well-being, particularly at key transition points in their lives
- Every child ready for success in school, with at least 90 per cent developing well across all areas of the Early Years Foundation Stage Profile by age 5
- Every child ready for secondary school, with at least 90 per cent achieving at or above the expected level in both English and mathematics by age 11
- Every young person with the skills for adult life and further study, with at least 90 per cent achieving the equivalent of five higher level GCSEs by age 19; and at least 70 per cent achieving the equivalent of two A levels by age 19
- Parents satisfied with the information and support they receive
- All young people participating in positive activities to develop personal and social skills, promote well-being and reduce behaviour that puts them at risk
- Employers satisfied with young people's readiness for work
- Child health improved, with the proportion of obese and overweight children reduced to 2000 levels
- Child poverty halved by 2010 and eradicated by 2020
- Significantly reduce by 2020 the number of young offenders receiving a conviction, reprimand, or final warning for a recordable offence for the first time, with a goal to be set in the Youth Crime Action Plan.

(DCSF 2007)

A subsequent report, '2020 Children and Young People's Workforce strategy' (DCSF 2008) was published in December 2008, stressing that professionals should be both 'excellent in their practice' and 'ambitious for young people' within a workforce based upon partnership and integration; how this is to be achieved in practice is not fully clarified within its content. How to keep up with such a relentless flow of legislation, policy and guidelines is a challenge for all senior practitioners in childcare and education, across all ages and stages. It is a good idea to sign up for the regular email circulars that are provided by the Department for Children, Schools and Families (**http://www.dcsf.gov.uk**). In order to have some knowledge of the background to legislative and policy developments, it is also necessary to keep up with current affairs, preferably by becoming a regular reader of a broadsheet newspaper, but at the very least by a daily browse on a good quality news website, such as those provided by the broadsheets, and/or the BBC. **It is the responsibility of the leading practitioner in every childcare/education setting to ensure that current guidelines are being followed on an ongoing basis.** The Local Authority is always available to provide advice, and the leading practitioner in a setting should maintain good relationships with their designated advisory teacher. It is hoped that experienced EYPs will also inhabit such advisory roles attached to the Local Authority in the not-too-distant future. It is probably appropriate to remind you at this point that the advice on legislation and guidelines in this book can only be as up to date as the publication date stated on the flyleaf!

Section 3: A brief international comparison of social legislation and its relative impact on Early Years practice

What other attitudes to social policy exist within other Western nations, and what can we learn from these with regard to the ongoing development of social legislation for children in England?

Attitudes to social policy of various nations can be seen very much in the light of whether they take principally an **individualistic** or a **collectivist** approach to governance and social policy. Britain has fluctuated to a great extent in this respect over the post World War II years, depending on whether it has been under a Conservative or a Labour government. Two opposing examples, one individualistic, one collectivist, can be provided in the approach to the provision of pre-school care and education taken by the USA and Sweden respectively.

Focus on policy and practice

Task Read and compare the following two examples. Make notes considering how these examples of practice relate to your own experience. Discuss with your fellow EYPS candidates, and work together in a group to research examples of policy and practice in other countries. When you have some further examples to compare, discuss the aspects of such policy and practice that reflect collectivist and individualistic ideals. You will find these to be oddly mixed within the policy and practice of some nations, especially the UK.

An individualistic approach – The USA: life, liberty and the pursuit of happiness

'We hold these truths to be self-evident, that all men are created equal, that they are endowed by their Creator with certain unalienable Rights, that among these are Life, Liberty and the pursuit of Happiness. – That to secure these rights, Governments are instituted among Men, deriving their just powers from the consent of the governed, – That whenever any Form of Government becomes destructive of these ends, it is the Right of the People to alter or to abolish it'.

(US government 1776)

These very famous words can be found in the US Declaration of Independence, and they demonstrate the culture upon which the USA was founded: that of the rights of the individual. Arrangements for pre-school care in the USA further illustrate the individualistic nature of its social structure.

- In 2002, slightly under half of the children under 6 in the USA were in some type of daycare; this figure had doubled since 1977.

- In 1995, there were 90 different childcare and early childhood education programmes ongoing in the USA managed by 11 federal (i.e. national government) agencies and 20 different offices. Melhuish (2006) calls this a 'non-system system'.

- There are no federal inspection systems for education and care settings for children under 6. Inspection arrangements differ greatly from state to state.

- Across the USA as a whole, provision for the under 6s is provided mainly by the private sector, by employers, charities and private profit-based businesses.

- State-funded provision is in place for very low-income (frequently non-working) families. This is, however, principally HeadStart, which was never designed as full daycare, but as a family education programme. Few HeadStart settings therefore offer full daycare services.

- Subsidies are available to help low-income working families pay for childcare.

- Tax benefits are given to middle- and high-income families to help them to pay for childcare.

- This hierarchy of state funding, subsidies and tax benefits outlined above tends to give rise to a three-tier system where children inhabit specific settings on the basis of parental income, with little mixing between socio-economic groups.

- In some states there are no regulations at all relating to the training of staff who work with children under 6. What information there is relating to the quality of care indicates that about half of the settings caring for children under 6 in the USA are of only 'fair' quality or below. There are no state provisions for maternity/parenting leave from work in the USA; individual companies make their own policies.

(Melhuish and Petrogiannis 2006, Cochrane and Clarke 2001)

A collectivist approach – Sweden: The People's Home

The Social Democratic political party has dominated the political landscape in Sweden from the 1930s until the present day. They espouse a similar political philosophy to the British Labour Party of the mid-20th century. Throughout the period between 1930 and the mid-1990s the Social Democrats successfully intervened in their national economy to maintain full employment in Sweden. The Social Democrat politician Per Albin Hansson proposed (1928) that Sweden should be a 'people's home. . . . a sharing, just community on a national basis where no one takes more than their share or stands outside the system of community provision' (Cochrane and Clarke 2001, p. 197). During the 1960s and 1970s Swedish welfare benefits and services expanded rapidly. High taxation of income paid (and still pays) for the Swedish welfare state. During the 1980s when the UK and USA were pulling back their state provision, Sweden's continued to expand.

Services for children and families in Sweden

- State-funded daycare is universally available for children under 7 and after-school care is universally available for children over 7. Parents pay a modest fee calculated on the basis of income.

- Swedish lone parents are much less likely to be designated 'poor' than they are in Britain and the USA.

- By the early 1980s over 80 per cent of mothers of children under 7 were in paid employment.

- In 1985 Swedes legislated to ensure that all working families had access to state daycare for children over 18 months. There is a current intention to extend this to *all* families, working or not.

- By 1998 73 per cent of children aged 1 to 5 were enrolled in pre-schools, which are open all year round, and for hours extending into the evening.

Swedish parental leave rights are as follows (from 1998):

- 360 days' leave from work allowed over the child's first 8 years at 80 per cent of salary. Parents may share this between them, but each one must take at least 30 days. This has become known as the 'daddy month'.

- A further 90 days' leave is allowed on reduced salary.

- Unemployed parents are paid for 450 days by the state over the child's first 8 years.

- Mothers get 50 days' pregnancy leave and fathers get 10 days' paternity leave when the child is born.

- Parents can take up to 60 days' paid leave per child per year to cover the provision of care when a child is ill.

Sweden has the most extensive public provision for pre-school and after-school care in Europe. It has an extensive national training programme in place for its Early Years workers. Nursery practitioners (*barnskotare*) take a three-year course; they can then choose to work as an assistant or take a further three-year course to become a nursery teacher (*forskollarare*).

(Cochrane and Clarke 2001, Melhuish and Petrogiannis 2006)

Studies carried out in the USA comparing children who have been raised principally at home with children who have been in daycare for long periods in their early years suggest that, when they turn 6 and enter formal schooling, their teachers note that those who have spent substantial periods in daycare in their earlier development are more aggressive and more inclined to develop behaviour problems (e.g. Belsky 2006). However, studies of Swedish children who have been in long periods of childcare during their early development find that they show little differences from those cared for mainly at home (e.g. Andersson 1992, Broberg *et al.* 1997). The indications are that it is the quality of care that is at the core of the matter rather than an inherent structural difference between home care and daycare. In summary, the basic social policy lesson to be drawn from this comparision is: 'you pays your money and you takes your choice', which is further illustrated by the summary comparison of social funding outlined below:

- Sweden has the highest level of social public expenditure in Europe, 33 per cent of their national income as opposed to 22.4 per cent in Britain and 15.8 per cent in the USA.

- Sweden has a much lower level of population designated as 'poor' than Britain and the USA, around 6 per cent, while this figure for Britain and the USA is around 17–20 per cent (depending on calculation). Statistics indicate that New Labour have reduced this figure slightly in Britain over 1997– present.

- Unemployment pay in Sweden is equal to 85 per cent of the average wage. Comparative figures in Britain and the USA are 67 per cent and 59 per cent respectively.

(Cochrane and Clarke 2001)

Clearly the Swedish model is one that many would like to emulate, but those who have a more individualistic political orientation fear the necessary taxation would suppress individual initiative and choice within the population. It is up to individuals to make up their own minds in this respect, and, at senior practitioner level, to be able to provide an informed, educated and considered opinion on national and international policy developments throughout the course of their careers in childcare and education.

It is suggested that those wishing to read further with regard to international comparison focus initially upon the 'Starting Strong' report parts I (2001) and II (2006), which is an extensive comparison of early years care and education in the Organisation for Economic Cooperation and Development (OECD) nations; also that they browse the current Te Whariki guidelines for Early Years Childcare and Education in New Zealand, for which there is sadly no room to detail in this chapter, but which uniquely manages to serve both as a platform for the Early Years curriculum and as an underlying, highly collectivist social philosophy. The Maori phrase which provides its title translates to 'a woven mat upon which all may stand'.

Focus on policy and practice

Task Once you have browsed the Starting Strong and Te Whariki documents, discuss the concepts of individualism and collectivism with your fellow EYPS candidates and colleagues, with regard to developing Early Years policy for children and families. Which political orientation do you lean towards, and what are your reasons? (Note: Do *not* expect to agree completely on such issues with all your colleagues – the point of this exercise is to initiate friendly debate!)

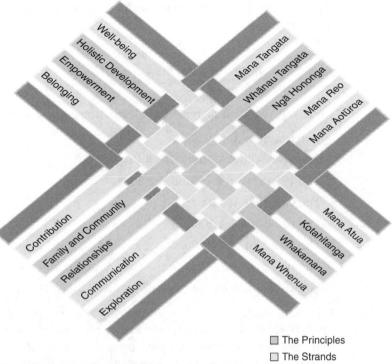

Figure 3.1 Te Whariki: the woven mat

Te Whāriki is a metaphor for the curriculum, which weaves together the principles, strands, and goals defined in the document. The whāriki concept recognises the diversity of early childhood education in New Zealand. Different programmes, philosophies, structures, and environments will contribute to the distinctive patterns of the whāriki.

Source: Te Whariki: National Early Childhood Curriculum Guidelines, published by Learning Media Ltd for the Ministry of Education, Wellington 1996.

Conclusion

How and why did social legislation and children's legislation develop in England?

The account above briefly covers 500 years over which concepts of social policy legislation developed in England, first of all with a focus upon basic human rights and needs, followed by a growing understanding of the special rights and needs of children and their families. As society has grown more complex, initially through industrialisation and later through technological change, the intricacy of social policy and legislation for children and families has developed simultaneously. Discerning reflective practitioners should keep in mind the caution of Alderson (2008) who suggests that much of such policy making and legislation relates more to controlling the activities of children and their families rather than to the collective provision of help and support. The knowledgeable, flexible practitioner should always be able to carefully balance the needs of individual children within the system concerned to ensure that, above all, the demands of statutory guidelines and curricula are never allowed to compromise the individual rights and needs of children and their families. *In particular, the practitioner's first responsibility should always be to the promotion of children's ongoing, healthy physical and psychological development.*

What are the key pieces of social policy legislation that will underpin the work of the first generation of Early Years Professionals, and how can they keep up with ongoing changes?

Currently, the main such pieces of legislation and policy in England are as follows:

- The Children Act 1989
- The Every Child Matters Green Paper 2003
- The 10 Year Plan for Childcare 2004
- The Children Act 2004
- The Childcare Act 2006
- The Children's Plan 2007
- The statutory guidelines of the Early Years Foundation Stage (2008)
- The 2020 Children and Young People's Workforce Strategy

Keeping up with ongoing changes is a challenge, but, as suggested above, signing up for the regular DCSF email bulletin at **http://www.dcsf.gov.uk** can be a key step in the right direction, alongside keeping up with current affairs, which helps to allow enough time to comprehend the reasons for, and to make preparations for change.

What other attitudes to social policy exist within other Western nations, and what can we learn from these with regard to the ongoing development of social legislation for children in England?

The key comparison here is between individualistic and collectivist philosophies of social policy, which in a democracy are very much a choice of the individual, and one which fundamentally underpins how they decide to cast their vote. It is not the purpose of this book (or author!) to influence your opinion in any political direction, but it *is* advised that you develop an informed opinion to underpin your work, particularly with a view to eventual promotion into a more senior role that may involve an input to policy construction at local, national and possibly even international level. A comparison between two Western nations is provided above, one that takes a highly individualistic approach, and another that leans more to the collectivist viewpoint. It is recommended that further reading be undertaken to reflect more deeply upon such comparisons, initially with a focus on the Starting Strong project (2001–2006) and the unique Te Whariki (1996) concept that underpins the early years education and care programme in New Zealand.

Endnote

It is hoped that you now feel confident about where to find up-to-date information relating to the main provisions of the national and local statutory and non-statutory frameworks within which children's services work, and their wider implications for early years (S04), and that you understand the sociological and historical bases and the content of the current legal requirements, national policies and guidance on health and safety, safeguarding and promoting the well-being of children and their implications for early years settings (S05) (CWDC 2006).

When I was 18, and hesitant about casting my first vote (incidentally, in the election that brought the Thatcher government to power for the first time), my father refused to give any advice beyond a broadsheet newspaper summary of the manifestos of the political parties and a warning: 'if you don't vote, then don't criticise'. This would seem the ideal parting advice to pass on to you: read widely and become more knowledgeable about politics and social policy in order to engage in the ongoing debate which, with only a few setbacks, has steadily advanced societal conditions in England for young children and their families over the 500 years leading up to the present. Post-'credit crunch' Britain stands on the brink of yet more societal change, as Western economies adjust; this may create changes to the ways that it organises its care for its youngest children. However, the expertise of Early Years Professionals will continue to retain its value, whether their principal work remains in collective daycare with children from families where both parents are in paid employment, or whether they increasingly work with disadvantaged families with young children, as unemployment numbers rise.

Focus on policy

Task How do you plan to keep up to date with current affairs and changes in the legislation and guidelines that apply to Early Years practice? Discuss plans and useful resources with your fellow EYPS candidates and colleagues, making sure to note the location of useful websites and resources in your Continuing Professional Development Portfolio, and ensure that you keep this list up to date. You may also find it helpful to set up a website 'favourites' list on your Internet browser program. You can start with the suggested reading list below.

Further reading

Alderson, P. (2008) *Young Children's Rights, 2nd edition.* London: Jessica Kingsley Publishing.

Bochel, H., Bochel, C., Page, R. and Sykes, R. (2009) *Social Policy: Themes, Issues and Debates.* Harlow: Pearson.

Cochrane, A. and Clarke, J. (2001) *Comparing welfare states: Britain in an international Context.* Berkshire: Oxford University Press.

David, T. (1993) *Educational provision for our youngest children (European perspectives).* London: Paul Chapman.

Glennerster, H. (2006) *British social policy: 1945 to the present, 3rd edition.* London: Blackwell.

Marr, A. (2007) *A History of Modern Britain*. MacMillan: London.

Melhuish, E. and Petrogiannis, K. (2006) *Early Childhood Care and Education*. Abingdon: Routledge.

Oberhuemer, P. and Wich, M. (1997) *Working with young children in Europe; provision and staff training*. London: Paul Chapman.

Pugh, G. (2006) *Contemporary issues in the early years, 4th edition*. London: Paul Chapman.

Stainton Rogers, W. and Roche, J. (1994) *Children's Welfare and Children's Rights, a practical guide to the law*. London: Hodder & Stoughton.

Websites

Barnardo's: http://www.barnardos.org.uk

Effective Provision of Pre-School Education (EPPE) project: http://k1.ioe.ac.uk/schools/ecpe/eppe/

Devon County Council: online document bank for childcare providers: http://www.devon.gov.uk/index/cyps/early_years_and_childcare/eycs/providers/doc bank.htm

OECD (2001) *Starting Strong Early Childhood Education and Care*. Paris: OECD Publishing: http://www.oecd.org

OECD (2006) *Starting Strong Early Childhood Education and Care* Part II. Paris: OECD Publishing: http://www.oecd.org

Ministry of Education (NZ) (1996) *Te Whariki: Early Childhood Curriculum*. Wellington: Learning Media: http://www.minedu.govt.nz/web/downloadable/dl3567_v1/WHARIKI.pdf

NSPCC: http://www.nspcc.org.uk

SureStart: http://www.surestart.gov.uk

UNICEF (2007) An Overview of Child Well Being in Rich Countries, available at: http://www.unicef-icdc.org/presscentre/presskit/reportcard7/rc7_eng.pdf

UNICEF (2008) The Child Care Transition: a league table of early childhood education and care in economically advanced countries, available at: http://www.unicef-irc.org/publications/pdf/rc8_eng.pdf

Journals

Children and Society

Children Now

Educational Researcher

Early Years Educator

Nursery World

Psychological Review

Early Years – an International Journal of Research and Development

References

Alderson, P. (2008) *Young Children's Rights*, 2nd edition. London: Jessica Kingsley Publishing.

Andersson, B.E. (1992) 'Effects of day-care on cognitive and socioemotional competence of thirteen-year-old Swedish schoolchildren'. *Child Development,* 63, pp. 20-36.

Barnardo's (2008) 'History of Barnardo's', available at: http://www.barnardos.org.uk/who_we_are/history.htm Accessed on 30/3/08.

BBC (2001) 'Children as animals: origins of anti-cruelty laws', available at: http://www.bbc.co.uk/dna/h2g2/A640810 Accessed on 30/3/08.

BBC (2008) Birth of the Welfare state, available at: http://www.open2.net/historyandthearts/history/theservice_welfare.html Accessed on 30/3/08.

Belsky, J. (2006) 'Effects of Child Care on Child Development in the USA'. In J.J. van Kuyk (ed.) *The Quality of Early Childhood Education*, pp. 23-32.

Beveridge, W. (1942) *Report to the Parliament on Social Insurance and Allied Services*. London: HMSO.

Broberg, A., Wessels, H., Lamb, M. and Hwang, C. (1997) 'Effects of day care on the development of cognitive abilities in 8-year-olds: a longitudinal study', *Developmental Psychology,* 33(1) pp. 62-9.

Cochrane, A. and Clarke, J. (2001) *Comparing welfare states: Britain in an international Context*. Berkshire: OU Press.

David, T., Gooch, K., Powell, S. and Abbott, L. (2003) 'Birth to three matters, a review of the literature', available at: http://www.standards.dfes.gov.uk/eyfs/resources/downloads/rr444.pdf Accessed on 29/3/08.

DCSF (2008) *2020 Children and Young People's Workforce Strategy*, available at: http://publications.dcsf.gov.uk/eOrderingDownload/7977-DCSF-2020%20Children%20and%20Young%20People%27s%20Workforce%20Strategy-FINAL.pdf Accessed on 20/12/08.

DfES (2003) *Every Child Matters* Green Paper. London: The Stationery Office.

Glennerster, H. (2006) *British social policy: 1945 to the present, 3rd edition*. London: Blackwell.

Marr, A. (2007) *A History of Modern Britain*. MacMillan: London.

Melhuish, E. and Petrogiannis, K. (2006) *Early Childhood Care and Education*. Abingdon: Routledge.

Ministry of Education (NZ) (1996) *Te Whariki: Early Childhood Curriculum*. Wellington: Learning Media, www.minedu.govt.nz/web/downloadable/dl3567_v1/WHARIKI.pdf Accessed 30/3/08.

National Head Start Association (USA) (2008) 'About the National Head Start Association', available at: http://www.nhsa.org/about/index.htm Accessed on 24/3/08.

OECD (2001) *Starting Strong Early Childhood Education and Care*. Paris: OECD Publishing.

OECD (2006) *Starting Strong Early Childhood Education and Care Part II*. Paris: OECD Publishing.

Shonkoff, J. and Phillips, D. (2000) *From Neurons to Neighborhoods*. Washington: National Academy Press.

SureStart (UK) (2008) 'SureStart: About us', available at: http://www.surestart.gov.uk/aboutsurestart/ Accessed on 24/3/08.

The Effective Provision of Pre-School Education (EPPE) project 1998-ongoing, available at: http://k1.ioe.ac.uk/schools/ecpe/eppe/ Accessed 29/3/08.

US Government (1776) The Declaration of Independence, available at: http://www.ushistory.org/declaration/document/index.htm Accessed on 31/3/08.

UNICEF (2008) 'The Child Care Transition: a league table of early childhood education and care in economically advanced countries', available at: http://www.unicef-irc.org/publications/pdf/rc8_eng.pdf Accessed on 20/12/08.

UK government publications

DfES	The Education Act 1870	HMSO
DoH	The Public Health Act 1870	HMSO
DoH	The Children Act 1889	HMSO
DoH	The Children's Charter 1908	HMSO
DoH	The Children and Young Person's Act 1932/33	HMSO
DfES	The Education Act 1944	HMSO
DoH	The Children Act 1948	HMSO
DoE	The Housing Act 1980	HMSO
DfES	The Education Reform Act 1988	HMSO
DoH	The Children Act 1989	HMSO
DfES	The Education (Schools) Act 1992	HMSO
Ofsted	Full Day Care: Guidance to the National Standards 2001	HMSO
Treasury	Every Child Matters: Green Paper 2003	HMSO
Treasury	The 10 Year Plan for Childcare 2004	HMSO
DfES	The Children Act 2004	HMSO
DfES	The Childcare Act 2006	HMSO
DCSF	The Early Years Foundation Stage 2008	HMSO
DCSF	The Children's Plan 2007	HMSO

4

Safe and equal in the setting and beyond

Jane George

Chapter overview

The standards addressed in this chapter are:

S18   Promote children's rights, equality, inclusion and anti-discriminatory practice in all aspects of their practice

S19   Establish a safe environment and employ practices that promote children's health, safety and physical, mental and emotional well-being

S20   Recognise when a child is in danger or at risk of harm and know how to act to protect them

(CWDC 2006)

The text will address the following key questions:

- What are the legal rights to equality for practitioners and children within the English early years workplace?
- What tools are available to an EYP to support the promotion of children's rights, equality and inclusion and how can these be used effectively to demonstrate and model anti-discriminatory practice?
- What practices can an EYP draw on to promote safety, health and well-being for children in an early years setting?
- What strategies can an EYP develop/use/contribute to multi-agency approaches to protecting children?

Disability as a 'deficit'

When I was twelve years old, I was thinking about growing up. Until that moment, I think I had somehow believed that when I grew up I would become 'normal', i.e. without a disability. 'Normal' then meant to me 'like my big sister': pretty, rebellious, going out with boys, doing wonderful, naughty things with them, leaving school, getting a job, leaving home, getting married and having children . . . I suddenly realised that my life was not going to be like that at all. I was going to be just the same as I always had been – very small, funnily shaped, unable to walk. It seemed at that moment that the sky cracked . . . The next two years seemed like a dark roller-coaster ride . . . My main preoccupation seemed to be desperately trying to deny the awareness of my difference, which had started on that day.

(Micheline Mason in Campling 1981, pp. 23-24)

Micheline Mason
Source: Allan Sprung

Introduction

As an EYP, and lead practitioner in a setting, creating an environment that protects the children's health and safety, and reflects and values diversity in society is your responsibility. The most important aim in this endeavour is for the children in your care to be supported in their building of a positive self-image, and to respect the feelings of others, whatever their culture, 'race' or ethnicity, and whether or not they have a disability. If these concepts are successfully communicated, the children will not enter adolescence perceiving the concept of 'normal' in the very limited fashion that had clearly been communicated throughout childhood to Micheline Mason, given her reflection in the paragraph above. The keys to this are the resources, activities and communication that you and your colleagues provide for the children and their families. Effective practitioners need to ensure that the environment they provide supports and values diversity through an awareness that is real and relevant, not tokenistic. In order to achieve this, practitioners may need to honestly examine and reflect upon any prejudices and biases they might hold. Practitioners may not always be aware of internalised stereotypes that can affect their expectations of children and families. The effective practitioner needs to question whether the setting does work to value diversity in children and their backgrounds and avoid a 'colour/disability-blind' approach, where treating children 'equally' is translated into treating all children 'the same'. Iram Siraj-Blatchford suggests that early years practitioners should make children aware they all have an identity that is individually different and that difference should be celebrated:

> A positive self-concept is necessary for healthy development and learning and includes feelings about gender, race, ability, culture and language. Positive self-esteem depends on whether children feel others accept them and see them as competent and worthwhile.

> (Siraj-Blatchford 2001, p. 104)

A young child's self-esteem is easily damaged (see Chapter 6) and research suggests that children as young as 2½ may show signs of discomfort with physical differences. By the age of 4, children from minority ethnic groups may feel unhappy with their appearance (Derman-Sparks and Ramsey 2006). Promoting and providing an inclusive environment that celebrates and values differences in identity, culture, religion, abilities and social practices is a difficult task, within a setting and without. No setting exists in a vacuum, but rather reflects the community it is a part of, with its share of discrimination, conflicts, issues over gender roles and ignorance with regard to disability (see Focus on practice boxes below). The effective practitioner, nevertheless, has to strive for and promote inclusive, anti-discriminatory practice by:

- identifying and addressing any practices that are discriminatory within the setting;
- promoting self-esteem and positive group identity;
- valuing children and adults for their individuality and ensuring a sense of belonging;
- respecting where children come from, what they achieve and what they bring to the setting.

This chapter will introduce these concepts through the following sections:

Section 1: Children's rights and employment rights: equality and inclusion, which focuses upon legislation and policy aimed at promoting equal opportunities in childcare and education settings.

Section 2: Practice examples relating to equal opportunities in action in three separate paradigms:

- Culture, 'race' and ethnicity
- Disability
- Gender.

Section 3: The promotion of health, safety and well-being in early years settings.

Section 4: Safeguarding as an essential multi-agency concept in early years practice.

Section 1: Children's rights and employment rights: equality and inclusion

What are the legal rights to equality and inclusion for children and practitioners within the English early years workplace?

To be able to move forward and discuss this multi-faceted question, it is essential to have an overview of how early years settings and practice have changed over the last 20 years. The earlier chapter on social policy gives a detailed summary of legislation for children and families but it is useful to have some additional notes from a practitioner's viewpoint on the ever changing world of Early Years, as we are now operating within a very different professional environment from the one that I (and maybe some of you) joined in 1987! To help us reflect upon both the direction and distance travelled over this time I have included a list of the main drivers for change, which have provided many of the challenges that we have risen to within the last 20 years. The contents of some have already been outlined earlier in the book:

- The Children Act 1989
- Every Child Matters Green Paper 2003
- The Ten Year Plan for Childcare 2004
- The Children Act 2004
- The Childcare Act 2006
- The Children's Plan 2007
- Constant change within the guidelines for the care and education of children under 5 which has included: the Desirable Learning Outcomes, Ofsted inspections, national standards for a range of early years/care environments, Early Learning Goals, the Foundation Stage, Birth to Three Matters guidelines and Every Child Matters, all of which have recently been encapsulated within the statutory Early Years Foundation Stage guidelines (2008).

In order to protect the equal opportunities of staff within the workplace, lead practitioners who have responsibility for employing and/or supervising and managing staff should be aware of the requirements of the following legislation:

- The Health and Safety at Work Act 1974
- Sex Discrimination Act 1975
- Race Relations Act 1976

- Amendments to the Sex Discrimination Act 1975 and the Race Relations Act 1976
- Sex Equality (Gender Reassignment) Regulations 1999 extending the scope of the Sex Discrimination Act
- Employment Equality (Sexual Orientation) Regulations 2003
- Employment Equality (Religion or Belief) Regulations 2003
- Employment Equality (Age) Regulations 2006

With regard to equality of opportunity for both children and adults within the setting we need to be aware of the following pieces of legislation:

- Disability Discrimination Act 1995
- The Disability Discrimination Act 2005
- Special Educational Needs and Disability Act 2001
- Special Educational Needs Code of Practice 2001

And, alongside the Children Acts of 1989 and 2004 which have already been introduced in Chapter 3, leading practitioners also need to be aware of the legal requirements introduced in the Protection of Children Act 1999 in order to produce appropriate professional safeguarding policies for childcare and education settings. We will repeat here the warning that appears in Chapter 3 – 'It is probably appropriate to remind you at this point that the advice on legislation and guidelines in this book can only be as up to date as the publication date stated on the flyleaf' – and you are similarly encouraged to keep up to date by reading quality newspapers/news websites and professional journals and circulars. All legislation (and some 'Green Paper' guidelines) that are currently relevant can be viewed by using the search facility on **http://www.parliament.uk/index.cfm**.

Focus on policy

Reflection *For EYP candidates with extensive work experience, it would be helpful at this point to reflect on your own responses to the changes that the Early Years workforce has experienced during your working life. For full pathway candidates, the further reading recommended at the end of this chapter and Chapter 3, combined with discussion with more experienced others, either within your workplace or with EYP candidate short pathway peers, would be beneficial.*

All Early Years settings (other than individual Home-based Childcare) are workplaces and as such must follow basic Health and Safety and Equality of Opportunity legislation and guidance. For example, The Health and Safety at Work Act

1974 sets the basic minimum standard to meet the safety needs of the workforce but additional to this as Early Years workers we have to address the physical environment, the resources and the levels of supervision to meet the safety needs of the children in our care. Given the role of the EYP in 'leading practice' we must also apply considerations of safety, inclusion and protection to colleagues, stakeholders and visitors. Consider the following incident and what your response to the situation might be.

Focus on policy and practice

Lena has recently achieved EYPS. Two months ago she was appointed as Deputy Manager in a private day nursery. She applied for this post as job advertisements for EYPs are currently quite rare, but she felt that, based on the job description, the setting was looking for a lead practitioner, even if the title was 'Deputy Manager'. (A number of EYPs in her cohort had also echoed her thinking.) She is still finding her feet in this long-established setting, working with some long-serving, qualified and experienced staff.

A few days ago, she witnessed a conversation between a placement student and his supervisor, Bev, the toddler room leader. The student spoke to Bev in a polite and respectful manner when he informed her that as a student his college allowed him 'authorised absence' for Eid celebrations. He informed her of the most likely date for Eid, about three weeks away, and promised to confirm the exact date as soon as possible. Bev refused the request and informed the student that if he took time off for Eid he would not be allowed to continue his placement.

Identifying good practice
Lena contemplates the following:

- What message does this give to the student?
- Is this a message from the setting or from one individual?
- Does the setting have a policy to cover the situation?
- What message does this send to the staff, children and families in the setting?

She finds the Employment Equality (Religion or Belief) Regulations (2003) on the Internet at **http://www.opsi.gov.uk/si/si2003/20031660.htm**, and notes the aspects of the situation that have violated legally required practices relating to equality of opportunity in employment. She goes to see the manager of the setting the following day and draws her attention to the situation. The manager expresses regret and says she will speak to the member of staff and to the student, and make sure he gets his Eid holiday. She thanks Lena, and asks if she will develop the staffing policies of the setting, which are very much in need of an overhaul.

Leading practice

Lena realises that the practice of experienced staff is often slow to change, so the following week, she asks Bev to help her prepare a series of multi-faith activities for the children, initially focusing upon Eid. At the end of the month, after consulting again with the setting manager, Lena gives a presentation to all the staff to discuss and finalise some new policies relating to their employment. The following day she overhears Bev telling another member of staff that it is not fair that 'they' will get 'their' holidays and 'ours' as well. Lena then mentions at the next staff meeting that it has come to her attention that some members of staff may not have understood that, while practice will be planned around the expectation that both staff and children will take holidays on the feast days of their religion, the relevant number of days have to be taken from the adults' annual leave allocation if they are on the payroll. When the local authority circulates a flyer advertising equal opportunities (diversity) training, Lena asks Bev if she will take the training programme with her.

Reflection

It is much easier if older members of staff can be persuaded to 'remain on board' as positive colleagues, given their many years of valuable professional experience. However, as national and international developments swiftly unfold within early years practice, there may be 'hiccups'. Aspects relating to equal opportunities are particularly vulnerable in this respect, as they are very open to misunderstanding, and may, in the worst managed cases, lead to destructive 'us and them' attitudes developing among groups of staff. If such an issue degenerates into a serious dispute, all members of staff are likely to be affected, which is in turn likely to impact negatively upon the day-to-day practice and 'atmosphere' of the setting. As such, it is always best to try to deal with such issues in a conciliatory fashion, persevering if your initial efforts meet with failure or only partial success.

Any setting that does not meet the safety, equality and protection needs of its workforce is highly unlikely to be able to meet the diverse needs of individual children and their families – which is why this point has been made at the beginning of this chapter, as it reflects 'starting at the beginning'! The importance of a *team* commitment to practice within the setting, and the leadership necessary to achieve this is discussed further in Chapter 10, 'Surviving validation', where the EYPS candidate's leadership of and other contributions to team coherence are presented as central concepts that must underpin both written and practical validation tasks.

What tools are available to an EYP to support the promotion of children's rights, equality and inclusion and how can these be used effectively to demonstrate and model anti-discriminatory practice?

Children's rights

The EYP needs to gain knowledge of the legal framework for their area of work within UK and European law; this can be achieved through specific training as part of the lead-in to EYPS validation or by personal study starting with the chapter 'Social Policy for Early Years' earlier in this book. There are a number of useful texts which summarise the legal frameworks that directly influence equality practice in Early Years including Griffin (2008) and Lindon (2006), both of which provide an introduction to the subject and some basic links between theory and practice as well as extensive lists of further reading, while Alderson (2008) gives a comprehensive overview of contemporary children's rights theory, practice and legislation.

One aspect that has remained constant for over 40 years is the voice of the Pre-school Learning Alliance (formerly the Pre-school Playgroups Association, see **http://www.pre-school.org.uk/**), working hard to keep 'learning through play' on the agenda for all children, regardless of culture or disability, when guidance from successive governments between 1988 and the present seemed to be trying to drop this agenda item, potentially depriving children of their internationally recognised right to developmentally appropriate play and leisure time (Jarvis and George 2008). It is especially pleasing to note that the recent Rose Report on Primary Education indicates the value of learning through play in school and not just in the early years, citing the contemporary research encompassed by the TACTYC play research seminar (2008). The European social charter (1961, 1996) guarantees rights to children from birth (and before) up to the age of 18 in respect of the following issues:

- Protection before birth via maternal health protection
- Rights of the Family
- Legal status of the Child within his/her family
- Criminal liability of and criminal law in respect of children to be addressed in a developmentally appropriate fashion
- Health protection of children
- Special protection of children – protection from violence, abuse and exploitation, with special protection for vulnerable groups such as those with special needs
- Right to education
- Prohibition of child labour
- Specific working conditions between 15 and 18
- Rights of migrant children

Children's Rights concepts also focus particularly on children's opportunities for developmentally appropriate participation in their wider society.

Documents which offer conceptual guidance on best practice in equality and anti-discrimination are found on the international, national and local stage. Internationally the key readings for any Early Years worker and especially an EYP come from the United Nations. The UN Convention on the Rights of the Child 1989 is an international agreement which sets out basic standards that signatory countries agree to uphold. Article 2 is especially important here; it gives children

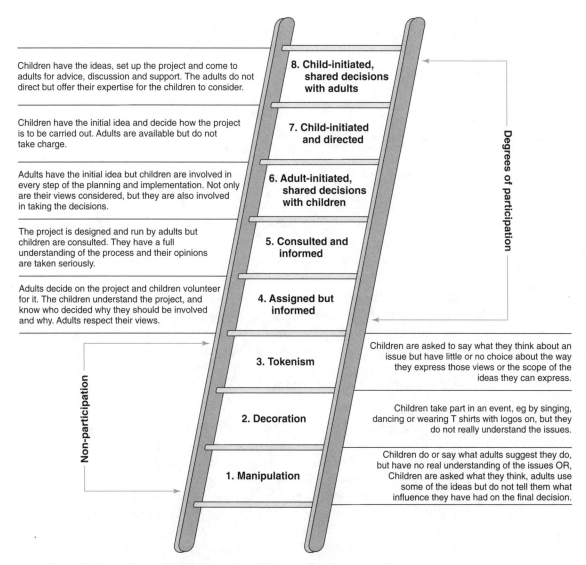

Children have the ideas, set up the project and come to adults for advice, discussion and support. The adults do not direct but offer their expertise for the children to consider.

8. Child-initiated, shared decisions with adults

Children have the initial idea and decide how the project is to be carried out. Adults are available but do not take charge.

7. Child-initiated and directed

Adults have the initial idea but children are involved in every step of the planning and implementation. Not only are their views considered, but they are also involved in taking the decisions.

6. Adult-initiated, shared decisions with children

The project is designed and run by adults but children are consulted. They have a full understanding of the process and their opinions are taken seriously.

5. Consulted and informed

Adults decide on the project and children volunteer for it. The children understand the project, and know who decided why they should be involved and why. Adults respect their views.

4. Assigned but informed

Degrees of participation

3. Tokenism

Children are asked to say what they think about an issue but have little or no choice about the way they express those views or the scope of the ideas they can express.

2. Decoration

Children take part in an event, eg by singing, dancing or wearing T shirts with logos on, but they do not really understand the issues.

1. Manipulation

Children do or say what adults suggest they do, but have no real understanding of the issues OR, Children are asked what they think, adults use some of the ideas but do not tell them what influence they have had on the final decision.

Non-participation

Figure 4.1 The ladder of participation

Source: http://www.niassembly.gov.uk/images/pics/centre3.gif

the right to a non-discriminatory life and equal rights within the convention whatever their race, ethnicity, sex, religion, language, disability, opinion or family background. A recent innovation in each of the four countries of the United Kingdom is the appointment of a Children's Commissioner. While the detail of the post varies between the countries, the focus is raising awareness of and promoting the rights of children and young people. Interestingly, Sir Al Ainsley-Green, who is the current (mid-2008) commissioner for England, has previously been involved with the playgroup movement.

Section 2: Equal opportunities in action

Equal opportunities in action: culture, 'race' and ethnicity

 Focus on policy and practice

An Ofsted Inspection Report on a private daycare setting had revealed most areas of care, practice and provision to be 'good' with only one graded as 'satisfactory', this focusing on 'inclusive practice' issues. The inspectors felt there was only 'limited' recognition of cultural diversity. The inspectors had taken into account the largely mono-cultural catchment area of the setting, but felt it was even more important in such circumstances to promote ideas of cultural diversity in preparing children for the wider world.

Andy, the setting Manager, met with his Lead Practitioner, Jon, to discuss drawing up an initial action plan which would then be rolled out to staff for their opinions and ideas. Jon told Andy that a colleague, who worked in a local authority maintained setting, had recently been given some training on new initiatives around inclusive practice, and offered to find out more about this. Andy said that he would also contact the local Early Years Service to ask for advice.

Identifying good practice

Andy had made initial contact with a local Early Years advisor, but had been too busy to follow this up, so Jon arranged a meeting with the Inclusive Development Programme Coordinator. After an interesting discussion, Jon came back with several ideas he felt could be included in their action plan. The advisor, Angelica, had mentioned the services of a teacher who supported Traveller Children, who would be happy to come and talk with the children. Although the setting didn't currently have any traveller children, Jon remembered that it had some years ago. Angelica also suggested the centre carry out a survey to discover international and multi-cultural connections within the centre's existing families, as, she reflected, there was a lot more 'diversity' in the construction of present-day families than had been the case during previous decades, and the current craze for researching family trees was also turning up some very interesting international and multi-cultural histories of which families had previously been unaware. She also felt that the increasing numbers of children from Eastern Europe now in primary schools would soon be reflected in early years settings, as some of these families settled permanently in the UK. Jon informed Andy of the outcome of his discussion with Angelica, and proposed that finding out about the 'diversity' of families of children attending the setting could be started with a topic on 'Myself'. He also felt, for the new children who would begin in September, that the information sheet each child filled in for their individual profiles should be more comprehensive, so that the full richness of the 'diversity' within children's family backgrounds could be identified and celebrated.

Leading practice

At the weekly meeting, all of the centre's staff were invited to comment upon the Ofsted Inspectors' findings. A number of them felt it was difficult to 'make diversity real' for young children if the culture used was completely outside the children's own experience. They referred to the celebrations for Chinese New Year that a student had promoted during a block placement early in the year, which staff proposed had 'flown above the children's heads' and that they had seen it as 'just another party'. Jon felt that was a little harsh, that the student had been genuinely attempting to look at another culture, and that the artefacts, clothes and food she had brought into the setting had promoted conversation and interest among some of the older children. He told the staff about his meeting with Angelica, and showed them a brief 'family tree' he had drawn of his own family's diverse roots, asking them each to complete something similar for next week's meeting.

On the topic of 'traveller children', the staff had mixed feelings. Reactions locally to traveller families had not been very positive over recent times, after one of the local authority sites had been closed down. This had resulted in traveller families choosing their own areas in which to stay, which had not met with the approval of some of the local residents. Jon reminded them that exposing children to cultural diversity was a key aspect of preventing their engaging in stereotyping and discrimination in their later development, and also a way in which parents might begin to learn about the

Figure 4.2 **The persona dolls**
Source: www.persona-doll-training.org

world outside their own cultural niche. He also reiterated a message from Angelica that she would be happy to come along and talk to staff and answer any concerns they might have.

The following week the staff's varied and interesting family trees promoted much discussion. It was realised by staff that they already had several sources of 'diverse culture' within the setting that they could use for the benefit of the children and support an action plan. The 'traveller children' topic was later enacted and became a success, with the teacher introducing a 'persona doll' that proved to be a favourite with the children, so much so that a member of staff volunteered to go on 'persona doll' training and several other such dolls were bought as resources for the setting.

Reflections

- *Do you consider the Manager's and Lead Practitioner's reactions to the Ofsted Inspectors' report were appropriate and adequate?*

- *Do you feel the Lead Practitioner led and supported the staff sufficiently in reflecting on their practice?*

- *Should there have been some involvement of parents/carers/the wider local community at any stage in drawing up the action plan?*

- *Have you experienced a 'mono-cultural' situation like the above? If so, how did that impact on your practice?*

As can be seen in the example above, Early Years practitioners have a series of tools available to them to assist in this task, but, as is often the case, the most effective tool is action based on a sound working knowledge of theory combined with reflection on practice. Local knowledge, gained through good working relationships with your local authority Early Years team, and effective local continuing professional development (CPD) are also invaluable to help settings and Early Years practitioners identify and respond to the needs of their communities. An EYP who aims to lead practice effectively will need this local information to help them develop a suitable service for the local community including knowledge of the local population – languages, cultures, religions, specific needs and knowledge of local services. Local authorities have also been tasked with creating EYP Networks, so it really is in your best interest to make yourself known to them as soon as possible so that you can benefit from the wealth of knowledge, training and services they have to offer!

Equal opportunities in action: Disability

Nationally, guidance for practice in equality is embedded within the Early Years Foundation Stage (2008). The Statutory Framework, item 1.14, gives strong emphasis to including all children, valuing diversity, meeting individual needs, and hands to us, the practitioners, the responsibility for removing or overcoming

Table 4.1 Deficit/Difference models of disability

Deficit model	Difference model
Disability is a deficiency or abnormality	Disability is a difference
Being disabled is negative	Being disabled, in itself, is neutral
Disability resides in the individual	Disability derives from interaction between individual and society
The remedy for disability-related problems is cure or 'normalisation' of the individual	The remedy for disability-related problems is a change in the interaction between the individual and society
The agent of remedy is the professional who affects the treatment for the individual so they can 'fit into' society – probably in a reduced capacity	The agent of remedy can be the individual, an advocate, or anyone who affects the arrangements between the individual and society

barriers children may face that could limit their ability to access opportunities to develop to their full potential. It is the practitioner's responsibility to make sure that the child can access teaching and learning, not the child's or the parents'. The Disability Discrimination Act (2005) outlines a clear set of responsibilities for practitioners which ensures that the defence that you did not know that a particular child had a disability/specific learning difficulty is unacceptable; the day-to-day curriculum/routines should be designed to be inclusive. The EYFS Practice Guidance, items 1.7 to 1.10, stresses the importance of meeting the *individual* needs of children and refers to 'personalised learning' and planning for the needs of specific children. The view of disability should be specifically that of difference rather than deficit. This can be expressed as in Table 4.1.

Focus on policy and practice

Pam Jarvis, one of the other editors of this book, reflects: I was once involved as a school governor in a school that pioneered inclusive practice during the early 1990s by taking in a child into Reception who had severe cerebral palsy, whom I will call 'Julie'. When Julie entered the school she was unable to walk, or to talk very much, but everyone who interacted with her realised that there was a keen intelligence working within, that had been nurtured up to this point by sensitive and patient parenting, and we worked very hard together to help her to realise her considerable potential. However, along the way, Julie's appearance met with some unfortunate comments from adults bringing other children to and from school, grandparents appearing to be particularly insensitive in this respect, perhaps because they had been socialised for the longest period in a society that viewed disability very much from the deficit point of view. Comments included references to 'the little crippled girl' and once a question as to whether she had come along with a parent to collect a brother or sister, and how kind the other children were being to include her in their play. When the person in question was told that Julie was a pupil at the school, the response was: 'But the teacher must spend so much time with her – how is that fair to the other children in the class?' These fears were only slightly ameliorated by the further information that Julie had a full-time special needs assistant! However, Julie (and the other children in her class) went on to thrive, and by the time she was 8 she was both walking and talking, and working within the normal literacy/numeracy range for a child of her calendar age.

Identifying good practice

One of the children in the older year groups of this school had a much older sister (whom we shall call Sandy), who had been born with severe spina bifida. When the admission of Julie raised the profile of special needs among the school community, Sandy, at that time in her mid-twenties, came to a parent–governors meeting to tell us her education story. There had been no concept of inclusion during her primary years, but as she moved towards secondary school age the Warnock Report on Special Educational Needs (1978) was published, putting inclusion firmly on the national education agenda. As such, Sandy and her physically disabled peer group in the 'special school' were all given a standard IQ test, the first test of academic ability that they had ever been given. Sandy scored around the 150 mark, indicating that not only was she not within the normal range . . . she was within the 'gifted' area of the IQ continuum. It was decided that, on the basis of this discovery and the rapidly changing policy on the education of what were then called 'handicapped' children, Sandy should attend a mainstream secondary school. Warnock famously stated in 1986: 'If I am to walk along a road, I need shoes; but there are those who need a wheelchair, or a pair of crutches, or a guide dog, or other things beside. These needs could be identified and met, and then off we could all go together'. However, Sandy's experience indicated that this was very much an 'ideal' notion in the education world of the early 1980s. On arriving at her secondary school she found that some areas of the campus were not negotiable in a wheelchair, and, due to her very slow walking speed, she found it difficult to arrive at different rooms within the time allocated between lessons for 'changeover'. After some initial confusion (as Sandy was the only disabled pupil within the school, and the first that it had ever admitted), the Headteacher decided that the teachers should start their lessons at the stipulated time and, if Sandy arrived late, she was not to be reprimanded, but that it would be her responsibility to 'catch up' from her point of arrival, without disrupting the rest of the class. This would not only now be designated extremely poor and exclusive practice – it would actually be illegal!

Leading practice

These two examples should help you to grasp the vast changes that have occurred within the whole education system over the past 30 years. As a leading practitioner within an early years setting, it will be your responsibility to ensure that the inclusion practice guidelines reflect the current laws relating to inclusion in education settings. It is hoped, however, that your aim would not simply be to comply with the law, but to move the inclusivity practice of the setting into the bounds of 'excellent'.

Reflections *Consider the following, making notes on these points:*

- *How might you design training for staff in an Early Years setting on the 'deficit/difference' model?*

- *How would you develop the policies in your setting to aim for excellence in inclusion?*

- *What issues might arise within your setting relating to the design of the building if you had a member of staff or a child with the same types of disability as Julie and Sandy? How might you deal with this?*

- *How would you deal with a parent or grandparent expressing highly anti-inclusive views, and how would you expect your staff to respond to such comments?*

Focus on practice

Wendy Holland, one of the other editors of this book, reflects: I recently regularly visited a student on placement in a setting that had been designated a Children's Centre Plus. As such, their intake included children with special educational needs, and on one visit we discussed three recent admissions to the 3–5 years room: 4 year old identical triplets, all of whom had been identified as being on the autistic spectrum. Their mother, a single parent, 'Pauline', had met with the Nursery Room's Lead Practitioner, 'Elizabeth', and 'Pat', the setting's SENCo (special educational needs coordinator), and expressed the wish that the triplets should remain together and not be separated into different class bases.

Identifying good practice

Pat was supported by an early years practitioner with special needs training and several teaching assistants, and the setting policy was to try to include children with SEN as much as possible in the daily routines, withdrawing the children into a small group only at the beginning and end of the day. Each child was usually allocated a class base and attempts were made to involve them at story or circle time, with support. Some staff felt concern at the prospect of the triplets being in one class base even with support. As the triplets displayed different levels on the autistic spectrum it was felt, in order to meet individual needs, it would be beneficial to separate them.

Leading practice

Elizabeth and Pat discussed this with Pauline, who was resistant to the proposal at first, but eventually agreed to a trial period. Over time, 'Tom', the triplet who showed the least overt autistic behaviours, managed gradually to access circle and story time within his class base. Initially his support worker would sit beside him, but after a period she was able to move away, as long as she remained in view. This had an effect on the rest of his play and involvement, as he gradually began to accept other children into his personal space. 'Peter', the triplet with most complex needs, was placed in a particularly creative class base, where his obvious talents for drawing and painting were stimulated and praised. He would quite happily access group times for short periods. 'Stephen', the triplet with the greatest need for cognitive and emotional support, preferred to play and explore in a one-to-one situation with a trusted adult, and would actively seek out the company of his brothers. Elizabeth regularly coordinated with the boys' keyworkers and subsequently collated and communicated all these developments on a daily basis to Pauline via a home–school diary to reassure her the triplets were happy, and enjoying their time in the setting.

Reflection

- *In this practice example, do you feel the mother's wishes were sufficiently respected?*

- *Do you feel the solutions reached supported each triplet's individual learning journey?*

- *Could this have been achieved by, as their mother had wished, keeping the triplets together?*

- *Was this a case of the triplets fitting in to existing routines and practice or a genuine attempt to meet individual needs?*

- *Have you experienced a similar difficulty in trying to meet individual needs within inclusive provision? If so, how did you deal with this?*

Task **Discuss the above with colleagues, and define what you feel is good inclusive and anti-discriminatory practice.**

Equal opportunities in action: gender

The use of the term 'Gender' (initially used as a linguistic term in some European languages) was converted by 1960s feminism to describe those aspects of behaviour that can be proposed to relate to culture and learned behaviour, rather than to behaviour programmed by nature, for example: long hair for women and short hair for men, and dresses for women and trousers for men.

There is a suggestion that adults treat children very differently, depending upon the child's gender. In a study by Condry and Condry (1976) a group of people were asked to describe the emotional behaviour of some 9 month old infants, who had been startled by a Jack-in-the-box. Those who had been told the infants were boys described the reaction as anger. If they thought the infants were girls, they described the reaction as fear. Similarly, if they thought some babies were boys, they encouraged activity, and chose male type toys; if they thought the babies were girls, they chose soft toys, and interacted in a more nurturant way.

Bio-evolutionary theories suggest that the genders have evolved differently to play different roles in reproduction, hence the enduring differences found between girls and boys in education are unlikely to change. However, the evidence suggests that there is a wide range of individual differences within this biology, so stereotyping is not useful, even if some aspects of gendered behaviour are linked to balances of hormones in the physical body (see, for example, Jarvis 2006).

Social Constructionist theories suggest that the genders are taught to behave in particular ways through socialisation. However, this is not a licence to attempt to 'programme' children in any way one decides is the 'right' way. It is necessary to try to understand the individual child's personality rather than 'train' him or her in a standard, gendered or relentlessly 'gender blind' way, which often generates frustration in children. Davies and Banks (1995) found that 4 year olds of both genders tended to respond to modern stories for children containing gender stereotype role reversals by presuming that counter-stereotypical characters in the text had 'got it wrong'. These authors reported subsequently interviewing a 4 year old boy about why he thought girls were different from boys. They quoted a long transcript from this interview, where the boy repeatedly responds to adult questioning by proposing that girls play different games that he finds boring, his final response being: 'I don't know, because they play different games to what we do. I told you that about two million times' (Davies and Banks 1995, p. 52).

Within a modern childcare and education setting, practitioners should be aware of complex modern gender issues, which rather dichotomously relate to avoiding stereotyping, while avoiding 'gender blind' practice, which does not recognise the typical differences observed between male and female toy preferences and play styles. There is currently some concern that, within the mainly female-directed environment of early years care and education management, there is some misunderstanding of boys' highly physical free-play activities, and a need for early years staff to have a deeper understanding of male modes of learning in the early years (DCSF 2007).

Focus on practice

Where a boy took an injury or a heavy fall and did not make a fuss, or dealt with a play fighting incident that injured another child in a responsible way, boys had a very subtle, but obvious way of showing approval and solidarity; a light touch in passing to the boy who had shown resilience in a difficult situation, often offered by another boy who both individuals within the interaction would see as having a more 'senior' role. For example, 4½ year old Rory received a hefty shove in the back during a football game from one of the larger, older players. He fell quite heavily, but got up and ran back into the football crowd, smiling. An older, Year 1 boy ran past and gently patted him on the back.

(Jarvis 2008, p. 188)

Identifying good practice

In the observation above, Pam Jarvis considers a very male mode of social interaction that she observed in her study of outdoor free play among children aged between 4 and 6.

Task Did you know that boys show approval/friendship in this way? Consider how you deal with play fighting between boys of this age in your setting.

Leading practice

Task Consider the behaviour policies and practices in your setting. Is there 'room' for boys to play in active and 'physical' styles within these, or might there be a possibility that the rules you are working within have curtailed such modes of play? How might you remedy this, while still upholding the setting's health and safety responsibilities (you should be very aware that this is not an easy task – see below).

Reflection *Paley (1984, pp. 115-16) reflected that superhero and 'bad guy' play is as natural and essential play for little boys as 'princess' play is for little girls, urging Early Years teachers to remember that everything is make-believe 'except for the obvious feelings of well-being that emerge from fantasy play' and that teachers 'are not princesses, and need not act as if the superheroes will pull down the classroom walls'.*

Task Discuss the above with your fellow EYPS candidates and colleagues, putting together a 'thinking document' relating to how you respond to boys' play-fighting activities and how you might develop your practice in this respect in the future.

Task What Sex is your brain? Take the BBC Quiz and find out! http://www.bbc.co.uk/science/humanbody/sex/index_cookie.shtml

This quiz is based upon the concept of different levels of testosterone having a subtle effect upon gendered behaviour. It is fun, but there is a more subtle message for those working in childcare and education. . . . Everyone is an individual and stereotyping, especially during early development, can therefore be very harmful.

Section 3: The promotion of health, safety and well-being in early years settings

What practices can an EYP draw on to promote safety, health and well-being for children in the early years setting?

Health and Safety

As noted earlier, settings have to be safe as workplaces under the Health and Safety at Work Act 1974. Until September 2008 we all relied upon the National Standards for different settings to ensure we met basic health and safety needs of the children in our care. Many settings opted to exceed the basic levels outlined in the National Standards and may have applied for and achieved national and/or local recognition for their good practice through a variety of quality measures. From September 2008 the basic standards for health and safety in childcare and education settings are in the Early Years Foundation Stage (EYFS) documents, as they have been drawn from the National Standards for Daycare (2001), see Chapter 3.

Focus on practice

Policy review

Task All potential EYPs must have a sound working knowledge of the Statutory Framework and Practice Guidance documents in the EYFS which are available at http://www.dcsf.gov.uk. The introduction of the EYFS in September 2008 should have prompted a review of all setting policies related to health, safety and child welfare to ensure that they are compliant with the most recent guidelines. Find out if this has taken place in your setting and how it was recorded; ideally dates of completed policy review and planned future review should be noted on the policy itself.

Reflection *Setting policy documents should give us clear guidance on minimum acceptable standards for health, safety and welfare including detail on staffing and suitable persons, risk assessments which should be carried out and essential first aid skills. Legislation, guidance and related policies will go some way to creating a healthy and safe environment for both children and staff, but it is often the individual actions of children and adults that compromise health and safety in the setting!*

Task Discuss the opportunities and challenges presented by the task above with your fellow EYPS candidates and colleagues.

An EYP, as leading practitioner in the setting, must consider:

- The resources they offer the children, which should meet both UK and European safety standards.
- The appropriateness of the selection of resources and activities for children at different ages/stages of development, as a developmentally inappropriate toy which is perfectly safe for the stipulated age group may still pose a significant danger to a younger child (for example, toys with small parts for infants who are still using their mouths to explore the properties of objects).
- The 'ground rules' for activities, and how it will be ensured that both staff and children understand and comply with these.
- The basic levels of supervision required for different activities.
- How to prevent children putting themselves or others in danger without undermining their judgement and self-confidence.
- How to support children to take increasing responsibility for their own health and safety
- How to be a good role model and demonstrate best practice in health and safety to children and adults.

Task Reflect on these points yourself, as an EYP candidate, with your validation cohort·and with the lead practitioner and the staff team in your setting.

Focus on practice

On a recent visit to a local country park I was lucky to observe a family at play. The two older boys aged (approximately) 4 and 6 years were playing a game of 'tig', running around the open grassy space. Zac, a younger brother aged (approximately) 2 years, ran after them trying to share their play. He ran quickly and confidently until he tried to change direction when he wobbled and leaned to one side but steadied himself and set off again following his brothers. He really struggled to slow down and stop, often relying on his brothers and parents to act as his brakes! He was temporarily distracted from the game by a small stream which he studied carefully, then he walked alongside the stream in the direction of flow for a few moments. He watched the flow intently but never stumbled or tripped as he walked along the edge of the low bank. His parents observed him from a discreet distance but did not distract him from his task. He stopped when he reached a small bridge and re-engaged his family when he turned to them and shouted 'pooh-sticks'!

The family then moved towards a 'living playground', an area of yew and rhododendron with paths and tunnels and dens. Zac followed his brothers through a gateway on to a narrow path, his parents again at a discreet distance. When he saw his brothers through the shrubs Zac turned off the path and headed directly towards them through the undergrowth. He displayed great skill as he picked his way between the low branches, finding firm footings and using the higher branches as handrails. He climbed a muddy bank using similar skills – finding footholds and supporting and balancing himself by holding on to branches. His parents and siblings watched on but left him to concentrate and work out his own path; they did not distract him by calling his name or offering a 'helping hand', help which could so easily have been his downfall. When he reached the top of the bank he glowed with pride, he stood up tall and looked back over his 'everest' and smiled. His achievement earned him lots of praise, in the form of attention and hugs, from his family.

Identifying good practice

I felt very privileged to observe Zac's play and reflected on what I had seen on the drive home. I considered that Zac had made extremely creative use of the resources offered to him, and he was supported in his play by people with whom he shared bonded attachments, who gave him confidence in his ability to explore and his judgement to keep himself safe as he challenged the limits of his skills. These factors made the afternoon's play an excellent child-led activity for Zac. Jarvis (2007) describes how important approval from slightly older males within the peer group is within the development of self-esteem of boys in the early years (see Gender Focus on practice box above), and as such Zac's skills, confidence and self-esteem would not only have been boosted by the successes in his play, but also because his achievements had been noted by his older brothers.

Leading practice

When I began reflecting upon the contemporary early care and education environment, I compiled a further list of questions:

● Would Zac have been offered this (or a similar) opportunity within an early years setting?

- Would he be spending time with more skilful, adventurous, older children within an early years setting?

- Would an early years worker have stopped this play as unsuitable for such a young child, or on the grounds of accident prevention?

- Would an early years worker have tried to help - calling his name or offering a hand - which may have been counterproductive, reducing the scale of his achievement?

- Would I, as a leading practitioner, have let this play reach its natural conclusion, and/or expect my staff to have done so? Would there have been any element of 'blame' attached to an adult observer, if the child had met with an accident?

Reflections *In reflecting on Zac's play on a family outing, we can consider how adults' reactions to children's play may vary, depending upon whether the setting is an informal environment where the caring adults are from the child's own family, and/or whether the setting is a formal, professional environment where the caring adults are paid professionals. In this case, the professional setting appears to struggle with problems that do not arise within the family environment. This is a complex issue, to which there are no easy answers, within the post-industrial culture of contemporary England, where practices are moving towards collective care during the working day for the majority of children under 5.*

Task **Discuss this issue with your colleagues, particularly with respect to how children's rights to exploration and 'limit testing' can be enhanced within your setting. I hope that this description of Zac's play has prompted you to reflect and question what your own practice might have been in this situation where both safety and inclusion should be equally important considerations.**

Brown (2008, p. 222) neatly encapsulates the practitioners' 'safety versus independence' dilemma:

> Once, when my wife was away in France, I collected my 5 year old grandson from school. As a special treat we went to Rowntrees Park where there is a variety of brightly coloured adventurous play equipment. He went straight to the top of the 'spider's web' (about 10 metres off the ground). Admiring his agility, I sent a text message to my wife telling her of our grandson's feat. Almost immediately I received a reply saying, 'Are you mad? Get him down!' In an instant my whole perspective on the situation changed, and I began to encourage him to come down . . . reaching through the ropes, he placed his hands on the central pole, but on surveying the scene, he pulled back and climbed back down the net (much to my relief).

Brown's grandson, like Zac, had a clear sense of his own abilities and was able to explore this to its limits, without taking over-ambitious risks. Logically, such a sense is likely to have been firmly inculcated by evolution within a successful species (a species that routinely takes risks well beyond its ability to cope is unlikely to survive for very long!) However, it is the balance between allowing children to take 'safe risks' and protecting them against accidents that we currently find very difficult.

There is at present a lively ongoing debate about the curtailment of risk-taking in the management of the current generation of Western children (Stephenson 2003), and the increasing adult management of their play activities, largely due to fears relating to health and safety. Corsaro (1997, p. 38) described this process as 'the institutionalisation of more and more children's leisure activities'. Adult fears relating to the injury of children in collective settings, particularly with regard to fears relating to the potential for parental litigation following even minor accidental injuries, too often leads to the over-swift intervention of adults where they perceive the smallest potential danger. It is very difficult within our current cultural climate to get such a balance 'just right' in practice, hence the many ongoing, complex debates around this issue:

> Risky play is difficult to theorise but essential for well-being; children need opportunities to push themselves beyond boundaries in familiar environments; schools and classrooms have become risk-averse places and this is detrimental to children's development and well-being.
>
> (Tovey *et al.* 2008, online)

Well-being

Chapter 2 is a good summary of basic child development and the factors that influence development, and it may be useful to refresh your thinking on social and emotional development and attachment before you explore the concept of 'well-being'. Well-being is not a new term but recently the term has taken on great significance in the world of Early Years. John Bowlby established the link between bonded relationships and a child's emotional well-being in the early 1950s. Since then others have contributed to this area of research (a summary can be found in David *et al.* 2003, the research report which underpinned the Birth to Three matters framework). Over time the emphasis has shifted from the mother as all-important to the quality of the pattern of care and attachments the child has within its daily environments. The EPPE project (1997, ongoing) identified that quality and consistency of personnel working with children was key to their well-being and development. The principal way that we measure children's well-being in early years practice is by careful observation of their behaviour within the setting.

 Focus on practice

Observation

Those of you who have studied childcare and education on previous training programmes may already be accomplished at child observation, particularly if you are already a leading practitioner within your setting. However, if you are relatively new to this professional area, especially if you are a full pathway candidate with little or no previous experience in childcare/education it is absolutely crucial that you develop good observational skills while you are on your EYPS training pathway, as not only will you need to carry out professional observations of children in your day-to-day practice, but one of your key roles will also be to support the development of observational skills in more junior staff. There are many good texts about child observation, some of which are listed in the further reading below.

Task Based on your reading of such texts, ensure that you understand the following basic observation techniques:

Diagrammatic: including tracking and sociogram, and that you are able to present your results on simple charts (e.g. bar chart, pie chart)

Sampling: including target child, focal child, time sampling, snapshot, event sampling

Observations using checklists: e.g. EYFS profile (DCSF 2008), High/Scope technique (Hobart and Frankel 2004, p. 139) and see the The Leuven Child Involvement Scale for Young Children in the Focus on practice box below.

Observations using photograph and video records: this must crucially include an understanding of conventional ethical practice when handling data generated in this way.

Participant observation: where you observe children while taking part in their activities (useful for understanding the event from the perspective of your own engagement)

Non-participant observation: where you observe children without participating in their activities (useful when you want to adopt a more objective orientation to the information gathered).

Collecting objective data

It is important to ensure that an acceptable level of **objectivity** is present in the observation records of the setting, relating to both individual children and specific areas. This can be ensured by:

- Carrying out regular non-participant observations
- Making sure that the child/area is observed by two or more members of staff within a two- to three-week period
- Carrying out 'paired' observations where two people observe the same area or child simultaneously
- Discussing any concerns that may arise from your observations with other practitioners on a 'need to know' basis (e.g. with the leading practitioner and/or another practitioner who has been asked to carry out observations on the same child/area).

Enacting more than one measure of the same person or area is called **triangulation**, and ensures some level of **validity** (if observation notes agree, you can be more confident that you are observing what you initially thought you were observing, for example that a particular child really is quick to anger, or an outside area always becomes very slippery after a light fall of rain) and **reliability** (if more than one person observes the same individual/area and arrives at the same conclusion, this enhances the possibility that the points raised are going to arise again in subsequent observations).

Having grasped the basic techniques, you must ensure that you can select and enact a suitable observation method to gather information relating to:

- Children's individual personalities and 'styles'
- Children's individual and collective needs
- How children learn
- How children interact with peers and adults
- Behaviour changes which may indicate illness or other underlying problems
- How to plan future practice and activities
- How children use resources
- How to pursue your own professional development

and to gather information about individual children's:

- Physical and sensory development
- Intellectual/cognitive development
- Language development
- Emotional development
- Social development
- Aesthetic/spiritual development

In early 2007, UNICEF produced the report 'An overview of child well-being in rich countries'. While many European countries (particularly those on the Scandinavian peninsulas) were high in the rankings, the UK was close to the bottom of the table along with the United States. The methodology of the survey has been questioned, but any evidence that our children may be experiencing a 'less than best' childhood should be unacceptable to any member of the children's workforce. In 2008 a review by the Child and Adolescent Mental Health Services, 'Improving the mental health and psychological well-being of children and young people', identified continuity of staff and professionals as important to children and their families, and workforce development as one of the challenges for the future. Recent work on well-being has been carried out in Belgium by Laevers (1997 and 2005) and this work has been incorporated into the Pen Green Framework for Engaging Parents (2008), using the Leuven Child Involvement Scale for Young Children (LIC-YC) initiated by Laevers and his colleagues. This is a framework with which you may be familiar, as it has been adopted by many childcare settings across the UK. For a full explanation of this scale see the relevant section of the following Focus on practice box.

Focus on practice

Example of an observation evaluation method: the Leuven Child Involvement Scale for Young Children (LIC-YC)

Pascal and Bertram (2004) used this as the observation method in their Effective Early Learning Study (EELS). A summarised description of their method is outlined below.

The Child Involvement Scale consists of two components:

- a list of 'involvement signals' and
- the levels of involvement in a 5-point scale.

The child involvement signals

Concentration: the level of attention the child directs towards the activity

Energy: the effort the child invests in the activity

Complexity and creativity: the level of competence the child shows in the activity, as measured against his or her previous best efforts; the consideration of whether the child is moving into his/her 'zone of proximal development' in engagement with this activity

Facial expression and posture: the intensity of the child's posture and facial expression. Does s/he appear to be completely absorbed in the activity?

Persistence: the duration of concentration that the child gives to the activity, and the ease/difficulty of distraction

Precision: the attention to detail within the activity

Reaction time: how quickly a child reacts to further stimuli within the activity, showing motivation and keenness

Language: how a child talks about a particular activity, e.g. does s/he ask to do it again, or state that s/he enjoyed it?

Satisfaction: how proud a child is of his/her achievements within the activity (Note: this does not have to relate to satisfaction with a specific product – it could be satisfaction with an experience).

Child Involvement Scale

The child involvement scale is to be used with reference to the involvement signals.

Level 1: Low Activity Stereotypic, repetitive and passive, with little effort or indication that the child feels that much is demanded. S/he is easily distracted, after which the activity is forgotten.

Level 2: A Frequently Interrupted Activity The child is engaged in an activity for part of the time, but spends approximately half of the observed period not paying direct attention. S/he is relatively easily distracted, after which the activity is forgotten.

Level 3: Mainly Continuous Activity The child seems busy at an activity but there is the feeling that 'something' is lacking and that the task is routine. S/he is relatively easily distracted, and may not return to the activity.

Level 4: Continuous Activity with Intense Moments There are some signs of intensity in the child's engagement. S/he can be interrupted, but not wholly distracted, seeking out and resuming the activity again following the interruption. S/he may resist interruption in some cases. Attention may fluctuate a little, but in general there is high concentration and focus.

Level 5: Sustained Intense Activity The child shows: concentration, creativity, energy and persistence for almost all the observation period. S/he shows little response to interruptions, and has clear motivation to continue the activity. The authors suggest that such observations are carried out via the time sampling method, observing a child for two minutes, and three times during two sessions during a given week, resulting in 12 observations.

Task Design a sheet for recording Child Involvement Scale data with your colleagues/peers and practise using this in your setting. (Note: Bertram and Pascal include a sample sheet in their report, p. 8.) You can use this method to assess individual children or to assess the general success of specific activities/areas of the setting. Keep this in mind as you move on to Chapters 5, 6 and 7.

Clearly, using this scale would come with all the warnings attached to observing children, and allocating a number to the behaviour can be subjective, but I think we can all agree that an unhappy child who is unhappy within its environment is unlikely to be learning from their experiences in the way that a child who is comfortable, secure and happy is likely to enjoy and benefit from their day-to-day experiences (see Chapters 6 and 7 for more information on this topic).

What are the implications of the rise to prominence of 'well-being' for early years practice and specifically for EYPs? What can EYPs do to ensure that children are supported by adults who can give the quality and consistency of care so necessary to support well-being? After you have read Chapters 5 and 6, reflect on the following points and consider your personal practice as well as your role as a lead practitioner.

- Your state of well-being and your ability to relate to and support others
- Your ability and willingness to model desirable behaviour with regard to building positive working relationships with children and their families
- Your skills as a keyworker working closely with specific children and families to optimise their experience in your setting
- Your ability to work with a team to create and operate an effective keyworker system in your setting. See Chapter 2.

Keeping 'up to date'

We all have a duty to the children and families that we work with to be up to date in our practice. Keeping up to date has never been easier; there is so much information available to us via the Internet as well as more traditional sources – the difficulty is finding the time to read it all or just to sift through it for anything relevant to you and your setting. Subscriptions to online information services are a simple way of getting the 'headlines', which should leave you time to read in more detail articles of specific interest to you and your setting. Nursery World, CWDC and government departments offer this service and it is free. If there are a number of you in your setting you could share out the reading and have weekly discussion groups to cascade ideas through your team. This would be a really good way of engaging all staff in planning and decision making.

Armed with all this information and working with your colleagues, the next step in the process is to review/create your setting's policies with regard to safety, inclusion and protection. It is vital to understand that policies are working documents; they are plans for action which all colleagues should follow under specific circumstances and they ensure a minimum quality of experience and consistency in practice. To be effective all staff need to feel ownership of the policies, they need to be consulted when policies are being written, they need to be committed to act within the policy and they need to be involved in the review (see Figure 4.3). Each setting should have a plan for regular review of all policies but should be flexible and be prepared to amend policies that are no longer effective as and when the need arises. This is an area that many EYP candidates have worked on for their validation tasks. The cycle of policy amendment should proceed as follows:

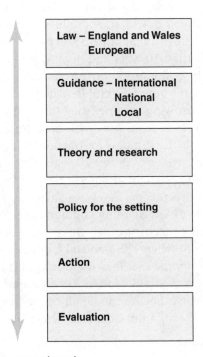

Figure 4.3 Cycle of policy amendment

Focus on practice

Task At this point you should investigate the policies in your setting and reflect on:

- What policies the setting has
- Are there other policies that you feel they should have?
- How are staff, children and families and the wider community informed about these policies and how effective is this communication?
- When were the policies last reviewed?
- How are staff inducted into working with these policies?
- How do the staff feel about the policies?

Reflection *What is your role as EYP, lead practitioner, in ensuring that the policies serve the needs of all involved with the setting and that they are carried out effectively and consistently?*

Section 4: Safeguarding as an essential multi-agency concept in early years practice

What strategies can an EYP develop/use/contribute to multi-agency approaches to protecting children?

In January 2003 David Batty wrote an article entitled 'Catalogue of cruelty' for the *Guardian* in which he outlined some of the 'most shocking' child killings in England since 1945. The majority were from the 1980s. He gives a brief overview of more than 10 cases and in all cases he identifies poor communication, breakdown in communication or just a lack of communication between agencies tasked with protecting children as contributing to their demise. While these cases make harrowing reading, they have all critically informed the child protection frameworks that we work with now; for example, the case of Tyra Henry in 1984 is noted as the stimulus for the production of new guidelines on child protection for social workers. Almost 20 years after this, the case of Victoria Climbié led to a thorough review of children's services, which was initiated by the Every Child Matters Green Paper 2003 (see Chapter 3), and an emphasis on multi-agency approaches to safeguarding children. The recent case of 'Baby P' has again created waves of concern through the whole early years workforce and through all the professions where children and families are in focus. We all await with interest the policy response that may result from this recent tragedy.

The Every Child Matters Green Paper identified five outcomes for children (0–18 years) that we should all be working to meet and which EYPs should lead on; to reiterate from Chapter 3, these are

- Be healthy
- Stay safe

- Enjoy and achieve
- Make a positive contribution
- Achieve economic well-being.

In this section of the chapter, and to promote your understanding of standard 20 of EYPS, our discussion will focus on 'Stay safe'. The aims noted in the outcome 'Stay safe' include ensuring children are safe from:

- Maltreatment, neglect, violence and sexual exploitation
- Accidental injury and death
- Bullying and discrimination
- Crime and anti-social behaviour

and that children have security, stability and are cared for by adults to whom they have bonded attachments (see Chapter 2).

To help us deliver the Every Child Matters Framework, the Government has produced the Common Core of Skills and Knowledge for the Children's Workforce (DfES 2005), which outlines the skills and knowledge practitioners need to action the ECM agenda. Under the heading 'Safeguarding and promoting the welfare of the child' we are told that:

> Those who work with children and young people have a responsibility to safeguard and promote their welfare. This is an important responsibility and requires vigilance. You will need to be able to recognise when a child or young person may not be achieving their developmental potential or their health may be impaired, and be able to identify appropriate sources of help for them and their families. It is important to identify concerns as early as possible so that children, young people, their families and carers can get the help they need. **As well as ensuring that children are free from harm, it is equally important to ensure their well-being and quality of life.**   (DfES 2005, p. 13)

The final sentence here is very important – for the majority of children the role of the childcare workforce is to ensure well-being and quality of life which will support the children to reach their developmental potential. Distressing and 'headline grabbing' cases like Victoria Climbié and Baby P are still thankfully in the minority; most safeguarding activity that Early Years Practitioners undertake on a day-to-day basis involves supporting children from troubled families who may lack understanding of children and childhood, rather than identifying life-threatening abuse. One final point here is that in addition to their role as a member of the children's workforce an EYP must also expect to lead the practice of other colleagues in this respect, as in all others.

Under the heading 'Multi-agency working' the Common Core states that:

> To work successfully on a multi-agency basis you need to be clear about your own role and aware of the roles of other professionals; you need to be confident about your own standards and targets and respectful of those that apply to other services, actively seeking and respecting the knowledge and input

others can make to delivering the best outcomes for children and young people.

(DfES 2005, p. 18)

The role of referral and multi-agency working is crucially important within safeguarding procedures. Unless you are employed within a local authority or other agency team with specific responsibility to deal with safeguarding issues, you will not be called upon to *diagnose* the safeguarding needs of individual children, but to *communicate* any suspicions to the agencies responsible for investigating them. Again for the EYP, this aspect of practice is also principally about your own actions and your role in modelling and leading best practice in others. It is vital that you understand how to professionally observe children in order to gather information on their progress and well-being. See Focus on practice: Observation box above.

Focus on policy and practice

Task If you are on an academic programme as a lead into or alongside EYPS training, it is very likely that you will have studied the Common Core (see Chapter 2) and used it within a Personal Development Planning module. If this document is new to you, it is one you really should get to know well. Your reflection task is based on this document. At this point it would be useful to familiarise yourself with the knowledge and skills requirements of the Common Core and carry out a personal audit/skills analysis comparing your skills and knowledge with those listed in the Common Core. How do you measure up? Do you feel confident to model and lead 'best practice' for both experienced and inexperienced colleagues? Do you feel confident to challenge 'less than best practice'?

As well as the documents discussed above, you should familiarise yourself with Working Together to Safeguard Children (DfES 2006) and the Common Assessment Framework for children and young people: Practitioners' Guide (CWDC 2007). You should also refer to the flow chart earlier in the chapter which shows the link between legislation, guidance documents and theory/research and policy and practice for, as EYP/lead practitioner/manager, drafting and evaluating policy and procedures on safeguarding children within your setting will most likely be your responsibility.

In terms of your own skills, the essentials are your ability to build good working relationships with parents and carers, your ability to communicate with a range of different professionals, your awareness of confidentiality and your 'trump card' – your observation skills. Time spent developing and honing observation skills will generate huge rewards for:

- **You** – you will learn so much from observing children and reflecting on your practice;

- **Children** – the better you know the children you are supporting, the better able you will be to meet their individual needs and the more likely you are to identify development and change;

- **Families** – demonstrating detailed knowledge and understanding of their children will support development of working relationships with parents/carers which can only benefit children in the long term.

Hobart and Frankel (2004) is a valuable text which you can use to further develop your observation skills; you may also find the more recent text, 'Childhood Observation' (Palaiologou 2008), one of the 'Achieving EYPS' series, useful in this respect. Many years ago, the idea that 'practise makes perfect' was lost to me when someone explained that 'practise did not make perfect – but it did make permanent'. The point that was being made was that unless your practise method was correct you would be embedding the wrong way to do the task, which would be counterproductive and could take a long time to correct. It is important to the development of your observation skills that you have a critical friend to give fair and honest feedback to help you develop your skills or at least prevent you from developing too many bad habits! For example, enacting an observation regime that recognises the importance of objectivity (see Focus on practice: Observation box above) is crucially important with respect to the safeguarding policy within a setting, as concerns raised with outside agencies will be taken far more seriously and progress more swiftly if a set of clear, objective and triangulated observation data is provided. You must also develop skills in dealing with constructive criticism with respect to both taking this from and providing this to colleagues, if you are to support and lead best practice in others.

Focus on practice

Mary and her family lived in local authority housing. During a period of regeneration all of the houses on her road were being renovated and many of the families had been moved to alternative accommodation but Mary and her family were still waiting.

Work on the empty houses started, and Mary's family were finding life difficult as they experienced frequent breaks in water, gas and power supplies and the area was, according to her Mum, 'like a building site'. The area was such a mess that a couple of weeks ago Mary had fallen over some wood the builders had left, hit her head on a wall and been taken to the hospital where she had had five stitches in a head wound and an overnight stay. The local health centre wrote to Mary's Mum asking her to bring Mary in for a follow-up appointment, just to check on the head wound, but the letter was never delivered. The delivery driver had looked at the houses in the road and decided that no-one would still be living there and eventually the letter was returned to the health centre. At the health centre the maternity cover health visitor eventually picked up on this missed appointment when she had 'got to grips' with her new job, but by this time it was almost 10 weeks since the original injury.

Identifying good practice

Mary started in an early years setting four months ago. Her keyworker Wasim recently told the leading practitioner Sarah that he is struggling to establish a good working relationship with Mary and her family. He tells her that the offer of a home visit before Mary started at the setting was politely but firmly refused. Mary's attendance is not good and she is often late. The explanations given for lateness and absence also seemed rather strange, for example the need to accompany her mother on regular shopping and launderette visits. He is also concerned about Mary's appearance and demeanour, as she appears dirty, sometimes smells unwashed, and she is always hungry, rushing to grab any food offered. He also shows Sarah a record he has kept of Mary's cuts and bruises and a head injury requiring stitches. She did not sustain any of these injuries in the setting.

Leading practice

Sarah reassures Wasim that he has acted appropriately. She thanks him for taking such an interest in Mary's family and applauds the very professional efforts that he has made towards building a good working relationship in a difficult situation. She advises him to take care to remain objective when recording, and not to jump to any swift conclusions. She commends his use of the setting's policies and procedures in guiding his actions to date. As she is the setting safeguarding coordinator, she asks him to continue his observations and recording and to continue working positively with the child and her family. She suggests that they meet again the following week to review the situation, reminding Wasim of the confidentiality of their discussions.

Reflection *Put yourself in Wasim's shoes. He has seen:*

- *home visit declined*
- *poor attendance and some lateness*
- *signs of neglect, hunger, dirty, smelly*
- *signs of injury.*

What would you do?

Task

- **Now think about your role as EYP/Leading Practitioner and how you would respond to Wasim.**
- **Consider your role as an EYP in a multi-agency team and how your perspective might change.**
- **As EYP in a multi-disciplinary team how might you support Mary and her family?**

I hope that from this reflection you will conclude that Wasim has one piece of a large jigsaw and how different his perspective is to the perspective of a member of a multi-agency team who, through their access to information generated by their cross-agency communication, recognise and appreciate the difficulties that Mary and her family are experiencing.

Armed with your knowledge of legislation, guidance and local policy and practice (see Chapter 3) and your knowledge of children gained from close working relationships with parents and carers (see Chapter 8) and your highly developed observation skills (see above and Chapter 5), you are in a good position to notice, observe and record changes in behaviour and demeanour which may indicate a child falling short of their potential, or a child/family experiencing difficulty. You may produce a vital piece of the safeguarding jigsaw relating to an individual child, or support one of your colleagues to do this; remember, if this had occurred within each of the cases cited in the frame of 'child protection tragedy', the problems leading up to the ultimate outcome may have been neutralised before the child came to serious harm. One thing is certain: you, like any other professional working with children and families, will produce only a part of the jigsaw and it is only when a number of pieces are put together through multi-agency working that a coherent picture is produced. We are a part of a multi-agency operation – playing a part in a a team far wider than our workplace. Therefore, we may build a picture which causes us to refer a child to the local safeguarding authority but, within the role of setting lead professional, to refer is the limit of our role.

Conclusion

This chapter has sought to answer the following questions:

What are the legal rights to equality for practitioners and children within the English early years workplace?

You have been directed to sources of information relating to the large body of policy and legislation relating to equal opportunities and safeguarding. These guidelines and directives change very frequently, and leading practitioners have a responsibility to keep up to date and be able to lead the setting in identifying the current, relevant guidance informing their setting's policy and practice.

What tools are available to an EYP to support the promotion of children's rights, equality and inclusion and how can these be used effectively to demonstrate and model anti-discriminatory practice?

The practice boxes and diagrams throughout this chapter should help you reflect upon this point; the content relating to observation skills and objectivity are particularly important. The point relating to modelling good practice is especially important for a leading practitioner, as within any setting (as within most areas of human existence) there is very much a culture of less experienced individuals 'doing what I do rather than what I say!' It might be useful to reflect upon this point with your colleagues to consider some (anonymised) practical examples.

What practices can an EYP draw on to promote safety, health and well-being for children in an early years setting?

The complex issues of safety vs risk and what constitutes 'well-being' have been discussed above. If you have to cover a work-based learning module in the course of your training, it might be worth considering a project in this area of policy, which is currently high on the Early Years reform agenda, and a subject of discussion in many different arenas, both academic and practitioner oriented literature; see, for example, Tovey (2007) and Pen Green (2008) respectively.

What strategies can an EYP develop/use/contribute to multi-agency approaches to protecting children?

The content of this section of the chapter draws heavily upon the Common Core (see Chapter 2) and should be read in conjunction with the legislation and policy outlined in Chapter 3, and with the section on multi-agency working in Chapter 8. As such, we have taken a multi-agency approach to informing you about multi-agency working! This is a topic that will remain current for the foreseeable future in Early Years, and is a key development driven by the advent of the EYFS. It subsequently creates a range of opportunities and challenges for the first generation of EYPs and all leading practitioners in contemporary Early Years settings.

Further reading

Griffin, S. (2008) *Inclusion, Equality & Diversity in Working with Children*. Harlow: Heinemann.

Hobart, C. and Frankel, J. (2004) *A practical guide to child observations and assessments*, 3rd edition. Cheltenham: Stanley Thornes.

Lindon, J. (2006) *Equality in Early Childhood Linking Theory and Practice*. London: Hodder Arnold.

Palaiologou, I. (2008) *Childhood Observation*. Exeter: Learning Matters.

Tassoni, P. (2008) *Practical EYFS Handbook*. Harlow: Heinemann.

Whalley, M. (2008) *Leading Practice in Early Years Settings*. Exeter: Learning Matters.

Websites

http://www.barnardos.org.uk/

http://www.11million.org.uk/?CFID=38069106&CFTOKEN=94998647 (The Children's Commissioner for England)

http://www.nspcc.org.uk/

References

Alderson, P. (2008) *Young Children's Rights*, 2nd edition. London: Jessica Kingsley Publishing.

Batty, D. (2003) 'Catalogue of cruelty'. Available at: www.guardian.co.uk/society/2003/jan/ 27/childrenservices/childprotection Accessed on 6 November 2008.

Brown, F. (2008) 'Playwork'. In A. Brock, S. Dodds, P. Jarvis and Y. Olusoga (2008) *Perspectives on Play: Learning for Life,* pp. 217–30. Harlow: Pearson Longman.

CAMHS Review (2008) *Improving the mental health and psychological well-being of children and young people.* Available at: http://www.dcfs.gov.uk/CAMHSreview

Campling, J. (1981) *Images of ourselves: women with disabilities talking.* London: Routledge and Kegan Paul.

Condry, J. and Condry, S. (1976) 'Sex differences: A study of the eye of the beholder'. *Child Development,* 47, pp. 812–19.

Corsaro, W. (1997) *The Sociology of Childhood.* Thousand Oaks, CA.: Pine Forge Press.

Council of Europe (1996) The European Social charter. Available at: http://conventions.coe.int/ treaty/en/Treaties/Html/163.htm Accessed on 3 January 2009.

CWDC (2007) 'Common Assessment Framework for children and young people: Practitioners Guide'. Available at: http://www.cwdcouncil.org.uk and at: http://www.everychildmatters.gov.uk/caf

David, T., Gooch, K., Powell, S. and Abbott, L. (2003) *Birth to Three Matters: A Review of the Literature.* Research Report 444. London: The Stationery Office.

Davies, B. and Banks, C. (1995) 'The Gender Trap: A Feminist Poststructuralist Analysis of Primary School Children's Talk about Gender'. In J. Holland, M. Blair and S. Sheldon (eds) *Debates and Issues in Feminist Research and Pedagogy.* Clevedon: Multilingual Matters, pp. 45–69.

DCSF (2007) *Confident, capable and creative: supporting boys' achievements.* Available at: http://publications.teachernet.gov.uk/eOrderingDownload/DCSF-00682-2007.pdf Accessed on 15 February 2009.

Derman-Sparks, L. and Ramsey, P. (2006) *What if all the kids are white?* New York: Teacher's College Press.

DfSE (2003) *EveryChild Matters.* Green Paper. London: The Stationery Office.

Griffin, S. (2008) *Inclusion, Equality & Diversity in Working with Children.* Harlow: Heinemann.

HM Government (2005) *Common Core of Skills and Knowledge for the Children's Workforce.* Available at: http://www.everychildmatters.gov.uk ref DfES/1189/2005.

HM Government (2006) *Working Together to Safeguard Children.* Available at: http://www.everychildmatters.gov.uk/socialcare/safeguarding

Hobart, C. and Frankel, J. (2004) *A practical guide to child observations and assessments,* 3rd edition. Cheltenham: Stanley Thornes.

Jarvis, P. (2006) 'Rough and Tumble Play, Lessons in Life', *Evolutionary Psychology,* 4, pp. 268–86.

Jarvis, P. (2007) 'Dangerous activities within an invisible playground: a study of emergent male football play and teachers' perspectives of outdoor free play in the early years of primary school', *International Journal of Early Years Education,* 15(3), pp. 245–59.

Jarvis, P. (2008) 'Building social hardiness for life: rough and tumble play in the early years of primary school'. In A. Brock, S. Dodds, P. Jarvis and Y. Olusoga (eds) *Perspectives on Play: Learning for Life,* pp. 175–93. Harlow: Pearson Longman.

Jarvis, P. and George, J. (2008) 'Play, learning for life: the vital role of play in human development'. In A. Brock, S. Dodds, P. Jarvis and Y. Olusoga (eds) *Perspectives on Play: Learning for Life,* pp. 253–71. Harlow: Pearson Longman.

Laevers, F. (2005) The Curriculum as Means to raise the Quality of ECE. Implications for Policy. *European Early Childhood Education Research Journal,* 13(1), 17–30.

Laevers, F. (1997) Forward to Basics! Deep-level-learning and the Experiential Approach, *Early Childhood Research Quarterly,* 12(2), pp. 117–43.

Lindon, J. (2006) *Equality in Early Childhood Linking Theory and Practice.* London: Hodder Arnold.

Palaiologou, I. (2008) *Childhood Observation.* Exeter: Learning Matters.

Paley, V. (1984) *Boys and Girls, Superheroes in the Doll Corner*. Chicago: University of Chicago Press.

Pascal, C. and Bertram, A. (2004) *Enhancing the Participation of Black and Minority Ethnic Communities in Childcare*, DfES, London.

Pen Green (2008) *The Pen Green Framework for Engaging Parents*. Corby, Northants: Pen Green.

Siraj-Blatchford, I. (2001) *Supporting Identity, Diversity and Language in the Early Years*. Milton Keynes: Open University Press.

Stephenson, A. (2003) Physical Risk Taking: Dangerous or Endangered? *Early Years*, 23(1), pp. 35–43.

TACTYC (2008) Summary from play research seminar, 2008. Available at: http://www.tactyc.org.uk/pdfs/2008_Colloquium_summary.pdf Accessed on 2 January 2009.

The Primary Review (2008) The independent review of the primary curriculum: interim report. Available at: http://publications.teachernet.gov.uk/eOrderingDownload/IPRC_Report.pdf Accessed 17 February 2009.

Tovey, H. (2007) *Playing Outdoors: Spaces and Places, Risk and Challenge (Debating Play)*. Buckingham: Open University Press.

Tovey, H. *et al.* (2008) Summary of Findings from Play Research Seminar, 2008. Available at: http://www.ttrb.ac.uk/attachments/8707ac44-4ba4-4986-ac21-1b95c287aa32.doc Accessed on 28 April 2009.

UNICEF, 'Child poverty in perspective: An overview of child well-being in rich countries', *Innocenti Report Card 7, 2007*. Florence: UNICEF Innocenti Research Centre.

Warnock M. (1986) 'Children with special needs in ordinary schools: Integration revisited'. In A. Cohen and L. Cohen (eds) *Special Needs in the Ordinary School*. San Francisco, CA: Harper & Row.

UK Government publications

Office of Public Sector Information: http://www.opsi.gov.uk (HMSO)

DoE	The Health and Safety at Work Act 1974
DoE	Sex Discrimination Act 1975 (and Amendments)
DoE	Race Relations Act 1976 (and Amendments)
DfES	The Education Reform Act 1988
DoH	The Children Act 1989
DoE	Disability Discrimination Act 1995
DoE	Sex Equality (Gender Reassignment) Regulations 1999
Ofsted	Full Day Care: Guidance to the National Standards 2001
DoE	Special Educational Needs and Disability Act 2001
DoE	Special Educational Needs Code of Practice 2001
DoE	Employment Equality (Sexual Orientation) Regulations 2003
DoE	Employment Equality (Religion or Belief) Regulations 2003
Treasury	Every Child Matters: Green Paper 2003
Treasury	The 10 Year Plan for Childcare 2004
DfES	The Children Act 2004
DoE	The Disability Discrimination Act 2005
DfES	The Childcare Act 2006
DfES	The Education Act 2006
DoE	Employment Equality (Age) Regulations 2006
DCSF	The Early Years Foundation Stage 2008
DCSF	The Children's Plan 2007

Part 3

Leading practice in the Early Years setting

5

Leading in children's learning and development

Wendy Holland

Chapter overview

The standards addressed in this chapter are:

S10 Use close, informed observation and other strategies to monitor children's activities, development and progress systematically and carefully, and use this information to inform, plan and improve practice and provision

S13 Make effective personalised provision for the children they work with

S14 Respond appropriately to children, informed by how children develop and learn and a clear understanding of possible next steps in their development and learning

S15 Support the development of children's language and communication skills

S16 Engage in sustained shared thinking with children

S21 Assess, record and report on progress in children's development and learning and use this as a basis for differentiating provision

S22 Give constructive and sensitive feedback to help children understand what they have achieved and what they need to do next and, when appropriate, encourage children to think about, evaluate and improve on their own performance

Relating to the standards we are focusing upon in this chapter, the following key questions will be addressed:

- What effective strategies can we develop for observing, assessing, planning, recording and reporting children's learning and development?

(S10, S21, S22)

- How may we use such strategies to promote effective personalised provision based on a clear understanding of child development and possible next steps in children's learning?

(S13, S14)

- How can we achieve effective practice in supporting children's emergent language and communication skills through sustained shared thinking and the provision of a language-rich environment?

(S15, S16)

Alice's progress

Alice, a twin aged 3 years, has been causing some concern. Her keyworker and Alice's mother have discussed how Paul, her twin brother, does all the talking for them. This practice seems to have increased since the arrival of their new baby brother. Alice's mother is particularly concerned about her language development and pronunciation. The twins are relatively new to the setting and Alice is still not separating well from her mother, despite her brother being there. Alice's keyworker has asked the Lead Professional, Jill, an EYP, to observe Alice for the afternoon.

At the beginning of the session, Alice settles after a tearful parting from her mother. She joins her brother at the water; filling containers seems to calm her and her sense of well-being appears to improve. Her levels of concentration and involvement appear to be high as she attempts to pour water from one container into another. Chelsea, a 4½ year old, comes to join them. She talks to Alice rather than Paul. Over the few short weeks Alice has been in the setting, she has tended to seem more at ease with the older children.

Chelsea moves away to a painting easel and Paul decides it is time to play outside. Alice hesitates for a moment, then joins Chelsea who is humming to herself as she paints. The painting area is a favourite area for the twins, and Alice soon becomes absorbed in mixing colours on a palate, staying by herself at the easel when Chelsea has gone outside. She changes her brush from one hand to the other while mixing, then painting. Jill eventually draws up a small chair by the easel and looks at the painting Alice is involved in, asking Alice about her painting. Alice explains, with a reasonable amount of clarity, that it depicts a mother monster with a demanding baby monster. Jill records in her participant observation (see Chapter 4) and evaluation that:

- Alice's level of well-being has been sufficiently high for her to feel confident to engage in activities on her own without Paul.
- She showed ease in the company of an older child.
- Her concentration and involvement while painting were sustained for longer than was usual for her.
- Her communication with the practitioner evidenced language skills to a degree she had not shown previously on her own, although some sounds were not yet fully articulated.
- The topic of the picture suggests that she is coming to terms with her mother's involvement with her baby brother.

Jill made an extra note to ensure Alice's progress was shared with her keyworker so that, when Alice's mother came to collect the twins, they could discuss the **processes** that Alice had been engaged in to produce her painting, rather than just presenting her with the **product**.

Introduction

Two key elements of the EYPS are: (a) a practitioner's ability to demonstrate and model their own good practice, and (b) showing clear leadership of this effective practice with staff in order to support children's learning and development. This chapter will signpost research findings which underpin such effective practice for the reader, as well as providing examples from practice which exemplify the characteristics of effective leadership. The focus will be on those standards that particularly identify the role of the practitioner in responding to the individual and holistic nature of children's learning, through the establishment of strategies for observation, planning, monitoring, assessment, recording and reporting, to enhance children's development. The use of such strategies in creating effective personalised provision will be examined. The importance of using such a framework to provide a language-rich environment, and the role of sustained, shared thinking between child and adult within that, will also be investigated.

What effective strategies can we develop for observing, assessing, planning, recording and reporting children's learning and development?

Before we consider which strategies to develop, we need to understand the rationale behind the need to observe, assess, plan, record and report children's learning and development. The Early Years Foundation Stage framework (DCSF 2008) provides us with such a rationale for the implementation of the Observation, Assessment and Planning cycle for children from Birth to Six years.

Planning, to be effective for children this age, needs to be closely linked to their interests. It also needs to be flexible enough to absorb and use those spontaneous moments of learning that occur daily with young children. At the same time, it needs to ensure that all children receive exposure to experiences and activities that promote each individual's journey towards the Early Learning Goals (see Chapter 2).

Observation is the means by which rich information can be gathered about each child (see Chapter 4). By doing close, regular observations, we can:

- determine children's particular interests, likes and dislikes
- identify any special or particular needs
- establish levels of well-being and involvement
- gain knowledge of newly acquired skills
- assess individual progression
- plan next steps for personalised learning.

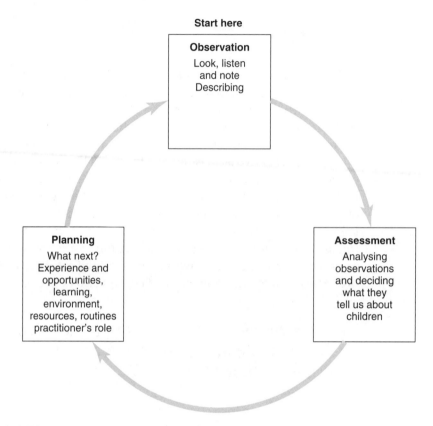

Figure 5.1

All of the above can be gained through regular participant observation while engaged in activities, talking with and listening to children. However, other forms of observation come into play; for example if there are concerns over a child's behaviour, event sampling may need to be employed and, by observing when a particular type of behaviour occurs, the triggers/causes for such behaviour identified. Concerns about areas of possible deficit or delay could involve the use of more detailed target child and/or focal child observations (see Chapter 4), in order to gather evidence to support further investigations by the Special Educational Needs Coordinator (SENCo). A key focus for such observations would be to consider the balance between the amounts of ludic (imaginative) and epistemic (investigative) play in which the child engages (Hutt *et al.* 1989), with a view to balancing this more carefully if the child is engaging in significantly more of one sort of play than the other.

On a broader level, observation can also highlight:

- gaps in resources that need to be addressed

- the imbalance between child-initiated and adult-led activities and experiences

- lack of sufficient access between indoor and outdoor environments for all children, including those with additional needs

- the need to provide more inclusive resources and activities to acknowledge and celebrate the diversity of children in the setting and the unique individuality of each child

- exemplary practice that can be cascaded to others or the need for further training in a particular area

- the need for more input from parents and carers to help support and develop the child's learning journey.

How we record observations is usually dependent upon the needs of individual settings. The EYFS CD-ROM includes examples of proformas and a template for a child's *Learning Journey* to use when observing. For new practitioners these can provide guidance and help in ordering the information they gather under such headings as:

- Context for learning
- What did they do?
- Links to Early Years Foundation Stage
- How did the adult support the learning?
- Next steps.

The importance of committing the observation to paper, as soon as possible, lies in the need to provide more reliability and validity. The perspectives of several members of staff, as well as parents and carers, also provide triangulation of evidence for a child's profile. With the increase in the use of ICT, forms of recording, other than written narrative, are increasingly being developed. The use of digital photographs, video and audio recording which can be shared with the home all help to effectively build a child's profile or record of achievement.

Assessment, the next phase in the cycle, is the essential analysis and review of what has been observed. In order for this to be effective, sound knowledge of how children develop and learn is necessary (see Chapter 2). An understanding of schemas (Piaget 1951, Athey 1990) will help the practitioner and parent recognise, support and extend the child's developmental stage (Pen Green 2005). For example, how often has a **transporting schema** (where a child is fascinated by moving materials from place to place) not been recognised in a setting or at home and ignored or stopped because it is messy or inconvenient, instead of being supported and extended? The use of scales of involvement and well-being (Laevers 1997, 2005 and see Chapter 4) can help the observer assess the level of learning (on a continuum from deep to superficial) that is taking place. Effective knowledge of the six EYFS areas of Learning and Development and their related aspects is essential, in order for the child's progress towards the Early Learning Goals to be tracked (see Chapter 2). This *formative* type of assessment, assessment *for* learning, is an essential ingredient when attempting to plan for personalised provision and next steps learning for the child.

The EYFS, as with the previous frameworks, provides clear guidance on assessment – Statutory Framework for EYFS (DCSF 2007). Ongoing observation and assessment in all six areas of Learning and Development provide a summary of each child's progress that informs their EYFS Profile. The Profile organises the early learning goals into a set of 13 assessment scales each with a nine-point scale. See Appendix 1 of Statutory Framework for Early Years Foundation Stage (DCSF 2007). The scales poster is also available at: **http://www.naa.org.uk/libraryAssets/ media/poster_v8_aw.pdf**. It is anticipated that most children will achieve the first three points before moving on to the early learning goals. For those children who will not reach level 3 during the EYFS stage, alternative assessment arrangements can be used.

Practitioners need to be aware that the scale points from 4 to 8 are not necessarily reached in a hierarchical fashion. Through personalised planning and provision related to their interests and experience, each child will reach his/her level through their own individual route. There is a consensus view that point 9 describes a child who is working consistently beyond the early learning goals. The EYFS Profile is a **summative** form of assessment, assessment *of* learning, as it identifies the levels reached by a child at the end of the Foundation Stage, but can also be used in a **formative** way to inform the Year 1 teacher's planning.

The Profile is one form of many available to record assessments (see Focus on practice box, ECERS and ITERS below). As with the previous profile document (Foundation Stage Profile 2003), some settings prefer to create their own specific document rather than using the EYFS Profile. However we document assessments, one important factor needs to be considered, that of ease of access for the child and parents/carers. Ongoing individual profiles or Records of Achievements have an important role in informing parents/carers of their child's continuing development. They also provide a vital opportunity for children to access their own learning and, in doing so, celebrate their achievements as well as being able to self-assess.

Practitioners need to familiarise themselves with other forms of assessment scales such as the Common Assessment Framework (DfES 2005) (CAF). Holistic

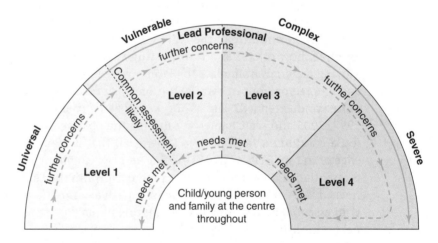

Figure 5.2 The Common Assessment Framework process

Source: http://www.nelincs.gov.uk/NR/rdonlyres/D32741B2-C1EA-4E11-AD72-8FB1C35B30C0/0/section2.jpg

provision and assessment of children requires new skills, or at least new ways of thinking. The CAF is not solely for children practitioners have concerns about, or for children with additional needs.

This assessment requires practitioners to make connections between the child's home experience and how the child experiences the setting to a degree that has perhaps not happened before. Rather than being simply a referral mechanism, it needs to be seen as 'an assessment which is linked to a referral' (DfES RB740) on the EYFS CD-ROM (DCSF 2008). In this way the underpinning agenda of Every Child Matters for more effective multi-agency working (now a statutory requirement in the EYFS) can be progressed.

Assessing quality of provision

The use of Infant/Toddler Environmental Rating Scales (ITERS) for children from birth to 30 months and Early Childhood Environmental Rating Scales (ECERS) for use with children from 2½ to 5 years helps when a setting wants to assess its provision in an holistic way, by looking at such items as space and furnishings, personal care routines, listening and talking, activities, interaction and parents and staff; these have been used and developed by several high-profile Early Years research projects on both sides of the Atlantic over the past 20 years, including EPPE – Effective Provision of Pre-School education (1997–2003) and REPEY (2003) (Sylva, Siraj-Blatchford and Taggart 2003). Training in applying these scales to a setting can be offered by local authorities.

Focus on practice

The **ECERS (Early Childhood Environment Rating Scales)** are constructed as follows:

ECERS-R is based on seven subscales:

- Space and furnishings
- Personal care routines
- Language reasoning
- Activities
- Interaction
- Programme structure
- Parents and staff.

ECERS-E is based on four subscales:

- Literacy
- Mathematics
- Science and environment
- Diversity.

These aspects are scored along a continuum:

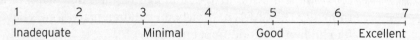

```
1       2       3       4       5       6       7
Inadequate      Minimal         Good          Excellent
```

The scales are used as follows:

1 = Inadequate

- Children's needs for health and safety are not met
- No warmth or support from adults is observed
- No learning is encouraged

3 = Minimal

- Children's basic health and safety needs are met
- A little warmth and support is provided by adults
- There are few learning experiences

5 = Good

- Health and safety needs are fully met
- Staff are caring and supportive of children
- Children are learning in many ways through interesting, fun activities

7 = Excellent

- Everything is good
- In addition, children are encouraged to become independent
- The teacher plans for children's individual learning needs
- Adults have close, personal relationships with each child

(Cryer 1999)

The **ITERS-R (Infant-Toddler Environment Rating Scale, Revised)** has seven sub-scales each of which yield a scale score, using the same scoring system as ECERS. The subscales are:

I. Space and furnishings

1. Indoor space
2. Furniture for routine care and play
3. Room arrangement
4. Display for children

II. Personal care routines

5. Greeting/departing
6. Meals/snacks
7. Nap
8. Nappy changing/toileting
9. Health practices
10. Safety practices

III. Listening and talking

11. Helping children understand language
12. Helping children use language
13. Using books

IV. Activities

14. Fine motor
15. Active physical play
16. Art
17. Music and movement
18. Blocks
19. Dramatic play
20. Sand and water play
21. Nature/science
22. Use of TV, video, and/or computer

V. Interaction

23. Supervision of play and learning
24. Peer interaction
25. Staff-child interaction
26. Discipline

VI. Programme structure

27. Schedule
28. Free play
29. Group play activities
30. Provisions for children with disabilities

VII. Parents and staff

31. Provisions for parents
32. Provisions for personal needs of staff
33. Provisions for professional needs of staff
34. Staff interaction and cooperation
35. Staff continuity
36. Supervision and evaluation of staff
37. Opportunities for professional growth

It is recommended that trained observers spend at least three hours observing and interview senior staff within a setting before applying measures from either scale. There are also manuals and grids that can be purchased or obtained from various local authority sources to ensure that the scoring measures are applied effectively.

(Harms *et al.* 2006)

Leading practice

As you can see, these are very detailed scales and staff wishing to use them to evaluate their own practice should seek training from their Local Authority in order to use the system properly. This would obviously be very useful for those who are already – or have an ambition to be – Leading Practitioners (LPs).

Task With the help of your colleagues and/or EYPS programme provider, seek out a training programme for ECERS and ITERS.

Planning, the other main ingredient of the learning cycle, is clearly dependent on effective **observation** and **assessment**. Planning can happen in a vacuum or be created by adults with more focus on meeting the dictates of a particular curriculum and learning outcomes. The danger is that an inflexible adult planning of environment and activities may lead to transmission teaching and a *passive* learning environment for children. Child development theory (see Chapter 2) and findings from contemporary research, such as the longitudinal study, Effective Provision of Pre-School Education (EPPE 1997–2003) and the REPEY report (DfES 2002), support the view that babies and young children are *active* learners. The focus on play-based provision in the EYFS acknowledges such theory and research. Planning that is informed by daily observations and assessments showing children's interests, and that involves, extends and challenges those interests, has been shown to be more effective in helping progress children's development.

The EPPE research highlighted above found that settings where practice showed evidence of a mix of planning for child-initiated experience, child-led experience shared and extended by adults and adult-led experience were **centres of excellence**. Regardless of geography or socio-economic status, children in these settings appeared to make similar learning journeys. The importance of sustained shared thinking between child and adult, the use of open-ended questioning and, again, an equal balance between what the child initiates and the adult leads is underpinned by the REPEY findings. Good planning allows for these things to happen on a daily basis. For this to happen, practitioners need to have a clear understanding of the relationship between the different types of planning used by a setting.

- **Long-term** planning ensures that all areas of Learning and Development are addressed, and usually covers the whole year. It will also look at the provision of resources for special occasions, celebrations, festivals, and visits either out of the setting or visitors to the setting. The overall balance of the curriculum, for example effective access to both outdoor and indoor provision and the necessary resources, special projects that may be undertaken with creative partnerships, or any project that requires time to evolve. Any improvements recommended by Ofsted after a report will be included in the school's long-term improvement plan.

- **Medium-term** planning can act as a bridge between long-term and short-term planning, covering a period from three to six weeks. In the Foundation Stage, activities and themes tend to be of shorter duration, in line with children's changing interests and abilities. Medium-term planning could look at the access to and fair distribution of resources, the balance of topics and areas of focus within the six areas of Learning and Development and the ratio of child-initiated to adult-led activities and experiences.

- **Short-term** planning usually includes what will happen within one week. The key factor, as mentioned earlier, is to ensure that it is flexible to allow for children to follow their interests.

No plan written weeks in advance can include a group's interest in a spider's web on a frosty morning . . . yet it is these interests which may lead to some powerful learning.

(DCSF 2007, p. 12)

In order for planning to support holistic and personalised provision, it needs to reflect an inclusive approach – not by treating all children equally, but by building differentiated provision in order for children to *access* activities and experiences equally, to create enabling environments for all (see Chapter 7). It must also be informed by the formative observations and assessments of children's development that occur daily, so that children's interests and potential next steps are clearly in evidence, alongside any adult-led activities to promote particular outcomes in the six areas of Learning and Development within the indoor/outdoor environment. (Examples of detailed short-term planning are available on the EYFS CD-ROM.)

A final element needs to be highlighted when looking at the planning cycle, that of **accountability**. As the EYFS has been given legal force under the Childcare Act 2006, settings need to ensure that all elements of the planning cycle are effectively in place. With regard to assessment and the EYFS Profile, the statutory arrangements allow for parents to receive a written summary of their child's progress against the early learning goals and the assessment scales and, where a parent requests it, a copy of the completed EYFS profile for their child. This may not differ too widely from earlier notions of good practice, where meetings were planned with parents to look at children's profiles/records of achievement before transferring to another setting.

Focus on practice

Reflection *Whether you are an experienced leading practitioner on one of the shorter pathways or a more recent entrant to the profession on the full pathway, you will no doubt have very quickly become involved in the planning within your current setting.*

Task Use your journal to reflect on your planning in the light of what you have learned so far in this chapter. Could you improve your planning? How would you go about this, with a 'real' rather than 'ideal' world orientation? See if you can arrange a session, either face to face or on a forum within your training provider's virtual learning environment (VLE) to discuss this with other EYPS candidates. You may also be able to continue this as an ongoing conversation, particularly if you can ask your tutors to set up a forum specifically for this purpose. In the college in which the editors of this book practise, such a forum has been set up in the 'Work based learning' area of the Early Years VLE.

Having looked at the separate elements of the planning cycle and their rationales, we can revisit the initial question: *What effective strategies can we develop for observing, assessing, planning, recording and reporting children's learning and development?*

Effective observation: leading practice

Having to lead and show effective practice in this vital area at a time of change, when old practices may need to be revised to ensure they meet the new requirements of the EYFS, can aid the EYP in developing new planning strategies for children from Birth to Five years. How can the EYP create effective strategies that lead and support the first element in the planning cycle, *effective observation*?

- They need to assess practitioners' knowledge and understanding of child development in the 0–5 year age range to ensure that observations are effective and appropriate. Through the current cascading of practice in accordance with the EYFS framework, possible areas of confusion or lack of knowledge could be highlighted and staff then supported through the provision of additional training.

- Practitioners who have previously used the Birth to Three Matters framework now have to observe with a different framework in mind, including the six areas of Learning and Development. The EYFS non-statutory guidance (DCSF 2008) does provide examples of how to 'look, listen and note' for ages from 0 to 60 months, situated within the six areas of Learning and Development. The EYP needs to ensure practitioners are guided and supported when using new information and forms of observation.

- The variety of observation techniques and their specific uses need to be understood and reinforced (see Chapter 4 and Focus on practice on ECERS and ITERS).

- Additional staffing needs to be factored into planning to allow for non-participant observations to take place when necessary.

- Differentiated proformas need to be created to meet the needs of differing age groups from babies to 4 and 5 year olds. The EYP needs to involve staff working with the various age groups, to ensure practitioners understand the new formats and requirements, and through discussion to create and own observation procedures and proformas that meet their specific needs.

- Staff observations of children other than by their key person need to be seen as common practice and in some instances planned for, in order to increase validity and reliability.

- The importance and use of information/observations made by parents/carers of the child in their home environment needs to be acknowledged.

- There needs to be agreed practice on the recording of observations and how they inform children's profiles and future planning by staff involved in the different age groups.

The above, if implemented, with the EYP involving staff so that they feel real ownership of new practices, could help to promote and embed systematic and effective observation strategies within a setting.

Effective assessment: leading practice

How can the EYP lead and support effective practice within the next element of the planning cycle, **assessment**?

- Staff knowledge and understanding of the areas of Learning and Development in the EYFS framework need to be identified, in order for observed patterns of behaviour to be formatively assessed and recorded under the six areas of learning, and against the early learning goals. The EYFS Practice Guidance (DCSF 2008) highlights stages from 0 to 60 months under 'Development Matters', giving a brief résumé of children's learning and development at a particular age/stage.

- Discussion of or introduction to practitioners of other scales of assessment, for example scales of involvement where assessment is focused on *process* rather than *outcome,* and children are involved in 'deep level learning' (e.g. Laevers 1997 and see Chapter 4). Such research suggests that children need to feel a clear sense of well-being in order for learning to be truly assimilated and accommodated.

- Practitioners need to be well versed in the range of schemas that children may demonstrate. The recognition and assessment of schema that show how children are trying to make sense of the world around them, through testing out their ideas by carrying out the same action in a variety of contexts and with different objects, is an important stage in children's development, and needs to be assessed as such.

- The EYP needs to ensure that practitioners are reflective and can self-assess honestly. The EEL (Effective Early Learning) Project run at Birmingham University by Pascal and Bertram (1997) considered the quality of adult interaction with young children, and offered a broad set of guidelines for effective self-assessment.

- The EYP needs to ensure practitioners are familiar with the Common Assessment Framework, and understand it as an assessment framework, prior to referring a child. This kind of assessment is pivotal in helping to promote the provision of personalised and holistic provision for children, and requires practitioners to listen to and establish real dialogue with parents. (Easen 1992)

- The EYP needs to be proactive in helping to create (perhaps through liaison with Local Authority Advisors) a profile of formative assessment for children that now spans from birth to 6 years. Not only will this help provide continuity of provision for individual parents and children to access, it will continuously inform personalised planning, and is now a statutory requirement under the EYFS framework.

- The EYP needs to help practitioners become familiar with the EYFS Profile (or its equivalent) as a summative assessment for each child at the end of the Foundation Stage. Staff must be assisted to understand that these statutory documents are moderated by the Local Authority as one assessment measure that is applied to the setting, and that they must always be easily accessible to parents. A summary of each child's achievements towards the Early Learning Goals must be provided before the child makes his/her transition to the next setting.

- The EYP also needs to model effective practice, by encouraging the use of profiles as a form of self-assessment with children to encourage self-evaluation as they progress on their learning journey.

- Infant/Toddler Environmental Rating Scales (ITERS) and Early Childhood Environmental Rating Scales (ECERS) may also form part of the EYP's strategies when holistically assessing the setting's provision (see Focus on practice box on ECERS and ITERS above). The assessment scales can be used with the help of staff, to improve provision by looking at specific areas of the physical environment, such as space and staffing ratios, furniture and resources as well as less tangible elements of the environment, such as interaction between child and adult, the quality of listening and talking, and available activities and planning.

Effective planning: leading practice

Leading and supporting effective practice in the final element of the cycle, **planning**, requires the following:

- The EYP needs to discuss with and support staff in implementing new planning structures, which incorporate the changes in planning and assessment required by the EYFS framework.

- By the creation of differentiated planning proformas that fit the individual needs of babies, toddlers and 3–5 year olds, the EYP can help practitioners promote personalised and holistic learning. By talking to parents, the baby room staff could produce charts that reflect individual children's routines for feeding and sleeping, including transitional toys, or special, calming language that is family specific and will put the baby at ease.

- The EYP needs to ensure that planning at whatever age/stage reflects individual needs in, for example, patterns of attendance, routines that might be directly linked to the diversity of a child's culture, knowledge of a child's attendance at other settings, when and who will collect the child and the special requirements of a child with any kind of delay or deficit.

- The EYP should recognise the need for flexibility in planning that allows for children's interests to inform future short-term planning, while reflecting on links between the medium- and long-term plans of the setting in relation to topics and areas of Learning and Development, supporting staff who are unsure or lack the confidence to divert from planned provision.

- Planning needs to be accessible and visible to all staff, so that roles and requirements are clearly discussed and represented, and planning and preparation time needs to be built into the planning timetable to allow this and other tasks (e.g. the upkeep of individual profiles) to effectively happen.

- The EYP needs to ensure that time is given to evaluation of and reflection on daily planning, through discussion by staff teams involved, in order that next-day planning can be revised/extended to meet changing and individual needs.

- Planning needs to be accessible to parents, too. An overview of planned activities could be placed on the parents' information board, which might also include enlisting help with resources, encouraging participation in setting events (baby massage sessions, for example), or setting visits to look at print in the environment for older children.

- As with observation and assessment, the EYP needs to value the input of practitioners. Planning that has been created through whole staff involvement is more likely to be effective than planning that has been imposed.

Focus on practice

Sunflowers and caterpillars

Sue, a relatively new practitioner to the Children's Centre, whose previous employment had been in a school nursery class, had attended training on outdoor gardening activities. The head had been particularly keen for a member of staff from the 3 to 5's room to attend, as the setting had just finished re-designing, with the help of parents, some of the outdoor provision to include raised beds for the children to plant and grow things in. One project Sue developed involved the planting of sunflower seeds, initially in plastic cups filled with compost, which were duly planted out in one of the raised beds and nurtured by Sue and the children. It was a particularly hot summer, and the sunflowers grew to enormous heights. Eventually it was time to harvest them and Sue had planned to link the event to several areas of learning and development. She and Christine, the setting's Leading Practitioner, had discussed the timetable and planning for this older group of children who were due to leave that summer, and it had been agreed they would benefit from a slightly prolonged time of focused activity after lunch, before going out to play and the arrival of the afternoon children. The cut sunflowers were going to join a display of yellow objects in the room, which included a print of Van Gogh's painting of sunflowers. Sue had planned to look at one of the sunflowers in some detail, indicating in her planning the vocabulary she intended to introduce and the learning outcomes she hoped to achieve. The rest of the flowers were arranged in a vase and placed in the middle of an area that had been prepared with some 'thick' paints which some children had helped to create earlier using powder paint and glue (the thickness of the brush strokes in the painting had been commented upon by the children, and the idea of painting with thick paint using thick brushes appealed to them).

The largest sunflower had been selected for examination, and placed on sheets of large white sugar paper on the floor. The tallest child in the group lay down next to it and the children estimated the flower was three times as tall as him. 'As tall as a giant,' was one reply. Sue reminded them how difficult it had been to cut them down. 'Like Jack and the Beanstalk', a child commented. Sue explained how the seeds in the seed head could be eaten, or planted, like they had a long time ago. She began to look at the flower, noting the 'hairs' on its long stem, its pale roots and the 'veins' in its leaves. 'We've got veins,' said a boy, showing Sue his hands. 'Yes', she replied, then continued examining the sunflower. 'Yours are blue and knobbly', insisted the boy. This comment was ignored. Christine, who had been asked by Sue to observe the activity for the children's profiles, sensed some of the children had lost interest, and were no longer following the examination of the sunflower, but were concerned rather with something small and moving. A caterpillar had crawled from under a curled leaf and was slowly making its way to the edge of the paper. The children's interest in the sunflower immediately evaporated and all eyes focused on the caterpillar.

Sue tried several times to draw the children back to the focus of her careful planning, eventually looking to Christine for support. But Christine joined in with the children's interest, suggesting they made a 'home' of some kind for the caterpillar, and food for it to eat, gently persuading Sue that the sunflowers could be enjoyed another day, and the children could still experiment with thick brushes and thick paint. Sue was reluctant at first and concerned that her intended learning for the children and her planning would need to be fitted in to another period of focused activity or discarded. She was eventually won over by the children's enthusiasm for the new class 'pet', whom they named Vincent 'after the man who painted sunflowers'.

Identifying good practice

Sue has shown elements of good practice in her initial training and the planting activity which had obviously been a continuing source of interest to the children. Her planning also shows she has tried to think about the learning outcomes for these older children who will be leaving the setting at the end of the summer. Her initial examination of the sunflower was interesting – getting the children to estimate its height and involving the children in an enjoyable way. Reminding them of the difficulties they had cutting the flowers down again taps into the children's imagination and interest, with the response about 'Jack and the Beanstalk'. Her introduction of new vocabulary starts well and again stimulates interest in the children, especially the boy who makes the connection between the veins on the leaf and the veins on our hands, which Sue should have explored in more detail. She does not, however, intend to be side-tracked.

Christine's refusal to support Sue in continuing with the sunflower activity also shows good practice. She is indicating to Sue that children's interests need to be listened to. The caterpillar had caught their imagination and interest. The planned activity could take place another time, when the children would be happy to re-engage with it. The resources Sue had prepared would not be wasted, as they could still form part of an activity in its own right.

Leading practice

Christine may empathise with Sue, who, having done the training, was keen to put it to use by planning projects for the newly developed garden area. The sunflowers had been a great success; not only Sue's group but the whole setting had enjoyed the sunflowers. Sue had obviously spent a lot of time and energy in planning the sunflower project, linking it in to the areas of learning and development with projected outcomes for the children, culminating in the activity she had asked Christine to observe in the belief that it would provide useful material with which to assess the children's understanding and learning. So Sue's reluctance to be side-tracked into a different focus was understandable; however, Christine needed to reinforce the need for flexibility, and the importance of letting children's interests influence planning.

After this incident, Christine asked for Sue's help in developing the 'Vincent the caterpillar' project. Sue soon became caught up in planning activities and resources around the life-cycle of the butterfly, as the children watched in fascination its building of a cocoon and its final transformation, not into the anticipated beautiful butterfly from the storybooks they'd listened to and the pictures looked at and searched out with Sue's help on the Internet, but a brown moth. The children were still fascinated as they released 'Spiky' the moth into the garden.

Reflection

- *Do you agree with Christine's decision?*
- *Could she have achieved her intentions in a different way?*
- *Did Christine's lack of support of Sue undermine her role as a Leading Practitioner?*
- *Was it more important for her to illustrate the need to be flexible?*
- *Was Sue at fault in planning and resourcing her project in advance?*
- *Was Sue right to try to challenge these older children, who were due to leave the setting, in the manner she did?*
- *Had her previous experience in a Nursery Class attached to a school predisposed her to view planning in a different way from Christine?*
- *Did the extension of the children's interest in the caterpillar justify Christine's actions?*

Task Try to reflect on the above, as well as other issues you feel this example raises, and where possible discuss these with peers. Consider too, have there been instances when circumstances out of your control have adversely influenced your own planning? How did you deal with them?

How can we use such strategies to promote effective personalised provision based on a clear understanding of child development and possible next steps in children's learning?

Personalised provision leads to effective personalised learning. The EYFS framework describes it thus:

> . . . providers to reflect the rich and personalised experience that many parents give their children at home. Like parents, providers should deliver individualised learning, development and care that enhances the development of the children in their care . . .

(DCSF 2007, p. 9)

In order for the EYP to lead and support practitioners in creating such an 'enabling environment' for every child, thorough understanding of child development needs to be modelled to and expected of practitioners. Only by understanding the norms within a range of behaviours can the practitioner identify the needs of individual children, and become alert to potential deficit and delay. Sheridan (1997) produced norms for children's development that have been widely used and adapted. Criticism of these norms consisted of the fact that they were too prescriptive in stressing age-appropriate levels of behaviour. The EYFS framework in its non-statutory practice guidance provides a more generous overlap between expected behaviours for children from birth to 60 plus months (see Chapter 2), the first 'norm' or age stage beginning at birth to 11 months, followed by the next which starts at 8 to 20 months, and so on. This overlap allows for the range of abilities within any particular age stage. However, the EYP needs to ensure that the sequences that run through these norms are used with caution. Some babies will not crawl before they walk; not all children will process language in the same way, perhaps electing to be mute until they are ready to speak. Nature and nurture will combine and interact to create the *unique child* (also see Bronfenbrenner's work in Chapter 2).

The EYP's responsibility in leading and supporting practice here depends upon their ability to ensure practitioners take all these factors into consideration. Home visits before a child is admitted to the setting, though sometimes expensive in having to provide supply cover, provide essential information about the child. In their home environments, parents often feel more relaxed, freely providing information about particular transitional toys, family language, friendships that have been formed with children already attending the setting. For babies and very young children, it could focus on their likes and dislikes when having nappies changed, their feeding and sleep habits, the way they prefer to be held or rocked. Such information can be gleaned during setting visits, but parents are sometimes ill at ease filling in an information sheet in a more formal situation, with the bustle of the setting around them. The home visit can also help the practitioner understand the child's position within the family, their relationship with other siblings, parenting styles, the family's position within the wider community, any possible fears the parent might already have about their child; in addition, expectations parents/carers might have regarding the setting and 'education' in general can be identified. It can also create a particular bond between the practitioner and child. Seeing this new adult in his/her home environment builds trust and helps the child during the transitional phase from home to setting.

This information, combined with initial careful observations and assessments during the child's settling-in period, can help the practitioner to provide and plan for effective personalised provision for that child. Looking at behaviour according to where it falls within a particular age norm against a particular area of learning and development is only part of the picture when trying to create personalised, holistic provision. What this will show is an individual child's particular learning style, so we can plan basic provision to allow for those children who are more visual or kinaesthetic in the approaches to investigating their environment. Such information will also help the practitioner to understand the schemas in which they are currently engaged, to help them make sense of the world. The amount of time children need to accommodate and assimilate ideas will vary, so the routines of the day should not be inflexible (see Chapter 7). Time should be built in to planning to allow for children to dwell for extended periods of time on a project or activity or to revisit projects/activities the next day. Children's creations need to be valued and their persistence in trying to build a model should be encouraged. They should not rush to finish and their creation should not be discarded at the end of the day during a hasty tidying-up routine (see the section on the Reggio Emilia approach in Chapter 6). If personal provision is carefully tuned, children's levels of well-being and involvement will rise and deep personal learning will occur.

Flexible planning around children's interests, too, should ensure diverse practice to encompass and celebrate the diversity of children's backgrounds and experiences within the setting. The use of sustained shared thinking with children as they create their products will show their understanding of process and give practitioners a clearer view of the next steps in provision needed for the child to progress, which may include revisiting an area of learning and development time and again until they have successfully assimilated and then accommodate the process. Keeping profiles up to date and regularly reviewing with children their own profile again helps to personalise provision through aiding the child to self-assess and see what their next challenge/step might be.

Personalised provision for children who may be giving cause for concern needs to be structured as soon as possible. Again this will have been arrived at by early conversations with parents/carers prior to the child's admission, or during the settling-in period. The child may have come from another setting or been assessed by another agency, and this needs to be taken into consideration when planning provision for the child. The EYP needs to ensure that practitioners are clear about the policies and procedures involved when a child is giving cause for concern, involving **early years action, then early years action plus and finally statementing: http:// www.teachernet.gov.uk/management/atoz/s/senidentificationandassessment/**

If the child already has a statement, the setting needs to ensure the additional financing can provide appropriate ratios of staff and resources to meet the needs of the child with SEN. If the child is giving cause for concern, and is not statemented, for example a child with behavioural issues or language difficulties, the EYP can discuss with the keyworker how to personalise provision to improve the situation for the child, using behaviour strategies that are already in place, in the first instance, or developing a new system of rewards that relate to the child's interests. The use of baby signs, Makaton or Picture Exchange Communication System (PECS) (Callcentre 2008, online) might be introduced for children with slight language delay. If further investigation is needed the EYP can liaise with the SENCo, keyworker and parents to arrive at an Individual Education Plan (IEP) for the child, to provide personalised provision that addresses the child's particular issues, as well as their overall development. IEPs must be reviewed at regular intervals; research suggests that many children will require temporary additional help at some time during their development. This requires staff to be alert and supportive of parents to ensure they understand the necessity for such temporary measures. It is the EYP's role in leading and supporting practice in this area to model good practice and ensure that staff feel comfortable, voicing and being proactive on behalf of a child they have concerns about, so that personalised provision can be adequately established for that child.

Focus on practice

George had been a 'precious' baby in both the medical sense, being delivered prematurely at 28 weeks, and in the emotional sense, as the long-awaited child of older parents. He began in the Toddler Room at the setting, his parents having been loath to let him go, until financial necessity forced them to. George's behaviour had caused some concerns from the beginning. He was not intentionally aggressive to other children or adults as long as they did not attempt to persuade him to join in activities, meal times, or any other routines of the day. His reaction was initially to show frustration, then attempt to run away and hide. 'George ploughs his own furrow', Grace, his keyworker, had said to Janet, the setting Leading Practitioner, during one of their discussions about George, adding: 'Of course, it doesn't help when his parents don't have any routine with him at home.' Janet suggested she and Grace talk to his parents about George's lack of routine. His parents arrived late for the meeting, which meant George was present during their discussion, and it soon became apparent to Janet and Grace that they had little control over George's behaviour. Both parents looked exhausted, due partly to George's lack of sleep routine.

Janet and Grace both offered suggestions for helping ease George into some kind of routine. The parents were grateful and promised to try the methods suggested. Janet also asked if the setting SENCo might observe George, at the same time calming fears that anything more than immaturity and lack of routine were at the root of George's behaviour. George's parents did not manage to encourage him into a routine, and the SENCo, after observing George, agreed with Janet's initial diagnosis that George's behaviour was a product of his immaturity due to his premature birth and lack of routine at home, suggesting they should try to get the parents to cooperate. When George was due to transfer into the 3–5 years room the suggestion was made to his parents that he would benefit from a longer stay in the Toddler room, but his parents were adamant they wanted George to 'go up with his friends'. In the 3 to 5 room, where the planning and focus were on more adult-led activities that challenged children's learning and development, more demands were placed upon George to join in activities and be sociable. This in turn led to more behaviour difficulties. 'He just ignores you', his new keyworker had said to Janet, asking if Janet would observe George to see if his behaviour was simply due to the transition into a new room with new expectations or if any other triggers for George's behaviour could be identified.

Identifying good practice

Janet observed George over a period of days. He had a cold and a cough, which his keyworker described as 'semi-permanent'. Janet noticed that George tended to engage in solitary play, but would on occasion choose to play alongside particular children who were, in the words of one staff member, 'noisy and boisterous', and 'not a particularly good role model for George'. Janet noticed George would sometimes stand very close to a child and peer into their face if he wanted to communicate with them. His language skills were immature for his age, some sounds being entirely absent from his speech, and some children would turn away, but George would gently turn their faces back to him. During one observation, a child playing with musical instruments dropped a cymbal, which stopped most of the children nearby in their tracks. George, however, had his back to the incident and carried on building a tower with plastic blocks. Janet felt George's hearing needed to be investigated and, after speaking with the SENCo, contacted his parents.

Leading practice

After his hearing assessment, George was found to have a severe conductive hearing loss in both his ears, and an operation for grommets to be inserted was arranged. Janet researched information on grommets and knew they were sometimes only partially successful (not like fitting a pair of spectacles). She informed staff and, on George's return, asked his keyworker and other staff in the 3–5 room to note down any differences in his behaviour. 'He keeps putting his hands to his ears', one member of staff noted. But his keyworker recorded, 'he now stops, turns and looks at you when you call his name.' Janet decided to arrange a meeting between herself, George's keyworker, the SENCo and George's parents. He was still operating at a less mature level than his peers. So an Individual Education Plan was agreed for George, with reviews every two months. Initially, there seemed to be no difference in George's behaviour. After four months one of the grommets had worked its way out, and at an IEP meeting with parents they confirmed that they were managing to establish a routine for George, and really felt the staff support was making a difference.

Reflection

- *Did Janet, along with other members of staff, too easily accept that George's behaviour was the result of (a) being premature and (b) being the only child of overprotective parents with a 'permissive' approach to parenting?*

- *Could one of the reasons for George's behaviour, i.e. his conductive hearing loss, have been detected earlier?*

- *Did Janet, his keyworker and the SENCo handle the situation with the parents appropriately?*

Task Discuss the above and any other queries you might have about this situation with your peers/colleagues if possible. Have you been in a similar situation where behaviour issues have been wrongly or inadequately dealt with? As the EYP in this situation, what steps would you have taken?

How can we achieve effective practice in supporting children's emergent language and communication skills through sustained shared thinking and the provision of a language-rich environment?

The EYP, in order to lead and support practice in this area, needs to have a sound knowledge of the possible developmental stages children go through in acquiring language and communication skills (see Chapter 2 and associated reading). Again, as with the use of developmentally appropriate stages, caution must be used. For many children, however, a sequence of development can be evidenced, and the EYP needs to familiarise him/herself with these general stages. Research into the kinds of language we use as practitioners with children can also have an important effect (Bernstein 1976, Tough 1974). From the baby's attempts at early vocalisation to the rapid fire 'why?' question of the older child, children naturally engage in trying to communicate with significant others in their lives. The EYFS practice guidance suggests that effective practice in encouraging children's developments in this area of learning requires **positive relationships** to be built with **people who have meaning for them** (DCSF 2007, p. 39). Without the sense of security and trust such relationships engender, it is suggested that communication and language skills may not fully develop in the young child (see reference to 'Genie' in Chapter 2). It is the EYP's task to lead and support practitioners in creating such warm, trusting, **enabling environments**, through, for example, establishing open and trusting relationships with parents/carers, accepting and using their specialised knowledge of the child's daily routines, the forms of language used by the family that the baby or child responds to best. Where a child comes from a home where the principal language spoken is not English, it can help to request tapes/CDs in the baby's home language. Ensuring the keyworker for a child fully understands the importance and remit of their role is also essential in ensuring that babies and young children entering the setting can experience a warm, supportive, trusting environment.

Within such key relationships, a baby will learn to link sounds and voices to the new routines of their day, for example music being played during nappy changing, as well as the practitioner's calm voice, or a favourite story being read before they fall asleep. In a trusting, caring relationship, children will more readily express feelings, thoughts and ideas. The EYP needs to ensure that planning and organisation incorporate daily opportunities to explore language through rhymes, songs, poetry and stories, and for older children to access fiction and non-fiction materials, and that the language accessed is also reflective of the diverse nature of children's individual personalities and cultures. Books and signs around the setting written in their home language will enable children from diverse backgrounds to feel welcomed as part of the community, creating an environment rich in language for every child. The *Hundred Languages of Children* suggested by the Reggio Emilia (1998) schools implies that children's communication is not limited to the use of speech, but can be seen through dance, music, mark-making, drawing, modelling, painting, expression and body language, to name but a few. Young children learn best when all their senses are engaged.

The EYP needs to lead and support practitioners in promoting this rich language environment, through the use of 'conversations' and early 'proto-conversation' turn-taking with babies and toddlers (see Chapter 2), daily sessions with rhymes, songs sung in diverse languages and repetitive and familiar stories, linking sound to movement as children become more mobile. Song books can be created for parents to use at home to encourage familiarity with rhymes and language, accompanied by pleas for help in compiling story sacks, songs and rhyme bags. As children progress they can be encouraged to 'read' a story to peers, or recreate a familiar story with such visual aids as home-made puppets and props and magnet boards; to listen to and act out story and rhyme tapes, as well as having access to books both fiction and non-fiction, big books, pop-up books, board books and interactive multimedia sources. Musical instruments can be used to emphasise the beat and rhythm of language, tapping out the beats, for example, in a child's name, trying to repeat a pattern played by an adult or peer. Later still comes the introduction of different uses of language for different audiences; the chance, time and encouragement to discuss, argue, share experiences, re-tell narratives in the correct sequence, showing an understanding of language patterns in stories. Children in a rich linguistic environment with access to a range of printed materials will begin to link sounds to letters, using their growing phonic knowledge to write simple words. Any language-rich environment needs print in all its forms, with outings, perhaps, into the local community to look at print in the wider world – the huge neon sign naming a supermarket or the street name of where they live. The EYFS practice guidance devotes more pages to this area of Learning and Development (Communication, Language and Literacy) than any other, giving numerous examples of how effective practice can be achieved.

Alongside this exposure to and experience of language, the EYP has to look at how practitioners use language with children in their daily practice. Both the EPPE and REPEY research studies emphasise the importance of using language in sustained shared thinking with children. As Siraj-Blatchford *et al.* (2002) suggests, this is not always an easy thing to achieve: 'The challenge in enquiry is to interact with the child so as to capture their interest and attention without telling them to stop what they are doing'. The use of certain forms of language by the practitioner is also highlighted, particularly the form and phrasing of questions e.g. the use of open-ended questioning: *I don't know, what do you think? or what would happen if we did . . . ? or what rhymes with. . . . ?* The EYP needs to model and support practitioners in the *art* of open-ended questioning. The EPPE findings (2003) showed that, even in those 'centres of excellence' where very good practice was reported, only approximately 5 per cent of questions used by practitioners were of the open variety. Practitioners need to plan for such shared thinking to happen, but also to seize the spontaneous moment from some child-initiated experience. For the practitioner to be genuinely involved in shared thinking with a child, they need to understand the world from the child's perspective.

 Focus on practice

Zahir's world

Susan, the setting Leading Practitioner, had been monitoring the profiles of the 4 to 5 year olds who would be leaving the setting to go to school after the summer. She had already had a discussion with the keyworker responsible for Zahir, a 4 year old who, against the setting's advice, would be leaving that summer. His keyworker, Josie, explained why his profile which had started so promisingly, with his observations showing a lively and active boy, interested and engaged in a number of areas of development and learning, suddenly seemed to decrease and were almost non-existent for the last few months. Around that time Zahir's mother had become seriously ill, and had been undergoing tests involving short stays in hospital. Zahir's aunt, who usually collected him, spoke very little English, and the dialect she spoke was not well understood by the member of staff who acted as interpreter in these situations. Zahir's father did speak good English, but on the rare occasions he collected Zahir he was in a hurry, reluctant to discuss the situation. Zahir had become reclusive, preferring to be at the design and technology table, building quite intricate, solitary models that he did not want to discuss. In the outdoor area he spent his time making larger models, re-arranging milk crates, tyres, hollow blocks and any other building material to hand. When other children offered to help or showed interest in his building, he would shout at them, often becoming excitable, using his home language. At times when the member of staff was asked to interpret, she would say he did not want anyone near, adding that he was too old to be using his 'mother tongue' in the setting environment, and the family should be helping to teach him English. While not openly defying the adults in the setting, he would only take part in focused activities reluctantly, refusing to communicate, except for the briefest of exchanges with other adults or children. Story time was the only time he seemed to give his full attention, listening intently to the stories, but again refusing to role-play or take part.

Identifying good practice

Susan decided to read the story in Zahir's room one afternoon. She took in a large empty cardboard box, telling the children they needed to listen carefully to the story so they would know what to do with the box afterwards. She read the story 'This is Our House' by Michel Rosen, where a group of children from a block of high-rise flats find a large empty cardboard box. They argue over what it should be – a boat, a plane, a house. In the process of arguing they wreck the box, then decide to work together to rebuild it into 'our house'. Zahir had sat listening intently to the story. As soon as it had finished, he leapt up and said, 'mine', attempting to put his arms around the cardboard box. Several other children began to argue and pull at the box. Susan got their attention by telling them they were behaving just like the children in the story. This cardboard box was now also in need of repair. The children carried it over to the design and technology area and began to repair it, under Zahir's minimal instructions. The children trusted Zahir as he always built interesting models which others tried to copy. Susan began to take some pictures of the process with a digital camera, then remembered the setting had recently acquired a video camera. By this time, the group had decided not only to repair the box but to make it into something under Zahir's direction. When Josie returned, Susan suggested that she video the proceedings, but Josie was unsure how to use the camera; she had been absent for the training due to illness and had not caught up. Susan continued taking digital images, but when she tried to show Zahir what she had taken and engage him in conversation, he looked away and continued with his task. The video camera, however, did catch his attention, along with the rest of the group. After they had been filmed for a while, Susan would stop filming and ask some children to talk to the camera.

'Like on the news', a child suggested. Susan agreed. Afterwards she showed the 'interview' back to them. Zahir had refused to take part until he saw the re-run, then he became animated, trying to explain his vision for the 'skyscraper house' his 'team' were building. In his excitement he slipped into his home language, then corrected himself, answering Susan's questions about windows, doors, lifts and stairs, as she probed how and why they were making a 'skyscraper house'.

Leading practice

Reflecting on the situation Susan notes the following:

- The issues around Zahir's behaviour should have been picked up sooner, not left until he was due to leave the setting.
- This had resulted in a sad little boy developing defensive behaviour. His sense of well-being had been allowed to reach very low levels. He had shown involvement (in model making), but this had almost been a displacement activity to hide from what was really troubling him.
- No real attempt had been made to discuss or talk with members of Zahir's family.
- There were issues that needed addressing around staff in the setting and the use and encouragement of home language.
- There needed to be some system whereby, if staff missed important training through no fault of their own, a way of inducting them should be found.

After discussion with the deputy manager the following course of action was decided:

- As well as the usual observations based on areas of development and learning, scales of well-being would be introduced (see the Leuven Scale in Chapter 4). Susan, who had used these in her last employment, would organise training for the staff.
- Better procedures for talking with and involving parents needed to be established. With only one part-time member of staff able to speak Urdu and Punjabi, the setting was limiting its ability to reach out to the increasingly diverse community it now served. The deputy manager said she would discuss with the manager the possibility of employing another bilingual member of staff who would work both in the setting and as a family support worker.
- Clear guidelines would be drawn up with regard to the use and encouragement of home language, and this would need to be reflected in the wider setting environment.

Task With your colleagues/fellow students consider the following points:

- What actions by Susan can be seen as 'good practice' in the above scenario?
- What other choices were available to her?
- If the manager does not agree to the employment of another bilingual member of staff, how will the setting deal effectively with communicating meaningfully with families from culturally diverse communities?
- Some settings have an increasingly diverse population; for example, a setting we visited last year housed children speaking more than 20 different home languages from Africa, Asia and Eastern Europe. How might a Leading Practitioner develop an inclusive approach towards these children and their families?

Conclusion

What effective strategies can we develop for observing, assessing, planning, recording and reporting children's learning and development?

(S10, S21, S22)

This chapter has emphasised the vital importance for the EYP to ensure the establishment of sound knowledge and understanding by staff of the **planning cycle**; the importance of good practice in the ongoing **formative observation** of children, and the linking of information collected through various kinds of observation to the assessment of each individual child's needs, in order to create personalised learning for the child. **Planning** should therefore allow for, in the **short term**, careful observation by staff of groups of children and the individual child, in order to provide activities and experiences that promote learning for every child on their journey towards achieving the Early Learning Goals (ELGs). Clear, whole school planning needs to be created to inform staff, provide proformas and promote discussion of, for example, resources, school trips, festivals, and the use of both indoor and outdoor spaces. Above all, in line with the play-based emphasis of the new EYFS framework, planning needs to be **flexible** enough to take into account children's individual interests. **Triangulation** of observations obtained by several members of staff, not only the child's keyworker, will provide the necessary **reliability** and **validity**. **Formative assessment** of young children from 0 to 5 years is an essential and statutory requirement of the EYFS framework. Assessment scales that recognise involvement and well-being as well as assessments against the six areas of learning will help to provide a holistic view of the individual child's development. The EYFS Profile can be seen as a **summative** document, detailing the stage the child has reached in relation to the ELGs by the end of the Foundation Stage, which will help with the child's transition to Key Stage One. Knowledge of the ITERS and ECERS scales can also help the practitioner assess and improve the environment and support good practice (see Focus on practice box above). An understanding of the Common Assessment Framework is necessary for practitioners to be able to respond to children about whom they may have concerns. **Recording** of observations and assessments can take many forms; often a setting will design its own proformas to meet its particular circumstances. Again, in the new EYFS, this is a statutory requirement. Examples of proformas for observing, planning and assessment can be accessed on the CD-ROM accompanying the EYFS guidance. **Reporting** children's achievements and development to parents has been and continues to be a statutory requirement (at least once a year). Other agencies, for example local authorities, Ofsted, and certain government departments, also require information such as the data from EYFS profiles for individual settings. Reporting also happens on a daily basis, between members of staff, between staff and parents and, most importantly, between practitioners and children, in order to help each child become self-reflective.

How may we use such strategies to promote effective personalised provision based on a clear understanding of child development and possible next steps in children's learning?

(S13, S14)

Knowledge of child development theories, research and initiatives is essential for **personalised** care and learning to take place. This has to be applied in conjunction with a sound understanding of the personal circumstances of each child. Bronfenbrenner's (1979) theory of the relationships within a family, between a family and settings and the larger world, Baumrind's view of parenting styles (in Oates, Lewis and Lamb 2005), Dunn and Kendrick's (1982) work on sibling relationships, all show the necessity for the practitioner to be knowledgeable about each child's individual circumstances if effective personalised provision is to be established. **Working with parents** and carers to establish effective personalised learning for the child is essential, together with ongoing formative observation and assessment. **Shared thinking** between the practitioner and child helps extend the child's development and learning potential, through the use of open-ended questioning. Allowing time for a child to revisit projects and self-reflect must be built into the routines of the day, if real and effective personalised provision is to be achieved.

How can we achieve effective practice in supporting children's emergent language and communication skills through sustained shared thinking and the provision of a language-rich environment?

(S15, S16)

As this chapter demonstrates, the practitioner needs a sound knowledge of the stages of **language acquisition** (see the Practice Guidance EYFS, DCSF 2008) for children from 0 to 5 years. The need for **positive relationships** to be established during the child's initial **transition** from home to setting is essential, with links to home provided by transitional toys, music or objects to reassure the child. Only in such a supportive and **enabling** environment, will children feel able to express themselves. The practitioner needs to recognise that children from 0 to 5 have *the hundred languages of children* through which to communicate with others, the diversity and variety of which needs to be recognised and celebrated by the practitioner. The provision of a **language-rich** environment, through book corners, story sacks, role play, puppets and regular sessions playing with language through rhymes and songs, are again essential for the development of a child's language. The real acknowledgement of the diversity of languages within a setting, as well as the celebration of that diversity and difference, is important for establishing positive relationships and a confident sense of self in young children. The means to create music, dance and rhythm as ways of expression, both indoors and out, need to be resourced. **Listening** to children and taking their questions seriously, sharing their thinking as they engage in activities and experiences, both self-generated and adult-led, are important in encouraging the development of a language-rich environment.

Further reading

Bee, H. (1997) *The Developing Child*. Harlow: Longman.

Bronfenbrenner, U. (1979) *The Ecology of Human Development: Experiments by Nature and Design*. Cambridge, MA: Harvard University Press.

Bruner, J. (1983) *Child's Talk: Learning to use Language*. New York: Norton.

Cohen, D. (2002) *How the child's mind develops*. London: Routledge.

David, T., Gooch, K., Powell, S. and Abbott, L. (2003) 'Birth to three matters, a review of the literature', available at:
http://www.standards.dfes.gov.uk/eyfs/resources/downloads/rr4444.pdf

Donaldson, M. (1978) *Children's Minds*. London: Fontana.

Lindon, J. (2008) *Understanding Child Development: Linking Theory and Practice*, 2nd edition. London: Hodder Arnold.

Nutbrown, C. (2006) *Threads of Thinking: Young Children Learning and the Role of Early Education*. London: Sage.

Oates, J., Lewis, C. and Lamb, M. (2005) 'Parenting and attachment'. In S. Ding and K. Littleton (eds) *Children's Personal and Social Development*. Oxford: Blackwell.

Piaget, J. and Inhelder, B. (1969) *The psychology of the child*. New York: Basic Books.

Smith, P., Cowie, H. and Blades, M. (2003) *Understanding Children's Development*. Oxford: Blackwell.

Vygotsky, L. (1978) *Mind in Society*. Cambridge, MA: Harvard University Press.

Websites

EPPE: http://www.ioe.ac.uk/schools/ecpe/eppe/

REPEY report: http://www.dcsf.gov.uk/research/data/uploadfiles/RR356.pdf

References

Athey, C. (1990) *Extending thought in Young Children: A Parent-Teacher Partnership*. London: Paul Chapman.

Bernstein, B. (1976) *Class codes and control*. New York: International University Press.

Callcentre (2008) Picture Exchange Communication System. Available at:
http://callcentre.education.ed.ac.uk/SCN/Level_A_SCA/Using_Symbols_SCB/Hot_PECS_News_HTA/hot_pecs_news_hta.html Accessed on 18 February 2009.

Cryer, D. (1999) 'Defining and Assessing Early Childhood Program Quality'. *The Annuals of the American Academy of Political and Social Science*, 563.

DCSF (2008) *Early Years Foundation Stage Practice Guidance*. Nottingham: DfES Publications.

DCSF (2007) *Statutory Guidance in the Early Years Foundation Stage*. Nottingham: DfES Publications.

DCSF (2007) *Early Years Foundation Stage Profile*. Nottingham: DfES Publications.

DfES (2006) *Common Assessment Framework*. Nottingham: DfES Publications.

DfES (2003) *Foundation Stage Profile*. Nottingham: DfES Publications.

DfES (2000) *Curriculum Guidance for the Foundation Stage*. Nottingham: DfES Publications.

Dunn, J. and Kendrick, C. (1982) *Siblings: Love, envy and understanding.* Cambridge, MA: Harvard University Press.

Easen, P. (1992) 'Parents and Educators: Dialogue and Development through Partnership', *Children and Society,* 21(5), pp. 376–89.

Edwards, C.P., Gandini, L. and Forman, G. (1998) *The Hundred Languages of Children: the Reggio Emilia approach – advanced reflections.* New York: Alex Publishing Co.

Harms, T., Cryer, D. and Clifford, R.M. (2006) *Infant/Toddler Environment Rating Scale,* Revised Edition Manual. New York, NY: Teachers College Press.

Hutt, S.J., Tyler, S., Hutt, C. and Christopherson, H. (1989) *Play, Exploration and Learning: a natural history of the pre-school.* London: Routledge.

Laevers, F. (2005) The Curriculum as Means to raise the Quality of ECE. Implications for Policy. *European Early Childhood Education Research Journal,* 13(1), pp. 17-30.

Laevers, F. (1997) 'Forward to Basics! Deep-level-learning and the Experiential Approach', *Early Childhood Research Quarterly,* 12(2), pp. 117-43.

Laevers, F. (1994) *The Leuven Involvement Scale for Young children.* Leuven, Belgium: Centre for Experiential Education.

Pascal, C. and Bertram, A.D. (1997) *Effective Early Learning: Case Studies of Improvement.* London: Hodder and Stoughton.

Piaget, J. (1951) *Psychology of Intelligence.* London: Routledge and Kegan Paul.

Rosen, M. (1996) *This is Our House.* London: Walker Books.

Sheridan, M.D. (1997) *From Birth to Five Years.* London: Routledge.

Siraj-Blatchford, I., Sylva, K., Muttock, S., Gilden, R. and Bell, D. (2002) *Researching Effective Pedagogy in the Early Years.* RB 356. London: DfES Publications.

Sylva, K., Melhuish, E., Sammons, P., Siraj-Blatchford, I., Taggart, B. and Elliot, K. (2003) *The Effective Provision of Pre-School Education (EPPE) Project: findings from the pre-school period.* London: Institute of Education.

Sylva, K., Siraj-Blatchford, I. and Taggart, B. (2003) *Assessing Quality in the Early Years Early Childhood Environment Rating Scale.* Stoke-on-Trent: Trantham Books.

Tough, J. (1974) *Children's use of language.* Education Review, 26(3), pp. 166–79.

6

Promoting emotional security and positive behaviour

Wendy Holland

Chapter overview

The standards addressed in this chapter are:

S07 Have high expectations of all children and commitment to ensuring that they achieve their full potential

S17 Promote positive behaviour, self-control and independence through using effective behaviour management strategies and developing children's social, emotional and behavioural skills

S23 Identify and support children whose progress, development or well-being is affected by changes or difficulties in their personal circumstances and know when to refer them to colleagues for specialist support

S25 Establish fair, respectful, trusting, supportive and constructive relationships with children

S26 Communicate sensitively and effectively with children from birth to the end of the foundation stage

S27 Listen to children, pay attention to what they say and value and respect their views

S28 Demonstrate the positive values and attitudes and behaviour they expect from children

Relating to the above standards, the following key questions will be addressed:

● What effective strategies can we develop that reflect our high expectations of all children and our commitment to ensuring each child achieves his/her full potential? How do we create fair, respectful and supportive relationships while achieving such effective practice?

(S07, S25)

● What effective behaviour management strategies can we create to support the development of children's social, emotional and behavioural skills? How do we effectively demonstrate the positive values, attitudes and behaviour we expect from children in practice?

(S17, S28)

- What constitutes effective practice in the identification and support of children whose development, progress or well-being is affected by changes or difficulties in their personal circumstances? What strategies do we need to establish and implement to ensure that, where necessary, appropriate specialist support is provided?

(S23)

- How can we develop practice to ensure effective and sensitive communication with children through listening to and respecting the views of children from birth to the end of the foundation stage is achieved?

(S26, S27)

Providing for John's individual needs

John had attended the children's centre since he was 2. Now at 3 years of age he was about to move into the attached nursery for 3 to 5 year olds. It was essentially the same building his elder brother and sister had attended several years before when it had been an LEA nursery school. John's brother and sister had been seen by both parents and nursery staff as exceptionally able children, the label 'gifted' having sometimes been applied to them, especially in relation to their early reading and number skills. As his parents had been vocal about their two older children's achievements and 'gifts', they were equally open and forthright about their disappointment in John's apparent lack of literacy and numeracy skills. The Centre had found John to be a quiet child, 'almost reclusive', one member of staff had said, given to sudden short outbursts of 'difficult' behaviour. On looking through the new entrants' profiles, Angela, the centre's EYP, felt that John was making age/stage appropriate progress in most of the six areas of learning. What did concern her, however, were his keyworker's comments regarding his reclusive nature, punctuated by sudden acts of aggression towards either staff or children. Often he would soil himself after such an episode, which nearly always seemed to occur at the end of the day. The soiling was seen by his parents as a particularly 'backward' step, even after Angela tried to explain that transitions sometimes had this effect on a child and they should be patient. John's parents got into the habit of expecting to talk at some length on a daily basis to his keyworker or, failing that, another member of staff about their son's progress, often making comparisons, within John's hearing, between him and his elder siblings. When his keyworker discussed this with Angela, she suggested the keyworker made more regular close observations of John. These highlighted his interest in dinosaurs and model making, as well as his skills on the computer and on the outdoor apparatus. He particularly liked to find original ways to negotiate the obstacle courses and spent time setting up complicated 'dens' from twigs and other materials at hand. However, John's parents were not responsive to his keyworker's reports of such positive activities; what they wanted to see was some clear evidence of writing or mathematical skills.

In discussion with John's keyworker, Angela subsequently suggested an approach similar to one she had seen developed at Pen Green Children's Centre, where children were filmed engaging in play-based activities, and this material was then used in discussions with parents/carers to provide insight into children's learning through play. She suggested they should include film of John building one of his special dens, which could then be used to inform parents during the twilight sessions that had been arranged for looking at the new EYFS framework. John's parents were regular visitors at the twilight sessions, and after watching the evidence (especially their own son being quite articulate about something that really interested him) their views began to change. This resulted in more praise and celebration of the activities their young son engaged in and, while still remaining proud of their older offspring, they began to accept and enjoy John's uniqueness. Slowly, this had a positive impact on John's behaviour and his aggressive outbursts gradually began to lessen.

Introduction

As can be seen from the above scenario, the standards to be focused upon in this chapter are those that particularly identify the role of the practitioner in having high expectations of all children, both in their behaviour and in each child's ability to achieve their full potential. The practitioner's role in developing children's social and emotional competency will be examined, through their use of effective strategies which promote positive behaviour, self-control and independence. In helping children to develop to their fullest potential, focus will also be placed on the practitioner's role in identifying and supporting children whose progress, development and well-being are affected by changes or difficulties in their personal circumstances. The remit of the practitioner's role in the referral process for children who may need specialist support will also be discussed.

The positive values, attitudes and behaviour this particular group of standards reinforce will only be achieved effectively through the establishment of trusting, positive relationships with children. How such fair, respectful and constructively supportive relationships can be developed will be examined. In particular, the practitioner's role in communicating sensitively and effectively, through careful listening to children and valuing their ideas and contributions, will be investigated. This chapter will, as in previous ones, signpost relevant research findings which underpin effective practice for the particular standards being addressed, as well as providing examples from practice which exemplify the characteristics of effective leadership. The Further reading list suggests texts that will provide a more detailed approach to some of the key issues discussed here.

What effective strategies can we develop that reflect our high expectation of all children and our commitment to ensuring each child achieves his/her full potential? How do we create fair, respectful and supportive relationships while achieving such effective practice?

For the practitioner to address these questions we need to look at the following:

- Sound knowledge of the emergent principles, theories and research underpinning child development (also see Chapter 2)
- Secure knowledge of the individual child through home visits, meetings with parents and carers
- Observations, assessments and the planning of personalised provision (also see Chapter 5)
- Good inclusive provision which challenges stereotypes that may inhibit development, whether from parents, practitioners, other agencies or children themselves (also see Chapter 4)
- Establishment of positive relationships which take into account children's levels of well-being and involvement, as well as practitioners' levels of engagement and support
- How we in the UK can learn from the best practice embedded in international approaches to early childhood care and education that support and challenge the child's development and learning (also see Chapter 3).

In order to develop effective strategies that reflect our high expectations of children, it is essential we understand each individual child. As stated in previous chapters, the practitioner needs a sound knowledge and understanding of child development in all areas – cognitively, linguistically, emotionally, socially and physically. With such knowledge, the practitioner needs to be able, through observation, to identify individual stages of development, in order to provide appropriate challenges for the child. Sound knowledge of the child's **prior learning and experiences** has to be in place, before reasonable, achievable and challenging expectations can be created. The gaining of such knowledge takes energy and commitment. The detail needed is not found in a single proforma that a parent or carer might have hastily or anxiously filled in when the child first attends a setting, or a brief observation of the child during the initial settling-in period. In order for the information to be detailed and meaningful, a holistic review of the child's experiences needs to be undertaken.

Ideally, this would begin with a home visit prior to the child's attending the setting. A wealth of information can be gained from such a visit:

- How the child relates to the significant others in his/her home environment
- How he/she communicates with parents/carers, younger or older siblings
- The quality of such relationships: are they warm, affectionate, supportive?

- What kind of behaviour strategies does the parent/carer use?
- What kinds of parenting style(s) does this suggest and how can we provide support and balance of experience for the child?

Parents may feel more at ease in their home environment, better able to tell you about the child's particular likes and dislikes, or the important routines of their day. They may discuss, too, any possible concerns they might have, which they have not really voiced yet to anyone 'official'. The practitioner is not there to judge, but to gain a picture. As the EPPE study (2003) has shown, it is what parents **do** to support their children's development and learning and how they do it that is important, more important than other influences such as the parent's occupation, education or income. Within the security of the home, rather than the strangeness of a new setting, the practitioner, hopefully, will be able to create the beginnings of a positive relationship with the child that will transfer when that child eventually arrives at the setting. Leaving a toy, game or book or the child to enjoy and bring with them, during their settling-in period, is one way of creating what needs to be a trusting, warm and respectful relationship.

It is not only the child who needs to feel comfortable enough to engage, but the parent too. As Every Child Matters states:

> The bond between the child and their parents is the most critical influence on a child's life. Parenting has a strong impact on a child's educational development, behaviour and health.
>
> (DfES 2003, p. 39)

There may be barriers, spoken or unsaid, that make the particular relationship between practitioner and parent/carer more problematic. The parent/carer might, as a child, have undergone difficult experiences within their family and/or the education system. In the case of very young children, the parent might be afraid, consciously or subconsciously, of their role being usurped, for example because the practitioner witnesses the child's 'milestones' first. Good, open and honest rapport needs to be established from the very beginning so that such sensitive issues can be explored. Essential is a real recognition too, by the practitioner, that the parent/carer is the child's first and enduring educator, whose intimate knowledge of the child will, if shared, provide the practitioner with the kind of detailed knowledge and understanding to be able to create an exciting, engaging environment that reflects the child's interests, while stimulating and challenging them within the areas of learning and development.

The cultural diversity of families needs to be acknowledged and celebrated. Questions about the use of home language and English, for example, might need to be raised. A review of research on bilingualism (Siraj-Blatchford and Clarke 2000, p. 30) suggests numerous advantages to being exposed to more than one language from birth. Whitehead (1996) is quite clear the research findings suggest that language mixing in the early years is not an indicator of 'muddle and inadequacy', but rather that children are making choices in how to express their feelings. She further suggests that,

It is absolutely essential that early years carers and educators respect the languages of the young children for whom they are responsible. This must go deeper than vague goodwill or tolerance.

(Whitehead 1996, p. 21)

If a home visit is not possible, for example because of insufficient staff to provide cover, or the visit is not wanted by the parent/carer for any number of reasons, the practitioner needs to ensure that they take time to talk with those parents/carers when the opportunity arises to gain a fuller picture of the child's prior knowledge, experience and interests than the usual admissions documentation generally provides.

A strength of good inclusive practice is that it challenges stereotypes and misconceptions of all kinds. This includes the possibly lower expectations that parents/carers, practitioners and children themselves may have about what is possible or achievable. A new parent might perhaps be finding it hard to adjust to their child's attending the setting and is being overprotective. This may well be preventing the child from settling in and taking full advantage of all the setting offers. It is the practitioner's task to explain this sensitively to the parent. It may be that an inexperienced practitioner is 'taking over' children's activities, thinking they are helping children who are 'struggling', when what they are really engaged in is the celebration of their own artistic talents! Again it is the Lead Practitioner's duty to model and explain good practice, while not dampening enthusiasm. In the case of children about whom there are concerns, or who have already been statemented, the Lead Practitioner needs to ensure that all parties involved communicate. The setting's **Special Educational Needs Coordinator (SENCo)**, the child's parents/carers and any other relevant agencies, when discussing and creating the child's **Individual Education Plan (IEP)**, need to ensure that expectations of the child are realistic and achievable. Such a plan will need to be revisited on a regular basis to assess the child's learning and development and ensure progress is built into expectations.

In attempting to raise expectations for each and every child, the practitioner should not accept stereotypical thinking, regardless of where it originates, but look at each child with knowledge and understanding of their capabilities, interests and particular learning styles and plan to promote and encourage whatever next steps are relevant and appropriate. The EYP needs to lead and support practice in this area by demonstrating through their own planning and assessment how differentiated progression is possible and, indeed, necessary for each child.

We need to keep in mind the **personalised learning needs** of the child when considering how to develop and challenge their learning (see EYFS CD-ROM Learning and Development section for age-staged progression across the six areas of learning towards the **Early Learning Goals**).

- The observation, assessment and planning cycle (see Chapter 5) is essential to maintain in order for the practitioner to be informed of children's individual interests and needs as they change and develop.
- Triangulation of team observations, through discussion at daily planning meetings, guides the planning of appropriate and challenging adult-led, child-led

and adult-extended activities, within rich, supportive and well-resourced continuous provision (see summaries of EPPE and REPEY findings, Chapter 5).

- Careful observation also identifies not only developmental stages but the levels of an individual child's self-esteem and involvement (see Chapter 4, the Leuven scales of well-being and involvement).

- Observation of staff levels of sensitivity and engagement (see EELS research scales of staff engagement in Chapter 4) also provides material for reflection on practice. It is the Lead Practitioner's duty to ensure all members of staff are aware of the need to promote a consistent and committed whole setting approach to principles, policies and practice.

The EYP also needs to be knowledgeable about best practice within international approaches to early years care and education, in order to enrich practice within the UK by reflection on their own principles and practice. The Reggio Emilia pre-schools in northern Italy promote the picture of the child as 'rich' in imagination and abilities, a curious and determined investigator and researcher of the world around them, whose questions are taken seriously.

Focus on policy and practice

The Reggio Emilia approach

The Reggio Emilia approach was initially created in the mid-20th century in a political context in which it was conceived as a reaction against fascism. Louis Malaguzzi, its creator, left the state school system to become involved in community initiatives in Reggio Emilia, a region of Northern Italy. The approach was pluralistic, involving children, parents, teachers, administrators and politicians. It took its influences from social constructivism (e.g. Vygotsky 1978), and aimed to develop children's knowledge through a collaborative partnership. Its opposition to standardisation, outcomes, targets and focus upon economic productivity means that the approach is often difficult to integrate into current Western curricula – a point that should make us consider where our own pedagogic practices have been heading over the late 20th century and first decade of the 21st century.

The child is viewed as rich in potential, strong, powerful and competent and able to develop their own theories about the world and how it works – a self-confident explorer/investigator with a sense of curiosity and the freedom of spirit to venture beyond the known/given. S/he is believed to have the capacity to explore such ideas in collaboration with other children and adults, using a 'hundred' languages with which to express themselves, including sign, art, dance etc., all of which are equally valued. Great emphasis is placed on adults and children learning together, valuing each others' opinions, viewpoints and interpretations. The welfare of young children is seen as the collective responsibility of the community, creating feelings of 'ownership' among all involved.

Children are encouraged to be aware of the present, build on the past and look to the future, and priority is given to setting aside the necessary time for children and adults to discuss and debate and reflect. Revision and reflection are considered central to children's learning, therefore projects unfold at the child's own pace. Children are encouraged and expected to concentrate for long periods of time from a very young age, while caring adults spend much time documenting, interpreting and sharing information with colleagues and parents. There is no set curriculum; both children and adults are viewed as researchers, and adults give great respect to children's theories and hypotheses, allowing children to make mistakes. It is common to find an artist in residence in Reggio Emilia settings, working with the children to express their ideas in art and craft forms.

Practitioners are expected to try to understand children's learning processes rather than acquire skills and knowledge that they will then expect to 'transmit' to children in turn; the practice of teaching is not seen as being about how to transmit information, but about developing understanding of how children learn. They are encouraged to meet and talk with people working outside the boundaries of education – for example, scientists, musicians, writers, architects – and both to take ideas from such professionals back into the setting and to invite those who are willing to visit and share their knowledge with the children. Reggio Emilia practice is distinguished by its rejection of hierarchical staff structure, externally imposed policies, manuals and curriculum guidelines.

The Reggio Emilia learning environment is designed to give space and light, with white walls, mirrors, three-dimensional pyramids and light tables. Above all, within the social constructivist model of learning, the environment must be flexible. The dining room is at the heart of the school, with the kitchen area visible at all times, underlining the importance given to preparing and sharing food. The furniture is multi-functional and open to modification, so that the children shape the room, and in turn the room shapes them (Rinaldi in Cadwell 2003). There is always an *atelier* (art studio or area) and a creative and discovery area available, containing a range of materials that are not for 'set' or restricted activities but intended to lead to investigation.

Identifying good practice

In the Reggio paradigm, practitioners are seen as *facilitators* and *researchers* who help children make sense of the world. A question like: '*Where does the water come from*' (perhaps asked by a young child seeing water pouring from a tap) might lead to the child's being challenged to find out. Donning hard hats, young children between 3 and 6 years, accompanied by practitioners/facilitators, might begin a field trip to investigate the setting's plumbing system and develop a project around the properties of water. The Reggio Emilia pre-school approach sees the environment as a *third teacher,* where the environment is carefully planned and resourced to encourage light and space and challenges the children to use it imaginatively and autonomously, with free-flow movement both indoors and out. If we are to have high expectations of children and their achievements, we need to provide similar environments rich in resources and potential.

Leading practice

- What value is placed on children's theories/ideas in your setting?
- How are different learning styles accommodated?
- How do children use their many 'languages of expression'?

Task Consider these questions with your colleagues and peers, and, on the basis of your answers, consider how you could improve practice in your setting, particularly so that children are given more uninterrupted time, allowing them to leave unfinished investigations, knowing that they can return to them later, and that not all will be tidied away at 'tidy-up time', and then deemed 'finished'.

Reflection *What problems might a Reggio approach create within a regime that runs on the statutory guidelines of the EYFS?*

Task Consider this point with your colleagues and peers, and how you might come to a satisfactory conclusion in terms of developing good practice, while maintaining the statutory requirements (Note: This may not be an easy prospect!).

 Focus on practice

Peter's progress

Peter was a summer born child. When he was just 3 years old, he attended a local nursery as his mother, a single parent, was new to the area and had found part-time work. She was anxious for Peter to take advantage of his full afternoon entitlement as soon as possible, and appeared reluctant to adhere to the setting's settling-in policy of a gradual introduction for new children. Parents were encouraged to stay until their child was settled for the first couple of weeks, and return to collect their child a little earlier each afternoon, until it was felt by practitioner and parent that the child was ready to separate for the whole afternoon session. So it was with reluctance that the setting agreed to shorten Peter's settling-in period.

To the practitioners, Peter presented as a particularly immature child, who appeared to need to investigate new experiences orally (Freud 1965). When engaged in using PVA glue for the first time, he discarded the spatula, dipping his fingers into the glue pot and proceeding to eat the glue and anoint his face with it. The same process happened with play dough, sand, cornflour 'gloop', virtually every new substance Peter experienced. He spoke very little at first, pointing or nodding his requirements, showing his displeasure by sitting down and refusing to move, hitting out and occasionally trying to bite other children and adults. This latter behaviour would occur if he did not manage to have first choice of the 'trikes' outside. If left to his own devices, he would happily ride silently round and round all afternoon. He was particularly restless at the end-of-session story time, so much so that practitioners had to ask his mother to revert to collecting him earlier, until he was happy to concentrate for slightly longer periods. She was distressed by this, informing staff that she was putting Peter into nearby daycare after his nursery session had finished, because of the demands of her job, and was not sure if this new setting could accommodate the earlier finishing time. So nursery staff persevered with Peter's distracting behaviour at the end of the day.

Over time, the slow level of progress in Peter's behaviour and communication skills began to concern some staff, but it was difficult to arrange time with his mother, who now had a full-time job, and had arranged for Peter to attend daycare before and after his time at nursery. Notes sent with the daycare staff at the end of a session were rarely replied to, and when meetings were arranged his mother often did not turn up. At staff meetings, when Peter's development was discussed, the view was often expressed that his immaturity was due to his young age and the number of changes he had had to surmount in a relatively short time. The fact that he preferred to spend his time outdoors engaged in physical activities was regarded as normal 'boyish' behaviour.

Identifying good practice

Helen, a newly appointed EYP, took particular interest in the young boys who were in their final term at the nursery. There appeared to be a staff culture that supported leaving the boys to their 'boisterous' outdoor play — a view underpinned by the belief that this was necessary, given the formal provision that awaited them in the reception class of the neighbouring primary school. Helen, who was familiar with the contemporary debates around boys' underachievement, having recently read the Primary National Strategy guidance for Early Years practitioners on supporting boy's achievements (DfES 2007), decided to look in detail at the profiles of all the boys who would be going through the transition to the mainstream school's reception class at the end of the semester. Peter's profile was of particular interest to her. Towards the end of Peter's final semester at the nursery, Helen managed, where staff had been previously unsuccessful, to arrange a meeting with Peter's mother, by being flexible and staying behind one afternoon. At the meeting, she tried to suggest that Peter should delay attending the neighbouring primary school in September, when he would be almost a year younger than most of the children in his reception class, explaining that his young age and personality were better suited to another term at nursery. His mother replied that this was the first she had heard of it, as none of the other staff had mentioned the possibility of Peter staying 'back', and, anyhow, she felt Peter was 'ready' for the 'proper work' experience the mainstream reception class would provide.

Leading practice

Having looked at all the boys' profiles, Helen noted they related to the six areas of learning mainly through lots of photographs of the children engaged at the sand and water trays, creating models with recycled materials, enjoying outdoor activities, or using construction both large and small within the setting. Some profiles contained examples of emergent writing and painting, or artwork done on the computer accompanied by scribing from setting staff to explain the process the children had been engaged in. A few examples of the boys' attempts at number recognition had also been recorded. The contents of Peter's profile were particularly sparse. What Helen noted was the circular schema that seemed evident when looking at the few examples of his paintings and emergent writing and his physical play. Helen decided that, in order to encourage the leavers to engage effectively in the development of their emergent writing skills, the outdoor provision needed to reflect more what was available to children inside the setting. Initially, she would put out large sheets of paper, either anchored on the ground or fixed to a wall, informing staff that these 'graffiti zones' would hopefully encourage the boys to mark-make outside. She also encouraged staff to set up and engage in role-play situations outside where emergent writing was needed (a ticket office for the train, receipts for petrol at the petrol station and menus for the alfresco coffee shop/café). Although Peter did access these new resources and activities, his input was limited, until the week Helen planned *looking for mini-beasts* as an ongoing outdoor activity. With the use of magnifying glasses and collection boxes, the children went on mini-beast hunts and Peter found a ladybird, or rather a ladybird found Peter. Helen watched as this boisterous boy stood perfectly still, arm extended, as the tiny creature slowly crawled up his arm, on to one hand, then the other and finally into the collection box another child held at the ready. Peter took his find into the classroom, lying full length in the carpet area, watching the creature inside the Perspex box. Staff commented it was the quietest and the most calm they had ever seen him. Later that day, he began painting the circular shapes staff had got used to seeing him produce. This time, however, there were circles within circles and curly lines spiralling around the circles. Helen was called in by a member of staff who proudly showed her Peter's creation and the adult scribing alongside it describing the 'ladybird' Peter had painted. He began a small production line in the days that followed, producing painting after painting, until his mother, on one of her rare visits to collect him, suggested he painted something else, looking for support from Claire, the new young member of staff handing her yet another of Peter's ladybird paintings. Claire, trying to be supportive to a parent she had been told was rather 'difficult', agreed it was perhaps time Peter tried to draw something else. Helen, on hearing of the incident, decided to approach the manager of the nursery about delivering some staff training. A number of areas of development concerned her:

- The limited use made of the children's profiles to guide planning for both individual and whole group development.
- The laissez-faire approach to boys' development and learning, particularly their inability to persist with difficulty, their fine motor skills and emergent writing. Taking good practice from the EYFS guidance, she hoped to introduce to staff the idea of 'learning diaries'.
- The need to revisit work on understanding and supporting children's individual schemas.
- The need to have a more equal and sustained approach to partnership with parents, to ensure that those parents who were hard to reach due to work or other

commitments were not discriminated against when it came to discussing their child's interests and developmental needs.

Reflection

- *Is Helen right to challenge the staff perspective on boys' 'boisterous' outdoor play being necessary in this situation? How might the staff react to yet more 'paper work'? Is she going too far too fast?*

- *Was she being unreasonable in her expectation of staff to accommodate 'hard to reach' parents with more flexibility? How might this have affected the relationship between Peter's mother and the setting?*

- *Discuss with other members of your cohort what changes Helen might make to staff use of children's profiles in planning.*

Task Discuss the above and any other queries/questions you feel this scenario raises with peers/colleagues where possible.

What effective behaviour management strategies can we create to support the development of children's social, emotional and behavioural skills? How can we effectively promote the positive values, attitudes and behaviour we expect from children in practice?

(S17, S28)

Standards 17 and 28 focus on the behaviours of both adult and child and also the behaviour management strategies used by both adult and child to develop and promote positive behaviour. The potential EYP must demonstrate the ability to:

- Consistently apply a behaviour policy that has clear boundaries and concise rules, on a daily basis, and one that sets reasonable, age-appropriate expectations of children's behaviour.

- Promote children's self-control and independence and demonstrate they can plan for opportunities to develop children's social and emotional skills.

- Give children opportunities to be responsible, make decisions, errors and choices, while continuing to feel secure.

- Help children to develop skills of negotiation in solving problems with other children and model such skills appropriately.

- Set a tone of high expectation of individual behaviour by being assertive and challenging unacceptable behaviour, making it clear to the child that it is the behaviour that is being focused upon and not the child him/herself.

- Support children who attempt to talk through conflicts and seek resolutions that are fair and equitable.

In showing leadership and support of others, the EYP needs to:

- Demonstrate the importance of positive values and attitudes, by actively promoting and modelling strategies to encourage appropriate behaviour in both staff and children.
- Reinforce the need for consistency in creating boundaries, and applying rules with both colleagues and parents/carers.
- Show the ability to be able to preempt potential behaviour problems through effective management of the physical environment, experiences, activities and resources, including sensitive scheduling of daily routines.
- Demonstrate through their own professional behaviour the importance of punctuality, time-management and reliability, as well as skills in listening, empathy and respecting differing views.
- Recognise the importance of working in partnership with parents/carers, and with appropriate professionals from other agencies, in order to help children with particular behavioural difficulties to fully access the provision.

Before we look in detail at the above desired requirements, we need to consider the wider picture of child development (see Chapter 2). As has been reiterated previously, it is only through a sound understanding of child development that successful practice can be achieved. This is certainly the case when looking at behaviour management strategies.

For babies and infants the practitioner needs to have a clear understanding of what is appropriate and age/stage related behaviour, in order to create effective behaviour strategies. The practitioner needs to pay attention not only to the child's cognitive, linguistic and physical development but also to their *emotional competency* (Denham 1998). It is through the development of the child's emotional competency that empathy for others, self-control, perseverance, social awareness and sensitivity can be encouraged (Goleman 1995). Research suggests (Dunn 1993, Barnes 2001, Smith, Cowie and Blades 2003) that children by the age of 2 years have developed 'person permanence' as well as the basic emotions. Between 4 and 5 years personal emotional styles become established and from 3 years the development of social emotions, for example the ability to empathise, has begun (Harris 1989). Research also suggests (Barnes 2001, Dunn 1993) that where parents/carers talked to their infants and young children about their feelings, children were more likely to talk about their own and others' feelings from 2 years of age.

Another important aspect related to emotional competency is the theory of mind, the beginnings of a child's ability to understand that other people have 'minds' feelings and an internal self (see Chapter 2). For the child this means tuning in to the fact that others will have desires, needs or feelings that may be different from their own. Along with this growing appreciation of themselves and 'others' as distinct and different, children placed in regular social situations outside the family environment need to develop the skills to organise and/or control their own emotions and behaviour to facilitate their interactions with peers.

Maccoby (1980) describes the basically impulsive nature of young children's behaviour and their limited ability to sustain attention. The average attention spans in physical play she identified as:

- 30 seconds at 2 years
- 42 seconds at 2½ years
- 55 seconds at 3 years.

Control and organisation of young children's impulsive behaviour needs careful handling and the understanding, for example, that a 2 year old, experiencing the emotional 'storms' that are frequent at this age, needs to be soothed and calmed before they can re-engage with others in the world around them. The 'coping strategies' that children themselves develop in order to control and organise their behaviour are not simply maturational, but influenced by their social environments in both negative and positive ways. Practitioners, for example, need to be aware and wary of any cultural or social stereotyping that may happen in a setting, either between children, staff or parents/carers. Research has shown that children as young as 2 and 3 years develop an understanding of and reactions to skin tone and gender which can result in cultural/racial stereotyping or, for example, gender stereotyping of types of play or toys or behaviour. Any and all of the above can have a definite and sometimes lasting effect on children's self-identity and consequently their behaviour and emotional competence, as well as their cognitive growth and development, as discussed in the previous chapters (Laevers 1994).

The practitioner's ability to respond positively to children's behaviour requires the ability to openly and honestly self-reflect. Webster-Stratton (2000) argues that practitioners need to be able to distinguish between their own feelings and thoughts, as well as be aware of their negative and positive thoughts in any conflict situation. The ability, after such reflection, to find ways to manage their own emotions and responses will make them more effective practitioners in meeting the children's needs.

What does knowledge and understanding of the above mean for the practitioner? Perhaps we should now return to the Standards for S17 and S28 at the beginning of the section on behaviour and apply what the above theory and research together with further initiatives suggests to the creation of effective practice.

The EPPE report (2003), in looking at 'excellent' settings, found they had adopted discipline/behaviour policies where staff supported children in rationalising and talking through their conflicts, using a 'problem solving' approach, supported by a strong behaviour management policy which all staff understood and to which they all adhered. In the less effective settings it was found that there was often no clear response to children's misbehaviour and/or conflicts and, on many occasions, children were told to stop or distracted.

One of the recommendations of Ofsted (2005) in a report on managing challenging behaviour was to underline the need for consistency among staff in the way expectations of behaviour are set and maintained.

An extract printed in the EYFS Primary National Strategy document on developing positive relationships by Julian Grenier, the head of Kate Greenaway Nursery

School (http://www.kategreenaway.ik.org/), proposes the need for 'consistency and a whole-staff approach . . . as a team we need to ensure that we are being fair and consistent' (2008, online).

In terms of leading and supporting practice, then, the potential EYP needs to ensure there is a whole-team consistency in implementing behaviour policies/strategies for effective practice to occur. This, of course, requires discussion, a feeling of ownership on the part of staff, and agreement with the philosophies on children's behaviour that underpin the policies created. It requires, too, support for an individual practitioner by other members of the team. Again, as Grenier (2008, online) suggests, 'nothing undermines a staff member more than when their careful work with a child is dismissed as "fussing" or "spoiling."'

The relevance and age appropriateness of behaviour policies/strategies is also key when considering good effective practice. Thinking back to the research on emotional competency, to ask a 2 year old to 'say sorry' will not mean much to the child, who may not even be able to understand the words, when a hug might be much more effective. 'Why did you do that?', when aimed at a child too young to be able to articulate reasons for their actions, is inappropriate, especially as on occasion their inability to reply is seen as stubbornness and seen as further evidence of misbehaviour! Age appropriateness needs to be built into every successful behaviour policy, especially as within many early years settings practitioners are dealing with the full age range from birth to five years. The EYFS in its Learning and Development section gives guidance on what to look for in terms of age/stage appropriate behaviours and the good practice that supports children's behaviour and self-control.

Assessing children's emotional competency and therefore their ability to understand and comply with the setting's behaviour policies can be achieved through observations in the same way information on cognitive development is gathered (see Chapter 4). Again the EYFS guidance gives suggestions of what to look for and notes that are age/stage related. In this way, individual behaviours can be more accurately understood and steps to help the child progress developed. The practitioner needs to provide experiences that help young children understand how adults and other children are feeling, and also experiences/activities that challenge the child's own interpretation of events and explanations of other perspectives. The Primary National Strategy's programme, *Excellence and Enjoyment: social and emotional aspects of learning* (see http://www.standards.dfes.gov.uk/primary/publications/banda/seal/), is comprehensive and linked to early years practice, providing the practitioner with numerous examples of good practice in encouraging young children to build positive relationships, feel good about themselves and others, and talk about their thoughts and feelings.

Helping children to resolve conflict by rationalising and talking through their feelings, as the EPPE research (2003) suggests, fosters children's ability to identify what they and others are feeling, and so realise the impact of their actions on others, helps them find solutions to problems, and builds self-esteem. The High/Scope (2003) approach, which some Early Years settings in the UK have adopted, similarly emphasises this need for children to reflect on their own behaviour, not through isolating the child, but by encouraging the child to discuss the problem with the adult or others involved.

Sometimes, for example in the case of bullying, other strategies are needed. The use of empathy or persona dolls (see Chapter 4) is an effective resource here, where issues relating to behaviour management can be addressed. If a child is being bullied, or is the one being aggressive to others, this can be explored through the use of the 'doll', without specifically identifying the child/children involved. This allows for the unacceptable behaviour to be effectively discussed without 'naming and shaming' or embarrassing either the child being bullied or the child doing the bullying, building an awareness that, while the behaviour is disapproved of, the child as an individual is still valued. To act otherwise would damage the child's sense of self-esteem and self-worth, and could well lead to progressively more 'difficult' behaviours as a result. Often, while the doll is being passed round for 'comfort', the child responsible for the unacceptable behaviour will console the doll and offer advice.

As mentioned earlier in this chapter, the environment is an essential factor in children's development. The EYFS, in its promotion of 'Enabling Environments', clearly states the importance of what is sometimes called 'the third teacher' (see earlier reference to pre-schools in Reggio Emilia). Ensuring that the environment has enough space, light and resources both indoor and out for children to explore and be challenged by can be a stabilising factor in behaviour management. Overcrowding around an area of continuous provision, for example, can be easily remedied by establishing 'fair' rules with the children on the numbers allowed access at any one time. As with adult participation in policy making, children's input in helping to create 'class rules' also shows positive results. Scarce or poorly planned resources can again cause unnecessary conflict. If the scarcity cannot be remedied very quickly, for example the provision of extra tricycles in the outdoor area, then, again, rules for fair use of the equipment need to be clearly established. The use of a visual reminder, for example a large egg-timer, again with the children's cooperation, helps reinforce fairness and responsibility in turn-taking. Planning activities/experiences can also affect children's behaviour. If the day is over-planned, being divided into too many routines, this can create conflict, with children having insufficient time to establish themselves or settle into areas of provision, time to finish or reflect on the processes they are engaged in. Alternatively, if too much time is allocated to very young children being expected to sit still, for example during overlong 'circle' or 'carpet' times, this too can lead to conflict and behaviour management issues. Planning, like the behaviour strategies themselves, needs to be age/stage appropriate. Again, involving children in the planning can have a positive effect, with ownership creating respect for and interest in the planned activities.

Involving children in the behaviour management strategies, where they have to take some responsibility for their implementation, is also successful. A 'kindness' tree, where young children discuss and elect who they feel has done a kind act that day, a 'happy smile' chart, where children decide, depending on their feelings about a particular incident, to display a happy or sad face, the shared responsibility for a class 'pet', all provide children with the chance to reflect, take responsibility for their behaviour and act autonomously.

Focus on practice

Nathan, a 4½ year old boy of mixed race (a white English mother and black West Indian father), was not his usual cheerful self. Catherine, the EYP at his setting, mentioned this to his keyworker at a staff meeting, when the children who were due to transfer to mainstream schools that September were being discussed. Most of the other 'leavers' were showing signs of real confidence at being the 'big children' at the setting. Nathan, however, had become uncharacteristically withdrawn. His keyworker told Catherine that she had discussed this with his mother, who was herself baffled at the change in Nathan. She had put it down to his realising he would soon be leaving the nursery and unfortunately having to say goodbye to some of his friends who were going to different mainstream schools. Later that week, Nathan's father came to collect him. He no longer lived with Nathan and his mother, but was still, it seemed, amicably involved in the childcare arrangements.

Identifying good practice

The keyworker mentioned her concerns about Nathan's withdrawn behaviour to him, but he dismissed it as 'a phase', saying he had started taking Nathan to a local judo club 'to toughen him up a bit'. Apparently Nathan really liked learning judo. Catherine, who continued to observe Nathan, suggested that his keyworker built in some one-to-one time with him. It was during such a quiet one-to-one session in the book corner that Nathan confided that he didn't really like going to the club. He loved doing the judo and being with his dad, but one of the other children there had called him 'bad names'. When asked if he'd told his dad, Nathan shook his head.

Leading practice

In discussion later with Catherine it was decided that the keyworker needed to make time for a conversation with Nathan's parents. In the meantime, Catherine suggested she used one of the persona dolls at circle time that day. The keyworker chose the traveller doll, Anya, whose long red hair and colourful clothes were always commented upon by the children. She had been introduced to the group some time ago by a teacher who supported traveller children and who was very knowledgeable about their lives and customs. The keyworker told the group that Anya was particularly sad because, after she had moved to a new area with her parents, she had been excited about going to her new school, but when she arrived the children had been unkind to her and called her names because she looked different, with her long red hair and colourful traditional clothes. The keyworker passed Anya around the group, asking them to say something kind to make her less sad. She observed Nathan as he watched intently as each child talked to the doll. When it came to his turn, he told Anya she was 'beautiful' and kissed her red hair. The keyworker told them Anya was feeling a lot better, then asked what Anya should do about the children who had been unkind. 'Tell the teachers . . . tell her mummy and daddy . . . tell them to stop making her sad . . . or her daddy will come and shout at them.' The last bit of advice had come from Nathan, who seemed more energised than he had been for weeks. Some of the children decided they were going to draw or paint a picture especially for Anya to cheer her up. Nathan drew a super-hero holding Anya's hand.

Reflection

- *How well do you feel Catherine and the keyworker handled Nathan's situation?*
- *What other action might they have taken?*
- *What advice would you give to the keyworker, when meeting with Nathan's parents over this issue?*

Task Discuss the above with your colleagues and peers. If you have little experience of dealing with such situations, try to find an opportunity to ask more experienced staff to discuss some past examples of their practice in this area with you.

What constitutes effective practice in the identification and support of children whose development, progress and well-being is affected by changes or difficulties in their personal circumstances? What strategies do we need to establish and implement, where necessary, specialist support?

(S23)

In order for this standard to be demonstrated effectively, the practitioner needs to have a positive and trusting relationship as well as sound knowledge of individual children. Through ongoing observations and formative assessment the practitioner will come to know the uniqueness of each child and the personal factors that may help or inhibit that child's development, 'tuning in' to the child's particular needs. Observations that focus not only on developing cognitive, linguistic, creative and physical abilities, but on the child's levels of well-being and involvement can reveal underlying tensions or difficulties the child may be experiencing as a result of changes in their personal circumstances. Practitioners need to be aware of the complexity of what constitutes a modern-day 'family'. The issue around divorce, with the resulting need to accommodate step-parents, step-brothers and -sisters in extended family situations, or becoming a one-parent family; the trauma linked to separation or bereavement; the emotional upheaval that can accompany the birth of a sibling or a mother's post-natal depression or the long-term illness or disability of a family member are some examples of this complexity. Research into the effect of such trauma and transitions on young children highlights the importance of extended care and support networks. Young children will not be able to articulate the difficulties such changes and transitions involve and may respond with uncharacteristic behaviours. It is the practitioner's responsibility to provide a calm and supportive environment for a child having to deal with such change, encouraging the child to express their fears and frustrations, through, for example, the use of empathy dolls/puppets and stories. Parents/carers who are themselves experiencing some of the trauma of the above changes may not want to talk or communicate, and may well be in need of help, advice and support themselves. It is an essential part of the good practice that Every Child Matters (2003) promotes, for practitioners to work in partnership with parents/carers, establishing trusting relationships that support the child and his/her family not only in the everyday sense, but through difficult periods and transitions. If such a relationship is created initially, the practitioner is in a position to help and support both the child and the family, by listening and then helping them where necessary to receive appropriate specialist help. In leading practice, the EYP needs to ensure that practitioners know how best to offer help and support, but also the appropriate boundaries in such sensitive situations (see Chapter 4).

The longitudinal EPPE research (2003) supports effective working with parents, pointing to the excellence of those centres that work in unison with parents, and the positive outcomes for children and parents that were the result of such open partnerships. Bronfenbrenner's 'Human Ecology' theory (1979) clearly supports the interdependent and interactive nature of the relationship between home environment and school (see Chapter 2). The EPEY (2003) and KEEP reports (2005) reinforce this message too, as does the continuing research and work undertaken with parents/carers at Pen Green's Children Centre (**http://www.pengreen.org/**).

Having established an open, honest and trusting rapport with parents can aid the practitioner where concerns about an individual child's development emerge. Working with children from birth to 5 years may well mean it is the practitioner/keyworker who is the first to voice such concerns. Discussion of these initial concerns with parents can help provide a holistic picture of a child's behaviour within the setting and in their home environment. It may be that parents/carers have been dealing with 'difficult' behaviour from a child without saying anything to staff, in the hope that maturation would solve the issues. In such a case the child with behavioural difficulties can be helped, through the creation of consistency in terms of clear boundaries being reinforced both in the setting and, with parents' cooperation, at home. Individual behavioural and educational plans can be created with input from parents, the keyworker and SENCo, to support children in the setting and at home, with parents having a clearer understanding of their role. All this can be achieved if an effective partnership with parents/carers exists, where the parents trust the perspectives of practitioners but also feel they are listened to. If parents are involved in their child's learning journey, they will be more willing to accept advice and any specialist help that is suggested, rather than possibly raising barriers, being in denial and resisting the support and advice offered.

The EYP needs to ensure that colleagues are informed about any particular transitions that can influence a child's holistic development, and are knowledgeable about the processes involved in applying Early Years Action or Early Years

Action Plus (see **http://www.bbc.co.uk/schools/parents/life/sen/statements/sen_ whatnext.shtml**) to a child's needs. Leading Practitioners must understand and have confidence in seeking out appropriate specialist help; in some instances this might involve the use of the Common Assessment Framework (CAF) (see Chapter 5). Most importantly, the setting needs to offer a calm, caring environment that supports children and their families in achieving the most positive outcome possible.

Focus on practice

David, a tall, energetic, 4½ year old child from a white working-class family, and Amin, a delicate, 4 year old Asian child, both of whom had attended their local early years setting since they were 3, recently became friends. They were not in the same group, but as soon as the outdoor provision was opened each morning they spent their time together. At first glance, it seemed to some of the practitioners who were making observations of the children in their play that Amin was the leader and David the follower in their games. It was David, however, who was the first to pinch and hit one of the children with SEN, and Amin who followed his example. The first incidence went unrecorded, as the child with SEN could not vocalise, and the adults on duty were otherwise engaged. It wasn't until the mother of a child on the autistic spectrum complained about the red marks on her daughter's arms that staff became extra vigilant. David was seen to kick out at a child with partial sight, when the child's support worker was temporarily occupied tying another child's shoe lace. David was asked to say sorry, but he refused and was taken inside to sit down until he felt able to apologise. Amin, who had not been seen to be directly involved, was allowed to continue to play uninterrupted. After a short interval he went inside to David's group, where he and David played quietly together with the cars and road mat. The incident was forgotten and David wasn't made to apologise. This 'bullying' of the children with SEN went on for some weeks before practitioners, during a casual conversation at a staff meeting, picked up that a pattern of behaviour was emerging with the two boys and the setting's special needs children.

Identifying good practice

An investigation of both boys' profiles by the Lead Practitioner, Janet, showed that the profiles were not up to date. Further conversations with their keyworkers revealed nothing to suggest reasons for the boys' behaviour, so both the boys' parents were asked to come in independently to discuss matters. It was revealed during the meeting with Amin's parent (only his mother attended; her English was poor and she was obviously embarrassed and reluctant to talk), with the help of a bilingual support assistant, that she was three months pregnant but had not wanted to say anything yet, as a previous pregnancy had miscarried at 16 weeks. She did admit, however, that Amin knew about the baby as he had had to change rooms to prepare for the new arrival. During her meeting, David's mother told Janet that David had been trying to pinch and hurt his baby sister, now 5 months old. His mother had not mentioned it, as she was hoping he would 'grow out of it'. Janet explained sensitively that, although the boys' behaviour had not been in any way acceptable, some insight had now been gained as to the possible causes of it. Both boys in their own ways were suffering from low self-esteem and low self-worth, which often happened during and after the arrival of a sibling.

Leading practice

Janet told the parents that the boys would be closely monitored but would also be praised and rewarded for any good behaviour they demonstrated. She asked that the parents try to show them as much affection as they could in order to bolster their child's self-esteem. After her conversations with both parents, Janet talked to the boys' keyworkers, who complained that it was difficult to keep up with the amount of 'paper work' now required of them, and that admin duties already cut into what could be used as consultation time with parents/carers. Janet decided to consult with the head of the setting about accommodating periods for the up-keep of profiles within the existing timetable. She also wanted to raise at a staff meeting the difficulties some staff were having in finding time to interact effectively with parents/carers, with a view to finding solutions to closer working with parents.

There was a noticeable improvement in Amin's behaviour within a very short space of time. The home corner in his group was changed into a baby clinic and lots of focus and discussion, stories and rhymes were taking place around the importance of having a new brother or sister. One of the 'casualties' of this improvement in Amin's behaviour was his brief friendship with David. David continued to be aggressive to other children, but somewhat indiscriminately now. He was being sent in from outdoor play for aggressive behaviour during nearly every session. His keyworker asked for another meeting with his mother, but a reply arrived saying she was too tied up with the needs of the baby. In discussion with Janet, it was decided to ask if a home visit would be possible. This was agreed, but, when David's keyworker and a nursery assistant visited, David's mother seemed exhausted and unwell. On their return, both the keyworker and nursery assistant expressed concern – the phrases 'a bit depressed' and 'tired all the time' had been used more than once as David's mother had tried to explain and apologise for the unwashed clothes and neglected housework, adding that David's father encouraged his son's 'manly' (aggressive) behaviour, which was frequently aimed towards her and his baby sister. After further discussion with Janet and the head of the setting, it was agreed that the help of a community family support worker would be enlisted. This proved successful, for after a few visits it was established that David's mother was suffering from severe post-natal depression. She subsequently received treatment and the family received the support it needed, a consequence of which was the gradual lessening of David's aggressive behaviour.

Reflection

- *Do you feel that this situation was dealt with effectively by the Lead Professional?*
- *How do you feel the boys' keyworkers fulfilled their roles, (a) initially and (b) subsequently?*

- *Do you feel the setting's behaviour policies were being implemented effectively?*
- *What is your opinion of communication between staff in the setting?*
- *How do you feel the setting responded to the needs of a family requiring extra support?*

Task Discuss the above and any other issues this scenario raises for you with colleagues/peers. Again, if you do not have a long experience of practice and dealing with such issues, try to discuss this with a colleague who can give you some examples from their past practice.

How do we develop practice to ensure that effective and sensitive communication with children from birth to the end of the Foundation Stage is achieved? How can the EYP lead and support practice in listening to, valuing and respecting what children say?

(S26, S27)

In order to develop meaningful and effective communication with children, we need, as with other areas of development, to have a sound knowledge and understanding of the theories and research that underpin children's acquisition of language. Chomsky's idea (1965) that infants are born 'pre-wired' may be one aspect of language acquisition, while Bruner (1983) and other more recent researchers would argue that language is essentially embedded in the social and emotional environment of infants' lives (see Chapter 2). It is important for the practitioner working with very young children to be aware of the unheard 'voices' of infants, who may not talk until their second year. As practitioners we need to realise that the first three years contribute substantially to children's acquisition of language and therefore their ability to become skilful communicators. The early forms, models and experiences of language to which they are exposed will affect their ability to communicate as they develop (Bernstein 1976, Tough 1974). We need to recognise, for example, and support the proto-conversations between adults and babies, in anticipating turn-taking, a social skill that will be very important as they grow socially. We need to appreciate the pleasure a 1 year old child expresses while listening to and making sounds; often they mimic the sounds significant adults around them express. Vygotsky (1978) suggests this is more than simple mimicry, that it is necessary to create something new within the process of imitation. We need to assist and encourage the personal vocabulary a child at 20 months might begin to develop, 'tuning in' to their attempts at communicating with us. Praise, repeat and extend the emergence of one- and two-word utterances at around 18 months that can contain such sophisticated messages.

Celebrate the beginnings of diversity, as children start to communicate in their home language, for the languages children speak are all closely linked to their sense of identity and self-esteem. Listening respectfully and sensitively to their attempts at communication, at whatever age/stage, helps children define their sense of self and raises their sense of well-being.

Stern (1985) reinforces the importance of playful communication with babies and infants during daily routines, such as nappy changing, washing, the 'snuggling in' before sleep. In this way the practitioner reinforces the behaviour that mothers might intuitively engage in, treating their babies and infants 'as the people they are about to become by working in their zone of proximal development' (Stern 1985, p. 43). As practitioners we need to understand also the physical maturity necessary for children to articulate sounds we, as adults, can understand. Whitehead (1996, p. 13) suggests: 'By the age of four the physical maturity of the nervous system and the finer muscle control over the mouth, throat and tongue, and even the presence of teeth, make the young child's pronunciation of languages very much closer to the adult forms . . .'

Listening, then, is a vital skill for the practitioner to develop and a skill also to be encouraged in children themselves. The practice guidance for the EYFS (DCSF 2008), in the Learning and Development section on 'Language for Communication', gives examples of progressive developmental stages with advice on how these can be supported and promoted to meet the individual child's needs. In the 30–50 months developmental stage, for example, 'effective practice' revolves around choosing stories for children with repeated actions and replies, reinforcing the earlier turn-taking. As Meek (2000, p. 203) points out, 'children, discovering language and playing with it, meet its physical nature before its sense.' Hence it is important for the practitioner to share in the delight of rhythms and rhyme with children. The knowledgeable practitioner will also recognise in young children the ability to express through many other means what Magaluzzi calls 'the hundred languages of children' (2006). So, in promoting and supporting effective practice, we help children develop their ability to communicate and we listen. We listen because:

- children are entitled to have their views and experiences respected – they are people too!
- it informs us of children's real interests and concerns and how they feel about themselves, which in turn makes practitioners more reflective
- it is a vital part of establishing trusting, respectful relationships
- it makes practitioners sensitive to the diverse ways children perceive the world around them and their home communities
- it extends our knowledge of children as unique individuals
- it models for children the need to listen to others
- it helps us provide an environment in which all children feel confident and self-assured, safe in the knowledge that their thoughts, feelings and ideas will be taken seriously.

Kylie's voice

Kylie lived in a constantly noisy environment. A home visit revealed a spacious and clean environment with laminate floors and minimal furniture. A wide-screen televi- sion, its volume quite high, was the focus of the room. In the corner there was an aquarium with piranha fish in it. A large sofa, on which Kylie's teenage brother lounged, watching the television, two chairs and a glass coffee table and a display cabinet comprised the rest of the furniture. No toys or books were visible. The sounds of loud music filtered down from upstairs. French windows opened out on to a square of grass bordered by bushes. Under one was wedged a half-inflated foot- ball. A bicycle with stabilisers was propped against the nearside fence. A dog on a lead in the neighbouring garden ran up and down the length of the garden barking. Conversation was difficult above the noise, but the family members seemed comfort- able with it, raising their voices to be heard. When told by his mother to bring down Kylie's toys, her brother returned from upstairs with a plastic washing basket con- taining an assortment of Barbie dolls, a board book, some comics, felt-tipped pens, crayons and paper. Kylie began to draw radiating lines across the pad of paper while the adults talked. When asked a question Kylie would nod or shake her head. Her mother explained that she was always this 'shy' in front of strangers, usually you 'couldn't shut her up'. There was obviously a big age difference between Kylie and her brother, and her mother said she was pleased Kylie had been given a place in nursery, to help her make friends with children her own age, as there were no other young children in the neighbouring houses.

During Kylie's initial visits with her mother to the setting, or if work intervened and her 17 year old brother would accompany her, Kylie remained silent. She watched the other children intently, and when approached would seek out her brother or mother and sit on their lap. She investigated the areas of continuous provision and the inter- active displays within the room, as long as her mother or brother were close by. Staff suggested Kylie would need time to settle in and her mother agreed to make arrangements with work to enable this to happen at the beginning of the new school year in September. Unfortunately, when September arrived, Kylie's mother was not able to stay with her through a gradual settling-in period, as her employer would not agree to her having sufficient time off work. However, Kylie's brother, who was unem- ployed, was happy to bring Kylie to the setting and stay. He tried to encourage his sister to access the provision in his deep loud voice, which stopped a number of other children in their tracks, initially, but they soon adjusted to having him among them. Her brother would often model what Kylie should be doing with the dough, sand, water and paints, as well as 'play fighting' with some of the young boys, until asked to stop by the staff. Kylie would access the activities and basic provision, but, as soon as her brother moved, she moved with him. After two weeks, her brother ar- rived one morning and announced he would have to leave Kylie with staff, as he had got a job. Kylie clung on to her brother as long as possible. When he finally left, she didn't cry, but sat with her thumb in her mouth on a floor cushion in the book corner, pushing away staff and other children if they attempted to engage or comfort her. Her keyworker made valiant attempts to draw Kylie out of her obvious sadness, but she remained silent and implacable for the rest of the week. The following week, her mother rang to say Kylie had caught a bad cold and would not be attending until she was better. The task of bringing Kylie to the setting was then given over to her grand-mother, who was also caring for her other daughter's young baby and toddler, and was unable to stay. The keyworker noticed that Kylie's grandmother both asked and answered questions on Kylie's behalf, as her older brother had done. Kylie continued to spend her time in the relative quiet of the book corner, which had been made into a 'reading den' with its canopy and comfortable cushions. By this time, the other children had stopped attempting to include her in their play.

Identifying good practice

Being a resourced setting meant that a number of children with particular needs accessed all the rooms, accompanied by either the setting SENCo or a support worker. Ben, a child with autistic tendencies, also enjoyed the calm of the 'reading den'. Gradually, he and his support worker and Kylie, through the use of the Picture Exchange Communication System (PECS) (Callcentre 2009, online), developed their own signing system to communicate. Kylie's keyworker was concerned that this might delay Kylie's attempts to speak, and discussed her concerns with the Leading Practitioner. The Leading Practitioner suggested that, as long as language was being used in conjunction with the PECS to stimulate Kylie's communication skills, it should be continued for the time being, as Kylie seemed to be gaining security from it. Kylie began to use her voice a short time later, during a role-play session with Ben and his support worker in the home corner. Observing from a distance, her keyworker watched as Kylie repeated the words of encouragement that Ben's support worker was saying, while Ben engaged in the pretend play of making a meal for Kylie and his support worker to taste.

Leading practice

Later that day, when Ben had finished his half-day's attendance, Kylie's keyworker introduced her to an empathy doll, 'Susie', who had 'fallen on the way to school and hurt her knee.' While Kylie 'nursed' the doll, quietly speaking words of comfort, her keyworker read the story of '*On the way home*' (Murphy 1982). After reading the story through, the keyworker then asked Susie what she liked about the story and, in a soft voice, Kylie answered for the doll, moving its head and hands, while the key-worker listened attentively. Kylie's attachment to Susie was such that her keyworker decided to let Kylie take the doll home (having read the home visit report on the lack of toys). She asked Kylie to help her pack a bag for Susie, listening carefully to Kylie's suggestions about what the doll might need to go 'on holiday' to her house, noting, too, that Kylie was having some difficulty in pronouncing soft 's' sounds at the begin-ning and end of words. When other children attempted to join in with help and sug-gestions, Kylie backed away, but encouraged by her keyworker, who told the other children that this was a special task for Kylie, she resumed packing the doll's bag, her self-esteem restored at being given a 'special' task. When Kylie's grandmother came to collect her, the keyworker began to explain, but was soon listening to Kylie giving her own reasons for the doll's 'holiday' and what she and Susie were going to do. Her keyworker suggested that, when Kylie brought Susie back, they might like to tell everyone about the exciting time they'd had.

In discussion with the Lead Practitioner about the success of using the empathy doll, it was decided that this could be extended, involving sending the doll home on 'holiday' with a number of children. Kylie's keyworker also mentioned the slight difficulty Kylie displayed with articulation and it was agreed the situation should be monitored, and sound story sacks used both in the setting and at home.

Reflection

- *How well do you feel staff at the setting responded to Kylie's needs in settling her in to her new surroundings? How might this have been done differently?*

- *What are your feelings on the use of signing as an additional means of communication? Do you consider the keyworker's concerns were valid?*

- *How effective do you feel the use of the empathy doll was in this particular situation? In what other situations might it be used?*

- *Do you feel Kylie was listened to and her wishes respected?*

- *Have you experienced similar situations where new children have elected to remain silent? What strategies have you used successfully to encourage the child's communication skills?*

Task Reflect on how successful you have been in engaging with families who may have differing priorities, which makes partnership difficult to achieve. If you have not been in practice very long, try to observe a more experienced colleague in such an interaction with a family, and write your reflections on this in your journal. If you can then share these and discuss them with your colleague, this might help both of you to reflect further on the situation.

Conclusion

What effective strategies can we develop that reflect our high expectations of all children and our commitment to ensuring each child achieves his/her full potential? How do we create fair, respectful and supportive relationships while achieving such effective practice?

An effective Lead Practitioner, as is shown in this chapter, needs to have sound knowledge of how children develop and learn, and be aware of current emergent theory, research and initiatives. Armed with such knowledge and understanding we should be able to provide effective support for both children and families. Children do not grow in a vacuum. It is hoped that, from reading this and previous chapters, the importance of knowing the individual child and their family has been emphasised. The high expectations we have of children need to be established from the beginning, based on sound prior knowledge of the dynamics within the child's family and the interests and experiences of the child him/herself. Expectations built round some external model of achievement, which bear little relation to those experiences and interests, may well build in failure and a low sense of self-esteem. What constitutes 'full potential' should be related to each child's individual needs, rather than to some standardised 'norm'. The personalised learning through which a child achieves this potential should reflect, respect and value the diversity of their life experiences. By modelling respect and value for and of each child, you will raise that child's self-esteem and create the beginnings of a positive, trusting relationship that will enrich both adult and child. From such a safe, supportive base, with their confidence high, children will be motivated to engage with any appropriate challenges they are set. From the practitioner's perspective, the necessity for continuous formative observation and assessment of children should be self-evident. Through such essential information gathering, each child's learning journey can be supported successfully and possible concerns highlighted and acted upon.

Sharing such knowledge with parents/carers as the child's first educators is another essential aspect. Even if the response is not as supportive or positive as you would wish, most parents want the best for their children; it is within the translation of this wish that frustrations and misunderstandings can occur. We cannot be 'precious' or obtuse about sharing our particular knowledge and understanding of the child. Current research and practice underpins, time and again, how vital that relationship with parents/carers is for the child's development and learning. High expectations need to be understood and shared if they are to be achieved, and possible stereotypes or misconceptions about each child's abilities challenged. Realistic expectations based on prior knowledge, respect for and commitment to each individual child's needs and a working partnership with parents/carers will help create an environment where children will feel supported and respected, and as a result achieve their potential.

What effective behaviour management strategies can we create to support the development of children's social, emotional and behavioural skills? How do we effectively demonstrate the positive values, attitudes and behaviour we expect from children in practice?

Again, as a potential EYP, the practitioner must be informed about current thinking in child development, for example the recent studies in brain research, cortisol studies, the theory of mind, and emotional competency (see above and Chapter 2), which are enriching our understanding of the complex mechanisms that inform the development of babies and young children. With such knowledge, we can create more effective strategies for helping a child understand and develop control over their own feelings as well as developing their awareness of the feelings and needs of others.

We need, as practitioners, to accept that children's behaviours will affect our own responses, producing negative as well as positive thoughts and feelings. We must counteract prejudice and stereotyping that can trigger a number of negative behaviours, while accepting that we may have our own personal prejudices, by modelling positive behaviour and establishing fair and consistent rules and boundaries. Again we need to share these with parents/carers, in order to provide consistency across environments, as well as ensuring a 'whole setting' approach to implementing agreed behaviour policies that are age/stage appropriate.

Much contemporary research reinforces the need for young children to acknowledge their feelings and try with adult help to resolve conflicts, through experiences that might challenge their own perceptions of events, developing that all-important ability to empathise with another's view or expectations. The SEAL programme (DCSF 2005) provides comprehensive materials and examples of how to help young

Source: POD/Pearson Education Ltd.
Malcolm Harris

children feel good about themselves. From a positive sense of self they are then able to build positive relationships with others. The use of empathy dolls can help practitioners deal with unacceptable behaviours while still valuing the child as an individual. The environment itself can help promote sharing and turn-taking if well structured and resourced. An over-planned day can result in conflict and negative behaviours as children feel 'trapped' by unnecessary routines and structures that are more for the benefit of staff or external agencies. Involving children in the rules-making process, encouraging them to become self-monitoring and self-reflective, creates a less conflict-centred approach. Rewards can play an important role, as well as positive feedback and praise from adults, as long as it is specific rather than given indiscriminately. The care of a class 'pet', if possible, encourages young children to take responsibility for their own and others' behaviour. Many concrete examples of behaviour strategies can be given, but practitioners need to remember that effective strategies must reflect particular circumstances and the differing and complex individual needs of each child in their care.

Further reading

Bruce, T. (2004) 'Play Matters' in L. Abbott and A. Langston (eds) *Birth to Three Matters: supporting the framework of effective practice.* Maidenhead: Open University Press.

Edwards, C.P., Gandini, L. and Forman, G. (1998) *The Hundred Languages of Children: The Reggio Emilia approach - advanced reflections.* New York: Ablex Publishing Co.

Moyles, J. (ed.) (2005) *The Excellence of Play.* Maidenhead: Open University Press.

Nutbrown, C. (2006) *Threads of Thinking: young children learning and the role of early education.* London: Paul Chapman.

Smith, P.K., Cowie, H. and Blades, M. (2003) *Understanding Children's Development.* Oxford: Blackwell.

Tizard, B. and Hughes, M. (1984) *Young Children Learning: talking and thinking at home and at school.* London: Fontana.

Wood, E. and Attfield, J. (2005) *Play, Learning and the Early Childhood Curriculum,* 2nd edition. London: Paul Chapman.

Websites

http://www.everychildmatters.gov.uk/deliveringservices/caf/

http://www.ecm.gov.uk/multiageencyworking/

http://www.kategreenaway.ik.org/

http://www.pecs.com/

http://www.pengreen.org/

http://www.persona-doll-training.org

http://www.standards.dfes.gov.uk/primary/publicatlons/banda/seal/

http://www.surestart.gov.uk

References

Barnes, P. (2001) *Personal, social and emotional development of children*. Oxford: Oxford University Press.

Bernstein, B. (1976) *Class, codes and control*. New York: Schocker Books.

Bronfenbrenner, U. (1979) *The Ecology of Human Development: Experiments by Nature and Design*. Cambridge, MA: Harvard University Press.

Bruner, J. (1983) Child's Talk. Learning to Use Language. Oxford: Oxford University Press.

Cadwell, L. (2003) *The Reggio approach: bringing learning to life*. Columbia University: Teachers College Press.

Callcentre (2009) Picture Exchange Communication System. Available at: http://callcentre.education.ed.ac.uk/SCN/Level_A_SCA/Using_Symbols_SCB/Hot_PECS_News_HTA/hot_pecs_news_hta.html Accessed on 18 February 2009.

Chomsky, N. (1965) *Aspects of the Theory of Syntax*. Cambridge, MA: MIT Press.

Denham, S.A. (1998) *Emotional Development in Young Children*. New York: The Guildford Press.

DfES (2003) *Every Child Matters* Green Paper. London: The Stationery Office.

DfES (2005) 'Excellence and Enjoyment: Social and Emotional Aspects of Learning'. Available at: http://www.standards.dfes.gov.uk/primary/publications/banda/seal/pns_seal137805_guidance. pdf Accessed on 31 December 2008.

DfES (2005) *Common Assessment Framework*. Nottingham: DfES Publications.

DfES (2005) *Key Elements of Effective Practice (KEEP)*. 1021-2005G. Nottingham: DCSF Publications.

DfES (2007) *Primary National Strategy: Creating the Picture*. London: HMSO.

Dunn, J. (1993) *Young children's close relationships: Beyond Attachment*. Newbury, CA: Sage Publications.

Freud, S. (1965) *Normalcy and pathology in childhood: Assessments of development*. New York: International University Press.

Goldschmied, E. and Jackson, S. (1994) *People under three: young children and day care*. New York: Routledge.

Goleman, D.P. (1995) *Emotional Intelligence: Why it can matter more than IQ for Character, Health and lifelong achievement*. New York: Bantam Books.

Gopnick, A., Meltzoff, A. and Kuhl, P. (1999) *How babies think: the science of childhood*. London: Weidenfeld & Nicolson.

Harris, P.L. (1989) *Children and emotion*. New York: Cambridge University Press.

Hutt, S.J., Tyler, S., Hutt, C. and Christopherson, H. (1989) *Play, Exploration and Learning: a natural history of the pre-school*. London: Routledge.

Laevers, F. (1994) *The Leuven Involvement Scale for Young Children*. Leuven, Belgium: Centre for Experiential Education.

Maccoby, E. (1980) *Social Development: Psychological Growth and the Parent-Child Relationship*. New York: Harcourt.

Meek, M. (2000) 'Transitional Transformations' in E. Bearne and V. Watson (eds) *Where Texts and Children Meet*. London: Routledge.

Meek, M. (1985) *'Play and Paradoxes'* In G. Wells and J. Nicholls (eds) *Language and Learning: an international perspective*. London: Falmer Press.

Murphy, J. (1982) *On The Way Home*. London: Macmillan Publishing.

Ofsted (2005) *Managing Challenging Behaviour*. Ref 2363. London: HMSO.

Pascal, C. and Bertram, A.D. (1997) *Effective Early Learning: Case Studies of Improvement*. London: Hodder & Stoughton.

Schweinhart, L.J. (2003) *Benefits, Costs and Exploration of the High/Scope Perry Preschool Project*. Ypsilanti, MI: High/Scope Research Foundation.

Siraj-Blatchford, I. and Clarke, P. (2000) *Identity, Diversity and Language in Early Years*. Buckingham: Oxford University Press.

Siraj-Blatchford, I., Sylva, K., Mutock, S., Gilden, R. and Bell, D. (2002) *Researching Effective Pedagogy in the Early Years*. RB 356. London: DfES Publications.

Smith, P., Cowie, H. and Blades, M. (2003) Understanding Children's Development. Oxford: Blackwell.

Stern, D.N. (1985) *The interpersonal world of the Infant*. New York: Basic Books.

Sylva, K., Melhuish, E., Sammons, P., Siraj-Blatchford, I., Taggart, B. and Elliot, K. (2003) *The Effective Provision of Pre-School Education (EPPE) Project: findings from the pre-school period*. London: Institute of Education.

Thornton, L. and Brunton, P. (2006) *Understanding the Reggio Approach*. London: David Fulton.

Tough, J. (1974) Children's use of language. *Education Review*, 26(3), pp. 116–79.

Vygotsky, L. (1978) *Mind in Society*. Cambridge, MA: Harvard.

Webster-Stratton, C. (2000) *How to promote children's social and emotional competence*. London: Paul Chapman/Sage Publications.

Whitehead, M. (1996) *The Development of Language and Literacy*. London: Paul Chapman.

7

Transforming the environment for play and learning

Wendy Holland

Chapter overview

The standards addressed in this chapter are:

S08 Establish and sustain a safe, welcoming, purposeful, stimulating and encouraging environment where children feel confident and secure and are able to develop and learn

S09 Provide balanced and flexible daily and weekly routines that meet children's needs and enable them to develop and learn

S11 Plan and provide safe and appropriate child-led and adult-initiated experiences, activities and play opportunities in indoor, outdoor and out-of setting contexts, which enable children to develop and learn

S12 Select, prepare and use a range of resources suitable for children's ages, interests and abilities, taking account of diversity and promoting equality and inclusion

S24 Be accountable for the delivery of high-quality provision

Relating to the above standards, the following key questions will be addressed:

- What strategies can be developed to support the establishment of secure, stimulating and purposeful indoor and outdoor learning environments through planned and appropriate adult-initiated and child-led experiences?

(S08 and S11)

- How can we ensure children are provided with flexible routines that meet individual needs, in a well-resourced environment that takes account of diversity and encourages inclusive practice and provision?

(S09 and S12)

- What strategies need to be in place to guarantee accountability for the delivery of such high-quality provision?

(S24)

Introduction

This chapter will have as its focus those standards that exemplify effective practice in leading and supporting the management of the child's learning environment, where the 'environment' is viewed in an holistic sense, to include the child's emotional and social well-being, as well as cognitive and physical development. It will discuss the practitioner's role in establishing and sustaining a safe, secure, purposeful learning environment, both indoors and outdoors; an environment that fosters the child's sense of well-being and natural curiosity, and where the child's ideas and contributions are valued. The necessity for appropriate and flexible routines which incorporate a balance of child-led and adult-initiated experiences and opportunities will be discussed, as well as the need for routines that allow children time to follow their interests and support particular individual needs. Routines also need to be created that are flexible enough to reflect the different kinds of access to and time spent in the setting by individual children, thus promoting the very necessary sense of continuity for the child between home, the setting, and possible other provision the child attends. The practitioner's responsibility for ensuring the environment is developmentally appropriate and, where necessary, specially adapted resources that reflect diversity and promote inclusive practice will be focused upon, as well as the practitioner's statutory accountability to all stakeholders for the delivery and maintenance of high-quality provision.

Theoretical underpinning, relevant research findings and new initiatives that highlight effective practice for these particular standards will, as in previous chapters, be discussed, as well as further reading to support more detailed analysis of the issues considered.

What strategies can be developed to support the establishment of secure, stimulating and purposeful indoor and outdoor learning environments through planned and appropriate adult-initiated and child-led experiences?

In order to develop effective strategies we need, initially, to look at the theory and current research that have been explored in previous chapters that underpin new government initiatives in Early Years through the Every Child Matters agenda to explore and expand the child's learning environment. With this point in mind, consider the following practice example.

Babies at play

Rachel, the relatively new manager of a private daycare setting, housed in a large Victorian detached property, discussed with her Lead Practitioner, Alice, how best to improve the outdoor provision. Rachel has been in post for only two years and during that time has concentrated on improving the indoor provision and resources. The large but neglected outdoor area had been next on her agenda; however, with the statutory implementation of the EYFS she felt it was necessary to make changes sooner rather than later. The babies and young children attending the setting currently accessed the outdoors by being taken on regular trips to a nearby park and play area, as well as spending a limited amount of time with tricycles, scooters and prams on a small tarmac area at the front of the building. Alice felt some changes could be made relatively cheaply, as she had a number of contacts locally who could supply larger equipment such as tyres and milk crates, and suggested to Rachel that one of the trees in the grounds of the house could be made into a sitting log with sections cut for use as stepping stones. She also discussed re-organising the staffing rota, in order that outdoor play could be accessed more regularly. At a staff meeting, Alice discussed the proposed rota changes for outdoor provision, whereby one member of staff would be involved in a focused activity, while another practitioner monitored the children's play generally, with some flexibility if the numbers of children accessing the outdoors increased. Alice also suggested that the staff in each room took it in turns to plan for a whole week's outdoor activities. Some of the staff were resistant to the suggested changes. One practitioner, Mary, in particular, voiced concerns about the health and safety of the children, especially in parts of the garden that were overgrown; she also felt, along with other members of staff, that the weather was not always suitable for children to be outside. She added that the shed, situated round the side of the house, where the larger equipment was stored, was a long way to drag/carry the existing equipment and, if more heavy equipment was to be brought in, it would lengthen the setting-up and tidying-away time and might possibly lead to staff injuries. Generally, staff felt the existing arrangements, i.e. visiting the local park and play area, worked well enough.

Identifying good practice

Alice reminded staff of the new focus between indoor and outdoor provision that good practice demands in the EYFS. She suggested that some of the older children could help with tidying away equipment and felt the new arrangements should be trialled for a short period. The overgrown areas were fenced off temporarily and Alice modelled good practice by planning and implementing the first two weeks' outdoor activities. After each group had been responsible for one week's outdoor provision, staff met to discuss how they felt the new arrangements had gone. Some practitioners still had reservations, particularly if the weather was poor, and children had not come to the setting adequately dressed for it. Without some kind of covered area, attempting to mark-make or use small-world resources had proved difficult. The new staffing rota had also been hard to implement when members of staff had been absent.

Leading practice

Alice agreed that a covered area would improve things, but also reminded staff that it was not expected that the outdoors would exactly 'mirror' indoor provision, and that planning should include alternatives for differing weather conditions. She took the staff's comments back to Rachel and after discussion it was agreed that the outdoor provision needed more investment. The redevelopment would be staged, but the staff would begin to make changes to their practice to embrace the emphasis on more free-flow indoor/outdoor play. Alice suggested all-weather clothing should be purchased for the children, and it was also agreed that she and another member of staff would attend training on planning and resourcing outdoor provision currently being run by the local authority. The member of staff, Mary, who had shown most resistance to the proposed changes, was asked by Alice to attend the training with her.

After the training, Alice discussed with Rachel how best to tackle the outdoor provision, then she and Mary, who had finished the training more committed to outdoor provision, fed back to the whole staff. With Rachel's agreement, the following recommendations were made:

- Soft surfacing should be laid for a new climbing frame and separate slide.

- The area around the trees and shrubbery should be pruned back and cleared and plants inspected for 'safety', but left for such uses as a den-making area, treasure hunt trail and digging and planting activities.

- A veranda at the side of the play area should be made safe and roofed to provide cover in wet weather.

- A new shed should be situated next to the play area for storing equipment. Alice said this could be made multifunctional, by painting one wall of the shed with blackboard paint to encourage mark-making, and instruments hung on another wall to encourage musical activities outdoors.

Alice and Mary, through discussion and the use of a video from their training course, showed how clear and careful planning of outdoor provision could support the potential for children's learning and development in line with the principles of the EYFS.

Reflections

- *How do you feel Alice handled the changes proposed for the outdoor provision?*

- *Did the staff have reasonable cause for concern, or were they just being resistant to change?*

- *Should Alice have given time for more discussion with staff on the expectations for outdoor provision laid down by the EYFS practice guidance?*

- *Did Alice model good practice long enough for staff to adapt their practice?*

- *Did she give sufficient guidance on the new planning?*

- *Should staff have had more input on the proposed changes for the outdoor provision?*

Task Consider these questions with colleagues (a) before reading the chapter below and (b) after reading it. Discuss to what extent it has informed your views.

Active learning

The Early Years Foundation Stage guidance advances the importance of seeing babies and young children as **active learners** and the need for practitioners to encourage this natural curiosity and drive to discover the world by creating 'enabling environments'. Such environments help children to actively build meaning, make connections and construct new ideas about themselves, other people and the physical world around them (see Piaget's theories on 'assimilation' and 'accommodation' in Chapter 2). Athey (1990) refers to such attempts by children to make sense of their environment as 'schema', and the Reggio Emilia approach also

Source: POD/Pearson Education Ltd. Jules Selmes

refers to the environment as the 'third teacher' (see Chapter 6). The EYFS guidance considers that effective environments 'enable' children to engage in the creating and refining of such schema. Through the repeated activities of different schemas, children are able to act like scientists and/or researchers, discovering patterns, connections and links between a wide variety of phenomena; such active learning may well be 'interactive, messy, boisterous and often physical' (DCSF 2007, p. 2). This view of the child as an inherently *active* learner should underpin practitioners' attempts to personalise and individualise their provision.

Personalised learning

Practitioners need to be aware of the different ways in which young children access the learning experiences that an early years setting provides. Knowledge of the child's learning at home can help the practitioner to create more personalised provision. Carr (2001) suggests that a child's learning disposition may help or hinder their ability to access the resources and experiences provided. For the young child to want to explore his/her environment, the practitioner needs to ensure the experiences and activities the environment presents are meaningful to that child. The ability to choose, to make decisions is also an important factor in the child's active learning, as it promotes autonomy. Where provision is limited or not developmentally appropriate, children will quickly lose interest. The match between a child's interests and the experiences made available can best be achieved through close observation and assessment of the child, and the development of meaningful partnerships with parents and carers (see Chapters 5, 6 and 8). The personalised learning journey and the effective practice it promotes have many benefits. The child's interest is sustained and their learning developed. The practitioner's knowledge of what the child can do and what the next steps should be are also developed, and, if shared with parents and carers, creates a secure cycle of learning between setting and home. The trust that this creates helps the discussion, where necessary, of any particular needs or concerns either the practitioner or parent may have.

Creating a trusting relationship in this way impacts upon the child's emotional development, for an 'enabling' environment should not be just about cognitive and physical growth. Emotional competency and a sense of well-being are important factors, as Laevers (1994) suggests, in the extent to which a child will engage with their learning environment. A low sense of esteem has been linked by research (Pascal *et al.* 1995) to low levels of involvement and 'surface' learning.

The importance of play

The EYFS promotes play as the medium through which young children naturally learn.

> Observing children playing might lead one to assume that play is any or all of the following: a social learning device; a cognitive learning device; a physical learning device; fun and freedom; therapy; occupation while adults are busy.

> (DCSF (2007) Effective practice: Play and Exploration, p. 1)

A play environment, however free and unstructured it might appear, needs to be appropriately and adequately resourced and planned for. The effective practitioner should ensure that children have choice, not only in which activity/experience they decide to engage, but whether to do so on their own, with their peers or with adults. Sufficient space and time are vital prerequisites in an enabling environment where a range of activities should be on offer, some of which may be planned and led by adults, based on their knowledge of children's current interests, learning styles and stages of development. Such a rich, enabling environment, where practitioners allow children to dictate the pace and length of focus, and sensitively and subtly intervene and support, provides a safe, secure dispositional milieu, in which children can develop and learn. Each early years setting will have its own unique milieu, presenting to children a particular view of what it means to be an active learner in that particular environment. Effective practice needs to try to establish a place where children will develop and learn in their own unique ways. The flexibility of such a play environment

Source: POD/Pearson Education Ltd. Jules Selmes

encourages the development of: 'playful minds . . . the most suitable approach to future life in our fluid, multi-media, global society' (David and Powell 2005, cited in DCSF 2007: Play and Exploration, p. 1). Future research may indeed support the idea that learning through play helps children achieve specific Every Child Matters (ECM) (2003) outcomes; what contemporary research has already established is that children's play can be complex and multilayered. It helps young children solve problems and gain a degree of control in their ability to absorb new knowledge and create meaning (see Jarvis 2007).

The role of the adult

Longitudinal research such as EPPE (2003) and REPEY (2002) emphasises the importance of the adult's role when engaging with children. Practitioners who allow children to direct their own play spontaneously, knowing when to join in and when not to interrupt the flow of children's play and exploration, are enacting that vital 'scaffolding' of children's learning proposed by Bruner (1983). They are also displaying a trust and belief in children's abilities, reflecting the approach used in the pre-schools in the Reggio Emilia region of Northern Italy, where the child is seen as the investigator/explorer of his/her environment and the practitioners as facilitators and co-researchers with the child (see Chapter 6). If the practitioner acknowledges this need to learn from and with the child and communicates this new knowledge and understanding to parents and carers, an holistic and individually unique learning environment can be created (see Pen Green 2008, online) The EPPE report (2003) identified 'centres of excellence' where a mixture of child-initiated, adult-extended and adult-led activities/experiences prevailed. Through such strategies as 'sustained shared thinking' (REPEY 2002), it has been shown that the practitioner can extend a child's language and ideas, encouraging the child to perhaps reflect on previous actions/learning and thus promoting 'metacognition' (thinking about thinking). This ability of the child to reflect on their own experiences and prior knowledge and to self-regulate behaviour when interacting with peers is essential for the child's growth and development in all areas. The research also confirmed the centrality of play in a child's early learning journey.

The effective practitioner realises that different contexts can promote different kinds of play and learning, and will provide for both the ephemeral interests children may have and areas of more continuous focus. Settings must provide for what Hutt et al. (1989) describes as exploratory, inquisitive play ('epistemic') as well as creative, playful play ('ludic'), and recognise the differing responses required. Practitioners should avoid over-hasty intervention, particularly in epistemic play; trying to communicate verbally with a child might cut across some private world of concentration and thought that should not be disturbed. The effective practitioner understands that children sometimes need to have their own space, a space that is protected from their peers and adults.

Contemporary research into play itself (see Jarvis and George 2008) highlights issues in today's society with regard to children's more limited access to play in their physical environment. It is suggested that neighbourhood play has decreased due to higher levels of traffic and the perceived 'stranger danger' threat. Playtime in some schools has been reduced, making less time available for the all-important skills of negotiation, compromise and social debate to develop, all of which are underpinned by play (see Brock *et al.* 2008). The institutionalisation of very young children into private and voluntary daycare where access to outdoor provision might be limited, and the use of ICT games which can create isolated and solitary indoor play, all point to the possibility that the environment provided by an early years setting might be the only form of outdoor play experience to which a child has regular access.

Outdoor play

Standard 11 in the EYFS (2008 online) clearly reinforces the need for 'play opportunities in indoor, outdoor and in out-of-setting contexts, which enable children to develop and learn'. Outdoor provision needs to have the same depth and breadth of engagement by practitioners as indoor provision. Children play and express themselves differently outdoors and, if practitioners are to create environments that harness the uniqueness of each child, outdoor provision needs to be planned so that children are inspired, challenged and intrigued, providing an environment just as 'enabling', with as much thought and planning as the indoor environment. The movement-based learning that is involved in children's schemas such as transporting, connecting, trajectory and rotation is often well fitted to outdoor provision where the space to move and explore safely can be supported. With provision that is flexible and versatile, too, children can re-create and change their environment imaginatively, taking ownership of their play milieu. However, research indicates (Pen Green Conference 2004), that, although the evidence of children engaging in schema-based play (see Chapter 5) is more common in outdoor environments, adults tend not to support or extend children's explorations of them to the same degree as schema-based play observed within indoor environments. As Learning through Landscapes (2008, online) suggests, the practitioner's role here is crucial; they need to demonstrate knowledge, enthusiasm and commitment to ensure the best possible use is made of the outdoor provision. Centres should aim to offer and resource a wide range of holistic experiences for children outdoors, including areas where play is active, boisterous and noisy, and others that are calm and allow children space and time to reflect. Bilton (2005) suggests that boys particularly express themselves more effectively outdoors.

> If I have not yet learned to love Darth Vader, I have at least made some useful discoveries while watching him at play. As I interrupt less, it becomes clear that boys' play is serious drama, not morbid mischief. Its rhythms and images are often discordant to me, but I must try to make sense of a style that, after all, belongs to half the population of the classroom.
>
> (Paley 1984, p. xii)

White (2008) suggests there are six major ingredients that provide a rich and satisfying outdoor experience for young children:

- natural materials;
- growing and the living world;
- water;
- physical play and movement;
- imagination and creativity;
- construction.

Source: POD/Pearson Education Ltd. Jules Selmes

All of the above are central to the **Forest School** approach to outdoor provision, developed in Denmark in the 1950s, which is now gaining recognition within the UK. Many benefits have been demonstrated through this approach. It addresses the 'nature deficit' that many children may experience in today's society and encourages self-initiated learning with children engaged in experiencing a variety of skills like den-building, treasure trails, bushcraft, environmental art planting and growing produce, as well as adult-supervised activities such as building woodland fires, cooking and learning to work with knives. Children with language difficulties particularly seem to benefit, as research suggests children make significantly more utterances when outdoors; through improved communication they also develop their emotional literacy. This more kinaesthetic and flexible approach to learning experiences develops children's ideas and respect and appreciation for the natural environment (Cook 2008).

Creative partnerships

Not all settings are in a position to set up a forest school, requiring as it does appropriate and available land, and considerable financial support. An alternative could be found through **Creative Partnerships**, which have now been established by a number of Local Authorities in England as a result of the Every Child Matters agenda. Some Early Years services are involved in helping settings access environmental projects as part of this partnership. They are also helping to establish practice along the lines of the Reggio Emilia approach (see Chapter 6), with local artists taking up residence in a setting for a period of time to help foster a more creative approach to early years practice (Canterbury Nursery School and Centre for Families and Children 2006). The benefits of such creative partnerships with their focus on children's creativity are many:

- Children gain in confidence.
- They learn new skills that are not simply 'task-related'.
- They grow in emotional intelligence through learning to communicate their feelings and ideas to their peers.
- They have increased awareness of difference and diversity.
- They learn to collaborate and work as part of a team.
- The environment is seen as an effective 'third teacher'.
- There is a depth of interaction as a result of children's being given time and space to pursue their interests.
- The emphasis is clearly on process and not on outcomes.
- Children are encouraged to make judgements, become absorbed and be persistent.

Having an artist 'in residence' has an impact upon staff performance as well as that of the children. Adults need to feel 'delight and curiosity in discovering artistic opportunities . . . the more the child feels the pleasure of the practitioner, the more willing they are to let their own pleasure show' (Théâtre de la Guimbarde 2004). There is a need from the beginning of the partnership to establish, for example, that the artist is sympathetic to the setting in terms of its ethos and principles regarding children's learning and development as well as having an ability to communicate with and listen to children effectively. Practitioners and artists need to reflect by sharing their perceptions on what is or is not working within a particular project and why. Adults also need to reflect upon how much they themselves are learning from such creative experiences, demonstrating Vygotsky's observation that 'teachers' and 'learners' often construct learning together, again reflecting the 'Reggio' approach. However, production of 'documentation' in such creative enterprises can be difficult. Practitioners therefore need to find ways to capture important moments in a child's learning which may be transitory. Again, the practice of individual learning diaries for each child, as championed by the EYFS, could be one way of assuring that those moments are not lost.

Having an artist in residence, as well as introducing new skills and experiences – a potter's wheel, creating sculptures, drawing and painting with unusual media, can also help practitioners look afresh at the kinds of activities that regularly occur in an early years setting. **Storytelling** by children themselves, with props they have made, encourages listening skills in the audience and speaking skills in the storyteller. As well as helping a child's creativity, stories can also give us insights into influences and anxieties or actual events which the child is trying to make sense of. The creative use of **movement**, which involves all the senses – hearing, vision, taste, smell and touch, can lead to the extension of verbal and non-verbal means of communicating for a child. Such movement aids expression, balance, flexibility, strength and confidence in developing relationships. Research has shown how essential movement itself is for children's growth and development. Greenland (2000) suggested that human beings did not just live in their heads but, as playful physical beings, in their whole bodies, while research suggests babies and young children are biologically driven to seek the physical experience that will most benefit their particular stage of development. Lindon (2001) suggests that children's powers of concentration are disrupted rather than aided by the requirement that the child sit still for long periods.

Using **photographs** to record a process or achievement, or to confirm an acquired skill, are often the perspectives brought to photography by adults, rather than seeing it as an art form in itself. Children, however, do not necessarily need a permanent record. A camera can provide the child with autonomy; they choose what they wish to photograph. I observed children on a visit to the park to feed the ducks taking photographs of the patterns left by their trainers in the mud, not the ducks they were going to feed! Photographs can be used to help communication with parents, support metacognition in children by recalling their previous experiences, and, if there is no common language, photographs can be a clear aid to communicating meaningfully.

The spontaneous expression of children's imagination through a range of different media, helped by an artist's perspective, demonstrates the innate human drive to explore, develop concepts and solve problems that all children have: 'through their imagination children can move from the present into the past and the future, to what might be and beyond' (Duffy 1998). Children thrive in an environment that fosters **connections rather than separations.** Good early years practice does not force young children to pursue knowledge on separate paths. Making mistakes and trying again should also be built into the process, with no pressures to produce a perfect result. Only through such first-hand experience can increasing competence and the confidence to accept new challenges be developed. The same starting point will and should have different outcomes for individual children, if practitioners apply the principles of good practice developed within the EYFS guidance. Using mixed age groups of 3 and 4 year olds can work well, too, in creative enterprises. Working with an artist, it was found that the 4 year olds were able to concentrate for longer periods of time when fully engaged in their work and this could be seen to impact on the concentration of the 3 year olds in the group (Canterbury Children's Centre 2006).

Focus on practice

An artist in residence

Jane, the head of a local authority setting, had managed to secure funding for working with local artists. The Lead Practitioner, Cathy, had spent time in a Reggio setting in Italy during the previous year and was now trying to implement some of that experience into the setting's daily practice, with varied degrees of success. One of the principles Cathy was keen to address was the Reggio approach to allowing children to investigate processes, as she had felt for some time that the setting was putting too much emphasis on the children producing similar artefacts, often for the consumption of parents. One practitioner, Helen, clearly disagreed that the process in which children were involved was more important than product, her argument being that producing an end-product showed application and dedication.

Cathy was very enthusiastic about the thought of working with an artist for a two-week period. Themes that the setting were currently focusing upon were Light and Dark (reflecting the time of the year) and colours, again reflecting the changing colours in the world around them. Due to other commitments, Sue, the artist, was only able to visit the setting for a brief look round before beginning her time there. During a short conversation with Sue as she gave her a tour of the setting, Cathy discussed the current themes as they went around the different rooms, hoping to establish what kinds of focus Sue was intending to pursue, so that short-term planning could reflect this. Sue, however, was reluctant to commit to anything specific, and talked generally about wanting the experience with the children to be organic.

During the first week, Sue initially focused on showing the children how to create a simple weaving frame from wood and string, and then demonstrated the principles of weaving with strips of ribbon and material. The older children, especially a group of 4 year old boys, enjoyed using the hammers, saws and tools to create the weaving 'looms', but quickly lost interest in the weaving process itself. The older girls persisted, creating loose, interesting patterns from two or three lines of weaving with various materials. Eager to have 'evidence' of the artist's involvement with the children, Helen emphasised how important it was for them to 'finish' their work. A small 'factory' developed with Sue and Helen mounting a display of the children's efforts at weaving.

Identifying good practice

On seeing this, Cathy spoke with both Sue and Helen, separately. She reminded Helen, yet again, that it was the process of weaving that should be the focus and not the product. With Sue, she thanked her for her contribution, talked about how the weaving activity had helped some of the children with their fine motor skills as well as extending knowledge in other areas of learning like the turn-taking and conversation that had taken place with the 'communal' piece of weaving Sue had initiated. Lastly, she commented on the need to focus on process rather than product. Sue looked confused, stating that she had thought from what Helen had said it had been a necessary part of her work with the children to encourage this. After some discussion and clarification, Sue and Cathy agreed a focus for the following week, both feeling much happier.

In the final week, Sue introduced special inks for the children to use on sheets of acetate, using daylight and a light box to explore the colours the children had created. One child, Joseph, who was generally shy about communicating with his peers, became fascinated by how the colours could be layered over each other to produce another colour. He became quite animated about the colours he'd create.

'Magic, it's magic', he'd say, proudly showing anyone who would look at how the process worked.

Leading practice

At a staff meeting the next week, Cathy asked for observations from staff about how they had found the experience. Most of the staff had found the experience beneficial, that Sue had been very supportive and full of suggestions, saying they would look more creatively now at how they used resources, and that the presence of a 'creative' mind in their midst had stimulated creativity within the children. Even Helen admitted that 'process' without any obvious 'product' was important, as evidenced by Joseph's reaction to mixing colours. One member of staff did worry that the children who had made the most 'noise' when it came to choosing what to do had dictated the way a session had gone, suggesting that, next time, perhaps choosing the composition of a group working with the artist might be better.

Task

- List in order of importance the number of ways Cathy might have improved the outcomes of Sue's time in the setting.
- Consider whether Cathy dealt effectively with the situation created by Helen.
- How would you deal with the suggestion by staff about choosing the composition of groups of children working with artists?
- Discuss the above with colleagues, comparing lists and possible solutions.

How can we ensure that children are provided with flexible routines that meet individual needs, in a well-resourced environment that takes account of diversity and encourages inclusive practice and provision?

(S09 and S12)

In order to be truly inclusive and accommodate diversity, a setting's routines need to be flexible. Creating a balance between the safety and comfort provided by a regular routine and the need to meet individual children's needs is what effective practitioners must strive for. There is a statutory requirement for practitioners within the EYFS to provide holistic and inclusive provision for young children, which is underpinned by the ECM agenda and recent legislation, for example the Race Relations (Amendment) Act 2000, the Special Education Needs and Disability Act (SENDA) 2001, the revised Code of Practice 2002, the Children Act 2004 and the Childcare Act 2006 (see Chapter 4). The EYFS highlights the relationship with the 'wider community' in all its diversity that effective settings develop and engage in.

One of the ways in which a setting can demonstrate its commitment to its local community is by organising its daily and weekly routines to accommodate some of the particular needs of the families within that community. Through the creation of schedules and routines that are responsive to babies and young children's needs, and flexible enough to take into account the needs of parents/carers, effective settings promote children's learning and development as well as building positive partnerships with families. The effective practitioner will understand the rationale for differentiation, when it comes to a child who, for example, attends more than one setting or with extended attendance may need a different period of rest. The effective practitioner, too, will understand the need for routines established for babies new to the setting to ideally reflect home patterns for sleeping and feeding. Children with issues around bladder control, specific medical conditions and SEN will require a more flexible approach. This will naturally affect the daily and weekly planning undertaken by practitioners, especially keyworkers, to ensure that individual needs are catered for.

Transitions

In more general terms, effective practice also needs to allow children time to come to terms with periods of transition from home into a pre-school setting or into mainstream school, ideally with a period of 'settling in' characterised by flexible planning that is sensitive to children's and parents' needs. Allowing children sufficient time to follow their interests should also be reflected in the day-to-day routines of the setting. If the day is broken up too often or routines are so rigid they stop children from becoming engrossed in activities and engaging in deeper levels of thinking, they become counterproductive. Again it is the balance between the safety and reassurance that comes from knowing what happens next for a child, and the time and freedom to engage in the kind of 'epistemic' investigative play that a child's curiosity feeds on, as well as the more imaginative, creative 'ludic' play, both of which promote deeper levels of thinking and learning (Hutt *et al.* 1989). The need for such flexibility now embedded in the EYFS framework (2007) has to be understood and supported by all staff for it to be effective. The Lead Practitioner will obviously model good practice, but may need to address the issue of more flexible routines in order that all staff understand the benefits for children and families. Looking at children as individuals and planning to meet their interests and needs, while ensuring overall development and progression within the areas of learning and development, calls for creative planning on the part of the whole team. If the keyworker has established a good working relationship with parents/carers and discusses children's interests and preferences (some of which will be ephemeral, while others will be more embedded), planning to meet individual needs should be easier and the very important continuity between the setting and home created.

Focus on practice

Staff in the baby room of a Children's Centre complained to the Lead Practitioner, Joy, about the routine laid down for nappy changing. In the present routine, nappy changing took place over a relatively short period of time for all the babies. This had initially been decided as a result of the low numbers of babies attending the centre. However, the number had increased slightly, as well as the number of toddlers now attending the setting, although staffing levels had yet to be increased. This had put pressure on the existing practitioners, not only in having to change more children, but they now had to queue for changing facilities that had previously been sufficient for their needs.

Identifying good practice

Over the next week, Joy observed the nappy-changing routine and could see that both babies and infants were distressed as well as practitioners. The pressures of time and lack of facilities were turning what should have been a relaxed, enjoyable experience into one that was fraught and hastily executed. After discussing the issues with staff, Joy expressed the opinion that the routine should change to reflect the individual needs of babies and infants; ideally, the babies' routines should reflect as far as possible the routines of home, in line with EYFS guidance. All the practitioners agreed this would be the better option, but pointed out that this change would affect the rest of the daily routines, for feeding, sleeping and if, for example, a practitioner was involved in an activity or observation. After looking again at the daily routines, Joy agreed that more staff were needed to support a more individual approach to the babies' and infants' needs. As numbers in the toddler room were at present quite low, she would speak with the Manager about more flexible use of existing staff until new staff were appointed. In the meantime, she asked practitioners to support each other as much as possible when it came to organising observations and activities for children's profiles.

Leading practice

As a result of her discussion with the Manager, Joy was asked to look at the routines in the 3–5 room. One area which took up staff time was the preparation and serving of snacks at a particular time each morning. Joy had previously worked at a setting where a rolling snack routine had been in place. She discussed with staff the possibility of making such a change, citing her own positive experience. Rolling snack could involve the children in helping to prepare it, an activity with great potential for learning as well as acquiring skills. Rolling snack also met the requirement of meeting individual needs, where children accessed the snack when they wanted it, not at a specific predetermined time. It also, as had been the case in her former setting, helped children who came to the setting without having eaten breakfast or those children 'at risk', who could access food throughout the day if needed. Joy also pointed out other benefits; for example, it encouraged children's learning and development within other areas of learning such as conversation, making choices and turn-taking.

Source: POD/Pearson Education Ltd. Jules Selmes

Some staff were hesitant, raising health and safety issues, but Joy pointed out that, if snack preparation was seen as an activity in itself, it released members of staff from the duty of preparing snacks for all the children, and changed it into an activity they could share with the children – a much more productive use of their time. Again staff stated this change to the routine would affect the rest of the day; often snack time had released those practitioners not directly involved, providing time for other duties, such as catching up on observations and children's profiles. Joy agreed it was difficult to find time within the working day, but time was already put aside for preparation and planning. She suggested the 'rolling snack' be given a trial run for the following four weeks, and then reviewed.

Reflections

- *How do you feel Joy responded to the issue over the nappy-changing routine?*
- *Was the solution she proposed fair and workable?*
- *Do you feel she should have involved staff more?*
- *In being asked to look at staffing and routines by the Manager, do you feel Joy's suggestions for a 'rolling snack' would help alleviate staffing difficulties in the setting?*
- *Do you consider Joy introduced the idea of changes to the snack routine in a positive way?*
- *Should she have involved staff more?*
- *If you had been in Joy's position, what might your proposals to help solve the issues have been?*

Task **Discuss the above with colleagues and compare your solutions.**

Acknowledging the diverse needs of the wider community has been shown by longitudinal research such as EPPE (2008, ongoing) to enhance children's sense of well-being as evidenced in the development of their cognitive, emotional and social intelligence. The Early Years Transition and Special Educational Needs (EYTSEN) research project commissioned by the DfES (2003) also found that nurseries and integrated/combined centres that supported the local community had a positive effect on the achievement of all children generally and those children with, or 'at risk' of, SEN in particular.

Diversity

In relating to Standard 12, the practitioner needs to take into account the above issues of acknowledging diversity and promoting inclusive practice (see Chapter 4). By focusing on the uniqueness of each child and their interests, the effective practitioner can create an environment whose resources reflect the diversity of cultures and beliefs of the wider community – ensuring, through artefacts, books, activities and experiences that are shared with parents/carers, children will feel they, their cultures and beliefs are celebrated and valued. Providing labels and print in the environment written in children's home languages will help children come to understand the importance of print, and will also make parents/carers

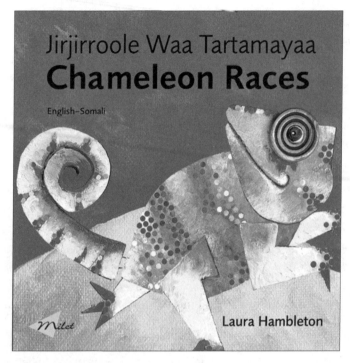

A dual-language book

Source: From Chameleon Races/English-Somali by Laura Hambleton (Milet Publishing 2005) Copyright: Laura Hambleton & Milet Publishing

feel more welcome. Dual-language books that are commercially available or made by the children and shared with their peers and family also promote a sense of self-esteem. World music and stories in different languages available on audio tapes for children to access and share, multicultural dolls, puppets, clothing representative of several cultures available in role-play areas, foods from different cultural cuisines, prepared and available at the snack table for children to taste and discuss, as well as the celebration of special festivals, are all examples that settings using good diversity practice adopt.

For children with Special Educational Needs (SEN), materials and space need to be adapted wherever possible, so they have equal access to indoor and outdoor provision safely. Tracking rails and tactile symbols can help the visually impaired child negotiate the indoor environment with more autonomy. Outdoor provision, using the senses of touch, smell and sound, perhaps through the building of a sensory garden, would support inclusive experiences. The use of an extensive range of communication systems in a setting including PECS (Picture Exchange System), Makaton, British Sign Language and Baby Sign (Callcentre 2009, online) helps hearing-impaired children and children on the autistic spectrum to feel included. Simple, practical additions like ramps or widened door openings give wheelchair-bound children easy access to indoor/outdoor provision. The Index for Inclusion by Booth and Ainscow (2002), for example, provides a clear checklist for settings to help them examine and expand their inclusive provision and practice.

Focus on practice

Accessing outdoor play

The baby and toddler room staff at a newly built Children's Centre complained to the Lead Practitioner, Jenny, about the difficulty of accessing the outdoor space, due to design 'problems'. A number of issues around 'architectural features' had emerged over the weeks since the setting opened and this was one more. Staff had found that a raised ledge supporting the doors to the outdoor provision was proving difficult to negotiate safely for children who were crawling or beginning to walk. Staff felt this was stopping the majority of children accessing the outdoor area. They also felt the area itself, while, having some good resources (large sandbox, tactile crawling track and small-scale climbing equipment on a soft surface), was not a particularly safe environment for babies and infants, containing as it did high concrete planters at each corner of the space.

Identifying good practice

After observing the children's behaviour, Jenny then discussed the situation with the Centre Manager who agreed that the planters would be fenced off as a safety precaution. Jenny met with staff to consider ideas on how the room could be adapted to help children access outdoor provision in line with EYFS guidance. One member of staff, Brenda, suggested that a low-level, customised ramp could be placed over the ledge during the time the doors were open. Jenny felt that would help the children who were walking, but suggested something softer was needed for those babies who were crawling and eager to be outside.

Leading practice

Jenny led the discussion on how this might be achieved, with staff finally agreeing on the use of foam blocks covered in blankets being laid over the offending ledge. Both the ramp and foam blocks were a success and this encouraged Jenny to discuss with staff the planning for outdoors. The planning in place had been 'patchy' due to limited access and lack of a 'rota' for identifying responsibilities in this area. This was addressed in line with EYFS principles on meeting children's individual interests and needs.

Reflections

- *Do you feel Jenny supported the staff's concerns effectively?*

- *Do you consider the solutions arrived at in enabling the babies' and toddlers' access to outdoor provision appropriate and adequate?*

- *Should Jenny have been more proactive if she was aware outdoor provision had been 'patchy'?*

- *Have you been in a situation where 'architectural features' have been an issue when trying to provide high-quality provision and practice? If so, how did you deal with them?*

Task Discuss this issue with peers and colleagues, especially if you have not yet had experience in such situations. Note their comments in your journal, and consider where such problems might arise in your own setting, and how you might deal with them.

What strategies need to be in place to guarantee accountability for the delivery of high-quality provision?

(S24)

In attempting to meet this standard, the EYP needs to show visible evidence of high-quality inclusive practice and provision, where the environment is viewed as an effective, enabling 'third teacher', supporting the cognitive, physical, emotional and social needs of children. The statutory requirements of the EYFS underpin each child's learning journey towards the **Early Learning Goals** and these need to be met and clearly demonstrated. The EYP is responsible for modelling and leading good practice in observing, assessing, planning and recording children's progress (see Chapter 5). Reporting this process to the stakeholders, most significantly the children themselves and their parents/carers, is an important part of practitioners' **accountability** for high-quality provision. The EYP is also accountable, through the progress of their own professional development and performance management, to senior staff and management, as well as external bodies. This accountability can be demonstrated in a number of ways. Practice that promotes and supports the vision or mission statement of the setting can be evidenced through the physical environment and routines that continuously demonstrate good practice, and through policies that are revised on a regular basis to take into account changes in legislation and government initiatives.

The EYP needs to highlight any specific training that staff may require to understand and embrace change and so ensure they are given the opportunity to improve their own professional development. This in turn should have a positive impact on the standard of provision in a setting. The EYP needs to take into account and act on feedback from parents/carers, through the use of, for example, suggestion boxes, regular discussion or noticeboards. This not only promotes a good working partnership, but also demonstrates flexibility and respect for stakeholders' views in the process of maintaining high-quality provision. Management, through performance review, can help the EYP to reflect on practice and provision and make any necessary changes. Drawing up improvement or action plans that are SMART (Specific, Measurable, Achievable, Realistic and Timebound), as a result of such feedback and reflection, will support and encourage reflective practice among staff. Again, the detail of such action plans need to be demonstrably open and accessible to stakeholders. Informing parents/carers through displaying such plans in the setting or through news letters or reports promotes transparency.

Conclusion

What strategies can be developed to support the establishment of secure, stimulating and purposeful indoor and outdoor learning environments through planned and appropriate adult-initiated and child-led experiences?

We have seen in this chapter how theories of development and learning that underpin good, effective practice are evidenced in the latest initiatives of the ECM agenda and the EYFS practice guidance. The young 'scientist/explorer' central to Piaget's vision of how children develop has now become the 'active learner' described in the principles of the EYFS. The role of the adult in supporting, sustaining and resourcing children's development echoes the work of Vygotsky and Bruner, demonstrating the crucial role the knowledgeable adult has to play in a child's learning journey. Being knowledgeable not only relates to content but also to context. The knowledgeable adult must understand sensitively how to engage a child in sustained shared thinking and must also recognise when not to intrude upon that deep-level learning that the solitary learner needs to investigate undisturbed. The 'enabling' environment that practitioners need to create in order for children to develop and grow effectively is reminiscent of the 'third teacher' approach grounded in the practice of Reggio Emilia pre-schools (see Chapter 6), an approach that sees trust and equality in relationships begin to develop, where practitioner and child go on a journey of discovery and research together. The need to personalise learning, to see children as holistic individuals, is now supported by numerous longitudinal studies and research into effective early years practice, as well as reflecting the five outcomes of ECM (2003). There is also the requirement to create secure environments where:

- Children's sense of well-being is nurtured and protected.
- The milieu is shown to support meaningful links with home in order to aid those potentially difficult moments of transition.
- Experiences are provided that are stimulating, intriguing and challenging, both indoors and outdoors.

All these factors have been shown to be integral to the most effective environments for the child's emotional, cognitive, social and physical growth and development. In such environments children can engage in epistemic and ludic play – play that is never undervalued by the phrase 'just playing', but seen as the multi-layered, complex problem-solving activity that it is. Play is now embedded in the principles and philosophy of good early years practice, as evidenced by the EYFS guidance. The opportunities for play in today's early years settings need to reflect the knowledge we now have with regard to the child's developing brain (see Chapter 2). Movement feeds the synapses in a child's brain, and the new emphasis on outdoor provision and the opportunities it affords physical development reflects this knowledge and understanding. It also reflects a realisation that today's children may suffer a 'nature deficit', as a result of Western post-industrial cultural mores and practice. Local Authority funding to improve outdoor provision, the launch of Forest School projects and creative partnerships are all attempts to redress the balance, to provide all children, whatever their individual needs, with secure, stimulating and purposeful indoor and outdoor learning environments.

How can we ensure children are provided with flexible routines that meet individual needs, in a well-resourced environment that takes account of diversity and encourages inclusive practice and provision?

(S09 and S12)

Flexibility is difficult to plan for but the necessity to accommodate children's individual needs is now grounded in legislation supporting the rights of the child and underpins the principles and practice of the EYFS. Routines need to be flexible enough to take into account those all-important links between home and the setting, whether it be the feeding and sleeping patterns of babies and infants reflecting the patterns and practice of home, or attempting to embed children's interests, however transitory, into short-term and medium-term planning. How to plan for the unexpected is a skill the effective practitioner needs to acquire and, when children's interests take hold, planning and routines need to be flexible enough to accommodate them. The mix of child-led and adult-led activities and experiences this process can create is shown repeatedly by research to be the best way of supporting children's learning and development. Planning and routines also need to support children at particularly vulnerable times such as the transition from pre-school to mainstream settings, or at times when their personal circumstances are temporarily difficult, for example the arrival of a new sibling, or the ill-health of a parent, or a death in the family.

When organising and resourcing the environment, the effective practitioner needs to take into account the free flow of play between indoor and outdoor provision. They have to ensure that all children have equal access to such provision and that the resources reflect the diversity of the wider community. If physical changes to buildings are required for children with particular disabilities, then, within reason, this must be swiftly undertaken in order to ensure that practice is inclusive. In supporting diversity, practitioners may need to examine their own beliefs and values to ensure that stereotyping does not take place. Treating all children equally does not mean treating them 'the same'. The values and beliefs of the wider community need to be embraced and, where there are difficulties and tensions, these need to be worked at for the children's sake. Difference and the richness diverse cultures can bring to a setting should be celebrated if an environment is to be truly inclusive.

What strategies need to be in place to guarantee accountability for the delivery of high-quality provision?

(S24)

Upholding the mission statement or vision for a setting depends on fundamental principles being agreed by all staff. In that way the delivery of high-quality provision can be maintained and sustained. The effective practitioner needs to be self-reflective and encourage such reflection in other staff. The willingness to undergo training in new skills or make changes to established practices needs to be modelled and other staff supported during such periods of change. Policies need to be up to date, expressing current thinking and legislation, in order for high-quality provision to be maintained. Being accountable to stakeholders, particularly children and their parents/carers, is a clear responsibility for the effective practitioner. Children and their parents/carers should have a voice in relation to the practice and provision of a setting, and their views acknowledged, taken seriously and acted upon. We are also accountable to such external bodies as the Local Authority and Ofsted. This is another area of responsibility, and the ability to respond to such inspections with positive action plans for improvement is a necessary skill that needs to be developed. Being able to maintain the identity, defend, reflect upon and sustain the delivery of high provision means that the effective practitioner is forward looking and never complacent about their practice and provision.

Further reading

Athey, C. (1990) *Extending Thought In Young Children: a parent-teacher partnership.* London: Paul Chapman.

Bilton, H. (2005) *Outdoor Provision in the Early Years.* London: David Fulton.

Canterbury Children's Centre (2006) 'Searching for Meaning'. Available at: **http://www.canterburycc.co.uk/meaning.php** Accessed on 4 January 2009.

Hutt, S.J. *et al.* (1989) *Play, Exploration and Learning: a natural history of the pre-school.* London: Routledge.

References

Athey, C. (1990) *Extending Thought In Young Children: a parent-teacher partnership.* London: Paul Chapman.

Bilton, H. (2005) *Outdoor Provision in the Early Years.* London: David Fulton.

Booth, T. and Ainscow, M. (2002) *The Index for Inclusion,* 2nd edition. Developing Learning and Participation in Schools, Bristol: CSIE.

Brock, A., Dodds, S., Jarvis, P. and Olusoga, Y. (2008) *Perspectives on Play.* Harlow: Pearson.

Bruner, J. (1983) *Child's Talk: Learning to use Language.* New York: Norton.

Canterbury Children's Centre (2006) 'Searching for Meaning'. Available at: http://www.canterburycc.co.uk/meaning.php Accessed on 4 January 2009.

Carr, M. (2001) *Assessment in Early Childhood Settings; learning stories.* London: Paul Chapman.

Cook, J. (2008) 'Setting up a Forest School', *The Teacher,* November, p. 43.

David, T. and Powell, S. (2005) 'Play in the early years: the influence of cultural difference'. In J. Moyles (ed.) (2005) *The Excellence of Play.* Maidenhead: Open University Press.

DCSF (2007) Early Years Foundation Stage Practice Guidance.

Duffy, B. (1998) Supporting Creativity and Imagination in Early Years. Burkingham: Oxford University Press.

Greenland, P. (2000) Hopping home backwards, body intelligence and movement play. Leeds: Jabado Publications.

Hutt, S.J. *et al.* (1989) *Play, Exploration and Learning: a natural history of the pre-school.* London: Routledge.

Jarvis, P. (2007) 'Monsters, Magic and Mr. Psycho: Rough and Tumble Play in the Early Years of Primary School, a Biocultural Approach'. *Early Years, An International Journal of Research and Development,* 27(2), pp. 171–88.

Jarvis, P. and George, J. (2008) 'Play, Learning for Life: the vital role of play in human development'. In A. Brock, S. Dodds, P. Jarvis and Y. Olusoga (eds).

Laevers, F. (1994) *The Leuven Involvement Scale for Young Children.* Belgium: Centre for Experiential Education.

Learning Through Landscapes (2008) Available at: http://www.ltl.org.uk/ Accessed on 15 February 2009.

Lindon, J. (2001) 'Striding Ahead'. *Nursery World,* November, pp. 12–13.

Lindon, J. (2008) *Understanding Child Development: Linking theory and Practice, 2nd edition.* London: Hodder Arnold.

Paley, V. (1984) *Boys and Girls, Superheroes in the Doll Corner.* Chicago: University of Chicago Press.

Pascal, C. *et al.* (1995) *Evaluating and Developing Quality in Early Childhood Settings: a professional development programme.* Worcester: Worcester College of Higher Education.

Vygotsky, I. (1978) *Mind in Society.* Cambridge, MA: Harvard.

White, J. (2008) *Playing and Learning Outdoors.* London: Routledge.

8

Leadership and partnership in Early Years

Sarah Procter, Lynn Bradley and Wendy Holland

Chapter overview

The standards addressed in this chapter are:

S29   Recognise and respect the influential and enduring contribution that families and parents/carers can make to children's development, well-being and learning

S30   Establish fair, respectful, trusting and constructive relationships with families and parents/carers, and communicate sensitively and effectively with them

S31   Work in partnership with families and parents/carers, at home and in the setting, to nurture children, to help them develop and improve outcomes for them

S32   Provide formal and informal opportunities through which information about children's well-being, development and learning can be shared between the setting and families and parents/carers

S06   The contribution that other professionals within the setting and beyond can make to children's physical and emotional well-being, development and learning

S33   Establish and sustain a culture of collaborative and cooperative working between colleagues

S34   Ensure that colleagues working with them understand their role and are involved appropriately in helping children meet planned objectives

S35   Influence and shape the policies and practices of the setting and share in collective responsibility for their implementation

S36   Contribute to the work of a multi-professional team and, where appropriate, coordinate and implement agreed programmes and interventions on a day-to-day basis

Relating to the above standards, the following key questions will be addressed:

● How can settings ensure that partnership working with families and carers is valued and embedded in practice?

(S29, S30, S31, S32)

- What is effective team working and how can it be delivered to ensure that children's development, well-being and learning are supported and enhanced by a range of professional backgrounds and perspectives?

(S06, S35, S36)

- What is effective leadership within an early childhood setting?

(S33, S34, S35)

The family in time (a 'focus' sheet from Pam Jarvis)

The family of the past	The family of the present	The family of the future

Was a traditional/extended family in the pre-industrial and early industrial period (to the early 20th century)	The liberation of women, including the rejection of full-time housework and childcare for paid work has brought about the development of the 'symmetrical family' where parents of both genders take equal roles (theoretically, but don't forget the female 'triple shift')	*This obviously has to be based on logical prediction:*
Was a 'unit of production' in the pre-industrial period – working life was carried out in or nearby the home, often with the whole family 'pitching in'		A continuing rise in 'alternative' family lifestyles
		Growing flexibility in gender partnerships focused upon shared child-raising, often outside formal marriage
Was a family of many brothers and sisters – parents had several children, but expected to lose one or two due to higher infant mortality (see typical large Victorian family picture above). From the mid 20th century onwards, contraception and better health care reduced the number of children born, but increased life expectancy.	There was a liberalisation of divorce laws in the Divorce Act (1969) followed by a growing divorce rate 1970–1990, and a subsequent rise in the amount of single parent, single parent + grandparent(s) and reconstituted or blended families	Emerging roles for older people, as the lifespan extends and people remain healthy and active for longer. These may possibly be associated with provision of care for grandchildren/great-grandchildren while parents are working
Marriage was for life, but the typical life-span was shorter than today	There is a growing rate of children born outside formal marriage (1980-present), and falling marriage rates	Expansion of artificial fertility techniques and associated legislation. May eventually allow completely 'test-tube' babies via the use of artificial wombs, and stem cell fertility techniques may additionally allow same-sex couples to genetically co-parent their own child.
The Industrial Revolution (1800–1850) brought the change of 'going out to work' for the adults of the family	There has been a rise in alternative family lifestyles (e.g. gay families, friendship group 'families')	
After World War II (1945 onwards) many families moved to new, single family sized houses in the suburbs and the cultural stereotype of the nuclear family with the 'instrumental' commuter father and 'expressive' housewife mother became the 'norm'	The typical family tree structure of the modern family is 'beanpole' like, with many single and two-child families but longer-lived members (see five generation 'beanpole' family picture below)	As the 'baby-boomers' born 1945–1965 retire, society will have to decide how to fund their pensions from a shrinking workforce, and as such baby-boomers reach the end of their lives, the British working population will start to fall . . . . unless a policy to encourage immigration of young people born from 1980 onwards is instigated in the near future
	Fertility techniques have been piloted that allow women to consider older first-time child-bearing	
	More people are remaining single and childless, meaning that we have both an aging and a falling population	

Sources (photos): Alamy Images: ClassicStock (l); Corbis: Gary Houlder (c); JUPITER IMAGES/BananaStock (r).

Introduction

In this chapter we are going to address the various ways in which Early Years Professionals can develop effective working relationships with other adults in order to ensure that outcomes for children are enhanced and improved. In particular, we will consider how EYPs can work effectively in partnership with parents and carers in the continually changing and dynamic family structures outlined in the focus sheet and also how they can work with staff from other professional groups and backgrounds as well as develop positive working relationships within their own teams. The skills, knowledge and values which support the achievement of these standards will be considered as well as how recent research supports effective practice. We will also consider how practitioners who are new to working in Early Years, and those without traditional 'leadership' roles within settings can contribute to the construction of a new perspective on leading practice.

Focus on practice

Josh's family

Josh, a 3 year old, whose family had recently moved into the area, began attending a private daycare setting in a reasonably affluent urban area of a city. His keyworker, Eve, noticed how his mother, Fran, who brought him in the mornings, seemed very reserved and reluctant to engage in conversation, making her younger child, a 10 month old daughter, the excuse for a quick departure. By contrast, his father, who collected Josh in the evenings, was talkative and generally pleasant, often apologising for being a little late. Josh appeared to settle into his new surroundings quite quickly, and formative observations soon began to show he had good communication skills and a facility for problem solving.

Identifying good practice

One morning, determined to share an observation with Fran, Eve attempted to draw her into conversation, but the younger child was crying and Eve quickly saw that Fran was on the verge of tears herself. Josh was also not as happy to leave his mother this particular morning, so Eve tried to distract him with his favourite activity of constructing with the large hollow blocks. She mentioned the incident to the setting EYP, Pat, who suggested a meeting with Fran, at a less hectic time than the morning 'meet and greet'. Eve thought she might mention this to Josh's father when he called to collect him that evening, but he was even later than usual, so late that Eve had been on the point of phoning Josh's home contact number. She had intended to remind Josh's father of the setting's closing time, but he'd been so apologetic and thankful, Eve had let the matter go.

In a casual conversation in the staff room, Eve mentioned to Pat how Josh's behaviour was beginning to change. The young boy's concentration, which had been remarkably good initially, was noticeably weaker, and he separated from Fran, whom she described as 'moody' and 'unpredictable', with increasing reluctance, adding: 'she's so different to Josh's father'. Pat asked if Eve had managed to set up a meeting with Josh's mother, to which Eve replied she had tried twice and each time Fran had not attended and made excuses afterwards. From other brief comments, Pat was beginning to worry about Eve's 'preferential' treatment of Josh's father. She suggested that, as something was definitely having an effect on Josh, it might be beneficial for Eve and herself to meet with both Josh's parents. Eve immediately defended the father, saying, as he ran his own company single-handed, it was difficult enough for him to find time to collect his son, let alone come to meetings, whereas Fran 'had all day'. Things were brought to a head one morning when Josh kicked out at another child and then tried to bite him. A meeting with his parents was arranged, but only Fran arrived. The meeting revealed several important facts that had not appeared on the admissions proforma or in initial discussions with Josh's parents. Eve and Pat learned that the family had moved to the area to be nearer Fran's family, so that she could return part-time to her job as a radiographer, but this had been put on hold as Fran had been experiencing prolonged 'constant tiredness' after the birth of her daughter, something she had not experienced with Josh. She felt Josh had picked up on this and was becoming a 'difficult' child at home. Although her sister was doing her best to help out with the children, she too was finding Josh's behaviour very demanding. Fran, who had seemed distressed and at times near to tears during the meeting, expressed real concern over the fact that Josh's behaviour was now 'public'. She had put it down to their moving away from the only place he'd known as 'home'. Pat reassured her that was possibly one reason for it, plus the additional stress of attending a new setting that all children experienced. She asked if Fran had seen her GP about the tiredness, but Fran replied that the family had only just become registered locally and had been trying to self-medicate with 'tonics'. She didn't feel she could 'trouble' a doctor with simple tiredness. At the suggestion that another agency might be able to provide temporary help (a family support worker), Fran was adamant that her own family was all the support she needed. When asked by Eve what her husband felt, Fran shrugged, 'He thinks I'll feel better when I'm back at work – it's me – I need to pull myself together.' Pat proposed that, with a 3 year old and an infant, there was little wonder she was tired, and suggested no-one would think she was 'wasting time' if she mentioned it at the family clinic the next time she attended. Pat proposed that the setting would continue to observe Josh and keep her informed of any new developments and that Fran and Eve could start a 'home/school diary' through which they could better communicate, given that mornings could be particularly 'hectic'. It was also agreed that there would be a meeting in a month's time 'to discuss how the whole family were getting along'.

Leading practice

After the meeting, Pat asked Eve how she now felt about the situation with Josh and his parents. When Eve began to suggest that Fran had a lot going for her – lovely home, supportive sister, great husband who supported her – it wasn't as though she had to go to work, Pat stopped her, saying she had a real concern that Fran was possibly suffering from some kind of depression and might need professional help. She also asked Eve to reflect on her relationship with both parents and ask herself why she was ready to forgive Josh's father his continual lateness, which had at times been extremely inconvenient for staff, but did not make a similar allowance for Fran's behaviour?

Eve did reflect and realised she had been biased in her approach. She made extra efforts with Fran, particularly on mornings when she appeared at the setting exhausted and strained, and did eventually speak with Josh's father about the inconvenience to staff that his continual lateness caused. When Eve tried to talk to him about Josh's behaviour, he became evasive, saying that was an 'area' his wife dealt with and he didn't want to interfere, adding that he felt sure Eve was doing a great job with Josh. Fran heeded Pat's words and went to see her GP, who diagnosed and began to treat her for mild post-natal depression. Josh's behaviour gradually settled and his sense of well-being and involvement began to increase. Fran began to appear less exhausted and was more willing to stay and talk with Eve about Josh's achievements, as well as communicating through the home/school diary. After Josh had been at the setting for six months, Fran found part-time work as a radiographer and introduced her sister, who would be collecting Josh in the afternoons, to Eve. Fran voiced her concerns that Josh's behaviour might 'dip' as a result of her returning to work part-time, but Eve reassured her that, even if Josh did react negatively to the changes in his routine, together they could support him through it.

Eve informed Pat of the change in circumstances, when presenting the changed paperwork for collecting Josh. Pat 'positioned' herself unobtrusively in the 'meet and greet' area of Josh's room occasionally and noticed a real difference in Fran's demeanour, something over the following weeks she was pleased to hear Eve comment on positively herself.

Reflections

- *How would you as a leading practitioner have dealt with Eve's rather 'one sided' attitude to Josh's parents? Here you could also reflect on gender issues, and consider if we are more likely to expect more from mothers than fathers, and the potential unfairness this raises.*

- *How might you continue to work with Fran if she completely refused to follow your suggestions to seek further professional help for her illness, and appeared to be increasingly depressed, to the point that you began to have concerns that the children's well-being may be at risk?*

- *What if Eve had not responded to Pat's suggestions in such a positive fashion? How do you think Pat should have moved on to manage the situation further?*

Task Discuss the above with your colleagues and peers. After considering the above, are any of you aware of having 'different rules' for mothers and fathers in your setting(s)? If so, how might you remedy this? Discuss with colleagues how you feel the above scenario relates to the standards focused upon in this chapter.

How can settings ensure that partnership working with families and carers is valued?

(S29, S30, S31, S32)

Families are the bedrock of society and the place for nurturing happy, capable and resilient children.

(The Children's Plan, DCSF 2007b, p. 5)

We are born into families, we create families, we live in families and we are buried by families. Families provide the basic social geography through which we negotiate our paths through life.

(Wasoff & Dey 2000, p. 1)

The above quotes suggest that the family is central and familiar, but 'the family' can have several meanings, as we outlined earlier. In fact, we could be said to live in several 'families': the nuclear family, the extended family and the ancestral family to name a few, all of which can and may impact upon a child's development. The EYP needs to be aware of the possible forms 'the family' might take when trying to meet the needs of individual children. The Office of National Statistics figures for 2001 showed families to be getting smaller with more 'only' children. The average age for first-time mothers is now 29. There has been a drop in the number of divorces (although the UK is still top of the divorce table in Europe) and a similar drop in the number of people getting married. Co-habitation is increasing as are the many and varied extended families with their complex relationships of step-children and step-parents, as well as an increase in the numbers of lone parents. This means that the practitioner could be dealing with a relatively new mother who is unsure of her own parenting skills, wary of the 'public' nature of the setting and feeling she is being judged on these emerging skills, or a more experienced mother who may not be able to articulate her real needs in the partnership. Many parents feel threatened by institutional contexts, by the agendas they feel are set by practitioners without sufficient consultation, and incomprehensible jargon used between professionals. This sense of 'insecurity' is sometimes aggravated by the media 'hype' which criticises parents for allowing their children unedited access to the Internet, for working too many hours, for being lone parents or divorced . . . the list is long. Practitioners need to be wary of being influenced by such media headlines into blaming parents for being too busy, stressed, disorganised, defensive or having poor relationships with their children, and try instead to empathise and see life from the parent's perspective.

The practitioner needs to establish the setting's policies while building a trusting partnership with parents. They also need to be aware of the impact of environmental factors on how a family functions. Obvious factors such as employment, health, housing will influence the functioning of every family within the setting's neighbourhood, in spite of many and varied government initiatives. Ghate and Hazel (2002) in their research describe the characteristics of families who may be 'at risk' as a result of 'poor' environments, 'poor' in this sense meaning not just poverty but also environments that do not have 'optimal parenting' conditions. While acknowledging that not all materially poor families live in poor environments, they suggest there is a strong link between 'geography' and 'deprivation'. In recent years the Government has tried to address such issues as child poverty and safeguarding issues through the Every Child Matters agenda, with the family's primary role of 'socialisation' at the centre of this initiative.

The multiplicity of factors involved shows the implausibility of trying to formulate one policy that will work to create a 'partnership' with all parents. There are some common denominators as Hall (1999) has found; early dialogue is essential and needs to be maintained. Such dialogue also has to be meaningful for both practitioners and parent/carers. It should empower parents by providing accessible information, advice, support and training. It should raise awareness about facilities and services through user-friendly media; how, for example, will the parent with poor reading skills or with English as an additional language feel if most information is only available in printed form? The crucial message here is how parents feel about these support services: 'The best services in the world will not necessarily enhance parents' ability to cope unless they are perceived as helpful and acceptable . . . to ensure that parents feel in control of the type of support they receive and the way in which it is delivered', Ghate and Hazel (2002, p. 262). These authors go on to suggest that problems arise when parents no longer feel 'in charge' of their children, in the sense that they are in some way handing them to someone else who will take over their care. In order to feel secure, they need to feel that there is a partnership in which the parents are the 'senior' carers.

Research has demonstrated convincingly that parental involvement makes a huge difference to children's outcomes (EPPE 2004). The impact of parental involvement can also have tangible benefits for parents, early education settings and the wider community. In this section we will consider how the EYP can support parental involvement in their child's learning and development in the setting and beyond. We will do this by examining some examples of good practice in relation to parental involvement including the work of the Pen Green Centre (PGC) in Corby, the Parents Early Years and Learning (PEAL) Project and the Birth to School Study: a Longitudinal Evaluation of the Peers Early Education Partnership (Evangelou et al. 2005). We will also be referring to support material on 'Positive Relationships' from the EYFS framework with regard to 'Parents as Partners'. International evidence found in the approach taken by the pre-schools in the Reggio Emilia district of Northern Italy, and the impact of such programmes as HeadStart and High/Scope in the USA (see Chapter 2) on creating successful partnerships with parents will also be discussed.

In creating open and trusting partnerships with parents, EYPs need to be able to reflect on their own values and beliefs in relation to parental involvement. As the EYFS suggests in 'Effective practice: Parents as Partners' (2007), some practitioners, in attempting to build partnerships with parents, may find certain parenting styles fit more closely with their own views, and they clearly need to reflect on this potential for bias. Experience of building relationships within diverse family situations where the practitioner may be from a different culture from the family, for example, can have an enriching effect on practitioners' perspectives and values. EYPs need to be prepared to move beyond traditional 'deficit' approaches, which appear to suggest that the professional's principal role is to compensate for some kind of inadequacy on the part of the parent. Such a 'deficit' model can lead to the creation of a partnership where the parent/carer is 'passive', which can in turn lead to resentment, if they feel that their role has been usurped by the professional. Reay (1998) suggests that this 'deficit' view can be particularly problematic in practitioners' perceptions of the abilities and interests of working-class parents, in relation to their children's development and education. He further suggests that, although both working-class and middle-class mothers invested time, effort, money, thought and emotion into their children's development and education, the difference that emerges tends to be the *effectiveness* with which middle-class mothers are able to access, shape and facilitate their child's care and education due to their greater 'cultural capital' (Bourdieu 1977). Finch (1984) in her study of inner city playgroups describes how '. . . middle class outsiders step in to take over playgroups which working class mothers cannot "manage" on their own. This fits neatly into the process of educating working class women in "proper" childcare practice.' Such perceptions can often understandably be perceived by parents to be patronising and/or tokenistic.

Children between the ages of birth and 18 years spend approximately 70 per cent of their lives at home with their 'first educators', so the home environment is obviously critical to their development and learning. The effective practitioner needs to understand each child's background and early experiences through both positively acknowledging the child as an individual and incorporating the child's early experiences in learning activities. The surest way to achieve this is, as suggested at the beginning of this chapter, through the development of an open, honest relationship with the child's parents/carers. True parental involvement needs to reflect a model of empowerment (Bax 2001, cited in Whalley *et al.* 2007). This model seeks to promote a parent's sense of being an active participant and co-educator in their child's learning and development rather than a passive recipient of information from professionals; this reciprocal relationship also enables the professional to become an active learner.

> The teacher is no longer merely the 'one-who-teaches', but one who is himself taught in dialogue with the students, who in turn while being taught teach . . . they become jointly responsible for a process in which they all grow . . . here no one teaches another, nor is anyone self taught. People teach each other.
>
> (Friere 1996, cited in Whalley *et al.* 2007, p. 156)

Friere, a South American educator, worked with impoverished and oppressed communities to develop an approach to education which sought to empower by encouraging participants in his programmes not to accept without questioning. This approach underpins the work at the Pen Green Centre where a similar model is used to enable parents to develop skills in critical reflection so that new knowledge and understanding can be co-constructed with the professionals employed in settings. The PGC was opened in 1983 in Corby in response to social and economic decline in the area resulting in poor outcomes for children and their families. The PGC developed a strong vision of a service which would 'honour the needs of young children and celebrate their existence. It would also support families, however they were constituted within the community' (Whalley *et al.* 2007, p. 3). While the PGC has been involved in many different types of parental involvement programmes since 1983, the *Parents Involvement in their Children's Learning Training Programme* (PICL) (Whalley *et al.* 2007) warrants further investigation here. Although it may be impossible for all EYPs to replicate the work of the programme in its entirety, an understanding of the approach could offer new ideas for practitioners. The PICL Programme seeks to support parents to develop knowledge, skills and understanding of their child's learning and development using a group work model. Concepts such as 'Involvement', 'Well-being', 'Adult style' and 'Schemas' are examined. Parents are also supported to develop skills in using video to record observations of their children at home. Parents and staff share video footage and written observations in order that the parent/carer and the practitioner can engage together in curriculum planning for the child, for both the home and the nursery. The PICL Programme has demonstrated that parents from any cultural or social economic background can be actively and meaningfully engaged in supporting their children's learning and development. See http://www.pengreen.org for more information about PICL.

The focus on and development of 'Parent Partnerships' within the 'Positive Relationships' theme and principles of the EYFS, and the development of such projects as Parents, Early Years and Learning (PEAL), Peers Early Education Partnership (PEEP) and its longitudinal evaluation, Birth to School Study (BTSS) (Evangelou *et al.* 2005), should alert the EYP to the Government's ongoing commitment to extending and improving the practitioner's ability to involve parents meaningfully in the education of their children. PEAL is a consortium project run by the National Children's Bureau (NCB), Coram (formerly the Thomas Coram Foundation for Children) and the London Borough of Camden, who have collectively developed a training programme for practitioners to help them work with families to ensure that parents are involved appropriately in their children's early learning. PEAL advocates the following elements as central to working with parents and families: authentic relationships, communication and partnership and the exploration of what is effective practice in the early years. PEAL supports practitioners in beginning the process of involving parents; this includes establishing the setting's values in relation to parental involvement, opportunities for parental involvement and helping the practitioner to reflect upon any skill or knowledge gaps they may have in relation to working with parents in this way. PICL is one of the tools a practitioner might use to begin the partnership process.

Parental involvement has been at the heart of the collective Early Years experience of children within the European context for centuries, initially informally, and then by the formation of cooperative groups in the post-World War II period until the present. The first pre-schools in Reggio Emilia, for example, were founded by parents and a range of opportunities for involvement continue to be offered to parents. 'Parent participation enables a communication network that leads to fuller and more reciprocal knowledge as well as to a more effective search for the best educational methods, contexts and values' (Malaguzzi and Penn 1997, p. 28). In the UK, the work of the Pre-School Learning Alliance, formerly the Pre-School Playgroups Association, can also be cited.

In the Reggio Emilia approach (Malaguzzi and Penn 1997), induction programmes for new parents ensure that parents are familiar with the layout of the building, the staff and, most importantly, that they understand the values, principles and philosophies that will shape their children's early learning experiences. Parental participation is nurtured through a range of methods to stimulate parents' interests and enable them to connect with the work of the setting. A day book, for example, uses photos to capture the children's significant experiences during the day. Extensive communication round the 'documentation' of children's learning and development is also an area where parents help by giving input and suggestions for future planning. They, alongside the teachers, are seen as co-researchers with their children and facilitators of their own children's learning journeys. Programmes like Early HeadStart (visit **http://www.literacytrust.org.uk/socialinclusion/ earlyyears/headstartresearch.html** for more information) and High/Scope in the USA (**http://www.highscope.org/**) again reinforce the vital importance of the active participation of parents in children's learning and development, particularly in communities such as Corby, in the sense that they are judged to be economically and socially disadvantaged.

The EYFS framework constantly reinforces the need for parental involvement to be seen as a fundamental element of early years practice that we need to develop. Through respecting the diversity of families, by establishing meaningful dialogue, by learning together through participation and co-researching, there is now a statutory expectation for partnerships between practitioners and parents to be effectively established in every Early Years setting. The resources provided within the EYFS Practice Guidance (2008), and contained on the associated CD-ROM, explore the many issues, challenges and dilemmas involved. Advice is provided that relates to how the practitioner needs to reflect upon and ensure their approach is inclusive and anti-discriminatory. It is emphasised that practitioners can come to understand the specific needs of parents, gain knowledge and understanding of particular lifestyles or beliefs, and establish some common ground around child-rearing practices through thoughtful and meaningful communication. There is also the need to ensure that practitioners, while trying to establish warm and friendly partnerships, maintain a professional attitude and do not become emotionally involved to the extent that they prejudice their role. As the EYFS states, 'sometimes inexperienced staff may make the mistake of trying to be a friend to parents rather than a friendly professional' (2007, p. 4).

Examination of research findings that identify and exemplify current good practice may help support practitioners in developing their own partnerships with parents. Discussions with other professionals both within and beyond their settings may also support the development of successful ideas and practices. The practitioner's own understanding of what parental involvement is and how it can be achieved needs to be grounded in the specific needs of the families that attend the setting through ongoing dialogue with all stakeholders.

Focus on practice

Sam and Cliff, parents working with parents

Sam works with her husband Cliff, running a small home-based childminding practice. Although Sam left school with few formal qualifications, she has worked hard
over the last seven years to achieve various qualifications in relation to early years
practice. Sam is now enrolled on the Long EYPS Pathway and is mentoring her
husband as he begins his NVQ 3. Sam and Cliff also employ two part-time assistants
for their childminding practice who are also enrolled on an NVQ 2 programme. Sam's
personal experiences of being a teenage parent and now step-parenting Cliff's four
children from a previous relationship have made her acutely aware of the varying
needs that parents and carers have in relation to parenting.

Sam and Cliff have been actively involved in many of the Early Years and Childcare
Partnership sub-groups, and Sam chairs a local forum for childminders. Sam has
undertaken some research with the other childminders about how they view their
partnerships with parents and carers.

Identifying good practice

Sam uses a staff meeting with Cliff and her two assistants to reflect on the relationships they have established with the parents who use their service. Following a
lengthy conversation they reflect on the values that they hope their practice demonstrates. They are inclusive in the way they recognise and respond to the differing
needs emanating from the diversity of families accessing their service. This is shown,
for example, through flexible routines that reflect children's home experiences and
family needs. The staff are professional, friendly and non-judgemental in their deal-
ings with parents, acknowledging, for example, cultural differences and values that
may impact on some childrearing practices. They attempt to empower parents by
showing that they value their perspectives, through frequent dialogue around
planned themes, visits, proposed additions or alterations to the environment,
providing the opportunity for parent participation in policy development and in
their children's profiles.

Sam has been involved in the PICL training; she attended a two-day training
programme with Leah, a parent who uses her childminding service. The training
programme offered both Leah and Sam the opportunity to acquire new knowledge,
develop new technical skills and have plenty of opportunity to discuss Leah's son
and his development and learning needs. Their shared observations about his development within his home and childminding setting have proved to be very enlighten-
ing and useful; Sam explains carefully how she will use these shared observations to
inform planning. As the course developed, Leah's confidence as a parent and carer
clearly grew and she asked Sam to support her in developing activities to encourage
her son's language development at home.

Following the training, Sam reflects on the benefits of being able to develop a range
of relationships with the parents of the children in her care. She reflects on other
successful parental involvement initiatives such as the Dads and Lads (+Lasses) day

225

trip to a local park which Cliff had organised, which resulted in a useful opportunity for him to speak to the dads about their children. This activity had resulted in a noticeable increase in fathers being involved in the drop-off and collection of their children. Kira, one of the assistants, has also been supported to produce a regular monthly newsletter, which is very popular. This provides information about forthcoming events, topics, visits and 'policy of the month' for parents to consider and feed back their suggestions.

Leading practice

Following these initiatives, Sam realises that building a 'community of practice' (Lave and Wenger 1991) is not only a valuable activity but helps strengthen her leadership abilities, and that the use of 'emotional intelligence' (Goleman 2000) is very important when developing partnerships and communicating with others. Together with her Childminding Network Coordinator, Sam discusses the findings from her research and they plan ways in which Sam can disseminate her research findings and practice back to the Network. Sam presents her findings to the Network group and the ensuing discussion is warmly welcomed by the majority. She is keen to contribute to improving practice by reflecting on key questions in an ongoing fashion, through her 'action research' within the setting, which she realises has the benefit of addressing her own Continuous Professional Development (CPD) needs as well as the CPD needs of her employees (see Chapter 9).

Task Think of new ways you can develop the practice in your setting:

- To encourage other practitioners to share their good practice in working with parents.
- To effectively enable fathers to be actively involved in their children's development and learning within the setting.
- What actions can the EYP take to ensure that parents feel empowered to contribute ideas, confident their ideas will be listened to?
- Ask yourself honestly, how often do you do this?
- What behaviours might *disempower* parents and carers?
- What learning communities are you involved in and what do they offer you? How can you replicate this opportunity for colleagues?

What is team working and how can it be delivered to ensure that the child's development, well-being and learning are supported and enhanced by a range of professional and lay perspectives?

(S06, S35, S36)

What is team working?

In any organisation, all members of staff make a contribution to the delivery of the service provided. Often individuals are expected to work autonomously, for example making appropriate decisions, taking responsibility if required in certain situations, and advising others on a specific or specialised work area. Traditionally, within many organisations there is a hierarchy in terms of roles and responsibilities, for example that between the classroom teacher, who increasingly manages practitioners of several different varieties within the classroom environment, such as teaching assistants, higher-level teaching assistants and 'nursery nurses' (or, in more modern parlance, Early Years Practitioners).

Rodd (2007) proposes that team work should involve the subordination of individual needs so that team members are able to fully engage in joint, coordinated activity in a concerted attempt to reach common goals, and that this is particularly important in early childhood services where a united effort is more likely to succeed in a complex arena which centres around families, their relationships and their feelings. This section will introduce definitions and concepts of teams and integrated team working and give an overview of the underpinning values and principles that enable integrated teams to develop and function effectively.

R. Meredith Belbin published 'Management Teams – why they succeed or fail' in 2004. Belbin set out to identify what made a good team, based on research in the UK and Australia. Eight key roles were identified and in successful teams all these eight roles could be seen in operation. Belbin concluded that, when selecting people for a team, filling the eight roles was as important as choosing technical skills or experiences. West (1994) proposes that the eight roles are as follows:

EXTRAVERT ROLES	
Outward-looking people whose main orientation is to the world outside, looking beyond the group and the task(s) in hand.	
Plant	The Innovator. Unorthodox, knowledgeable and imaginative, turning out loads of radical ideas. The creative engine-room that needs careful handling to be effective. Individualistic, disregarding practical details or protocol – can become an unguided missile.
Resource Investigator	The extravert, enthusiastic communicator, with good connections outside the team. Enjoys exploring new ideas, responds well to challenges, and creates this attitude among others. Noisy and energetic, quickly loses interest, and can be lazy unless under pressure.
Chairman	Calm, self-confident and decisive when necessary. The social leader of the group, ensuring individuals contribute fully, and guiding the team to success. Unlikely to bring great intellect or creativity.
Shaper	Energetic, highly strung, with a drive to get things done. They challenge inertia, ineffectiveness and complacency in the team, but can be abrasive, impatient and easily provoked. Good leaders of start-up or rapid-response teams.

INTROVERT ROLES	
Inward-looking people principally concerned with relations and tasks within the group.	
Monitor Evaluator	Unemotional, hard-headed and prudent. Good at assessing proposals, monitoring progress and preventing mistakes. Dispassionate, clever and discreet. Unlikely to motivate others, takes time to consider, may appear cold and uncommitted. Rarely wrong.
Team Worker	Socially oriented and sensitive to others. Provides an informal network of communication and support that spreads beyond the formal activities of the team. Often the unofficial or deputy leader, preventing feuding and fragmentation. Concern for team spirit may divert from getting the job done.
Company Worker	The Organiser who turns plans into tasks. Conservative, hard-working, full of common sense, conscientious and methodical. Orthodox thinker who keeps the team focused on the tasks in hand. Lacks flexibility, and unresponsive to new ideas.
Completer Finisher	Makes sure the team delivers. An orderly, anxious perfectionist who worries about everything. Maintains a permanent sense of urgency that can sometimes help and sometimes hinder the team. Good at follow-up and meeting deadlines.

(See http://changingminds.org/explanations/preferences/belbin.htm)

Role identification can be used as a team-building tool: it reinforces the fact that everyone is bringing something to the team, and that you all need each other if you are to be successful. Individuals have varying strengths and preferred roles; a good team leader will work to individuals' strengths and preferences. Although preferred roles are relatively unchanging over time, most people can happily perform two or three of the roles, sometimes simultaneously, and fill any gaps in the team's profile – clearly important if you have a team of less than eight people. The brief descriptions are of the 'pure' roles that are unlikely to be found in practice: what is seen 'on the shop floor' depends on the mix of preferred roles in each individual. Different roles are important at different times and an effective team will be aware of who should be 'centre stage' at a given time. You can link the Belbin roles to personality theory, where words such as 'Extravert' and 'Introvert' originated (see Chapter 2), but remember that the Belbin roles are rather less definitive. A marketing team might appear to be full of extravert, expressive and energetic people, but someone will still be able to act as the Company Worker or Completer Finisher.

> **Task** Visit http://www.businessballs.com. You will find that it offers a huge selection of team-building activities and team-building games that you can browse completely free of charge. If you are interested in personality analysis, you may also find the online test on http://www.humanmetrics.com/cgi-win/JTypes2.asp of interest, and you can find a deeper analysis of the Myers-Briggs 'types' on

http://www.geocities.com/lifexplore/mbtypes.htm. Remember, however, that personality theories are just that – theories, and that human beings are individuals, not 'types'. The only way to really work out how people respond to various situations is to get to know them.

Alongside having the right mix of roles and personality, teams also need other factors to maximise their potential. Csikszentmihalyi (1992) suggests that individuals and teams are most likely to achieve a state of flow when the following factors come together at the same time:

- Realistic challenges
- Attentiveness
- Clear goals
- Provision of informative feedback
- Involvement
- Sense of control
- A willingness to delegate and relinquish control
- Sufficient time.

In order to work together as a team, a group of people need to be aware that they are going to be, or are expected to be, working together. We cannot assume that individuals will recognise this, therefore the EYP may need to facilitate reflection time for team members to recognise their interdependence as well as their independence.

What is multi-agency/integrated working practice in an early years setting?

Children's experience in their early years has a major impact on their life chances. We can enhance this experience by increasing the availability of high quality early years provision and other health and family support services, as well as improving support for their transition into school.

(Children's Centre Practice Guidance, SureStart 2008, online)

This vision is driven by the Every Child Matters (ECM) outcomes and underpinned at statutory level by the Childcare Act 2006 (see Chapter 3). There is now a duty imposed on Local Authorities to deliver the ECM outcomes for all children, with additional duties being placed on Primary Care Trusts and Jobcentre Plus to work with Local Authorities to help children under 18 to achieve the five ECM outcomes of being healthy, staying safe, enjoying and achieving, making a positive contribution and achieving economic well-being. In order to achieve this, practitioners need to work with groups and individuals across services. Early childhood practitioners have always worked within a multi-disciplinary context because services for children and families have always been provided by a wide range of services that operate under the control of education, social work and health departments, that may be funded through private, voluntary or government sources.

However, simply having or being exposed to a range of professional expertise does not equate to integrated working, nor can we simply assume that those professionals work in collaborative ways to achieve shared outcomes for children and families. As we noted earlier, the Childcare Act (2006), ECM outcomes framework, the required Common Core skills for practitioners (see Chapters 2 and 3) and associated legislative frameworks now put a duty on Early Years services, education, social services and health in particular to work in synthesis.

Challenges

The challenges to effective integrated team working are not to be underestimated; they involve bringing together staff from a range of cultural and social backgrounds and frequently involve overcoming professional and/or cultural practice barriers to work towards common goals, maximising the benefits to children and families. Professions tend to create 'communities of practice' (Lave and Wenger 1991) in which certain ways of doing things and viewing the world outside are shared among people in a particular professional environment. There may also be profession-specific language that is used in the workplace that may be unfamiliar to practitioners from a different profession; for example, teachers' uses of acronyms like SATs (Standard Assessment Tasks), EBD (Emotional/Behavioural Disorder) etc. may not be familiar to health workers, and the emergency services' phonetic alphabet (Alpha, Bravo, Charlie, Delta etc.) may be everyday parlance to health workers but not at all familiar to teachers. Hence it can sometimes be difficult for practitioners from different professions to work together seamlessly. These are the not inconsequential issues, and they need to be addressed sensitively as we move on to complex multi-agency working within the Early Years environment. Evidence from the studies of Moss and Wigfall (2001) suggests that there are common barriers to effective team working: loss of individual professional identity, competitiveness, poor communication leading to feelings of isolation and resentment, lack of shared vision and understanding of desired outcomes; these factors are often underpinned by poor management and weak organisational structures, or the use of inappropriate leadership styles. Most importantly, the EYFS guidance on multi-agency working stresses the need to put the child at the centre when attempting to change or transform existing practices. Further advice and support for the establishment of multi-agency working is available on the EYFS CD-ROM, alongside related information such as the role of the Lead Professional in helping to establish the Common Assessment Framework (see Chapter 2), which recognises that the *child's* needs, not the adult's needs, are at the centre of practice in all Early Years environments.

Focus on practice

Jo, a Long pathway candidate, has been on placement at 'The Willows' Children's Centre. She is an experienced early years practitioner, having worked in a private daycare setting for over 10 years. The placement in this Children's Centre has given her valuable additional experience of working in close partnership with other professional groups. The Children's Centre also offers a range of in-house parental involvement programmes as well as outreach support within family's homes. Prior to arranging her placement, Jo spent time with her mentor in order to clearly identify her objectives for the placement. Carol, the Centre Manager, was then able to organise an induction programme for Jo which gave her an excellent opportunity to understand the policies and practices of the setting in relation to multi-agency and outreach working practices. Jo was impressed to find that the setting had established information-sharing and referral systems and working relationships across the various teams at the Centre and also with other practitioners and agencies which served the locality. The Deputy Manager, Heidi, was to mentor Jo during her placement and arranged to meet at the start and end of each day during her first week in the setting; during these brief meetings Heidi was able to answer any questions and ensure that Jo had a programme of work which met her broader learning objectives, including attending multi-agency meetings, attending a parents group forum and meetings with the other, non-daycare, staff teams working from the Centre.

After several weeks during which Jo discussed her observations and reflections with Heidi, Jo mentioned her growing concern about Angus, a quiet boy who often played alone and whose speech, on the rare occasions when he did interact with other children or adults, was difficult to interpret. He was reluctant to leave the setting when his mum, Sue, came to collect him. Jo had also observed that Sue looked tired, stressed and at times seemed unable to deal with Angus's behaviour. Jo asked Heidi if there had been any discussion about a possible referral to speech and language support for Angus as she felt there might be some question over language development delay. She also asked whether Sue attended any of the parenting programmes or received outreach visits. Heidi was interested to hear Jo's observations and questions and went to collect the child and family confidential records which were kept securely in the office. The file revealed some useful information; a referral to speech and language therapy had been made but needed to be followed up. The Centre had not undertaken any outreach visits to the family since their last keyworker had left two months previously, and whilst Sue had expressed an interest in more home visits she did not want to attend any Centre-based courses.

Identifying good practice

Heidi and Jo decided that Jo should work in the room with Angus on a one-to-one basis as well as in small groups to help support his language development. Jo made sure that she knew when Sue usually dropped Angus off and made direct contact with her, explaining that she was an experienced practitioner on placement in the Centre. Over the next few weeks Jo spoke to Sue on a daily basis about Angus's day in nursery; she also asked Sue about the sorts of things Angus liked to do at home; this received a positive

A 'magic bag'
Source: Le Kinder Club/Jane George

response from Sue who reeled off a long list of Angus's interests. Jo made sure that she gave undivided attention to Sue during these discussions and also suggested that some of Sue's observations were entered into Angus's personal nursery records. Sue was really interested in the observation sheets and was pleased and surprised to learn that her observations from home were being used to inform and enhance the setting's plan for Angus. Sue and Jo began to discuss their concerns about Angus's language delay and in turn how this affected his behaviour. Jo explained that she had been working with Angus and some of the other children using her 'magic bag' activity to specifically encourage listening and speaking skills.

Leading practice

After this particular meeting Jo went home and decided to type up instructions for parents and carers about the 'magic bag' and the various ways it could be used at home. Jo was careful to ensure that the instructions were presented in a way that a 'lay audience' would understand, while not being patronising. Over the following weeks Jo developed a range of other resources for parents so that they could carry on activities at home if they wished. The parents were being enabled to become part of an extended team.

Heidi also informed Jo that another Family Support Worker (FSW) had been assigned to Sue and Angus and that Sue had told the setting that she was happy for Jo to undertake a home visit. The home visit revealed that Sue had many anxieties and concerns including her own lack of qualifications and money problems, alongside her worries about Angus's language development delay.

It was agreed that Emma, the Family Support Worker, would make an appointment for Sue to see the Money Advice Worker. Sue also agreed that she would like to attend one of the Parenting Programmes but felt that she would prefer it if either Jo or Emma could attend with her. Emma said she would speak to Heidi and let Sue know as soon as possible. On their return to the Centre, Heidi and Emma wrote up notes about the visit and Emma emailed the notes and Sue's request to Heidi. The following week Heidi approached Jo and asked if she would be willing to attend the group meeting with Sue. They discussed the pros and cons of this level of support: was it sustainable, or might it create a dependency culture? Following a lengthy conversation they decided that it would be in both Sue's and Angus's best interests if Jo attended the meeting with Sue. Following each session, Jo met briefly with Sue to discuss the session's content, after which Jo commented to Sue how she appeared to be more confident about speaking in the whole group sessions, offering her opinions as well as appearing generally happier and less stressed. Sue told Jo that she had made friends with one of the other group members and they were meeting at each others' homes in between the group sessions; she also proudly announced that they had both enrolled on a Return to Work course and that she was considering going back to college in the autumn. Jo was also able to attend a meeting with the Speech and Language therapist with Angus where her detailed observations proved to be invaluable. The Speech and Language therapist was impressed with the language development programme which Jo had introduced through her 'magic bag' activity, suggesting some very helpful amendments. For the remainder of her placement, Jo met regularly with the Speech and Language therapist and made sure that she reported information about Angus's progress to both her colleagues and to Sue, with additional suggestions for activities that would support his language development. Heidi informs Jo that the Centre is very grateful for her help, particularly with Angus, over the period of her placement. Jo is delighted that she has been treated as a valued professional by the team, even though her role was that of a placement student.

Reflection

- *What skills and knowledge do you think effective workplace mentors need? (see Chapter 9).*

- *Do you work collaboratively at all times? If not, what 'blocks and barriers' to collaborative team working have you experienced, including working with practitioners from other agencies?*

- *In an early years setting where staff may work varied shift patterns and weekly hours, how can we ensure that all staff feel part of the team?*

- *How do you model collaborative working to others?*

Task Arrange a time when you can discuss the above questions with the manager of your setting, and then write some reflections on their answers in your journal. Over the following weeks come up with some ideas for improving practice and discuss these (tactfully!) with the manager.

What is effective leadership in the context of an early childhood setting?

(S33, S34, S35)

Early years setting leaders have traditionally been expected to adapt their role on a daily basis, moving between the direct care and education of children to lead administrator, being a member of a team, to leading and line-managing the team. In this scenario the demarcation lines between being a team colleague, a manager and a leader are fuzzy, to say the least. But expectations with regard to roles in early years practice are continuing to grow. Leaders in the diverse arena of contemporary early years now have to manage a vast area of care, health and family support as well as early education and simultaneously manage, deploy and develop staff with different professional backgrounds and qualifications effectively. This is clearly not an easy task, and it should be viewed against a backdrop of over £1.6 billion government spending on childcare and pre-school education since 1997. With this kind of financial investment comes a greater emphasis on accountability, as well as expectations of excellent practice within the setting. So in a time of change, flux and new, more ambitious expectations, we need to investigate what is meant by *leadership* in terms of the EYP's role, and how it is different from a traditional model which has tended to be much more about the management of a setting and its staff.

Whalley (2005) suggests that effective leadership within the context of early years settings demonstrates the ability to:

- enhance the learning and development potential of 0–5 year olds;
- encourage, enable and empower parents in their roles as parents and primary educators;
- develop and enhance the skills and knowledge and understanding of staff, including other leaders and potential leaders, to enable them to work in ways that are:
  - reflective, thus informing practice;
  - not professionally and/or personally 'role precious';
  - recognising the need to work across professional boundaries for the benefit of children and families;
  - innovative;
  - evidencing a commitment to ongoing professional development, of themselves and others.

(Whalley 2005, p. 10)

An EYP can demonstrate all of the above without necessarily line-managing any members of staff within a setting. Since the beginning of the 20th century, much has been written about how the individual can develop leadership behaviours which will 'get results' – with the proviso that the result desired may also be rather more complex than the rather behaviourally based management goals of the mid 20th century. Research indicates that there is no single behaviour, trait or style which defines 'good' leadership behaviour. Goleman (2000) suggests that we should think of leadership in terms of a range of styles, behaviours and traits which the accomplished leader will use appropriately rather as a professional golfer will choose the right golf club.

Goleman goes on to describe six styles which are linked to different components of emotional intelligence:

- The *Coercive* leader demands compliance.
- The *Authoritative* leader mobilises people towards a vision.
- The *Affiliative* leader creates an appropriate emotional climate.
- The *Democratic* leader builds consensus through participation.
- The *Pacesetting* leader expects excellence and self-direction.
- The *Coaching* leader develops people for the future.

Goleman links the successful application of these leadership styles to having six or more emotional intelligence competencies. Emotional Intelligence is described by Goleman (2000) as the ability to manage the self and relationships with others effectively. Table 8.1 sets out the specific capabilities and competencies described by Goleman in relation to Emotional Intelligence.

Siraj-Blatchford and Manni (2007), in their ELEYS (Effective Leadership in the Early Years) project, caution against the straightforward application of research

Table 8.1 **Emotional intelligence competencies**

Self-awareness	Self-management
• Emotional self-awareness • Accurate self-assessment • Self-confidence	• Self-control • Trustworthiness • Conscientiousness • Adaptability • Achievement orientation • Initiative
Social awareness	**Social skill**
• Empathy • Organisational awareness • Service orientation (N.B. the ability to recognise and meet customer needs)	• Visionary leadership • Influence • Developing others • Communication • Change catalyst • Conflict management • Building networks • Teamwork and collaboration

findings on effective leadership to Early Years settings, as many of these findings have come from research based in Primary and Secondary schools where 'outstanding leadership' has been unequivocally linked to raising achievement, alongside improving organisational performance. Children's Centres and daycare settings are rather different organisations where Siraj-Blatchford and Manni propose that the role of leader is correspondingly likely to be subtly different, requiring:

• **Contextual literacy** – situational leadership; consideration of the situation in which the leader operates and the people s/he is leading.

• A **commitment to collaboration** – where effective pedagogic and parental support are complementary, and effective integrated working arrangements are evidenced.

• A **commitment to the improvement** of outcomes for all children here through an holistic consideration for the child's development based on the recognition and awareness of the cultural context in which they live.

ELEYS also identified 'categories of effective leadership practice', regardless of specific setting, that were indicated by the findings of the REPEY case studies (Siraj-Blatchford *et al.* 2002):

• **Identifying and articulating a collective vision** achieved through the co-construction with children, parents and staff of shared beliefs, values and objectives.

- **Ensuring shared understandings, meanings and goals** through the ability to 'influence others into action'. A vision needs to be evidenced by effective practice.

- **Effective communication:** this requires transparency with regard to expectations, 'dialogue rather than monologue', consultation and reflection.

- **Encouraging reflection:** developing a 'community of learners' which goes beyond straightforward reflection to critically appraise practice and engage in ongoing professional development.

- **Monitoring and assessing practice:** monitoring and assessment of staff along with a collaborative dialogue was shown to be important in effective settings that took part in the ELEYS, as well as support systems such as peer observations.

- **Commitment to ongoing professional development:** this requires effective settings to provide intellectual stimulation for their staff as well as individualised support identified through ongoing training.

- **Distributive leadership:** self-esteem and staff morale can be heightened by leaders who work in a more collaborative and less autocratic way, involving staff in meaningful decision making.

> **Task** The specific recommendations for Early Years leadership above have many parallels to the emotional competencies described by Goleman (2000). Try to align the Emotional Intelligence competencies described by Goleman with the leadership role requirements outlined by Siraj-Blatchford and Manni (2007). What are the similarities and differences? Discuss with your fellow EYPS candidates and colleagues.

In her recent text, Leading Practice in Early Years Settings (2008), Mary Whalley concludes that there are still some key themes which need to be further explored in relation to early years leadership research:

- How important is leadership in the Early Years?
- What are the main roles of leaders in the Early Years?
- What are the characteristics of effective leaders in the Early Years?
- How much professional development and training is there for leaders in the Early Years?

Southworth (1998) suggested that leaders need to recognise the complexity of their role and understand that settings are dynamic rather than static organisations, which are continually evolving. There is also a need to recognise that contexts differ at every level; for example, they differ between individual children, families, local communities, socio-economic classes and cultures. Added to this is the ebb and flow of staff morale and energy levels; the arrival of new staff and students and the departure of others are just some of the factors to which settings need to continually adjust and make room for new energies, opportunities and challenges. The need for a Leading Practitioner to act as a combination of leader, supporter and innovator of good practice is today more necessary than ever. How this role will vary to some degree within each setting depends upon the factors Siraj-Blatchford and Manni outline above: contextual literacy, commitment to collaboration and improvement of learning outcomes; the EYP role was created to fill this niche.

Action research within early years settings can be a powerful driver in the quest to develop the right organisational climate. This not only offers continuing professional development (CPD) for the staff but also for the leader carrying out the research.

Focus on practice

Action research

Action research is a particular type of research methodology that developed over the last half of the twentieth century in education and health practitioner education. The basic method involves measuring a particular area of practice, enacting a change and measuring the impact of the change. This can be enacted on a 'loop' until the practitioner is convinced that the practice has been developed to an acceptable standard.

Task Access http://www.infed.org/research/b-actres.htm and read their introduction to action research. Make some notes in your journal about likely topics for action research in your setting. Discuss your ideas with your fellow EYPS candidates and colleagues.

It can be proposed that the drive towards multi-agency working needs to be balanced with the development of practice within individual professions and setting, as Frost notes:

> Efforts to improve children's services systems should focus on positive organisational climates rather than on increasing inter-organisational services co-ordination. This is important because many large-scale efforts to improve children's services systems have focused on inter-organisational co-ordination with little success and none to date have focused on organisational climate.
>
> (Frost 2005, p. 21)

If such an organisational climate is to be empowering and effective it needs to reflect some or all of the categories suggested by Siraj-Blatchford and Manni (2007) in their ELEYS project report (see above).

Task How can leadership impact on organisational climate? Think of some positive and negative examples from your own previous experience (not necessarily exclusively in Early Years) and discuss them with your peers.

Focus on practice

Peter is the Room Leader in the pre-school room of a large Children's Centre. He has recently completed his BA (Hons) in Early Years, and is about to start the validation process for EYPS. He has recently taken on a mentoring role for staff who are new to the setting; this means that he is spending considerable time in each of the other three rooms within the setting. Peter has become aware that his mentees are not following the setting's policies and procedures consistently. In particular, he has concerns about staff 'interpretations' of the setting's existing Behaviour Policy. This policy was written by a previous setting manager, and while it is quite clear that while staff know that a Behaviour Policy exists they do not necessarily understand it or agree with it.

Identifying good practice

Peter believed that many staff did not understand the relationship between a child's developmental stage and the typical behaviour within specific stages; he had witnessed some staff applying behaviour management strategies suitable for 3–4 year olds in the Baby Room. He raised his concerns during his regular supervision session with Lucy, the new manager of the setting. Lucy agreed with Peter that this was one policy that really had to be updated. Peter was mindful that a colleague from his EYPS candidate group had involved all the staff in re-writing her setting's Behaviour Policy. He described this process to Lucy; she agreed that enabling staff to be active participants in the process rather than handing them a copy of the finished product could result in shared and improved understanding.

Leading practice

The following week Peter asked staff to write comments on the white board in the staff room in response to his questions about issues relating to behaviour for different age groups, and the role of the practitioner and parents in behaviour management. While staff were initially self-conscious about this, they soon started contributing, and Lucy noticed that they were also having debates over these issues. Over the next few days the white board became full of ideas and suggestions which Peter incorporated into a draft consultation document. This was discussed with staff, with their suggestions being added, and clarification over areas of confusion or concern debated. After several more re-drafts, a final draft was accepted and it became a new Behaviour Policy which was both well received and understood by staff.

During this process, Peter also took the time to talk to parents about the Behaviour Management techniques they used at home, as he felt that consistency in practice between the home and the setting would be advantageous. Many parents expressed their concerns about their children's behaviour, and Peter's idea for an evening session on Behaviour Management was well received. Peter planned the session in conjunction with a local health visitor, who used the opportunity to catch up with some of the other issues and concerns parents had. Peter was delighted with the positive feedback from parents. When he read through the evaluation sheets that they had completed, he decided to organise further meetings around topics in which parents had expressed an interest.

Reflection

- *What policies currently need developing in your workplace/work placement?*

- *Do you think Peter's approach was equitable with regard to staff and parents, or could he have provided a similar board for parents' feedback, and then collated the two?*

- *In any collective Childcare/Education setting there will parents and children who do not 'come on board' in such an initiative – how can the leading practitioner support staff to maintain partnerships with such families?*

Task Discuss the above with your colleagues in your workplace/work placement. Consider how this example might be useful in developing the practice in your setting.

Conclusion

This chapter set out to address those standards which underpin the EYP's role in creating and sustaining effective working partnerships with parents/carers as well as other professionals or groups with specialist knowledge that can enhance the learning and development of children through multi-agency practice. Focus has also been placed on the role of the EYP as a 'leader' rather than as a manager, modelling good practice and supporting teams within settings. Literature, theories and research initiatives that support these standards have also been investigated and you have been asked to identify with and reflect upon practice evidence supplied through various scenarios. A number of key questions were asked.

How can Centres ensure that partnership working with families and carers is valued?

(S29, S30, S31, S32)

In attempting to answer the above question, consideration of what 'the family' means in contemporary Britain and its impact on children's learning and development was discussed. The need for practitioners to reflect on their own values and beliefs in order to develop meaningful and inclusive partnerships that value the diversity of children and their families was shown to be underpinned by considerable research into working in partnership with parents/carers. It established the need for practitioners to avoid a 'deficit' model of parents' abilities and instead recognise and celebrate parents as their children's first educators. The need for EYPs to lead and support practice in establishing real partnership with parents means going beyond a surface structure that simply involves them in supporting various practitioner-instigated activities within the setting. Empowered parents should be involved in decision-making and policy issues, and should be welcomed by practitioners as co-researchers and facilitators of their children's learning and development. It is the EYP's responsibility to lead staff away from a 'unilateral' relationship that can often exist between parents and a setting where information about children moves from staff to parents, and rarely in the opposite direction.

What is team working and how can it be delivered to ensure that the child's development, well-being and learning are supported and enhanced by a range of professional and lay perspectives?

(S06, S35, S36)

In attempting to answer the above question, consideration was given to how an effective team is defined and the roles within it. There is a need for the EYP to be proactive in encouraging reflection on the part of staff so that they recognise their interdependence as well as their independence, and in ensuring that practitioners feel valued as individuals while working collaboratively. The EYP, as leading practitioner, also needs to establish clear induction procedures for new staff and ensure that effective information-sharing systems are in place. The leading practitioner must also support staff sensitively within the setting to underpin the team's endeavour to address the individual and holistic needs of each child through multi-agency working. The recognition of the Government's initiatives to encourage effective multi-agency working is at the heart of the ECM agenda and is embedded in the EYFS practice guidance. This has been highlighted above, with some consideration of the challenges that multi-agency working might present, in particular overcoming professional barriers to achieve a common aim, while simultaneously developing the day-to-day work of core specialist teams.

What is effective leadership in the context of an early childhood setting?

(S33, S34, S35)

The traditional roles of the leading practitioner within an Early Years environment were examined along with the need to develop the new role of the EYP. Theories and research underpinning concepts around effective leadership were examined, for example Goleman's (2000) ideas on the links between emotional intelligence and successful leadership. The findings of the Effective Leadership in the Early Years (ELEYS) project undertaken by Siraj-Blatchford and Manni (2007) were also considered. Finally, the complexity of creating a successful 'organisational climate' as suggested by Frost (2005), in the full range of contemporary early years settings, with all their diversity, was investigated. A final word from Whitaker offers a concise and realistic definition of the complexity of a leader's work:

> Leadership is concerned with creating the conditions in which all members of the organisation can give of their best in a climate of commitment and challenge. Leadership helps an organisation to work well.

(Whitaker 1993, p. 74)

Further reading

Anning, A. *et al.* (2007) *Developing Multi-professional Teamwork for Integrated Children's Service.* Maidenhead: Open University Press.

Daly, M., Byers, E. and Taylor, W. (2004) *Early Years Management in Practice.* Oxford: Heinemann.

Frost, N. (2005) *Professionalism Partnership and Joined up thinking in frontline children's services.* Totnes: Research in Practice Series.

Johnson, S. (1998) *Who Moved my Cheese? An amazing way to deal with change in your work and in your life.* New York: Vermillion.

Rodd, J. (2007) *Leadership in Early Childhood,* 3rd edition. Maidenhead: Open University Press.

Siraj-Blatchford, I. and Manni, L. (2007) *Effective Leadership in the Early Years Sector (ELEYS) Study.* London: Institute of Education.

Whalley, M. (2008) *Leading Practice in Early Years Settings.* Exeter: Open University Press.

Websites

ChangingMinds: **http://changingminds.org/explanations/preferences/belbin.htm**

References

Adair, J. (1987) *Effective Teambuilding.* London: Pan.

Alder, S. in Laney and Packer (eds) (1994) *Managing Women: Feminism and Power in Education Management.* Buckingham: Open University Press.

Anning, A. *et al.* (2007) *Developing Multi-professional Teamwork for Integrated Children's Service.* Maidenhead: Open University Press.

Atkinson, M. *et al.* (2002) *Multi-agency working – a detailed case study.* National Foundation for Educational Research.

Baumrind, D. (1966) 'Effects of Authoritative Parental Control on Child Behaviour'. *Child Development,* 37(4), pp. 887–907.

Belbin, M. (2004) *Management Teams – Why they Succeed or Fail.* Butterworth-Heinemann.

Bourdieu, P. (1977) 'Cultural reproduction and social reproduction'. In J. Karabil and A. Hasse (eds) *Power and Ideology in Education.* New York: Oxford University Press, pp. 487–511.

Cameron, C. (2004) *Building an Integrated Workforce for a long term vision of Universal Early Education and Care.* Daycare Trust.

Chivers, J. (1995) *Team building with Teachers.* London: Kogan Page.

Csikszentmihalyi, M. (1992) *Flow; The Psychology of Happiness,* cited in Leadership Concepts and Analytical Tools, NCSL (2006).

Daly, M., Byers, E. and Taylor, W. (2004) *Early Years Management in Practice.* Oxford: Heinemann.

DfES (2003) Every Child Matters: Norwich: TSO.

EPPE (2004) Effective Pre-school Education. Available at: http://www.surestart.gov.uk/_doc/P0001378.pdf Accessed on 28 April 2009.

Evangelou, M., Brooks, G., Smith, S., Jennings, D. and Roberts, F. (2005) *The Birth to School Study: a longitudinal evaluation of the Peers Early Education Partnership (PEEP) 1998–2005.* London: DfES.

Finch, J. (1984) *Education and Social Policy.* London: Longman.

Frost, N. (2005) *Professionalism Partnership and Joined up thinking in frontline children's services.* Totnes: Research in Practice Series.

Ghate, D. and Hazel, N. *et al.* (2002) *A National Study of Parents, Children and Discipline.* London: Policy Research Bureau.

Gilbert, P. (2005) *Leadership – Being effective and remaining human.* Lyme Regis: Russell House Publishing.

Goleman (2000) 'Leadership that gets results', *Harvard Business Review,* Issue 3. Available at: http://www.hcmglobal.biz/pdf/leadershipthat.pdf Accessed on 15 February 2009.

Hall, J. (1999) *Resolving Disputes between Parents, Schools and LEAs: Some examples of best practice.* London: DfEE.

Harris, B. (2004) 'Leading by Heart', *School Leadership and Management,* 24(4), pp. 391-404.

Lave, J. and Wenger, E. (1991) *Situated Learning: Legitimate Peripheral Participation.* Cambridge: Cambridge University Press.

Malaguzzi, L. and Penn, H. (1997) *Comparing Nurseries: Staff and Children in Italy, Spain and the UK.* London: Paul Chapman.

Martin, V. and Rodgers, S. (2004) *Leading Interprofessional teams in Health and Social Care.* London: Routledge.

Moss, P. and Wigfall, U. (2001) *More than the sum of its parts? A Study of a multi-agency child care network.* National Children's Bureau/Joseph Rowntree Foundation, London.

Muijs, D., Aubrey, C., Harris, A. and Briggs, M. (2004) 'How do they manage? A review of the research in early childhood,' *Journal of Early Childhood Research,* 2, p. 157.

Northouse, P. (2004) *Leadership: Theory and Practice,* 3rd edition. London: Routledge.

Pugh, G. and Duffy, B. (eds) (2006) *Contemporary Issues in the Early Years.* London: Sage.

Reay, D. (1998) *Class work: Mother's involvement in their children's primary education.* London: University College Press.

Rodd, J. (2007) *Leadership in Early Childhood,* 3rd edition. Maidenhead: Open University Press.

Rodd, J. (1996) 'Towards a typology of leadership for the early childhood professional of the early twenty first century'. *Early Childhood Development and Care,* 120, pp. 19-26.

Rodd, J. (1997) 'Learning to be Leaders: perceptions of early childhood professionals about leadership roles and responsibilities'. *Early Years,* 18(1), pp. 40-46.

Scholtes, P. *et al.* (2003) *The Team Handbook.* London: Oriel.

Siraj-Blatchford, I. and Manni, L. (2007) *Effective Leadership in the Early Years Sector (ELEYS) Study.* London: Institute of Education.

Siraj-Blatchford, I., Sylva, K., Muttock, S., Gilden, R. and Bell, D. (2002) *Researching Effective Pedagogy in the Early Years.* Norwich: DfES.

Southworth, G. (1998) *Leading improving primary schools.* London: Falmer Press.

SureStart (2008) Children's Centres Practice Guidance. Available at: http://www.surestart.gov.uk/ improvingquality/guidance/practiceguidance/ Accessed on 15 February 2009.

Thornton, L. and Brunton, P. (2005) *Understanding the Reggio Approach.* London: David Fulton Publishers Ltd.

Wasoff, F. and Dey, I. (2000) *Family Policy.* London: Gildredge Press.

West, M. (1994) *Effective Teamwork.* The British Psychology Society.

Whalley, M. *et al.* (2007) *Involving Parents in their Children's Learning.* London: Paul Chapman Publishing.

Whalley, M. (2008) *Leading Practice in Early Years Settings.* Exeter: Open University Press.

Whalley, M. (2005) *NPQICL Pedagogical Leadership.* Nottingham: National College for School Leadership.

Whetten, D., Cameron, K. and Woods, M. (1996) *Management Skills Series - Effective Motivation, Effective Delegation, Effective Conflict Management.* London: Harper-Collins.

Whitaker, P. (1993) *Managing Change in Schools.* Milton Keynes: Open University Press.

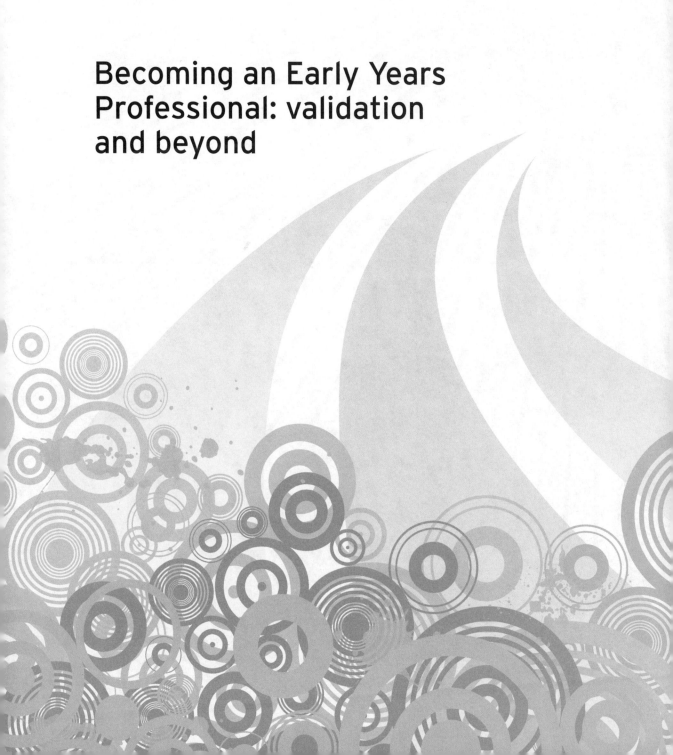

Part 4

Becoming an Early Years Professional: validation and beyond

9

Managing your placement supervisor, mentor and your own continuing professional development

Poonam Cant

Chapter overview

The standards addressed in this chapter are:

S37 Develop and use skills in literacy, numeracy and information and communication technology to support their work with children and wider professional activities

S38 Reflect on and evaluate the impact of practice, modifying approaches where necessary, and take responsibility for identifying and meeting their professional development needs

S39 Take a creative and constructively critical approach towards innovation, and adapt practice if benefits and improvements are identified

(CWDC 2006)

The chapter will approach this in the same format as Chapter 1, by considering key points and examples that relate to candidates on specific EYPS pathways, with an emphasis upon those within work placement situations, rather than in paid employment. These key points are as follows:

- The role of a placement supervisor
- The role of a mentor
- Expectations of an EYPS candidate
- Managing the relationships with supervisors and mentors well
- Approach while in placement.

Florentyna's 'CPD'

Florentyna had just finished her Foundation Degree in Early Years, and during her application process to take the BA (Hons) top-up in Early Childhood Studies her interviewer asked her whether she wished to sign on additionally to the Early Years Professional Status Long Pathway, as in so doing she would get half of her degree fees paid as she worked within an eligible setting. Florentyna discussed this with her supervisor at work who agreed that this would be a very good idea. In her subsequent conversation with the training centre, Florentyna was asked whether she had equivalent qualifications to GCSE English and Mathematics from the school and college qualifications that she had from Poland, where she had grown up. The training centre offered a service that would inform her of the English equivalents of these qualifications (via a UK agency called 'NARIC', see **http://www.naric.org.uk/index.asp?page=15**). When Florentyna's results came back, she discovered she had the equivalent of GCSE Mathematics at grade C or above, but not GCSE English. She was concerned at first that the training centre would not take her on to the BA (Hons) or the EYPS, but they explained that they would certainly be able to do so; however, Florentyna would need to gain GCSE English or an equivalent qualification before she could enter the validation process for EYPS. She was referred to a key skills tutor at the centre to discuss various options towards GCSE English or equivalent. The course leader for the BA (Hons) Early Childhood Studies explained to Florentyna that this was the first stage of her 'CPD' – continuing professional development, which she would discuss with her tutors, mentors and placement supervisor throughout her BA (Hons) and EYPS training programme. In particular, her GCSE studies would address Standard 37 by developing her skills in literacy.

Introduction

At this point, Florentyna's next questions would be likely to be: 'who will be my mentor?' and 'how will I be expected to work with them?' This chapter will attempt to provide basic answers to these questions. Candidates are assigned a supervisor and mentor to help them during their placement. The supervisor is the candidate's direct line manager. Those who are in paid work like Florentyna will already have a supervisor, while those who enter work placement will be allocated to a supervisor on arrival. The mentor may be a more experienced colleague within the candidate's setting, or a qualified EYP who has been employed by the training provider to mentor the candidate. As such, the supervisor and mentor have slightly different roles but they share a common goal of preparing the candidate to be successful in gaining EYP status. They play a facilitation role to ensure that the candidate has appropriate experiences and opportunities and they also prompt and support the candidate in their professional development, which will include activities within the workplace and external training.

The role of a placement supervisor

The placement supervisor is responsible for professional decisions concerning the candidate's progress, performance and assessment. Within the setting they are likely to be team leaders and first line managers. As such, they familiarise the candidate with the setting, staff and policies and procedures. Once placement has begun, they take an interest in how the candidate is performing and delivering against agreed objectives and act as a facilitator to ensure the candidate attends meetings and team discussions of relevance and gains the experience needed.

The supervisor is likely to set the candidate specific tasks during placement and to subsequently direct and guide the candidate in the performance of these tasks. Supervisors do not usually perform the tasks themselves but the activities they undertake may model good practice and share responsibility. They are available to discuss the approach the candidates will adopt, and their conclusions and ideas. Supervisors also provide a managed environment where goals are set, meetings are scheduled, resources are allocated and deadlines are set. As the relationship develops, the supervisor is likely to provide personal support as well as feedback on progress. They will also help to write a professional development plan for the candidate once they have observed them in practice and identified areas for improvement.

The role of a mentor

Mentors are usually well-established practitioners with significant leadership experience. They are likely to be Early Years Professionals and will have therefore been through the assessment process and possibly be assessors themselves. They can help to clarify understanding of the standards and the evidence required, but they must not give detailed advice or coach the candidate in any way. They can also be helpful in supporting staff at the setting to understand the EYP assessment process, the tasks candidates are likely to get involved with, and the standards against which they will be measured.

The role of the mentor is to provide encouragement and to act as a sounding board. For example, sometimes a candidate may wish to discuss how to overcome difficulties with negotiating with staff in the setting in order to obtain the experience they need. Mentors support candidates to find solutions rather than solving problems for them. They also act as a facilitator to help candidates to identify gaps in their knowledge and to gain opportunities for any additional experience they may need. They may help the candidate to consider and seek options within or external to the setting.

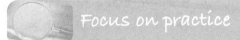

Focus on practice

Full pathway candidate Janine is on placement in a Children's Centre and is aware that in order to meet the standards she needs to build relationships with parents and be able to lead and support others in this aspect. As she is new to the setting and has little experience of working with under 5s, she discusses this with her supervisor. The deputy manager seems very reticent to let Janine talk to parents immediately. Janine does not know how to approach overcoming her reservations, so she discusses this with her mentor. The mentor prompts Janine to think about why the deputy manager may have concerns and then urges her to think of ways she can address them. Janine researches possible training and talks to other practitioners; she then decides that she should approach the manager again but this time with a plan and justification. She clarifies her understanding of the standards she aims to meet with her mentor, and she explains these to her supervisor. With a clearer understanding the supervisor decides to set Janine a project on improving working with parents within the setting. This not only involves consultation with staff, parents and other professionals but also enables Janine to improve her skills as she attends some formal training on working with parents. Janine and her supervisor agree that she will run workshops with staff and parents and cascade the training material to her colleagues.

Reflection *Janine has used her mentor for support to successfully overcome issues she has faced in getting her setting to support her in the activities she needs to undertake. The mentor has helped Janine to think about the solution herself and to structure her thoughts in the form of a plan and training. Providing her supervisor with a justification has helped towards a solution that not only develops Janine's professional understanding, but produces wider benefits to the setting. Janine will now be supported in working on a project which will prove invaluable for her EYP written tasks, tour visit and documentary evidence file, and the setting will improve the quality of its provision – a win-win situation.*

Expectations of an EYPS candidate

An Early Years Professional is defined as a highly skilled practitioner who raises the quality of provision in an early years setting. As such, whatever the training pathway, EYPS candidates in paid work and on placement will be expected to be 'self-starters'. The expectation will be that you have the potential to swiftly become a confident and knowledgeable practitioner with the ability to meet objectives, complete tasks and deliver results to a given deadline. You will be expected to provide leadership and support to change, shape and improve practice in the setting and make a real difference. The supervisor, staff in the setting and mentor will quite rightly have very high expectations of you, hence they will set challenging tasks and expect tangible results.

The supervisor is usually a very busy individual with a demanding job role and schedule. They will not have time to nurse you through placement. They will expect you to highlight your own needs and have the ability to work out solutions for yourself, with an ability to overcome potential barriers. You will be expected to possess suitable time-management and project-management skills to deliver the tasks assigned to you. In other words, on a day-to-day basis, it is likely that they will expect you to manage yourself.

Work placement supervisors will expect you to have a high level of knowledge about the Early Years Foundation Stage welfare requirements and practice guidance, and to quickly build a strong working knowledge of the setting's policies and procedures, what you are doing within these, and standard concepts of Early Years best practice (see, for example, the references to KEEP and the Common Skills Framework in Chapter 2). However, in the early days, the supervisor should expect to have to coach full pathway candidates in particular to relate all this to the day-to-day practice of the setting.

You will be expected to work alongside regular staff at their placement, striving to achieve the aims of the setting hosting the placement, while continually reflecting on and trying to improve your own skills and your contribution to the placement. The supervisor will not expect to have to sort out basic issues around team working, as they will expect you to be mature and empathetic in your approach.

It can be very difficult for EYP full pathway candidates to gain the respect and credibility of others, let alone 'lead and support' if they do not have much experience of working in an early years setting. To overcome this, such candidates should familiarise themselves with their colleagues and empathise with them as this is vital to their own success. All EYPS candidates, whatever their pathway, should recognise that their needs and rights and those of others have equal importance. You should adopt a style of communication that your colleagues are comfortable with, ensuring that you consult with all stakeholders, e.g. children, managers, other practitioners and parents. You should try to foresee problems and attempt to solve or overcome them before they become an issue. Most importantly you should show respect for yourself and others. If you can demonstrate that you work well with colleagues, the supervisor will be confident that you have the potential to lead and support change.

 Focus on practice

Before short pathway candidate Thomas starts his placement he analyses gaps in his experiences, his strengths and weaknesses and identifies that he needs to gain experience of working with babies. He discusses this with his supervisor and they arrange a period of time where he works exclusively in the baby room. He discusses areas of provision that he is uncertain about, e.g. feeding, nappy changing etc., with his supervisor and she ensures that the room leader is aware of gaps in his experience.

Together they formulate a step-by-step plan to ensure that he will steadily gain knowledge and experience. He establishes a good rapport with the staff in the baby room and takes time to understand how each person likes to work. He takes time to observe, as part of his training, and he offers to help where he sees staff are struggling. He makes himself familiar with the policies and procedures of the setting and the allocation of duties across the setting and in the baby room. He shadows each member of staff for a period of time to increase his awareness about their practice and the guidance offered by the setting. He asks detailed questions about the children and their routines and the manner in which this information is gathered. He listens to staff and sensitively asks questions to increase his knowledge. While undergoing this process he notices that routines are not formally updated with parents. Rather than raising this with management he talks to staff first and realises that they are asking for the information and that it is recorded in the daily diary used to exchange information, but that there is no formal mechanism to update the routine board, which means the information can be out of date. He talks to staff, and volunteers to do this, with the result that they are grateful; they see the merit in doing it but feel they do not have time, so his input to the setting is perceived as highly positive by all concerned.

Reflection *Thomas has analysed his own professional development to identify gaps in his experience and discusses them with his supervisor, enabling her to facilitate the acquisition of the skills he requires. He uses different methods to familiarise himself with policies, procedures and practice within the setting. He takes time to get to know his colleagues and respects them by helping them, listening to them and consulting with them, which means that when he does wish to initiate change they are willing to listen and can see the merit in his actions. As the supervisor can see positive changes there will be increased confidence in his capabilities.*

Managing the relationship with supervisor and mentors well

You must manage the relationship successfully with your mentor and supervisor to ensure that the support and input needed are timely and secured. It is vital to remember that all parties share the same goal, which is for you to be successful in developing professionally and in achieving EYP status. Relationships should be managed well by all parties, as, while they are generally rewarding, there is the potential for frustrating elements to creep in that may build up to confrontation. You should always make sure that you understand what the supervisor expects of you and that you make best use of the time allocated to you. You can help to meet this goal by trying to:

- Think for yourself by setting your own objectives, drafting plans, reflecting and analysing practice, and regularly discussing these with your supervisor and mentor, making revisions where agreed.

- Arrange formal meetings and remember to arrive well prepared and on time, as you are not the only demand on the supervisor/mentor's time.

- Plan for meetings to ensure that you use the time efficiently. If necessary, email information in advance, and summarise discussions to avoid misunderstanding and to highlight any issues.

- Be honest, as placements are a period of training and you are unlikely to get everything right first time. Even though discussing errors can be very uncomfortable, by keeping the supervisor and mentor informed you will gain their respect and also be able to discuss avoiding similar scenarios occurring again. Avoid blaming others for difficulties experienced – while you are unlikely to be to blame for all problems arising, you are unlikely to be completely blameless in all situations. Considering where you could have done things better is at the core of reflective practice and therefore constitutes a key point that informs CPD. If you are experiencing difficulties, the supervisor and mentor are there to help you. The worst scenario is that a lack of progress is interpreted as a lack of enthusiasm and effort.

- Keep a sense of perspective on any feedback that the supervisor/mentor gives you, as they are trying to improve your performance. You must use this as a learning process and actively ask for suggestions on how to improve. You should respect and follow the advice given, as the supervisor and mentor are more experienced, and the supervisor in particular knows the setting and its staff, children and parents better than you do. This means that a solution that may appear promising in the abstract may not be feasible within a particular setting at a particular point in time. Full pathway candidates especially should remember that 'perfect world' solutions are unlikely to be helpful in a 'real world' practice environment.

- Take the initiative by inviting feedback rather than waiting for the supervisor to offer it or criticise. You should ask questions that show that you are independent and can respond to feedback, e.g. Am I doing enough? Where can I improve?

- Discuss reflections and analyses to ensure that you are fully supported to identify development requirements or initiatives that need to be worked on.

- Show that you are enthusiastic and passionate about your work and the setting. By going the extra mile, you will gain the respect of others.

- Plan your work to ensure you have enough time and resources to meet deadlines, particularly those set by the supervisor.

 Focus on practice

Long pathway candidate Rohana identifies that she has little experience of working in the pre-school room. She also has no multi-professional working experience. Before she starts her EYP training she meets with her supervisor and they agree to meet every other week. Before their first meeting Rohana identifies her personal aims and what she needs to do to meet the standards. During their first meeting they discuss her personal objectives and gaps in her knowledge and experience. The discussion enables the supervisor to identify possible tasks/projects that Rohana could lead, not only to close these gaps in her skill set but also to support more junior staff. Rohana takes notes of their discussion and next time they meet they agree two specific tasks and analyse whether or not they need resources, training and staff involvement. They also discuss timescales and 'deliverables'. Rohana emails a summary of the meeting to her supervisor as well as possible obstacles and plans to overcome these. While undertaking one task, Rohana realises she has upset a member of staff and makes the supervisor aware of this. During a meeting they discuss how Rohana should repair this relationship, which she does successfully. She also researches training and resources and uses a progress report as the agenda for the following meetings. She ensures that she is prepared for each meeting and sets a clear agenda each time which covers progress to date and issues. She makes most meetings and, when she cannot, she takes the initiative in rearranging for a mutually convenient time. During the meeting Rohana seeks input on her progress, and learns that the supervisor would like her to change her method of communication from a newsletter to staff to a workshop so that she can get a more comprehensive input from all who work in the setting.

Reflection *Rohana has identified her own objectives and has set up regular meetings. She takes time to read and familiarise herself with the standards and has thought about what she needs to do to ensure she meets them. By being clear, she quickly gets agreement for her role. By taking the time to prepare and document their meetings, she is able to update her supervisor on progress so that they are left with more time during the meeting to discuss her approach and outcomes of her work. As a result, Rohana develops professionally as she is receiving more qualitative input. Her honest approach and her quest for feedback enable her to adapt her work flexibly to suit the setting and get better results.*

Approach while in placement

You should show an element of personal enterprise by seeking areas of opportunity where you can initiate change in order to drive continuous improvement. The setting supervisor will almost certainly have an idea of aspects of practice that are ripe for development and, given the constraints on their time, may be grateful for someone else to take the lead on these. You should work with the supervisor to identify skills or projects that are needed and which you can lead and be responsible for. These projects can provide excellent material for the written, documentary and tour elements of the EYPS assessment process as well as bringing significant benefits to the setting (see Chapter 10).

To ensure that you manage the supervisor and mentor well during your placement, you must take a structured approach to your work while completing tasks set by yourself and your supervisor. To produce quality work, that will bring positive change to the setting and that you can use for EYP assessment, you should regularly document your work and make ongoing reflections and analyses thereon to bring about improvement. The professional journal (see Chapter 1) is a very useful vehicle for this. If you do this well there will be significant benefits to the setting and you will gain an understanding of your immediate professional development and more long-term continuing professional development. The following simple guidelines may help you to structure your work.

1 Plan

You should start by using an objective approach to reflect on what you have done in the past and where you are now. You should list the skills and resources available and how they have been developed to allow you to establish strengths and weaknesses. Once you have done this you should align yourself with the professional challenges you are likely to face. Any skills gaps identified require an action in your development plan. If you are taking an academic qualification alongside your EYPS training, the Personal Development Planning or Personal Planning and Development module within this qualification should support you in this endeavour.

You should analyse what brings out your best performance and ensure that you operate on projects that use your skills to the greatest advantage, while facilitating a conducive environment. You should be aware of the views of others such as managers, colleagues and parents and what they have said about your performance, your strengths and areas for development. You should consider where you would like to go in the future and then scrutinise your strengths and weaknesses, and find ways within the standards to address these.

You should spend adequate time thinking through your aims, objectives, options and actions, considering these in the light of a SWOT analysis of your existing skills and the relevant workplace (Strengths, Weaknesses, Opportunities and Threats). You should set objectives, plan actions and manage time and resources effectively in order to achieve personal and organisational goals aiming for and attempting to achieve high standards. You may also find the use of Specific, Measurable, Attainable, Realistic and Time-based (SMART) targets helpful in this endeavour.

2 Research

You should take time to research and know the way the setting is organised and to become familiar with its policies and procedures. By understanding the mission statement and the aims and objectives of the setting, you can determine possible ways that you can help your supervisor achieve them by making a high-quality contribution. A sound knowledge of the Early Years Foundation Stage and concepts of best practice are essential (see Chapter 2), but in addition you should keep abreast of current thinking and critically evaluate options that may be relevant for implementation in the setting. You should develop your knowledge and skills by researching, analytically reviewing and discussing areas of provision.

3 Prepare

You should visualise your performance before you start, to enable you to foresee any issues and allow you to mitigate them. You should talk to other staff in the setting to enable you to consider the best way to go about your tasks. It may be advisable to shadow experienced practitioners for a period of time to gain the benefit of their knowledge and approach. You should take time to identify the skills, people, resources and time available and consider funding, training needs etc. and how they are going to be secured. A collaborative approach is more likely to result in successful implementation.

Ensure that all options have been considered before a proposal for resources is put forward, as the nature of Early Years work means that there are considerable demands on resources. To get support for resources or training you need to help your supervisor by providing a justification. You need to 'sell' the proposal by making it relevant to the project and show that it will make a measurable difference to practice by improving standards and/or quality. The mentor may be able to help in this thinking process by acting as a 'sounding board'. If a proposal enables additional or enhanced skills to be acquired then it is more likely to be supported.

The project plan should demonstrate considerable benefits to the children and the setting to ensure that you get support from all staff for the project. It is important to draft an action plan so that all work is clearly linked to achieving the objectives and to break the work into manageable steps and 'deliverables'.

Focus on practice

Standard 37: Develop and use skills in literacy, numeracy and information and communication technology to support their work with children and wider professional activities.

Short pathway candidate Rosy reviews the EYP standards and identifies that her weakness is her ability to 'develop and use skills in literacy, numeracy and information and communication technology to support her work with children and professional activities'. She discusses this with her mentor and they analyse which areas are most likely to be needed for her role as a practitioner and for the projects Rosy is working on. They determine that the setting has invested in resources to promote the use of ICT but they are not being used by staff or the children as effectively as they could be. Having referred to the EYFS, Rosy suggests to her supervisor that she undertake a project which focuses on use of ICT while working with children, as this is referred to specifically in the Knowledge and Understanding of the World (KUW) learning goal. Rosy agrees to lead a project on identifying ICT equipment available and how to use it as part of their work with children. Rosy and her supervisor decide that Rosy will use Microsoft Word and Excel to plan the project, produce project updates, prepare guidance and training notes for staff. They include an objective of training in Microsoft office packages on her development plan. They consider the options and decide that rather than attending a formal training course Rosy will have access to the nursery administrator, who is skilled in this area.

They also identify that there is a general need to build the confidence and skills of practitioners in ICT. They subsequently agree the primary objective of the project is to train the staff to use ICT in their work with children. Rosy takes this away and produces a set of smaller steps, having consulted with other practitioners in the setting, before she starts any practical intervention. For example, they agree that one of the steps will be 'evaluating training options on products available for use in the setting' and include this in the plan. Rosy then agrees the resulting project 'deliverables' with her supervisor and they agree these will form the agenda for future meetings and updating on progress.

Reflection *By considering her own shortfalls and discussing them with her supervisor, Rosy realises that she shares this weakness with her colleagues. This results in her leading a mutually beneficial project for the setting. Clear objectives and 'deliverables' are set and Rosy uses ICT to keep the supervisor informed. This should lead to a good working relationship throughout the project and, provided the 'deliverables' are met, should lead to a satisfactory result. Rosy increases her confidence and is able to use ICT in her work meeting the standard. She is able to use the project as a subject for a written task and has documentary evidence for her file in the form of project plan, minutes, training notes etc.*

4 Perform

You should use your intuition and be confident in your own abilities, reinforced through practice and training; however, you should welcome feedback and suggestions for improvement. By breaking challenges down into smaller achievable steps or tasks, you should consider options at each stage and try to ensure that you have adequate time to think and reflect. You should have confidence in your own judgements, but you should discuss your analysis and approach with other staff in the setting to gain feedback. Wherever possible, you should consider innovative and creative practice and use your initiative to demonstrate your adaptability and problem solving. It will help the supervisor if they can rely on you to use acquired knowledge and work cooperatively with the staff in the setting, as this means the project will have longer lasting value.

5 Communication

You should communicate effectively throughout with the supervisor and all those with whom you interact, including (sometimes especially) those with whom you collaborate in a multi-agency fashion, using a wide range of appropriate methods. For example, you should use speech, writing, technology and behaviour effectively in order to present and exchange opinions, ideas and information. Effective communication will earn you significant respect within and outside the setting.

6 Teamwork

You should work with others in order to establish and achieve common goals. By forming effective working relationships with staff in the setting and getting them involved in projects you are more likely to be successful. You will be able to undertake a variety of roles, both collaborative or in a leadership role, if you are successful in forging good relationships.

You should cooperate by sharing ideas and encouraging others to contribute theirs. If you work in synergy with others and share responsibility through challenges, collectively you will deliver more and make more of an impact. You should identify the contribution of others honestly to your mentor and supervisor so that they also get recognition. You should try to anticipate potential for conflict and aim to remove it or mitigate it. By playing to people's strengths and as a reliable and trusted member of the team, you will be able to lead and support others. If you know and understand the specific team dynamics within a setting (see Chapter 8), you can build on this to develop your leadership qualities.

7 Reflect

You should take a step back and analyse your actions, causes and effects. The professional journal is an ideal vehicle for this purpose (see Chapter 1). You should consider:

- how effective your planning and preparation was
- your research and whether or not you could have implemented/may in future implement other methods
- your style of participation
- how you effectively obtained, recognised and validated the contribution of others
- what you observed and whether or not you took an unbiased view when watching and listening
- your decisions, actions, strengths and needs for further development
- how well you analysed events, actions, responses and behaviour and whether or not you did this objectively
- the learning gained not only by yourself, but by colleagues, children, parents and relevant others
- building the learning gained into effective planning for the future.

 Focus on practice

Standard 38: Reflect on and evaluate the impact of practice, modifying approaches where necessary and take responsibility for identifying and meeting their professional development needs.

While working on placement, full pathway candidate Jim observes that the children play well when the age groups are mixed. But within this setting, the children are normally segregated by age: babies, toddlers and pre-schoolers. After several conversations with both his mentor and his supervisor, he decides to work on a project looking at adopting a multi-age approach in the setting for specific activities. He also plans to use this as the basis for his practitioner research assignment on the postgraduate certificate he is taking alongside his EYPS training. He receives a lot of negative criticism from the other practitioners, as they believe it is too difficult to facilitate group activities, but his supervisor has read many articles about the topic and is keen to introduce the concept to the nursery.

Jim and his supervisor decide to trial some activities with children from each age group to determine whether or not it is a feasible initiative. Having trialled a few different activities it becomes apparent that the multi-age approach is very successful for quite a few activities and that it was worth introducing this to the setting. To convince other staff, Jim produces a purpose-designed version of the report that he has written for his module assignment, which summarises the research he has conducted and his reflections upon the trials performed, their results and what was gained by each of the parties impacted, e.g. the children, staff and parents. He discusses this with his module tutor, mentor and supervisor, and makes some minor revisions based on their advice before sharing it with his colleagues. His reflective piece identifies some issues, but convinces the other practitioners of the merit of mixing age groups for certain activities and persuades them to trial it. The practitioners become willing to experiment with this approach, and it becomes part of their short-term planning. Jim becomes very interested in this area of practice, and decides to visit a setting that has fully adopted an integrated multi-age approach, to further his knowledge in this area.

Reflection *Jim has used his research and reflection on play to identify an opportunity to change and improve practice. His reflective practice allows him to identify issues which can be overcome, and is very useful in persuading others to embrace change. He produces a variety of purpose-designed training materials on this specific area of practice, using these to communicate his ideas to colleagues, and, in so doing, also helps them to develop their practice and that of the setting. When he achieves his EYPS he engages in CPD by becoming an expert within this area of practice, via collaboration with other settings, initially within his own location and then within a wider geographical area. Jim moves on to study for a Master of Early Years degree, which gives him the opportunity to collaborate with one of his masters module tutors to write a journal article on the multi-age approach.*

8 Review

Effective mentors and supervisors will regularly ask the EYPS candidates with whom they are working the following questions:

- What did you want to achieve?
- What actually happened?
- What went well?

- What didn't go well?
- What would you do differently next time?
- Did you identify ways to sustain a commitment to development?
- Can you identify how you have changed and added value to the setting and to practice?
- Can you demonstrate that you have contributed to change which has benefitted the setting?

It is also extremely useful to use the professional journal to reflect on these points on an ongoing basis, so you have already reflected upon the answer to these questions before you are prompted to do so by your supervisor and/or mentor.

Focus on practice

Standard 39: Take a creative and constructively critical approach towards innovation, and adapt practice if benefits and improvements are identified.

Having completed half her time at placement, full pathway candidate Freya decides to assess her skills by carrying out a review of people's perception of her as a practitioner. This is an innovative approach, never used before by the setting, but Freya has used it before in her previous career in marketing. She wishes to use the information she collects to enable her to review her progress and performance to date with her supervisor.

She decides to adopt a '360-degree' approach and solicit the views of her past work colleagues, other practitioners and managers both directly and indirectly involved with her day-to-day work, other professionals working in the children's centre, parents and the children. She also asks a colleague to take detailed observations on her personal practice and leadership skills.

Having collated all the information, Freya analyses all the points and, where possible, determines the reasons for views expressed. She identifies examples of good practice and areas for improvement for her supervisor. It was apparent that Freya was highly regarded within the setting but that the parents were not aware of her work and influence within the setting apart from the information from their children and their limited exposure to her as an individual. However, she realises that, using this approach, she has not managed to give a clear picture of the tangible results her work has delivered or the benefits of the changes to practice she has inspired. Neither does it reflect Freya's own concerns about her limited experience in leading a team discussion. She decides to list these and add them to the agenda for discussion.

Freya concludes with her supervisor that she must add a development objective to her personal plan, and that this will be leading a team debate. They also agree that she can take on more responsibility and get to know the parents by running a workshop for them on the EYFS, which will feed into the work that volunteer parents carry out within the setting. This will bring benefits to the parents, the children, the staff and the setting. Freya and her supervisor agree to use the 360-degree approach at her next review as it has given them valuable information. Freya's supervisor will also recommend this approach to her other senior staff.

Reflection Freya has used an innovative approach to assessing her skills but, recognising that it does not give a complete picture, she has used her initiative and collated more information for her meeting as this also raises development points. By using these methods Freya has made her supervisor's job much easier and has added some important development objectives for herself to ensure she continues to improve professionally.

9 Continuing Professional Development (CPD)

Reflective practice will enable you to:

- develop intuition
- increase effectiveness of observation
- identify strengths and weaknesses
- avoid repeating mistakes
- avoid blame and encourage respect for delivering practice.

It is important for you to set yourself developmental objectives focused on your professional competence, either on your own or with your placement supervisor. Continuing Professional Development (CPD) is essential for Early Years Professionals to maintain, improve and broaden their knowledge and skills and develop qualities to enhance their professional life.

You should seek a wide variety of opportunities, not just academic/formal training courses (as we saw in the example of Jim), to improve your professional competence. You should plan to undertake a broad range of activities specifically chosen to better equip you professionally. Some ideas include:

- analysing and employing innovative practices
- attending workshops
- networking with other EYPs or other professionals working with children
- visiting other settings and shadowing professionals working in other settings or in other professions with children
- seeking professional accreditation or quality assurance and getting noticed for your professional expertise.

Conscious updating of professional knowledge can also be achieved by pursuing qualifications, attending seminars or courses and undertaking research. You should learn by continual reading, and reflecting on your own practice as well as shadowing that of others. Multi-agency working can also be highly instrumental in developing senior practitioner skills within the contemporary Early Years environment, and building most directly upon those skills that EYPs most specifically hone through their highly multi-agency focused professional training.

We hope that, in focusing upon the final three EYPS standards, this chapter helps you to negotiate the complex web of skills and relationships that Early Years Professionals need to build to succeed in the multi-agency workplace of the future. The remaining chapters will look forward to the validation process, and listen to a wider range of voices from Early Years Professionals reflecting upon their thoughts about gaining Early Years Professional Status, and the wide range of future professional roles that may be open to them in the children's workforce of the future.

Further reading

Cottrell, S. (2005) *Critical Thinking Skills: Developing Effective Analysis and Argument.* London: Palgrave MacMillan.

Hobart, C. and Frankel, J. (2004) *A Practical Guide to Child Observation and Assessment.* London: Nelson Thornes.

Melhuish, E. (2006) 'Policy and research on preschool education and care in the UK'. In E. Melhuish and K. Petrogiannis (eds) *Early Childhood Care and Education, International Perspectives.* Abingdon: Routledge.

Mitchell, H., Wild, M. and Swarbrick, N. (2007) *Early Childhood Studies Reflective Reader.* London: Learning Matters Ltd.

Northedge, A. (2005) *The Good Study Guide.* Milton Keynes: The Open University.

Redman, P. (2005) *Good Essay Writing (A Social Sciences Guide).* London: Sage.

Schon, D.A. (1983) *The Reflective Practitioner: How Professionals Think in Action.* New York: Basic Books.

Journals

Children Now

Early Years Educator

Educational Researcher

Nursery World

10

Surviving validation

Jane Guilfoyle

Chapter overview

This chapter will address the following key points and questions that you are likely to focus upon as you consider your progression to Early Years Professional status validation:

- The Gateway Review and the Assessment process:
  - What is it?
  - When does it happen and how much of my time does it take?
  - What can I expect to have to do for the validation process?
  - What is the Gateway Review, exactly?
- Preparing for the Gateway Review?
- Preparing for the written tasks
- Preparing for the setting visit.

Candidate reflections on validation

Sunita EYP (previously validation only candidate): At the time I probably hated it and thought: God, this is a ridiculous exercise, but actually with the benefit of hindsight I can see that it was quite a valuable exercise . . . It was quite a good way of assessing people skills and their ability to tackle situations, and in fairness they are the types of situations that you do face, and they are difficult situations, so . . . in hindsight I think it was a very good way of selecting people that were appropriate to get through the EYP process . . . It helps you to understand what you have done, where you have shown true leadership and possibly identify areas where you could improve, same with innovative practice, the biggest thing I got out of it was the reflective side, and I think that is a skill that doesn't come up earlier on in your education with child care. So I think it was a really valuable skill to take back and I think having done the EYP process now, I do engage in reflective practice a lot more.

Mandy EYP (previously long pathway candidate): One of the most nerve-racking things I've ever done in my life. I was absolutely petrified . . . But yeah, I got through it . . . it's up to you to go out, and if you really want that qualification and that status, you're going to have to go out and grab it, it's not going to come on a plate.

The Gateway Review and the Assessment process

What is it?

The process consists of briefing and preparation for assessment and the final assessment itself. Briefly, it comprises the formative Gateway Review and the summative five written tasks and follow-up setting visit.

The preparation for, and completion of, the Gateway Review and the final assessment are common to all four pathways towards Early Years Professional Status. This process is the same for all candidates, whatever the length of the pathway and training they have followed. It is the same irrespective of the provider they have chosen. It is the same whatever setting the candidate is working in and encompasses the full age range of the EYFS, i.e. work with babies, toddlers and young children. It has been designed to maximise national consistency in the judgement of a candidate against the Standards and to provide a credible basis for the internal and external moderation of results.

When does it happen and how much of my time does it take?

Candidates start the validation process when they are ready for assessment against the Standards. This means that the timing of the briefing, preparation and final assessment will vary from pathway to pathway and from candidate to candidate.

For the Validation Pathway, both Gateway Review and the final assessment are completed within the four months allotted. For the Short, Full and Long pathways, the Gateway Review can be completed at any stage during the training. As it is a formative or developmental process, the training provider will determine the most appropriate time for it to take place. Anecdotally, it would seem that most providers carry out the Gateway Assessment in the later stages of the programme taken, to allow candidates the maximum time to develop the necessary skills. The summative assessment, that is the completion of the written tasks and the setting visit, must take place during the final four months of each of these pathways.

In the early days of EYPS, a period of three months was allocated to validation. The extra month added to this period reflects the logistical difficulties for centres and candidates in moving through this process. It was perfectly possible for a candidate to complete the whole process calmly in three months provided they didn't take any holiday, move house, start a new job, fall into poor health, have a family issue or experience any of those other things that life throws at us. A further month does allow a little extra time to deal with the unforeseen, but it remains that the validation process is a period when close focus on the tasks in hand is needed. To balance this, it must also be pointed out that those candidates who are ready for validation, having acquired the necessary skills, knowledge and experience, move smoothly through the process with relative ease and even some enthusiasm and enjoyment! This is the time when the centre's careful recruitment, guidance, selection, training and mentoring of candidates comes together and hopefully pays dividends.

Six and a half days are 'officially' allocated to a candidate for the validation process and the finance for some paid cover for the setting is provided to sustain this. It is crucial that even the most confident, experienced candidate has full access to this allotted schedule and that elements are not dispensed with because of other priorities. Some providers operate a flexible system of minimum attendance at a centre for preparation days with peers, but in addition require the completion of individual tasks with feedback by email. In addition to these preparation sessions, further individual candidate time will be needed to reflect on strengths and weaknesses before the Gateway Review, to complete the written tasks and to make arrangements for the setting visit. How much time this takes depends on individual circumstances, for example how accustomed a candidate is to reflective practice and how quickly they write.

What can I expect to have to do for the validation process?

Early Years Professional Status validation process: the steps

Note: *The order may vary slightly from centre to centre.*

Step 1	1 day in training centre
	Exploration of the role of the EYP
	Detailed consideration of the 39 standards
	The Forward Agenda
Step 2	Candidate in Early Years Setting (employment or placement)
	Exploration and self-review against the standards
Step 3	1 day in training centre
	Briefing on the written tasks
Step 4	Time in Setting to agree material for tasks and to further develop opportunities to gain experience
Step 5	1 day in training centre
	'Practice' for the 4 Gateway skills assessment tasks, i.e. Personal Interview; Presentation and Group Discussion; Staff Interview and the Written Exercise
Step 6	Time in Setting
	Preparation of self-analysis against the standards. Form to be sent to Centre for use by assessor during the Personal Interview
Step 7	Half a day in training centre
	Assigned time to be observed and assessed across 4 exercises (Gateway Review)
Step 8	Time in Setting
	Receive written feedback from Gateway Review and action plan for further development
Step 9	1 day (*or equivalent*) to write up tasks and reference material to standards
Step 10	1 day in training centre
	Review written tasks with peers
	Prepare for the Setting visit by an assessor
	Finalise date for the Setting visit

Step 11	Time in Setting
	Select and brief witnesses
	Make practical preparations for visit
Step 12	Send copies of all 5 written tasks and other documentation to the Centre to be forwarded to the assessor for consideration before the visit
Step 13	Time in Setting
	Five and a half hour visit to Setting by assessor
	Document check; tour of setting; witness evidence

What exactly is the 'Gateway Review'?

The 'Gateway' is a centre-based assessment process that aims to assess and provide feedback on a candidate's professional leadership skills. This review consists of four exercises and a written reflection, all of which are similar to those used extensively in education, health and the private sector. The purpose of the process is to check that the candidate understands the Standards and to assess the three skills listed below (*EYP Candidates' Handbook,* CWDC, September 2008). These skills are generic to working at level 6 (full graduate level) and fundamental to meeting the Standards.

The skills

1 **The ability to make decisions on the basis of sound judgement:**
   - thinks beyond the immediate problem and avoids 'quick fix' solutions
   - concentrates on what is the most important thing
   - makes appropriate decisions, using the available information but seeking further information when necessary
   - bases decisions on agreed principles and policies.

2 **The ability to lead and support others:**
   - gets ideas agreed, whether one's own or those of others
   - improves practice by motivating others to achieve agreed aims
   - recognises and develops the potential of others
   - proposes clear strategies for improvement as a change agent.

3 **The ability to relate to, and communicate with, others:**
   - communicates clearly, both orally and in writing
   - listens to others' concerns and responds appropriately
   - shows respect for others in a sensitive manner
   - manages own feelings and needs.

On the designated day, the candidate will find themselves booked in for a session of approximately 2–3 hours. All candidates will be asked to complete the same exercises, but the order in which these take place may vary. Each exercise lasts for approximately half an hour. Ideally, each candidate will receive an individual timetable.

Candidates are asked to take part in:

The Personal Interview

This is an individual one-to-one personal interview with an assessor that explores a candidate's experience with respect to the Standards. The candidate will have previously been asked to forward an analysis of their progress against the Standards to date and it will be the assessor's role to discuss this, check understanding of the Standards and the level of the candidate's recent and present work.

The Written Exercise

This involves written responses to practical issues and scenarios appropriate to the candidate's day-to-day work. Candidates will find themselves with a small group of their peers, in examination-style conditions. They will then be presented with an Early Years leadership focused written scenario and asked to respond in writing to five or six short items connected to this. As only 30 minutes are allowed for the whole exercise – reading, thinking, responding – time-management is extremely important. Bullet points may be used but responses must be detailed enough to allow the assessor to make a judgement. Consideration is given by the assessor to the accuracy of the writing in terms of legibility and meaning.

The Interview with an Actor

In this the candidate will conduct an interview with a professional actor who is briefed to perform as a member of staff, a parent/carer or a fellow Early Years or multi-agency professional. This will take place on an individual basis with only an assessor and the actor present. Before starting the interview, the candidate will be given a briefing sheet and will have 10 minutes to read it and prepare for the interview which should last approximately 15 minutes.

The Group Exercise

For this the candidate will be in a room with a small group of peers, whom they may or may not know, and two assessors. First each candidate will deliver a short 4-minute presentation. Guidance will have been given on this beforehand and a single side of A4 summarising the main points can be used. Following from this, the group will discuss the presentations and draw some conclusions. Candidates need to be aware not only of their own performance but also of the impact of their contribution on others.

Written Reflection

Before leaving the review the candidate will be asked to spend a short period of time completing some pre-formatted questions, which guide reflection on their experience of the four exercises. These comments are borne in mind when the assessors are preparing individual feedback.

Feedback

No feedback, verbal or written, is given on the day of the review. Each candidate will receive, as soon as possible, written feedback on each of the exercises. This feedback does not form part of the final assessment but it is crucial guidance for further development.

Preparing for the 'Gateway Review'

Have I fully considered the range and depth of the standards?

Feedback from candidates who have experienced the Gateway process highlights the fact that they find the Personal Interview session with the assessor very positive and useful. Preparation beforehand includes a briefing on the Standards and candidates should consider early in their pathway the nature and scope of the Standards. They should complete a self-review against each of the Standards and, although later they will be evidencing the Standards holistically, they should ensure they have explored each one fully and considered a breadth of ways in which they might be able to meet it.

For example, fully explore:

Standard 18: Promote children's rights, equality, inclusion and anti-discriminatory practice in all aspects of practice

Are you able to?

- Identify what you consider the key principles in delivering anti-discriminatory practice.
- Explain how the whole team in a setting are involved in putting the principles into practice.
- Explain how staff members are supported in challenging discriminatory attitudes displayed by children or their family members.
- Identify the range of resources and guidance materials required by a setting in implementing anti-discriminatory practice.

Am I able to summarise my own strengths and weaknesses in terms of each of the groups of Standards?

For the Gateway Review, candidates will be asked to analyse the groups of Standards, i.e. Knowledge and understanding (S01–06); Effective practice (S07–24); Relationships with children (S25–28); Communicating and working in partnership with families and carers (S29–32); Team work and collaboration (S33–36) and Professional development (S37–39) (*Guidance to the Standards for the award of Early Years Professional Status,* CWDC September 2008), and indicate which ones they will find easy to meet and why, and which might need further work before the assessor's visit to their setting. As indicated previously, the assessor will receive a copy of this analysis prior to the interview and their role will be to discuss it and probe the understanding of the candidate.

Following are two examples that might form part of this summary.

Candidate A is an experienced practitioner and was on the first Validation Only pathway prior to the implementation of the EYFS framework; she writes:

Groups of Standards about which I am most confident and why	I am very confident about my *Effective Practice (S07–S24)*. I work hard to provide a welcoming environment that is emotionally and socially inviting and intellectually and physically stimulating. I take overall responsibility for planning activities but I involve all staff to promote the framework and curriculum effectively for the children and to ensure continuity of care and a high quality of education. I motivate staff by presenting myself as a good role model and constantly evaluating and improving practice. Routines are in place but I ensure they are flexible to achieve the best outcomes for the children and allow for adult-led and child-initiated activities. I plan activities around themes and core stories suitable to the age and stage of development of the children in my care. I capture their achievements by way of photographic evidence, written observations etc., from which I create a file to help parents and other professionals, involved in their care, understand their progress and next steps. Most of all I endeavour to generate a thirst for learning by having fun and having high expectations of them based on a sound relationship and understanding of them as individuals.
Groups of Standards about which I am least confident and why	There are no groups of standards that I do not feel comfortable with; however, I need to complete some work in order to be up to date with S05 and S20. This is due to some recent changes in publications. I now need to complete some further reading and review one of the setting policies to be fully up to speed with the most recent legislation and practices. I will also need to consult with the setting team and carry out some staff training to ensure the whole staff team is working towards the same goal.

Candidate B is on the Full pathway; she writes:

Groups of Standards about which I am most confident and why	*Effective Practice (S07–S24)* I am confident that I am delivering effective practice and am recognising through my reflections and observations where improvements and changes can be made in the setting and my personal practices. I have led on the provision of a number of stimulating activities for children of different age groups and of various stages of learning development. This has made me more aware of the differences in children at their various learning stages and the steps that can be taken to extend their learning. I have been flexible in my approach to these activities if the children have not wanted to join in and have made sure that those who have been interested have been able to access the activities, including those with limited movement, for example. I have provided a supportive and positive environment for the children to enjoy activities and have frequently joined them in their play and learning to help them to develop their learning and understanding of their world. I have evaluated provision with colleagues and developed activities that have been popular.

Groups of Standards about which I am least confident and why	A group of Standards that I feel I lack confidence in is *Professional Development (S37–S39)*. At the moment I feel that I have not had enough experience in developing the use of numeracy and literacy. I have had the opportunity to develop and use ICT within my practice with regard to the video camera I am using when observing children, and have been able to cascade this practice to my colleagues. I have also been able to encourage the use of photography in other areas, for example display work rather than merely for observation purposes. I feel that I am still developing my abilities as a reflective practitioner and because of this I feel that I would lack confidence in identifying and meeting the professional development needs of others, although I feel capable of identifying and in turn putting into action steps to further my professional development.

The completion of this document, the Standards Reflection form, may be a stress flashpoint for some candidates. It may have to be completed under duress of time; it may bring home that the assessment process is 'real' and imminent; it may bring an uncomfortable focus on 'self', which some candidates are unused to and uncomfortable with; it may bring home the realisation that further experience or focus on a particular aspect of practice is still needed. Providers can give further guidance during preparation sessions, and mentors and peers are useful sounding boards.

Am I confident about identifying and outlining how to lead good practice when presented with scenarios?

Less experienced candidates may find it challenging to see beyond the immediate problem when they are presented with scenarios and asked to make appropriate decisions, as they have less understanding of wider issues. They must, however, ensure that they are confident about the agreed principles and policies that form the framework for decision making in Early Years settings. The following is an example for general discussion and reflection; it is not in the same format as the Written Exercise encountered at the Gateway Review. It is for practice and reflection.

Focus on practice

Kushi's 'Critical Incident'

Kushi is the manager of a small day nursery that is located within a large converted terraced house. It has a large, enclosed garden at the back to which the children have free, supervised access during dry weather. The front door is accessed from a flight of steps that lead down to the pavement outside. The setting is located on a moderately busy road in a suburb of a large city. The front door is secured by a code-operated lock that is deliberately placed too high for the children to be able to access. Staff at the practice know that the front door is to remain closed at all times.

The children's rooms are on the ground floor, the basement is used for storage, and the rooms for food preparation, staff room and office are on the top floor.

When the setting first opened, the owners had not intended to divulge the front door entry code to anyone but staff; however, as the children arrive and leave at very different times during the day, it was eventually decided that parents would be given the entry code if they would agree to ensure that the door was carefully closed after entry, and to sign a form promising not to divulge the code to others. The code is changed regularly, and Kushi carefully maintains an ongoing database of code rotation, and past/present code holders.

On this particular day, Kushi is coming down the stairs after her break when the front door opens and a very young woman whom she does not recognise walks through the door. The woman then walks into the toddler room, leaving the front door and the toddler room door ajar.

Response

- What would you do?
- What underlying issues does it raise?

Kushi moves quickly to close the front door. She then walks quickly into the toddler room, closing the door behind her, to find one of the staff in conversation with the young woman. Kushi intervenes, informing the woman that she is the manager of the setting, and asking politely what she is doing here today, as she does not remember that they have previously met. The woman informs Kushi that she is Vicky, the aunt of one of the children, Nathan, and that she has arrived to pick him up early, as her sister (who is in the middle stages of pregnancy) has been unexpectedly admitted to hospital.

Response

- What would you do?
- What underlying issues does it raise?

Kushi explains that she is not able to release children to an adult who is not listed by the setting as a carer, and that before releasing the child to his aunt's care she will have to check with the designated carers that it will be OK to do this. Vicky begins to argue that she must take Nathan now, as her sister . . . But Kushi continues to quietly but firmly insist that she must follow agreed procedure, and takes Vicky to a waiting area, asking her deputy manager to ring the designated numbers for Nathan's carers. When no answer is forthcoming, Kushi asks Vicky for the details of the hospital to which her sister has been admitted, and manages to ensure, through the hospital staff, that Vicky *has* been asked to collect Nathan by the designated carers. She then subsequently releases Nathan to Vicky's care.

Leading practice

As the leading practitioner in the setting, Kushi now needs to reflect on the situation that has occurred. She notes that:

- The divulging of the code by a parent to a non-designated adult has resulted in a situation arising that has endangered all the children in the setting. If Kushi had not been coincidentally coming down the stairs when Vicky let herself in, one or more of the children could have emerged on to the street through the open door.

- The situation then developed to a point where senior staff in the setting were put into a position where they were unable to avoid adding an extra problem for a family already trying to deal with a crisis situation.

She subsequently discusses the situation with her deputy manager. They decide on the following course of action:

- The owner of the setting will be asked whether the entrance can be restructured so that adults collecting children must pass through two doors, the outer one being unlocked, allowing them into a toughened glass 'porch' area, with the inner one remaining securely locked until opened by a member of staff.

- In the meantime, the entry code will be changed and parents/carers will have to ring at the existing front door. Kushi will construct the letter explaining the reasons for this (without reference to the specific incident).

- Parents will receive a completely separate communication asking them to update their 'emergency contact' record, with a specific reminder that it is particularly important to update this with the setting at times where there is some amount of change ongoing in the family, such as pregnancy, moving house etc.

- Kushi will ring Nathan's first named contact when the family emergency is over and express regret for any stress added to the event concerned, but also tactfully explain the situation that arose in the setting, and request during the conversation that the family are very careful to update Nathan's contact records during this time, so that a similar situation does not arise again.

Task **Discuss the points below with your fellow validation candidates:**

- **How far does Kushi demonstrate the three generic level-6 skills outlined earlier?**

- **The course of action that Kushi and her deputy manager agreed to ensure that this situation would not occur again is only *one* set of choices; there would be other, equally useful ways to respond. Try to find an opportunity to discuss with colleagues or fellow candidates how you would collectively decide to deal with a situation of this nature.**

- **How should Kushi and her deputy manager respond if the owner of the setting decides that they are not prepared to spend the necessary money for the entrance modifications?**

Some candidates find the scenario with the actor daunting and become anxious; others find it unrealistic and are uncomfortable with it because of this. Again, concerns about these issues can be raised during the preparation session and a practice activity gone through.

Focus on practice

Staff interview

Brief for practice of role-play

You are an EYP at the 0-5 years Happy Days Nursery. You have been at the nursery in your current role for six months and have been working, with the full support of the nursery owner, to improve practice in the baby room. You have run some twilight sessions for the whole staff to share good practice but there remains a concern about the quality of the interactions with the babies. Traditionally, this area has been staffed by the youngest and least experienced practitioners. Consequently, there has been a high turnover of staff in this area.

You are about to meet with Carol, who is the longest-serving member of staff at the nursery. She is currently leader of the pre-school room. She is a competent and skilful practitioner and has a lot of influence at the setting. You, and the owner, want her to move to lead and motivate the team in the baby room; you have tentatively raised this idea with her but she was not enthusiastic about the suggestion. You have decided that you need to meet with her to move forward with this.

Your task is to explore the issues, communicate your expectations clearly and agree what actions will be taken to bring about improvements.

The scenario should last about 10 minutes.

Task **Find a partner to play the practitioner, Carol. Allow them to decide how cooperative (or uncooperative!) they want to be. If possible, ask someone else to observe and afterwards consider what evidence there was for each of the three skills.**

The only other specific preparation to be completed individually prior to the Gateway Review is the sheet of bullet-points for the 4-minute presentation for the Group Exercise. Generally, the greatest challenge candidates face with this is keeping it within the allocated time and it is obviously sensible to have practised a timed delivery of the material (at an appropriate pace!).

What must be remembered about the Gateway Review is that a range of scenarios and exercises are used; it is rare that one candidate shines at all aspects and equally it is rare that a candidate demonstrates significant weaknesses in all four exercises. Remember, no one is perfect! Feedback from the review should be informative and constructive and should be discussed as soon as possible with a mentor or tutor. All feedback should make it clear whether weaknesses are significant or minor in importance. The majority of candidates are likely to be working at the appropriate level but the evidence may show that a candidate may not be on the most appropriate Pathway, in which case the candidate will be advised they should defer undertaking the assessment process or possibly embark on a longer Pathway. As a result of the feedback discussion, candidates should be clear about whether they need any additional experience in order to meet the EYP Standards and what actions they need to take in order to meet any Standards that are less easy for them to meet. Obviously, the nature and extent of any such additional experience depends on at what stage in the Pathway this review took place and how much time is available to remedy any gaps in experience or skills. It is best to listen to the advice of the training provider; there is no disgrace in taking longer to reach the goal, but, if the candidate does not have the necessary skills and practical experience, the next stage of the assessment process will certainly find them out.

Preparing for the written tasks

The next stage of the assessment process requires the candidate to undertake, document and evaluate a number of tasks, as a natural part of their work. A clear template of the requirements for their written accounts of the tasks is provided and word limits are set for each one. A concise and short portfolio of supporting evidence against the Standards is also required. The CWDC provide a 'Candidates' Handbook', which includes explanation of the rubric and coverage of each of the written tasks, an example on how to cross-refer to the Standards, and some guidance on the degree of depth and reflection required. Suggestions for supporting documentary evidence are also outlined. The exact nature of the guidance for the written tasks and documentation has evolved over the lifetime of the programme and will continue to do so. It is important that candidates follow and use the correct rubric, which should be supplied by the training provider. The general rule is that the guidance in place at the time of the candidate's initial registration to the EYPS Programme should be used.

The current (September 2008) structure of the tasks is as follows. It should be noted in particular that Task 4 has evolved from a focus on critical incidents to a reflective account of the candidate's personal practice with children. If you have been meticulous in keeping your professional journal (see Chapter 1) this should pay dividends now.

	Designated Age-range	Suggested Wordage
Task 1	0-20 months	1500-2000
Task 2	16-36 months	1500-2000
Task 3	30-60 months	1500-2000
Task 4	0-60 months	1500-2000
Task 5a, 5b, 5c	Focus: wider professional role	500-750 each

The tasks are snapshots of recent or current work. It is suggested that any tasks based on previous work or experience should normally have taken place within the past three years. In reality, unless copious notes were kept at the time, it is very challenging to write with the degree of detail and reflection needed unless the activities are fairly recent or contemporary. The quality and depth of the response to the five written tasks is of paramount importance and candidates should provide evidence for all the Standards in the five completed tasks taken together.

The following advice is very useful for potential EYPs.

Factors that make it likely that you can show the assessor you have met the Standards you have claimed:

- Produce comprehensive accounts that refer to policy and documentation
- Remember the importance of showing underpinning knowledge and understanding
- Include all the Standards
- Be succinct and specific
- Be clear and focused
- Make time to plan and do it; get some agreed time for feedback
- Consider 'who' was being led, 'why' the activity took place and 'who' will be used as a witness
- Think about and collect supporting evidence as you go along
- Include personal practice as well as leadership; show how you demonstrate this
- Make reference to current documentation and wider reading/research
- Include evaluation and outcomes
- Hit the deadlines
- Talk about 'I' not 'we', remember EYPS is focused on **leadership** rather than personal practice
- Consider word count
- Stick to age ranges in the rubric and make activities age-appropriate
- Make use of your reflective journal (see Chapter 1).

The documentary evidence should reflect everyday work activities by the candidate. The evidence should be numbered clearly and be easily accessible to the assessor who will have a maximum of 90 minutes to scrutinise this. The file of documentary evidence doesn't leave the setting but should be kept securely for six months afterwards. The following is an example of what was included by an experienced practitioner from the Long Pathway. This includes examples of a number of policies and procedures, which it was the candidate's responsibility to evidence she had drafted and written and to clearly link to appropriate standards.

D	Primary Source of Documentary Evidence
D1	Witness Statement - settling a new child
D2	Witness Statement - leading and supporting others in the use of outdoor play
D3	Outdoor play policy - explanation of the role of the adult
D4	Example of planning sheet being piloted for wider use
D5	Example of handout on number, reasoning and problem solving developed for staff training session

D	Primary Source of Documentary Evidence
D6	Investigation into complaint (Ofsted format) - copy to parents who made the complaint
D7	Letter to parents re. biting incident
D8	Observation of behaviour
D9	Behaviour Management Policy - outline of expected behaviour
D10	Inclusion Policy - explains roles and responsibilities of different people inside and outside the setting
D11	Quarterly Parents' Newsletter
D12	Action plan following from audit of provision and resources
D13	Example of planning sheet
D14	Admission Forms - settling-in procedures
D15	Play, Care and Learning statement - role of keyworker explored
D16	Planning and Assessment Procedures
D17	Example of personalised learning
D18	Example of language assessment records
D19	Anti-discriminatory Practice statement
D20	Policy on Nutrition and Food - importance of social and nutritional aspects
D21	Safeguarding Children Policy
D22	Witness Statement - led staff development session on the use of descriptive praise

In marked contrast to this, candidates on the Full Pathway will not have wide-ranging evidence from recent experience; their documentary evidence will be drawn from experience during their placements on the programme. As well as the suggested assessment records; plans; minutes of meetings; reports; case studies; observation notes; notes from parents and carers; memos from staff and other professionals; audits of resources; witness statements or testimonials, it would be appropriate to include copies of documents such as feedback reports from mentors who may have completed direct observation of the candidate's personal practice and/or leadership and support of other practitioners. While it is not appropriate to include academic written assignments completed during the course, it may well be useful to include documentary evidence that reflects the impact of the assignment on the setting, for example: team or staff minutes; revised policy or curricular statements; work plans; records of observations (see the example of Jim's project in Chapter 9). This linking is also a useful way for a Full Pathway candidate to add depth and a wider context to specific examples outlined in the tasks.

Preparing for the setting visit

Have you considered the following?

The needs of the witnesses

In terms of preparing for the setting visit one of the most crucial things to consider well ahead is the choice of witnesses and their availability. Three witnesses will be needed and possibly a fourth reserve. It is important to nominate people who have a range of knowledge of your professional skills, for example your line manager, a parent, a colleague who has been led and supported. It is also important to consider the witnesses' ability to articulate their knowledge and understanding of your professional role. Obviously witnesses must not be coached or led in any way but they will need to be appropriately briefed and, if necessary, reassured before the setting visit takes place. What form this briefing takes will very much depend on the needs of the witness and their background. All witnesses need to be encouraged to give specific examples of your abilities rather than general assertions – for example, explaining how you listen to children and value what they say on a daily basis rather than remarking that you communicate well with children. Access to witnesses at the appropriate time of the day may equally be a challenge. The order of the visit is laid down in the CWDC guidance, but the start time of the visit is negotiable and the availability of the witnesses may guide this. For example, for the following candidate the first choice of a witness was only available at lunchtime. This was accommodated by a later start time.

ANY CHILDREN'S CENTRE

Visit Timetable

Time	Length	Item
9.30 am	10 min	Arrival and introductions
9.40 am	20 min	First candidate interview: Standards
10.00 am	10 min	Presentation of supporting evidence file
10.10 am	45 min	Scrutiny of the file
10.55 am	30 min	Tour of the setting
12.10 pm	30 min	Assessor's writing and reflection time
12.40 pm	1 hr	Witness interviews:
		First Witness:
		Second Witness:
		Third Witness:
1.40 pm	30 min	Lunch
2.10 pm	30 min	Assessor's writing and reflection time
2.40 pm	30 min	Second candidate interview: Standards
3.10 pm		Visit concluded

The needs of the assessor

A quiet, private space is needed by the assessor to carry out the necessary interviews, scrutiny of documents, periods of reflection and recording. It is the candidate's responsibility to make the best possible arrangements. This can be challenging for some settings and requires forethought and planning. One candidate who had not considered this until the last minute suggested the assessor use her car! Fortunately, space was negotiated in an adjacent building.

The needs of the setting

Remember the visit can only take place with the consent and goodwill of the staff in the setting and they need to be kept informed about what is happening. The 'Tour' section of the visit can only take place when the setting is in operation and you need to think ahead and ensure it is carried out with courtesy and consideration for all. The date of the setting visit is set by the assessment centre and may be fairly inflexible; however, again it is your responsibility to communicate any major concerns or issues the setting has about dates or times.

The needs of the candidate

The assessor will be at the setting for 5 hours and 40 minutes in total and of that time you will need to be with him/her for approximately 2 hours in all. How your usual work role is managed needs careful thought and planning. For example, if you are supernumerary that day you may then be available to cover for colleagues who are 'out of commission' while giving a witness statement to the assessor.

You must also remember that the CWDC rules governing assessment mean that you receive no feedback on the day, and are given no indication of the outcome of the assessment, which can be very frustrating after all the hard work, planning and preparation!

An assessor's perspective

Verity has assessed candidates in every assessment period since EYPS began. Here are some of her reflections on her experiences

It's a serious occupation, but one that is usually full of the delights and surprises that working with young children can bring. There are occasional moments when you wish it was possible to comment on a particular practice, wanting to extend what is good practice into something excellent. Very occasionally it has been the obverse when certain activities or experiences have been entirely inappropriate or the kind of lazy or bad practice you wish never happened in the care and education of young children. Usually, those occasions are not the fault of the potential EYP, who sometimes has to work in less than ideal situations. The Government's hope in establishing the EYPS is to eliminate bad practice and raise the practice of all those responsible for the care and education of young children to the highest levels possible, an aim I'm sure the majority of us involved in early years provision all share. The new EYFS statutory framework and practice guidance are evidence of this intent, putting, as it does, the child at its centre. Many settings have now embraced it, and I have seen some laudable attempts to present its principles in a jargon-free way to parents and carers, through the use of colourful displays of children photographed in exciting and challenging experiences, or through the magic of ICT, a video running on a loop, of children 'playing', in the fullest sense of that word.

The best practice has looked with fresh eyes at previous methods of planning, observations and assessments and developed new, user-friendly proformas and techniques that reflect the emphasis on the use of formative observations and assessment that track and describe the unique learning journeys of individual children from birth to 5 years. The children's profiles have been a joy to read, with much evidence of shared thinking, open-ended questioning and the children's own words recorded and valued, so accurately demonstrating the stage a particular child has reached in their communication skills. Lesser practice has struggled to move from the previous frameworks and, as a result, is still fragmented and compartmentalised in its recording procedures and practice.

All settings have been faced with the issue of providing more effective outdoor provision, and I have witnessed some outstanding practice where EYP candidates have been at the forefront of inventive and creative uses of outdoor spaces. They have also pushed for changes, some quite radical, in established routines for set 'playtimes', which favour staffing needs rather than the needs of children, or what I call 'weather resistant' attitudes on the part of staff who fail to see the pleasure rain, puddles, wind and snow can have for children, if appropriately dressed.

EYP candidates, on the whole, have clearly demonstrated a child-centred approach, understanding that children being 'creative' doesn't mean the formation of a production line of the same greetings card, or miles of scrunched-up tissue paper pasted on to card cut-outs, so 'adulterated' that a child doesn't recognise his or her own handiwork. Praise and encouragement given for that first tentative attempt at marks on a paper or in the sand or chalked on the ground outside has demonstrated some real understanding of how children develop and learn. In the best practice, EYPs have achieved all this, through diplomacy and a real wish to be part of a team of practitioners who strive for excellence. Some settings providing placement experience have welcomed a knowledgeable and informed extra pair of hands, giving the EYPS candidate space and encouragement to trial new ideas. Other settings have stood back and waited, unsure what to expect, while a few have been resistant to the changes the Government has initiated.

Correspondingly, settings have had varied approaches to my visits. In some, the EYP has been handsomely supported, a room put aside for the assessor to work in quiet, with a table on which to spread considerable amounts of paperwork (there is quite a lot of documentation to consider!). A recent 'room' allocated to me as a visiting assessor doubled up as a 'themed' room for parties with piped music accompanying my every thought; another 'space' was found in a 'family room' at a children's centre, with very young curious faces appearing and giggling at intervals. In summer an outside area was found, quiet and secluded until a wind sprang up and the adjoining primary school had its playtime!

Some settings have shown clear evidence of such hard work and effort on the part of staff, not simply for my visit, I hasten to add, and I know any EYP would be supported and be surrounded by good practice. I find it amazing still, after many years in Early Years, that some very unpromising buildings can be transformed with a team will and determination into wonderful 'enabling environments' for children. It is obvious from the moment you enter that here young children are trusted and their ideas respected – often the EYPS candidate will have been a long-standing member of staff who had for many years been naturally following the ethos and principles underpinning the EYPS. There are so many examples: A 'kindness tree' where children decided as a group themselves who had done a 'kind' act that day, and deserved a place on the special tree; an EYP's very effective behaviour management strategy; a setting where difference and diversity were totally accepted. In this particular instance, the setting had a young amputee who was quite forgetful; during the tour, I heard several children call out: 'Everybody – look for Peter's leg – he's lost it again'. In another setting, children sat down to lunch still in 'role' as a fairy, a doctor and a fireman, showing how flexible rules allow for growth and continuity of play.

I have also witnessed less flexible routines where several energetic 3 year old boys ran round a room, being constantly told to 'stop it' and it 'wasn't time for play' when a perfectly adequate (and well-resourced) outdoor area was available. Thankfully the EYPS candidate spoke with the room leader and the children were 'released' into the fresh air. I know from later discussions that the EYP discussed changing the indoor/outdoor access of the room in question. I feel that this example perhaps captures why I feel very hopeful about the future of the EYPS and its impact on early years practice and provision. It is about changing attitudes and practices that needed to be reappraised in the light of what we now know about children's learning and development, and it is EYPs who will be the catalysts for such change.

Conclusion

So we have come to the end of this chapter, but not quite the end of the book. We hope, like Sunita and Mandy, that after going through validation (and possibly, like them, feeling quite stressed at some points of the process!) you will be rewarded with the news that you have achieved your Early Years Professional Status. When you started this book, this probably seemed like the conclusion to your journey. However, the writing team have to tell you at this point that it is really only the beginning! As such, you will find one more chapter in this book, where we turn the narrative over to those Early Years Professionals who gained their status with us over the past two years so that they can tell you 'what happened next' . . .

11

Concluding perspectives: Early Years Professionals talking – voices of the future

Pam Jarvis

Introduction: EYPs talking

In the autumn of 2008, I went to visit four of the Early Years Professionals whom I had taught over the previous two years, to talk to them about how they viewed their professional roles, and how they envisaged their futures. Two of them had received their Early Years Professional Status during 2007; the other two during 2008. Although they were a very small sample, they had trained on the full range of Early Years Professional Pathways, Validation Only, Short, Long and Full, and they inhabited a range of Early Years based occupations – a manager and a leading practitioner in two different children's centres in two different northern cities, a home-based childminder in a central urban district of one of these cities, and the owner/manager of a small daycare setting in a rural suburb located halfway between each conurbation. Two of them have subsequently moved on to become local authority advisors in the three months since the interviews took place, and another has become a leading EYPS candidate mentor, demonstrating the growing prestige of Early Years Professionals. The candidates discussed a wide range of points:

- Experiences of Gateway and Validation
- The role of developmental theory in the enhancement of practice
- The benefits of becoming an EYP
- The relationship between Early Years Professional Status and Qualified Teacher Status
- Multi-agency/integrated working, and the role of children's centres in re-energising communities
- Possible futures for EYPs.

Sunita's view of the contemporary Early Years arena

(We) need the right people in place (working with) the under 5s who understand we need self-confident . . . self-starters, children with a good self-esteem, (who) have the confidence to move forward in life, because those skills; those things that you are giving children will hopefully help them overcome several things, not just the transition to school . . . Hopefully they'll stand up in the gun cultures that they then might be living in, and hopefully they'll have the confidence to say 'I know what the right path is and this is what I'm gonna do.' Whereas possibly now . . . you see a lot of young people that, they're led into these things, you know, it's probably only 10 per cent that really want to commit, do all the bad things and the other 90 per cent are following like sheep. If we can give them . . . a bit more freedom to speak up, have that confidence, have that self-esteem, foster that independence, hopefully we can stop that happening in the future . . . . But it needs the right skills, people with the right skills in the early years . . . (children) need a good set of ethics and that doesn't come about from sitting down and doing worksheets, it comes about from fostering independence, improving self-esteem, (instilling) self-worth (and) problem solving.

The participants

(Professional roles stated were those inhabited at the time the interviews took place.)

- '**Sunita**' was the owner/manager of a well-established small daycare setting who had an existing honours degree in business studies. She had approached her EYPS through the Validation Only pathway.

- '**Lesley**' was an experienced early years teacher, and manager of a children's centre, who approached her EYPS through the Short pathway.

- '**Mandy**' was an experienced early years practitioner with 10 years of experience in childcare, having entered the profession at the age of 18, following her achievement of a 'nursery nursing' qualification. She spent the three years leading up to her EYPS validation studying on the Foundation Degree in Early Years and BA (Hons) Early Childhood Studies top-up, approaching her EYPS through the Long pathway.

- '**Sue**' was a home-based childminder who started her business four years ago. As she experienced increasing success, her partner left his job to become her partner in the business, and the following year they additionally employed some part-time staff. Sue had an existing honours degree in the social sciences. Once she and her partner had both achieved a level 3 qualification in Child Care and Education, she looked for a feasible way to gain postgraduate qualifications in childcare. The amount of release that her co-childminders were able to give her allowed her to approach her EYPS (and an associated Postgraduate Certificate in Early Years) through the Full pathway.

The methodology

The interviews were conducted in two offices (in the children's centres) and two kitchens (in the childminder's and daycare setting). I put a dictaphone on the table between myself and the participant, started with my first listed prompt (which was as near to an 'order of questions' as I got) and then we talked for approximately half an hour. The 'prompts' used were as follows:

- Comment on Gateway and Validation
- Immediate effects of becoming an EYP
- How you see your future as an EYP – opportunities and barriers.

At the time when the interviews were undertaken, Prime Minister Gordon Brown had very recently focused his speech at the Labour Party Conference (23 September 2008) on advances made in services for children, and my final question to all interviewees was: 'If Gordon Brown was sitting here instead of me, what would you say to him, in your role as an Early Years Professional?' Sunita's very thoughtful response was the quote used at the beginning of this chapter.

I transcribed the tapes on to Microsoft Word files as soon as I could when an interview was complete, and then erased the tape to protect the confidentiality of the participants. Where names were used, I changed these to pseudonyms while transcribing. Once the data set was complete I went through the printed transcripts, marking up themes that emerged from each interview.

The results are outlined below.

Experiences of Gateway and Validation

The candidates' comments on Gateway and Validation separated into several subthemes, one of which explored the very useful role of reflective practice, and another emphasising the need for solid leadership skills to underpin successful completion of the written and practical tasks within validation. The candidates' reflections on this topic also raised some potential issues and useful advice for candidates within specific professional situations:

I did think, you know, the different activities brought out different skills . . . And it did make me think, so I liked it and I did enjoy it! It's about discussing with people in a way that they do share with you . . . what I call archaeological digging. . . . You're reflecting back, trying to find out what's the root of the problem . . . I'm always . . . nervous in interviews anyway . . . when I had the second interview it was obvious that the assessor had really gone quite rigorously through the file and the questions . . . were ones that made me think . . . The things that were really powerful were when you reflected for the reflection sections on each of your written tasks, made you actually go 'Yeah. So what's good about that? What made me want to write about that? Where did that meet the Standard?'

(Lesley)

You're able to put across the things you've been proud of; the things that you've achieved . . . I do think that it does help you to properly examine your own skills . . . that . . . doesn't come up earlier on in your education with childcare, so I think it was a really valuable skill to take back, and I think having done the EYP process now, I do engage in reflective practice a lot more . . . I think the reflective practice element was really quite good. I think good practitioners do it anyway, but when you are forced to write things down and confront it, it does make you look at things differently. It did make me reflect on my practice, so from the business perspective I think the nursery went through some period of improvement, so that was good . . . The latest self-evaluation form that Ofsted have put out for the Early Years Foundation Stage is far more detailed and it is asking you to specifically look at areas and reflect on your practice, so the culture within childcare is moving that way anyway.

(Sunita)

It is about leading . . . It was that bit that was hard for some people who were younger . . . that leadership element.

(Lesley)

(The tasks) bring out areas where you've shown leadership.

(Sunita)

I do co-childminding – it would have been very difficult to show the assessor (around) and for me to come out for my interview on the same day if I hadn't got someone else to fall back on who could look after the children. Obviously I can't sort of sit there for an hour with the assessor while the children are here unwatched. . . . (If) you're a solo childminder with no one to fall back on it wouldn't be possible to do it unless you spread the assessment over two days. I had one day where the assessor did the interviews and another day when she did the placement visit . . . Had I not got co-childminders with me there is no way I could have done the course.

(Sue)

Mandy, who was unexpectedly made redundant eight weeks before her validation, and subsequently had to undertake her validation in a placement setting, made a point that Full pathway candidates may find very helpful:

I think you have to, if you're at that level, you need to make yourself known to everybody, you need to explain to them who you are, what you are here for rather than when you do your setting visit and you're going into a room and everybody's thinking who the heck's she? So I made a point I knew what was expected of me to be an EYP, so I made myself known to all the members of staff . . . I made sure I went and spoke to everybody else and explained who I was. I think I did that . . . for safeguarding as well, so the practitioners knew that if I was looking at a portfolio or something why, the reasons why I was doing that.

The role of developmental theory in the enhancement of practice

The two candidates on the longer pathways both made the point that the theory that they had covered in academic module delivery had been vital to their eventual success:

> As an EYP looking at the standards, I have learnt an awful lot more in being able to support practitioners . . . in using observations to plan for children's learning and development and to support their well-being as well . . . I did the BA to be in that role, so I'd be looking at that to support in future other candidates who are training, who are wanting to be at the level that I am at . . . and to show that it's not easy, but you can do it and there is support there for you . . . I think for example like the key person approach . . . it's very important in the EYP sense but unless you have done that higher level of learning you can't understand and reflect *why* it is so important. But by having that theory of development behind you, and the knowledge, I think you understand more and you appreciate things, why things happen . . . The EYP and BA help . . . build that knowledge for you.

> (Mandy, long pathway)

> It was a very good course to do; it really made you look at what you were doing and see why you were doing it . . . you do need the theory to back up the practical, I mean you need to be able to know and to justify, to explain why you're doing . . . I've been asked to justify various aspects of play-based learning, messy play for example, and I've been able to say . . . how it's building the children's confidence and self-esteem; the social theme (and) how it's sensory play and important for the mind . . . The thing is, I think, if you've not got the theory, if you don't know the background, you're not knowing why you're doing something. You're not knowing why there's a sand tray; there just *is* because there always has been . . . If you haven't got that background you don't know why it's important to let the children play in it.

> (Sue, full pathway)

The benefits of becoming an EYP

Two of the EYPs interviewed spoke of the positive impact that the award of the status had upon their professional confidence.

> Just in yourself, if you're one of the first people to do something . . . so you're a little bit pioneering.

> (Mandy)

> It's a confidence boost. Whereas previously you felt like you were in the shadow of school teachers, you're now able to sort of hold your head up higher and say well actually I'm qualified to an equivalent level to you so, you know, I'm no longer on that lower level rung, I'm on a par with you. There's been a business impact, in that every single . . . prospective customer who has come to us since I've got EYPS has signed up with us . . .

So it's quite a marketing tool if you like . . . You feel like you've got more authority to say the sort of thing that you're saying . . . It gives you that bit more credence; it gives you that level of authority.

(Sue)

Sunita, who has subsequently taken on mentoring work with EYPS candidates, also spoke of the energising impact of her new role upon her professional confidence.

I've benefitted personally - I've benefitted because I have been able to become a mentor and to work with a lot of candidates which is really stimulating, because I think it's another string to my bow . . . It means that you are seeing (candidates develop) in the same way that you are seeing children develop and you're seeing the fruits of your labour.

The relationship between Early Years Professional Status and Qualified Teacher Status

The most emotive and controversial thread that emerged dealt with the EYPs' frustration with the current confusion that exists over the relationship between Early Years Professional Status and Qualified Teacher Status (Early Years); consequently, it appeared that all of them viewed their current professional position very much through this lens. A document published after these interviews took place shows that UNICEF also recognises this point, not just as an issue for Early Years practice in England, but also within other European nations:

Benchmark 6 reinforces the training dimension of 'high quality care' by stipulating that a minimum of 50 per cent of staff in early education centres, including classroom assistants and all advisers and teachers, should have a minimum of three years' tertiary education, with specialist qualifications in early childhood studies or a related field . . . This benchmark . . . has had to be interpreted somewhat liberally in order to admit . . . countries such as France, Ireland, and the United Kingdom, where a primary school teaching qualification, with no special training in the developmental needs of pre-school children, is all that is required.

(UNICEF Child Care Transition report (2008), pp. 25–26)

This set of interviews with Early Years Professionals reiterated and expanded upon this point. Lesley, the only one of the group with Qualified Teacher Status alongside her Early Years Professional Status, took the most detached view:

I think you get some really good practitioners who have that rapport with children and then you can get some teachers that don't but . . . on the EYPS you get people who go 'Oh well, teachers!' and you take it personally, don't you, 'cos that's your profession! So I kept thinking they don't mean you, Lesley, they're just making a generalisation . . . They mean teachers who are very structured and (who) don't get imaginative play . . .

You know, an EYPS with a teaching degree or a teacher with EYPS, whichever way you want to put it, potentially has got the best of both worlds together.

Sunita had quite a lot to say on this topic, particularly to express her view that the Government currently misunderstood the different training that EYPs receive relating to the holistic care of very young children, as opposed to the overarching creation of a formal teaching and learning environment for children over 3 that Early Years teachers are trained to manage. In doing so, she expands upon the basic point that Lesley raises above, this time from the perspective of an EYP who does not share Lesley's dual EYPS/QTS professional identity:

One of the areas they (the government) really do need to look at is the skill sets that EYPs have, and why they are so important and so significant for under-5 year olds, and carry that through, because we've just had this debate about the teachers and the different way that they look at it . . . I think a lot of EYPs do look at the holistic development of the children, they do look at the routine of the day and use it, and exploit the learning opportunities, and I think that sometimes gets missed in a more formal school environment, and I think that that needs to be recognised as a slightly different skill set . . . how we're going to develop that workforce . . . we need appropriately skilled people . . . I think the thing is that, as an early years practitioner, you look very holistically at children and then the development is a huge part of that, it's a massive part of that, but you're looking very holistically at the whole picture. I think sometimes the drawback with teachers is that they come very much from an educational perspective; well, a child's development is not just based on the educational perspective . . . . Aspects of a child's day teach them a lot more, such as meal times, toileting, you know, simple things in life; the routine counts for a lot more than the education in inverted commas . . . What I'm saying is it's a massive learning opportunity, you know, fostering independence is a huge part of early years childcare and I think sometimes that's lost if you take too much of a teacher's perspective . . . They're not present at meal times, they're not present when children go to the bathroom, they're not present at sleep times in a nursery that's attached to a school . . . Whereas when you're working in a daycare setting, all of those things are hugely critical and, you know, whether you're looking at physical development, personal social and emotional development, there's learning opportunities through those opportunities that are highly significant, and possibly more important . . . That transition to school is much, much more difficult if the child has not had the freedom to become independent and hasn't been nurtured in that way . . . If they haven't had their self-esteem, their self-confidence and their independence nurtured from a young age, that battle becomes a lot harder . . . I think sometimes the angle that teachers bring doesn't take that into account.

Mandy spoke of the 'newness' of the EYPS qualification and the consequent issues raised:

Because it's a new qualification it's not going to be so widely known; it's not going to be so widely recognised. If someone says they've done a PGCE (Postgraduate Certificate of Education), everyone knows they're a teacher and they've got the qualifications readily available for that but the EYP is not currently that well known . . . (Then) you've got this EYP that comes in with a level 6 who's very used to the early years environment . . . and they may feel that they've been challenged or possibly undermined by teachers that are in the setting . . . (but) the people who already have a teaching qualification they're like 'why do we have to do it?' . . . because they're already at that level and have worked with young children for years. But . . . the EYP is for . . . working with children aged 0 to 5 years old . . . So I think maybe teachers who have been doing it for many years . . . being in schools, they're institutionalised . . . whereas the EYP is a holistic approach . . . well this is us in the new generation, and that's you from the old generation; this is the way you're thinking, well we're thinking in a new way . . . the old way of thinking will back down and they're going to have to realise that this is the way that the world is going . . . then the teachers who are supporting children's centres already may have to change their way of thinking and their way of working . . . I do think the children's centre agenda will open career paths and perhaps we need to look more carefully at how EYPs will fit into that coming from the child and the family basis, but fitting into different agencies.

Mandy raises several interesting threads above, particularly that relating to multi-agency working and the role of the children's centre, which is further discussed below.

Multi-agency/integrated working, and the role of Children's Centres in re-energising communities

The multi-agency working that is at the heart of Early Years Professional training was a key focus for the two participants who worked in children's centres.

Lesley had an optimistic view:

I think it will grow and be much more vast than people realise . . . with the integrated working in children's centres . . . We've taken on our children's centre workers; one has come from social care and one has come from health; both of them have nursery nurse qualifications. So as we're pulling in from health as new posts become available, it's understanding of children's development . . . that's going to be the base line and you're going to be able to move, I think, between health and education. So it'll open it up further (but) . . . we've got to get children's centres established; we've got to get multi-agency working, really working . . . You know we've really got to be working together. I do think hopefully all the edges will be blurred; there will be crossover and you will get people, for example, who might be on such as a health support team . . . who could perhaps go and do some stuff down at (the nursery associated with the children's centre). So . . . you do get this flow and sharing of practice, which has got to benefit the children if (we) have got more knowledge in different aspects.

Mandy, on the other hand, reflected upon some 'teething' problems:

. . . This integrated working . . . there are some pitfalls . . . Communication, even though we are . . . talking and multi-agency working and integrating, I think somewhere along the line there is a loophole. For example, my children's centre – we're supposed to support a specific demographic area. . . . The people who . . . know about the children's centre services . . . are actually coming forward but those people who don't, and the outreach workers . . . if they're not getting the statistics of who's being born into which area, who's moving to this area, what's changing, if we don't get that information and work in partnership with everyone, with each other, then those people are going to fall deeper and deeper into (poverty) . . . I think a lot of us (who) have worked in children's centres . . . are still relatively new, 'cos there's different phases of things and pilot projects going on all the time, whereas for some people it's they don't like change . . . everybody working together and joined-up thinking . . . It's very new to them; they're still sort of treading water and still a little bit unsure.

Lesley went on to talk about the positive ways in which she had worked with parents, and the subsequent development of the local community around her children's centre.

The working with parents would be essential, wouldn't it, in children's centres, 'cos that's the main thing. . . . This whole idea of the parents' voice being heard and shaping services so as children's centres become established if they're really doing that well, then the working with parents will be an absolutely key part of it . . . Recently we've had more and more mums, young mums funnily enough, 17 year olds, 18 year olds wanting to do the baby massage and the baby yoga. But that's only just started, you know, it has stayed quite affluent mums for a while, but now we've got mums from the local estate coming on, so hopefully that will change, but it just takes time doesn't it, you've just got to give things time for word to get out and somebody to try it . . . What is happening slowly is the conversations are not about . . . who's fallen out on the estate, although you do get a little bit of that. Conversations are about the children, when the children are playing parents are saying: 'Oh well, I've never noticed he did that before' and, you know, just this idea of talking about the children, the children are what we're here for. We are here for the parents and support how they make their social network and we have workers that can do outreach and stuff, but the conversations – just when you hear people talking about their children and enjoying their children . . . We give the community a chance to be a community instead of just a word. So they know each other, know your neighbours . . .

She went on to optimistically predict a potential emergent factor, as the children grew older:

. . . To be able to say to someone: 'I will come to see your Mum and Dad!' Most people see teenagers they don't know messing about, or even 11 year olds; they don't even say 'Oh you shouldn't be doing that!' It's like they're scared of them. They drive past, they won't stop the car, or they walk past, or cross the road, or whatever, and how ridiculous is that? . . . How ridiculous is that, that adults are scared of children? That whole sense of community which I think in this country we are losing and that is the social fabric that's missing, isn't it? That's where a lot of the problems are coming from . . . this is about parents and children . . . in the local community outside those doors there.

Mandy, working in a children's centre in a neighbouring city, made a very similar point, with an added appeal to keep the centre funding on an even keel.

Unfortunately if the money's not there to get all those parents out of poverty, some of those parents are slipping further and further into poverty and I think they (the

Government) need to put more money into outreach . . . and family support . . . there's a lot of funding posts out there that'll end in 2010. Those need to keep on going because . . . (otherwise) there is no way I'd be able to support the families I'm being able to support now. . . . if a family come to me I fill out a form with them, and (other services) will get in contact with them, look at their needs . . . And then they'd contact other agencies, and it's all about working together, so we all know . . . The other day this lady . . . she's in floods of tears because she couldn't thank me enough for the support I'd given her and for her children being in the children's centre. Her partner had left her, she was just completely all alone . . . you know it's a wonderful place to be in a children's centre, and I think Ed Balls (Secretary of State for Children, Schools and Families) needs to see that, rather than statistics on a piece of paper. He needs to see what is actually happening on a day-to-day basis and meet those people . . . or he won't see all that, he'll just see . . . a statistic . . . (Seeing this as a real situation) might make him realise that the good work is going on out there, and the money does need to continue because without government funding and support it cannot . . . Children's centres are heavily subsidised; if they're not subsidised, the children's centre is not going to be sustainable . . . We've got the lease here for three years, so really my job is only for three years, and if we're not sustainable we're not carrying on . . . You know my children's centre is filling up, like I said to you earlier, the nursery is just about full, but getting the staff there is a different matter.

Possible futures for EYPs

The participants were understandably cautious about predicting a future within the rather uncertain socio-political environment in which they found themselves, both in the new nature of the status that they had acquired, and in an international community which, at that time, stood on the brink of a major economic recession, created by events that had never been previously experienced within post-industrial societies. Nevertheless, they did have some interesting reflections on their future prospects.

The people in my (EYPS) cohort who were in private daycare . . . (there was) a younger girl . . . obviously a very good practitioner . . . she attends network meetings and she's always continually developing herself. I could see that, you know, in her career in the future she could come to do NPQICL (the National Professional Qualification for Integrated Centre Leadership), if she became a children's centre leader and she'd be well prepared for it.

(Lesley)

Some children's centres have put out ads specifically looking for EYPs . . . And I thought to myself, you know, fantastic, because the pay scales are moving, and people are recognising that EYPs have got something good to offer. On top of that I know that there is a union set up now as well (ASPECT, see **http://www.aspect.org.uk/about/eyp/**) and there's lobbying that will proactively look at pay and conditions and terms for EYPs. It won't just affect EYPs, it'll affect the whole childcare workforce, so I think all these moves in the long run will benefit all of us, and it might be that we don't see the fruits of it for a few years, but the immediate impact is starting to show . . . I think also the training aspects . . . as the EYP community widens and broadens, I think we can see some really good literature coming out and there might be an opportunity to just raise the game a bit in terms of how the whole leadership thing evolves in the nursery setting . . . I think that just bringing that element into the workforce will reap a lot of benefits . . . I think EYPs are in the slightly fortunate position, because there will be job opportunities that make more commercial sense, financial sense, to get an EYP in to do that job . . . . I feel that there will be opportunities on advisory levels within government positions . . . that will be required, because they can't train up all these EYPs and then have no one on an advisory capacity in the Councils to keep the momentum going.

(Sunita)

This last point has been borne out by two of the participants moving into local authority advisory posts (in teams within two different local authority areas) since these interviews took place.

The two participants who run their own businesses were also optimistic about their futures, and those of fellow EYPs.

I've obviously still been building my own business, and building up the number of staff, and I'm seeing my future sort of leading them through, getting them up to EYP and they're all at various points on the pathway; one is on second-year FD (Foundation Degree), one is on first-year FD and one is about to start (further education) level three. So they're on their progression routes . . . I have looked at possible academia teaching, and whether I do take that route or not I don't know yet, but yeah, I do see it as helping to develop others within the setting and outside . . . I do wonder if that's a sort of good point to start, like the ante-natal classes . . . to give parents ideas and guidance . . . they could be signposted at the ante-natal classes to the EYPs in their areas to give them more guidance and support, and perhaps just be a phone call away or something like that.

(Sue)

The EYP networking has been fantastic . . . we meet . . . once a quarter . . . you know we just discuss things that are happening out there in Early Years, and being able to relate to people on a similar level and talk to each other, and quite often the roles that we have within the settings are quite similar as well, so it's really nice just to be able to talk to another practitioner who is experiencing slightly different things. We bounce ideas off each other, so from that aspect it's been fantastic . . . the business has really benefitted.

(Sunita)

Conclusion

The message from this small group of EYPs is positive, despite the inevitable 'teething problems' that they are experiencing as pioneers within a new profession. As a researcher with a keen interest in the developmental processes of children of all ages, and the policies that underpin societies' support of children and families, I was particularly interested in the key societal role that these EYPs envisaged for children's centres, not only in caring for children in the present, but playing a major role in the development of whole local communities for the future. Given that these EYPs were working in a multi-professional integrated environment with families and young children aged in the full age range from 0–5, having received closely tailored training that facilitated their leadership within such environments, I was also very interested in their frustration at feeling that such expertise was being sidelined by a lack of recognition of their specialist training within the wider public arena. This aspect, I felt, led to the associated competition they perceived with early years teachers, trained within a different specialist arena, focusing upon the delivery of education for children aged 3–5 within a classroom environment. Given that this so clearly differs from the multi-agency integrated environment of the children's centre, which provides services for whole families, including care and education for children under 3, these EYPs felt understandably frustrated that teachers were nevertheless seen by some sectors of society as having inevitably 'superior' skills to EYPs, due to the long-established recognition of the teaching profession compared with the recent innovation of the EYP role.

Since these interviews took place, however, this point has been taken up by UNICEF (see above), and the prospect of international recognition of the value of Early Years Professional training, and its 'equal but different' relationship with Qualified Teacher Status, is a very positive note upon which to move forward into the future. As I have previously stated in Chapter 3, 'the expertise of Early Years Professionals will continue to retain its value, whether their principal work remains in collective daycare with children from families where both parents are in paid employment, or whether they increasingly work with disadvantaged families with young children, as unemployment numbers rise'. While conditions in the outside world may remain challenging for the foreseeable future, the professional prospects of the Early Years Professional remain bright, as their vital role in the provision of services for children and their families becomes more widely recognised. As more people enter the profession, it will become clear that EYPs have a crucial role, not only in improving the immediate lives of young children and their families, but in supporting the development of the initial cognitive, social and emotional competencies that allow human beings to become independent learners, to optimise children's opportunities across their whole developmental period, and additionally to help to regenerate cohesion within the communities in which they live.

As Mandy urges above, however, 'the money does need to continue', and it should be nationally recognised that the well-being of children, families and communities served by EYPs and children's centres relies upon continued support from government funding. It must be stressed that the money spent is actually a saving for society. The High/Scope Perry Pre-School study estimated that the saving to US society from a similar project undertaken in the USA (HeadStart) involving the establishment of children's centres for disadvantaged families and young children during the early 1960s was, by the early 2000s: '$258,888 per participant, on an investment of $15,166 per participant – $17.07 per dollar invested'. In particular, it was proposed that 93 per cent of this return was 'due to the large programme effect of reduced crime rates for programme males' (Schweinhart *et al.* 2005, pp. xvi–xvii).

If, in the light of this information, you return to Sunita's reflection which opens this chapter, you will see what an important profession you are seeking to join, not only in its benefits for young children and their families but for the nation as a whole. We wish you well as you complete your Early Years Professional Status and emerge into a world which will always need your skills, vocational dedication and enthusiasm.

Further reading

DCSF (2008) 2020 Children and Young People's Workforce Strategy. Available at: **http://publications.dcsf.gov.uk/eOrderingDownload/7977-DCSF-2020%20Children %20and%20Young%20People%27s%20Workforce%20Strategy-FINAL.pdf**

Schweinhart, L., Montie, J., Xiang, Z., Barnett, W.S., Belfield, C. and Nores, M. (2005) *Lifetime Effects: The High/Scope Perry Preschool Study through age 40*. Yipsilanti: High/Scope Press.

Shonkoff, J. and Phillips, D. (2000) *From Neurons to Neighborhoods*. Washington: National Academy Press.

UNICEF (2008) The Child Care Transition: a league table of early childhood education and care in economically advanced countries. Available at: **http://www.unicef-irc.org/ publications/pdf/rc8_eng.pdf**

References

Schweinhart, L., Montie, J., Xiang, Z., Barnett, W.S., Belfield, C. and Nores, M. (2005) *Lifetime Effects: The High/Scope Perry Preschool Study through age 40*. Yipsilanti: High/Scope Press.

UNICEF (2008) The Child Care Transition: a league table of early childhood education and care in economically advanced countries. Available at: http://www.unicef-irc.org/publications/pdf/ rc8_eng.pdf

Index

EXCITING EARLY YEARS & CHILDHOOD TITLES FROM LONGMAN

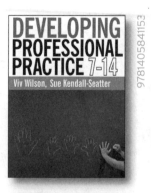

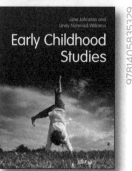
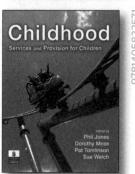